GUNSLINGERGIRL

PRESENTS

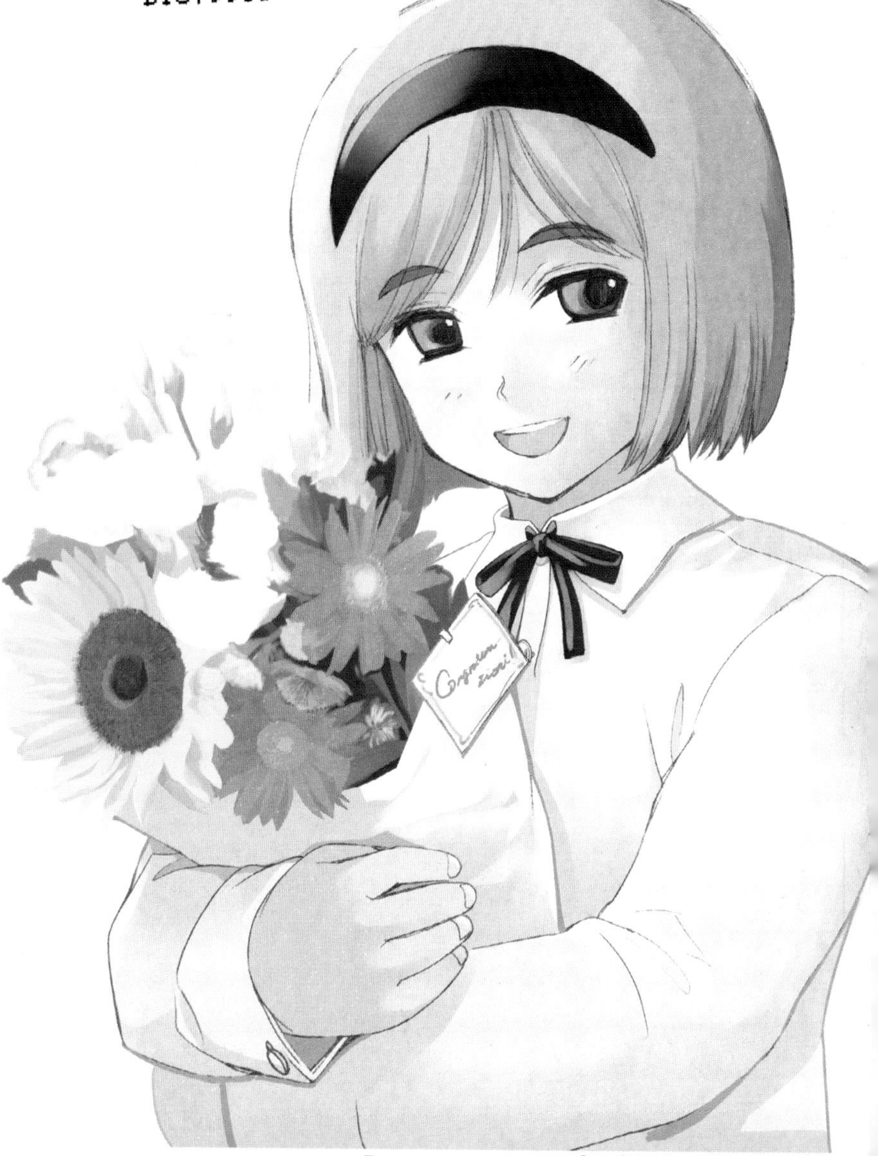

C O N T E N T S

Vol.3

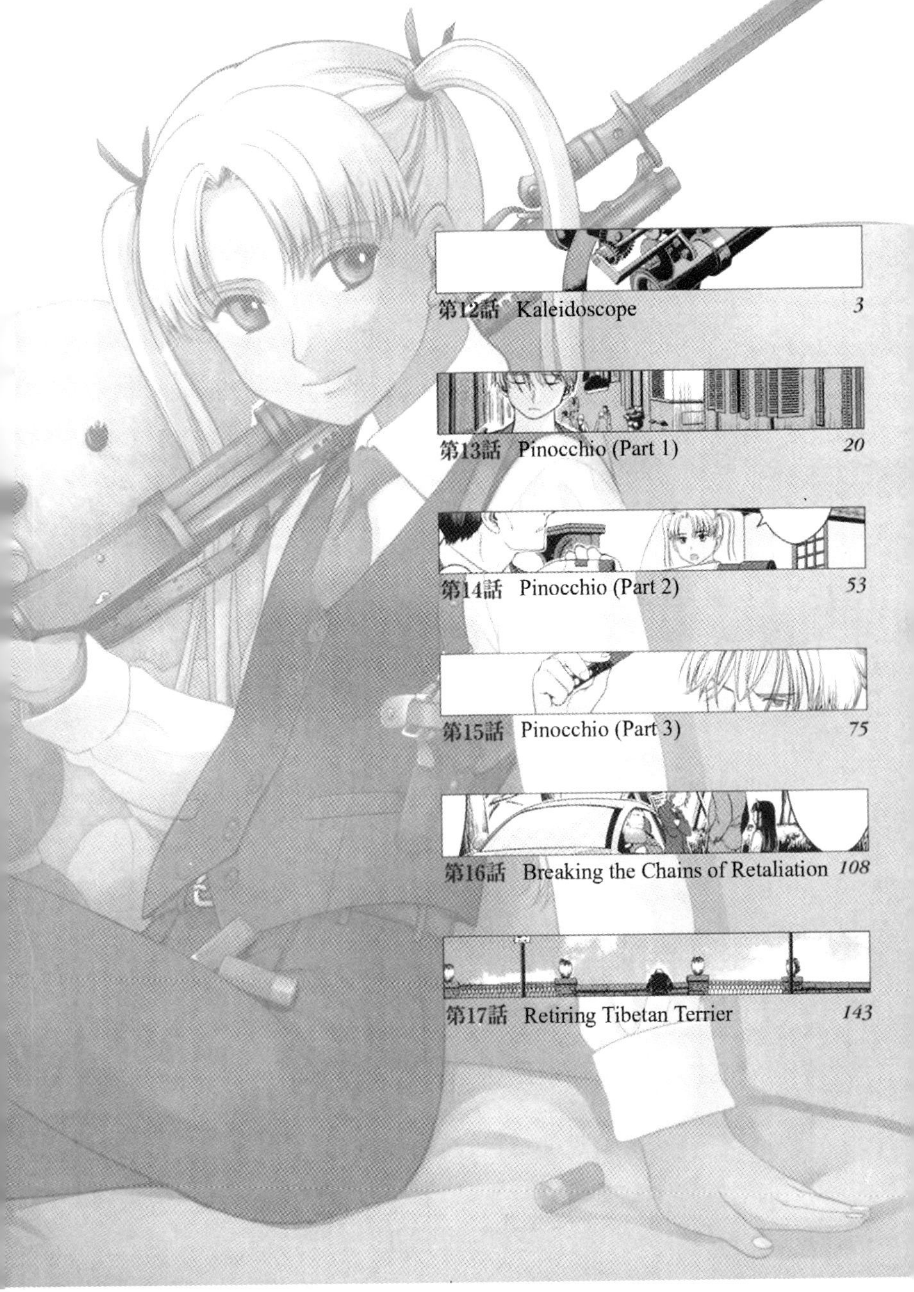

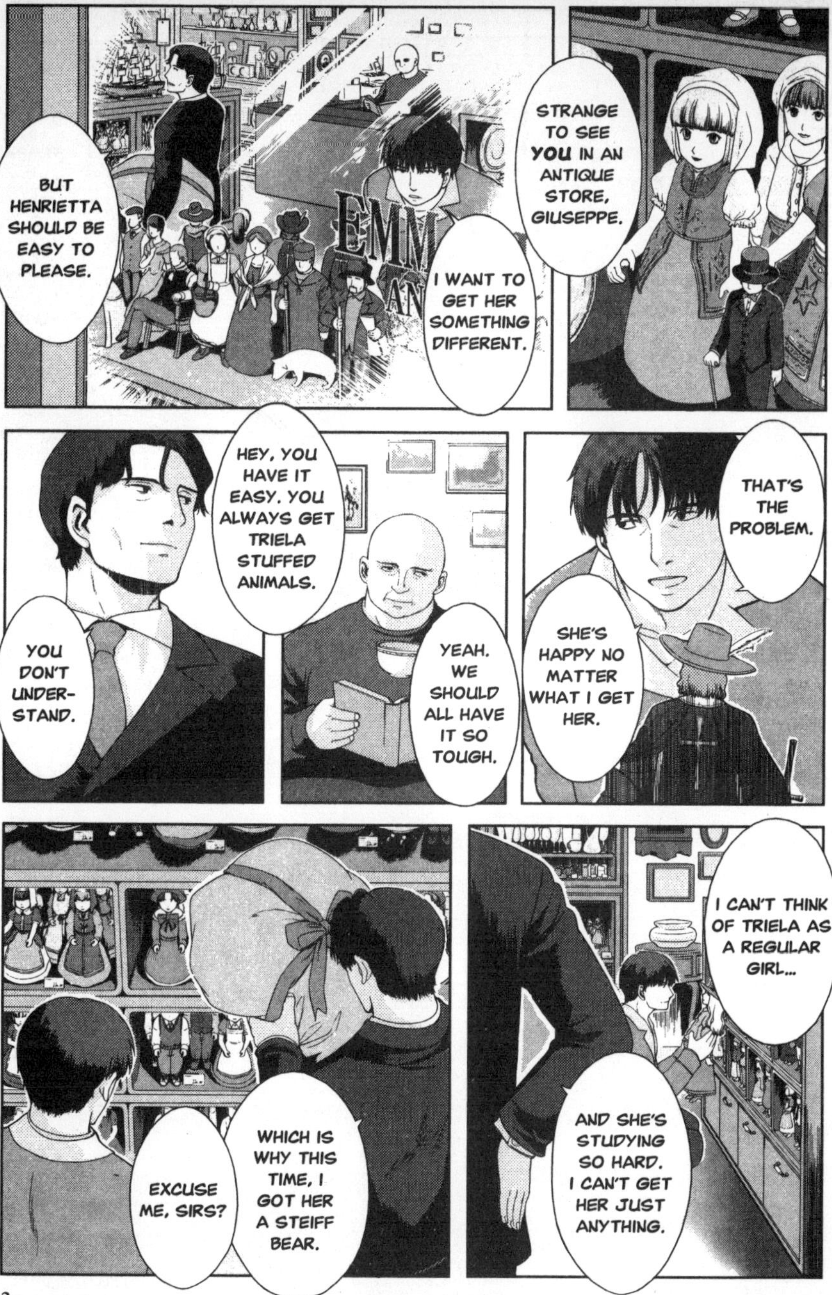
STRANGE TO SEE **YOU** IN AN ANTIQUE STORE, GIUSEPPE.
I WANT TO GET HER SOMETHING DIFFERENT.
BUT HENRIETTA SHOULD BE EASY TO PLEASE.
THAT'S THE PROBLEM.
SHE'S HAPPY NO MATTER WHAT I GET HER.
HEY, YOU HAVE IT EASY. YOU ALWAYS GET TRIELA STUFFED ANIMALS.
YEAH. WE SHOULD ALL HAVE IT SO TOUGH.
YOU DON'T UNDER-STAND.
I CAN'T THINK OF TRIELA AS A REGULAR GIRL...
AND SHE'S STUDYING SO HARD. I CAN'T GET HER JUST ANYTHING.
WHICH IS WHY THIS TIME, I GOT HER A STEIFF BEAR.
EXCUSE ME, SIRS?

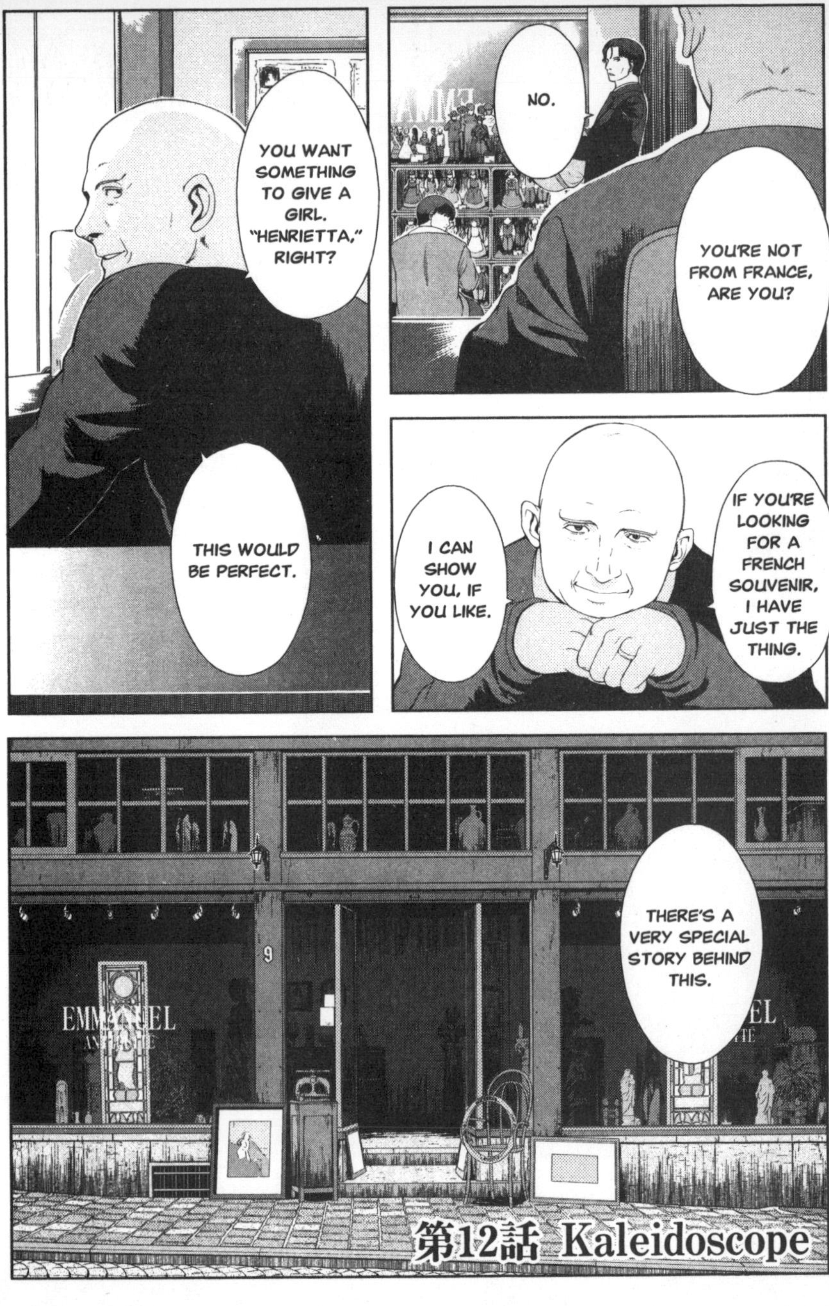
YOU'RE NOT FROM FRANCE, ARE YOU?
NO.
IF YOU'RE LOOKING FOR A FRENCH SOUVENIR, I HAVE JUST THE THING.
I CAN SHOW YOU, IF YOU LIKE.
YOU WANT SOMETHING TO GIVE A GIRL. "HENRIETTA," RIGHT?
THIS WOULD BE PERFECT.
THERE'S A VERY SPECIAL STORY BEHIND THIS.
EMMANUEL
9
第12話 Kaleidoscope

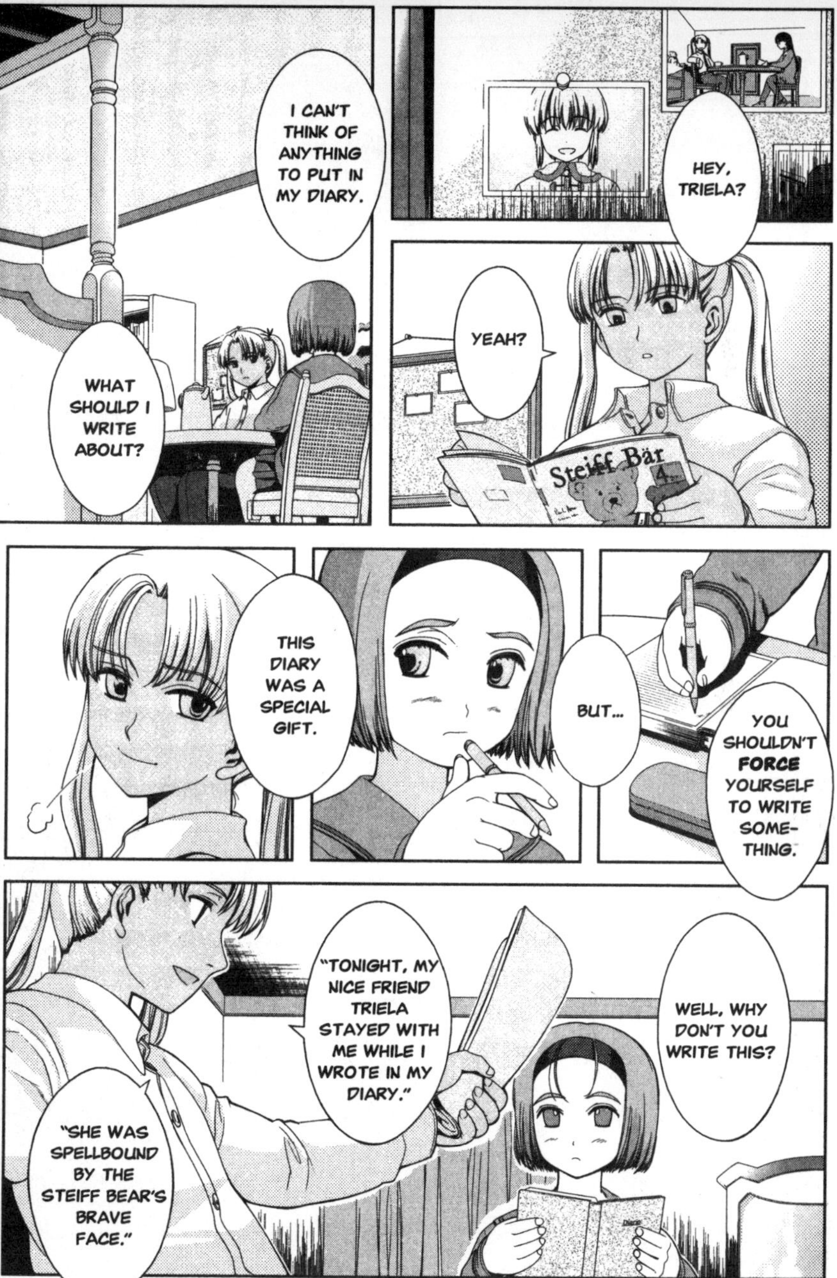
HEY, TRIELA?
YEAH?
Steiff Bär 4
I CAN'T THINK OF ANYTHING TO PUT IN MY DIARY.
WHAT SHOULD I WRITE ABOUT?
YOU SHOULDN'T **FORCE** YOURSELF TO WRITE SOME-THING.
BUT...
THIS DIARY WAS A SPECIAL GIFT.
WELL, WHY DON'T YOU WRITE THIS?
"TONIGHT, MY NICE FRIEND TRIELA STAYED WITH ME WHILE I WROTE IN MY DIARY."
"SHE WAS SPELLBOUND BY THE STEIFF BEAR'S BRAVE FACE."

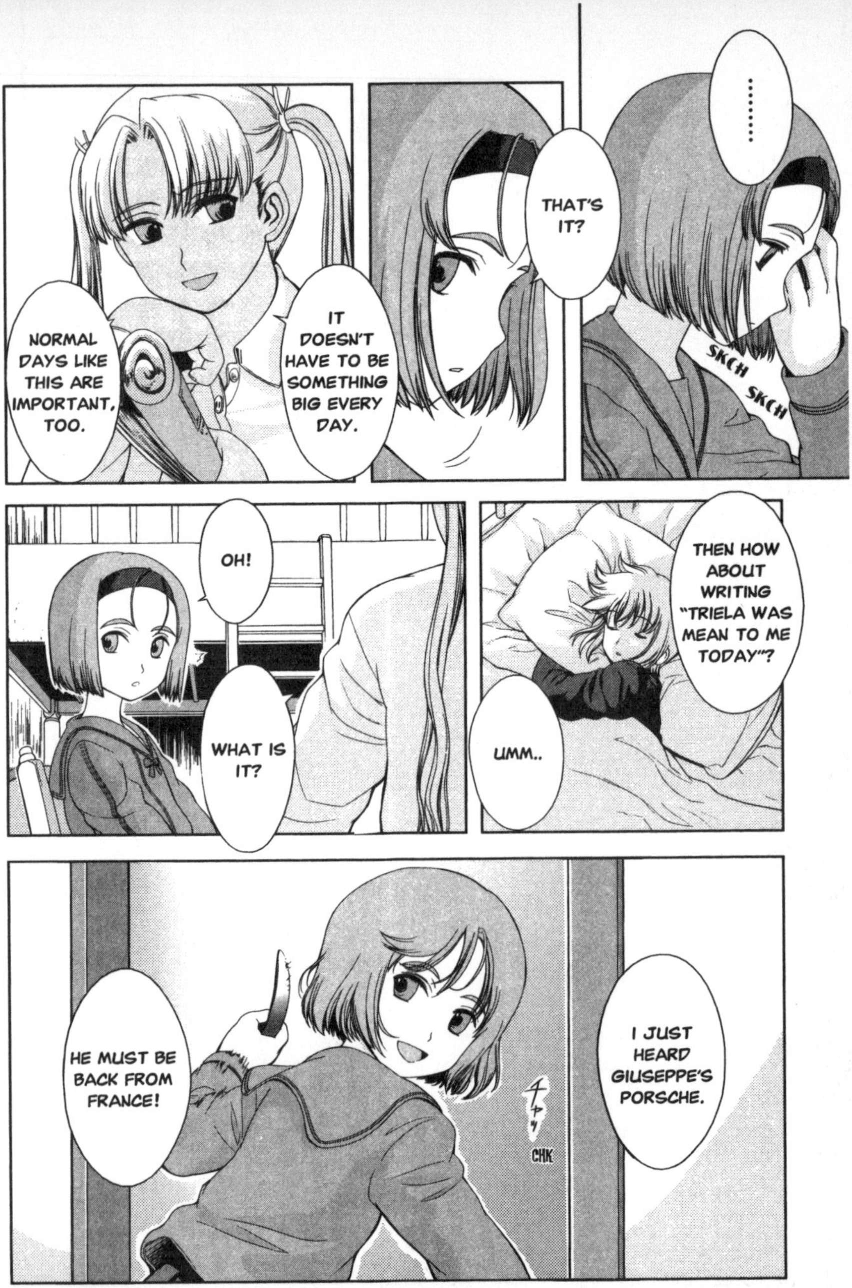
......
SKCH SKCH
THAT'S IT?
IT DOESN'T HAVE TO BE SOMETHING BIG EVERY DAY.
NORMAL DAYS LIKE THIS ARE IMPORTANT, TOO.
THEN HOW ABOUT WRITING "TRIELA WAS MEAN TO ME TODAY"?
UMM..
OH!
WHAT IS IT?
I JUST HEARD GIUSEPPE'S PORSCHE.
CHK
HE MUST BE BACK FROM FRANCE!

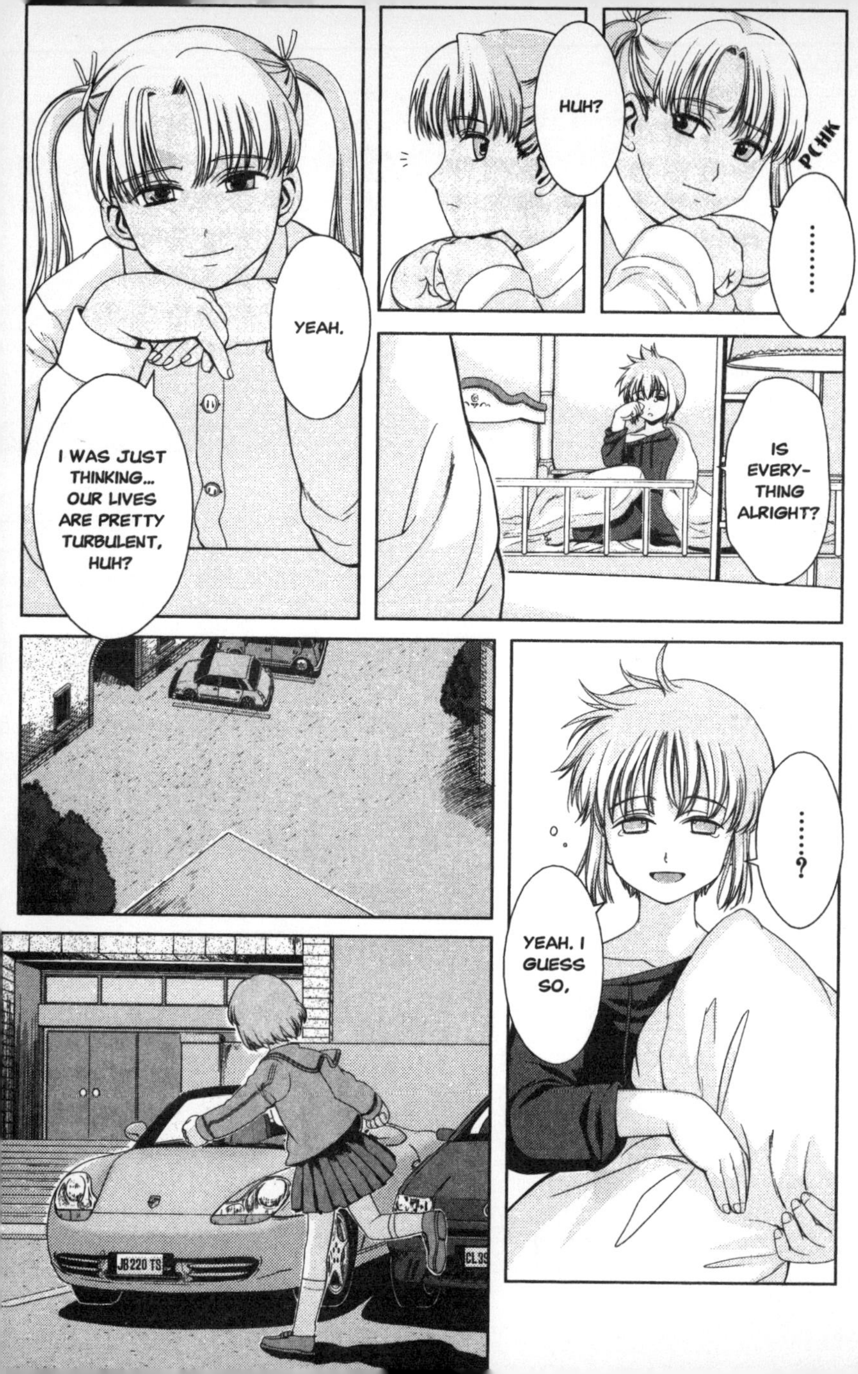
I WAS JUST THINKING... OUR LIVES ARE PRETTY TURBULENT, HUH?
YEAH.
HUH?
PCHK
......
IS EVERY-THING ALRIGHT?
......?
YEAH. I GUESS SO,
JB220 TS

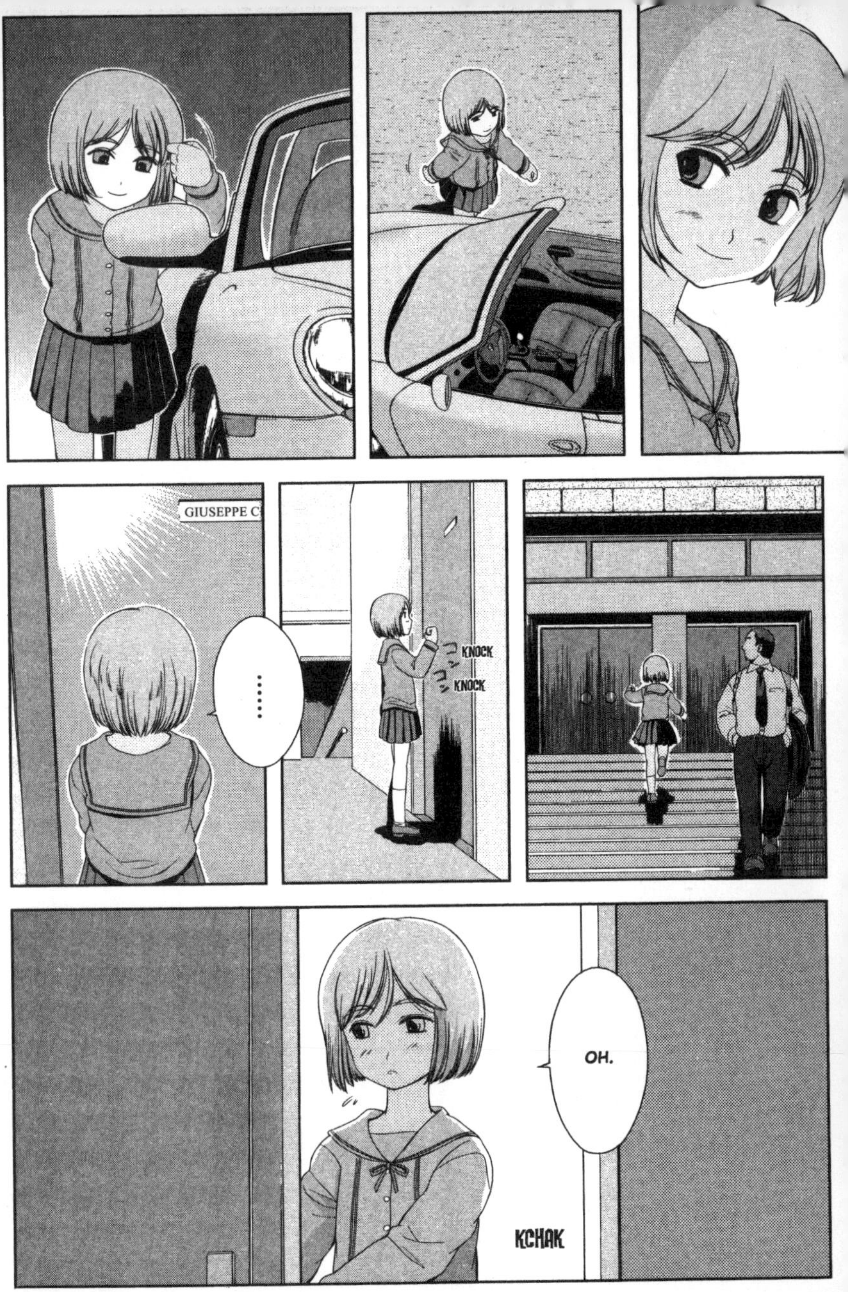
GIUSEPPE C
......
KNOCK
KNOCK
OH.
KCHAK

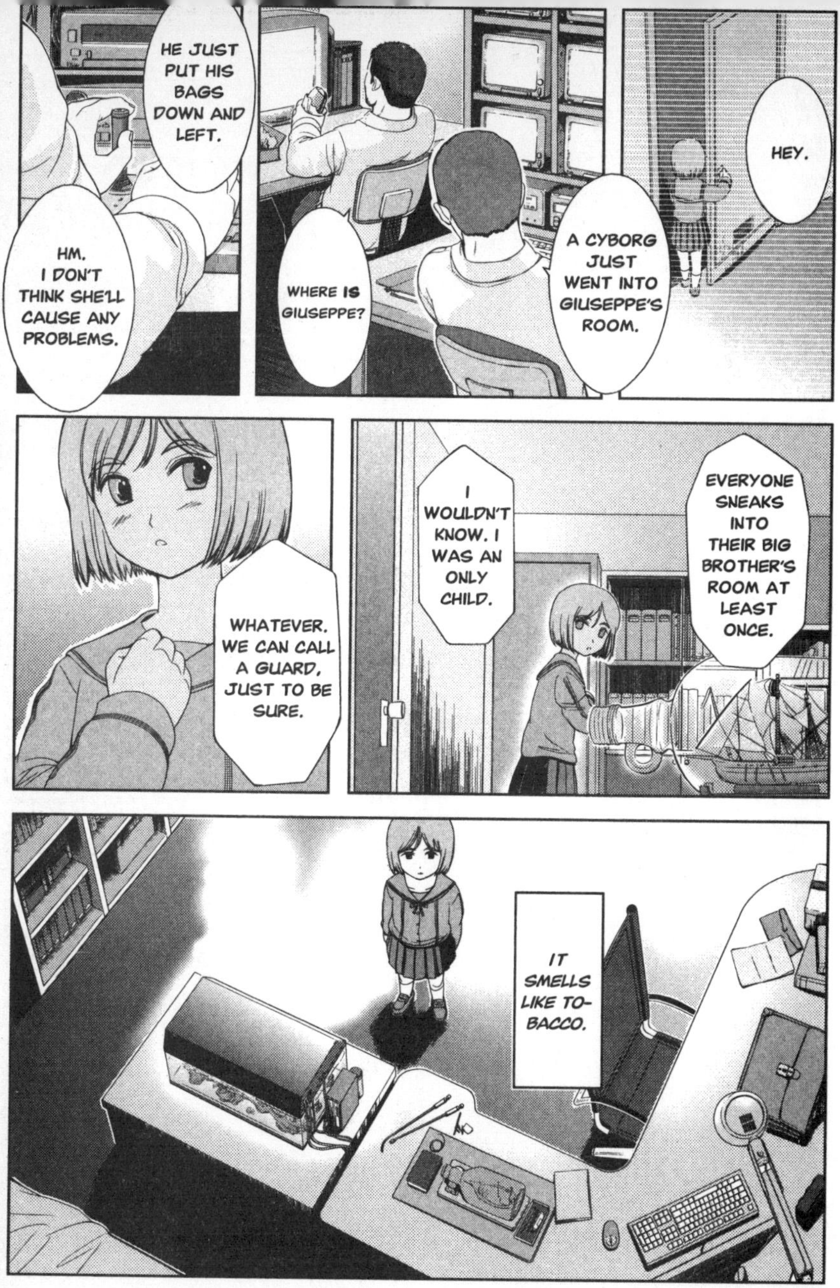
HEY.
A CYBORG JUST WENT INTO GIUSEPPE'S ROOM.
WHERE IS GIUSEPPE?
HE JUST PUT HIS BAGS DOWN AND LEFT.
HM. I DON'T THINK SHE'LL CAUSE ANY PROBLEMS.
EVERYONE SNEAKS INTO THEIR BIG BROTHER'S ROOM AT LEAST ONCE.
I WOULDN'T KNOW. I WAS AN ONLY CHILD.
WHATEVER. WE CAN CALL A GUARD, JUST TO BE SURE.
IT SMELLS LIKE TO-BACCO.

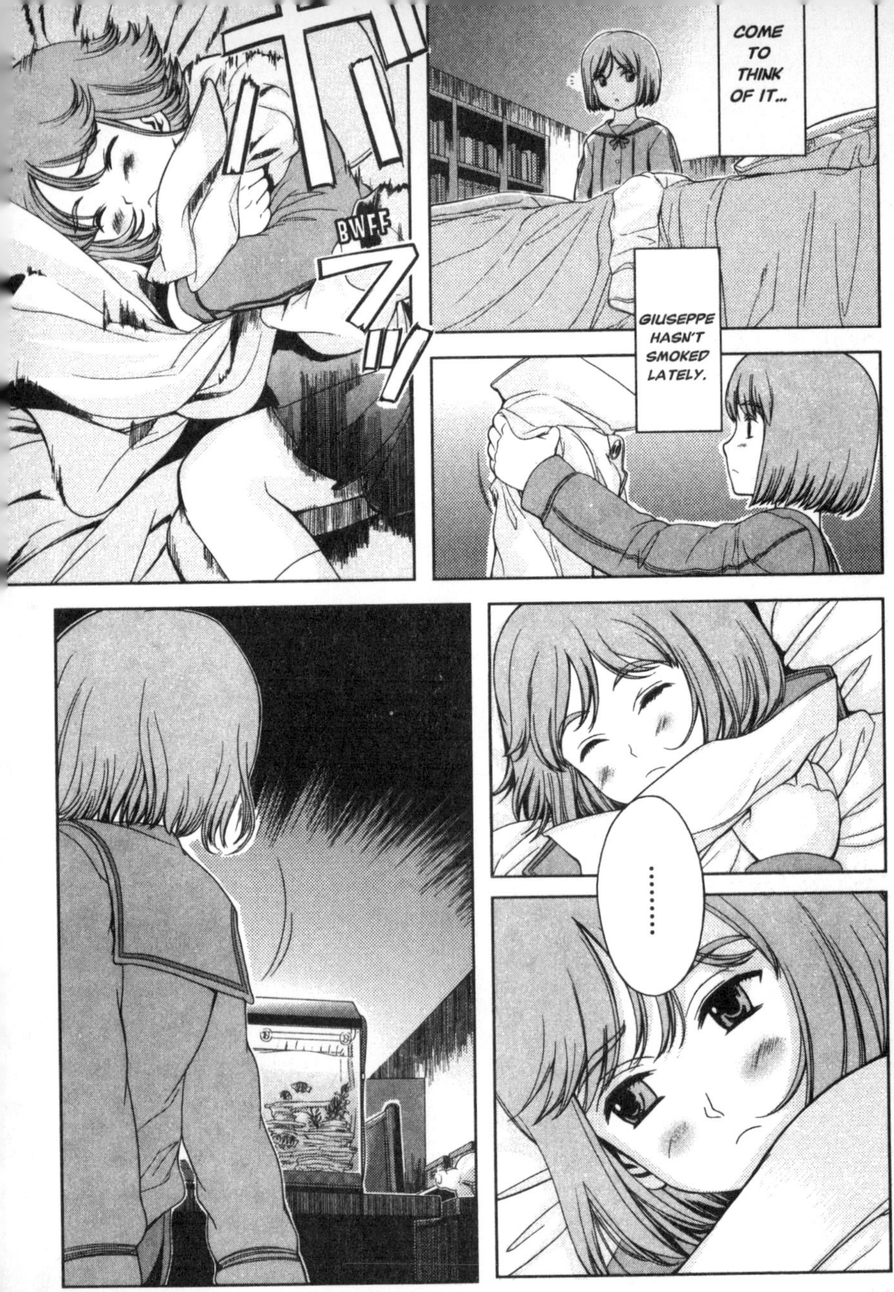

COME TO THINK OF IT...
GIUSEPPE HASN'T SMOKED LATELY.
BWFF
....

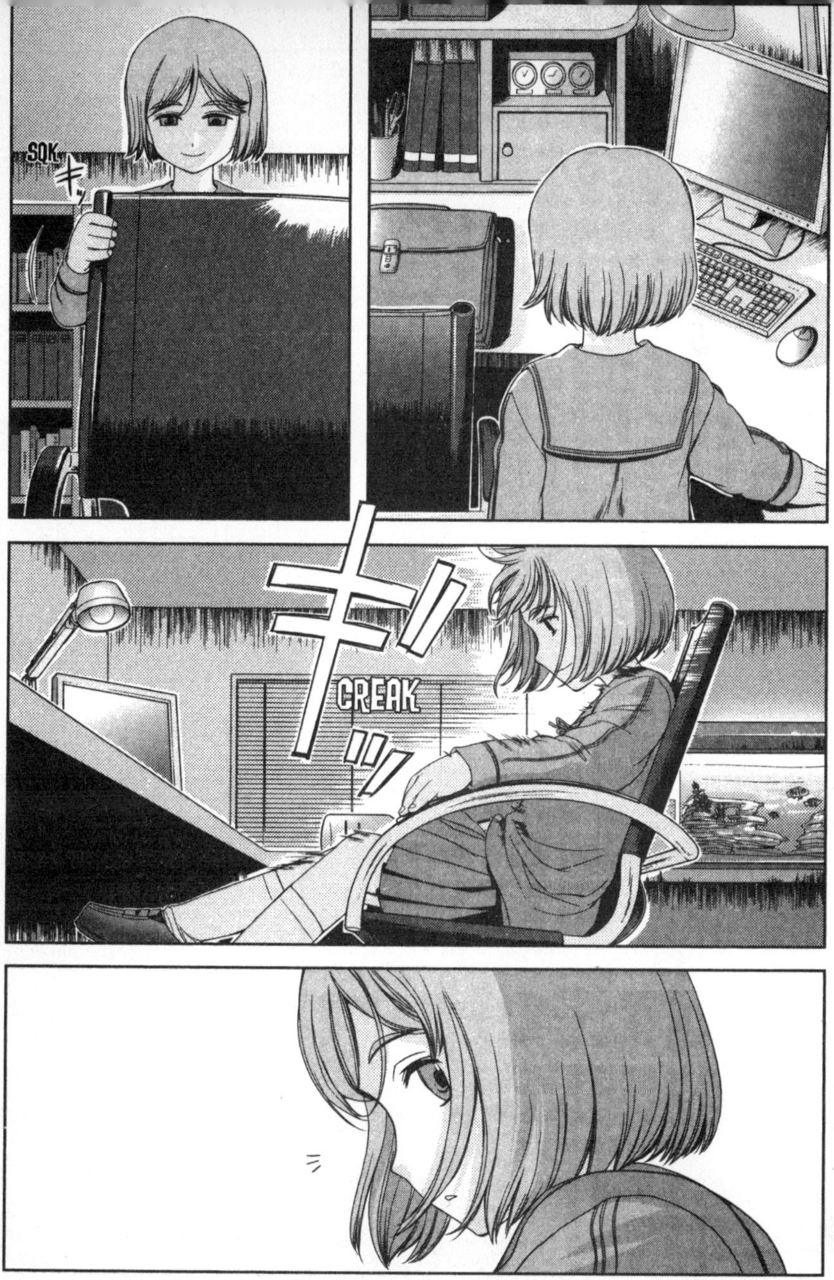

SQK
キ
CREAK

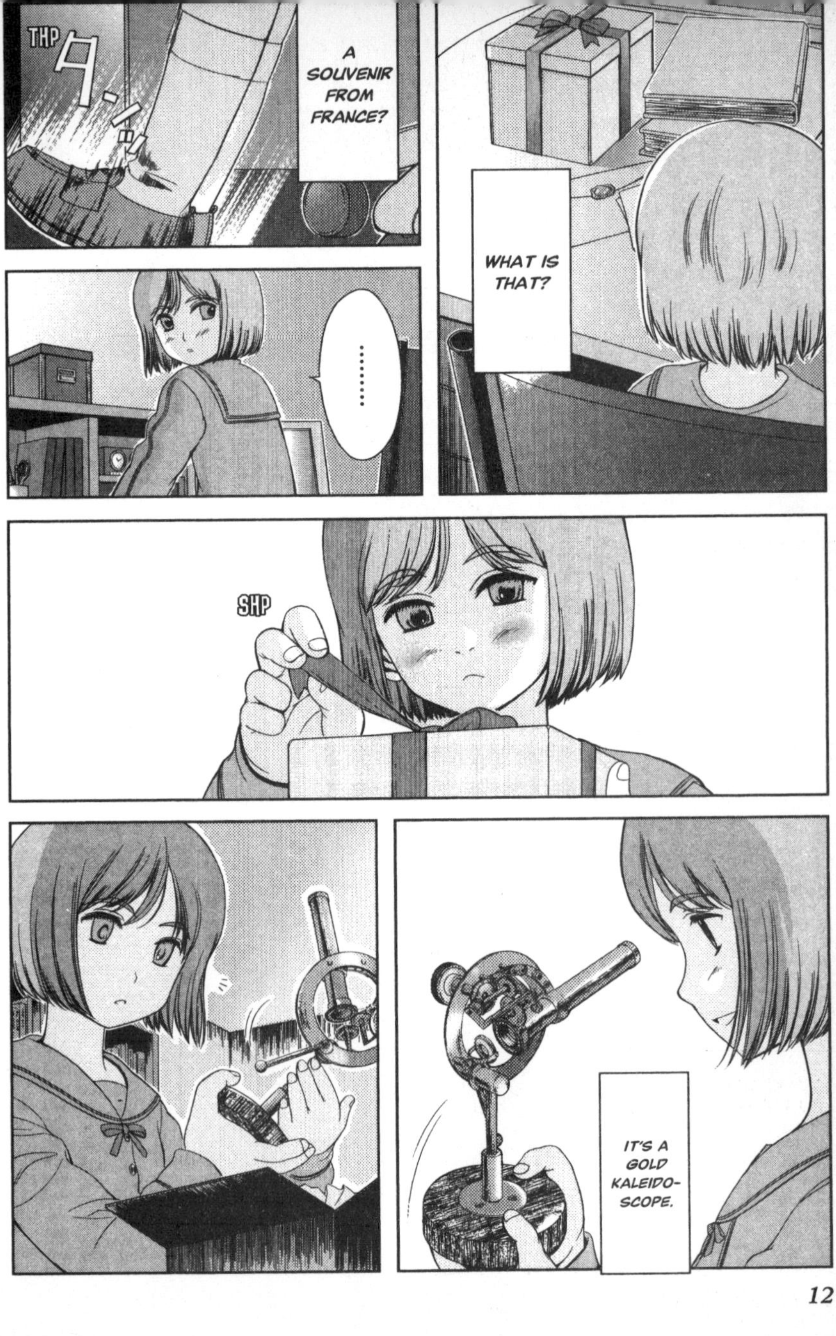
WHAT IS THAT?
THP
A SOUVENIR FROM FRANCE?
....
SHP
IT'S A GOLD KALEIDO-SCOPE.

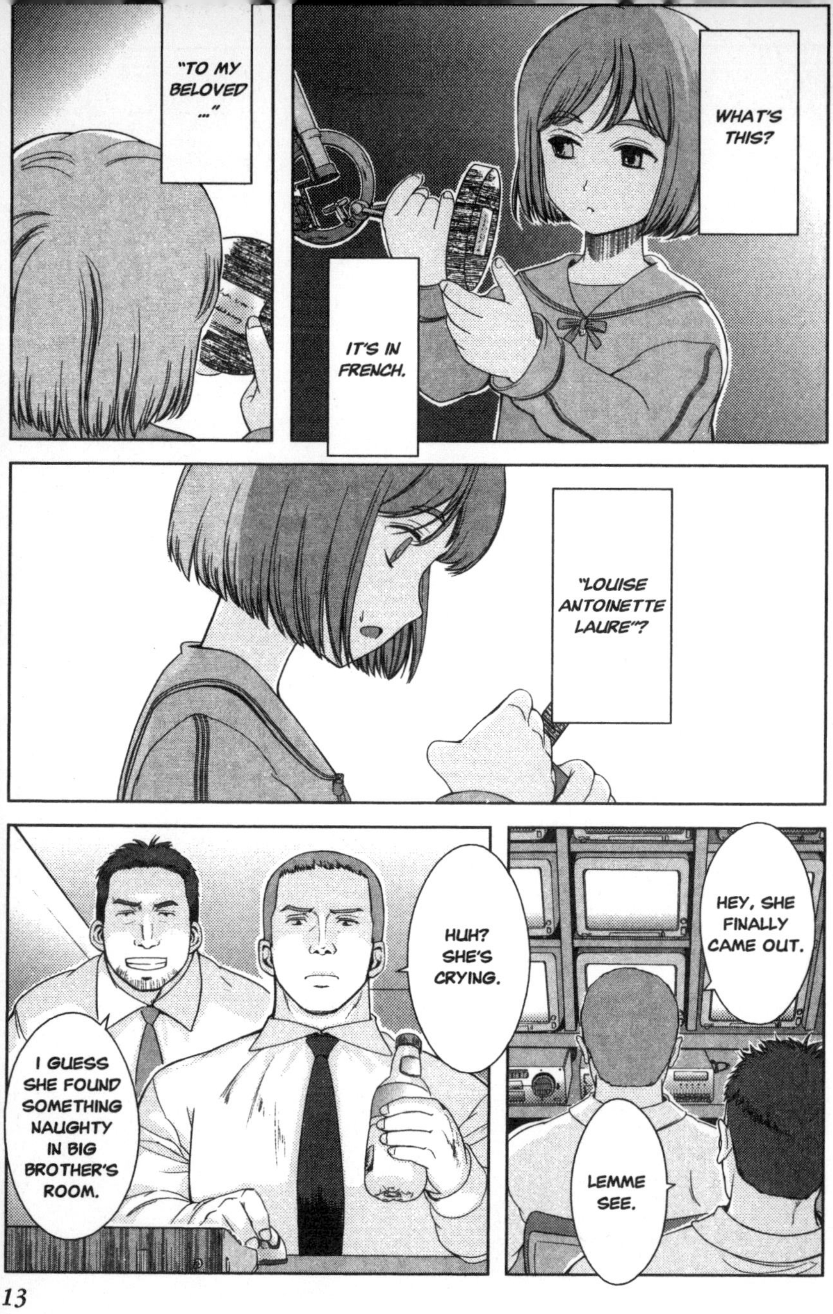
WHAT'S THIS?
IT'S IN FRENCH.
"TO MY BELOVED ..."
"LOUISE ANTOINETTE LAURE"?
HEY, SHE FINALLY CAME OUT.
LEMME SEE.
HUH? SHE'S CRYING.
I GUESS SHE FOUND SOMETHING NAUGHTY IN BIG BROTHER'S ROOM.

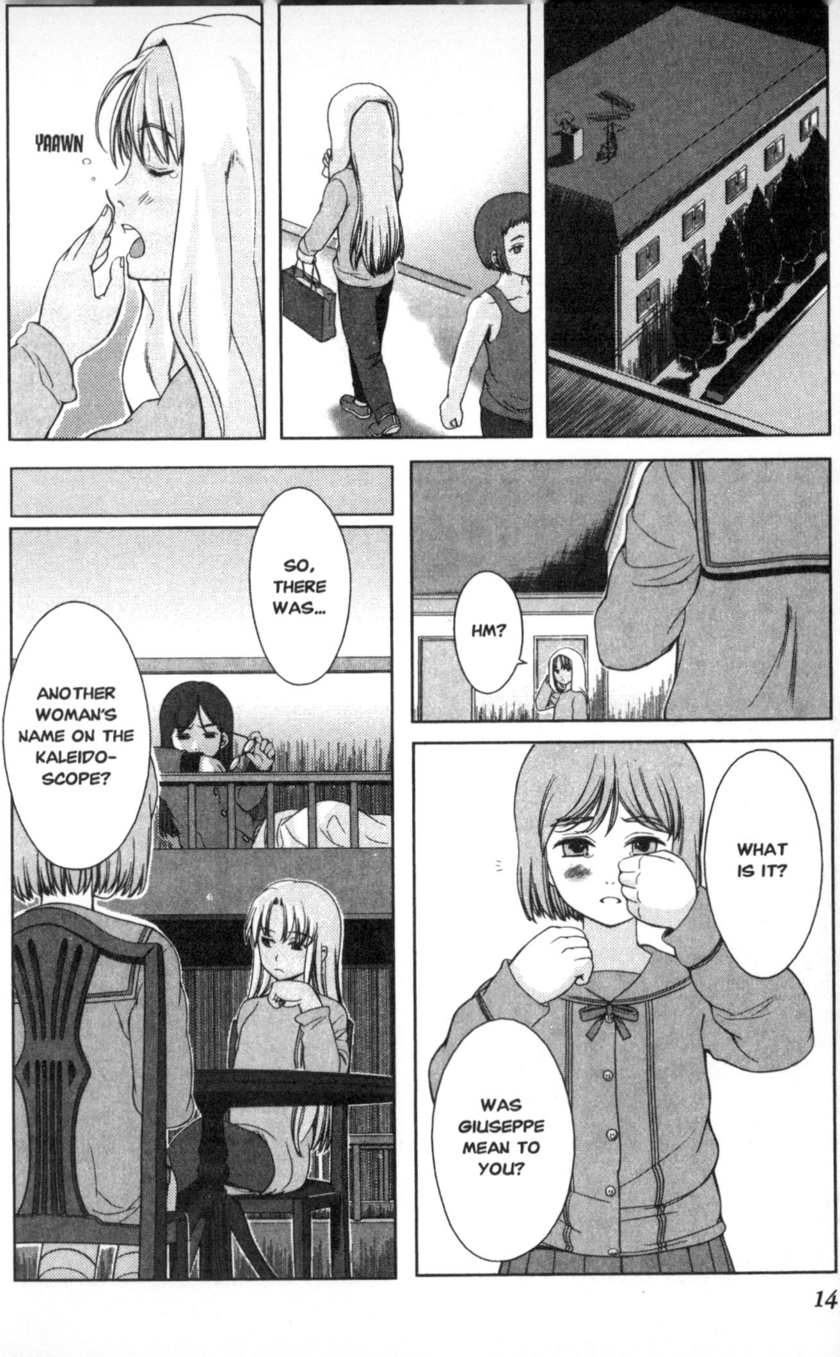
YAAWN
SO, THERE WAS...
ANOTHER WOMAN'S NAME ON THE KALEIDO-SCOPE?
HM?
WHAT IS IT?
WAS GIUSEPPE MEAN TO YOU?

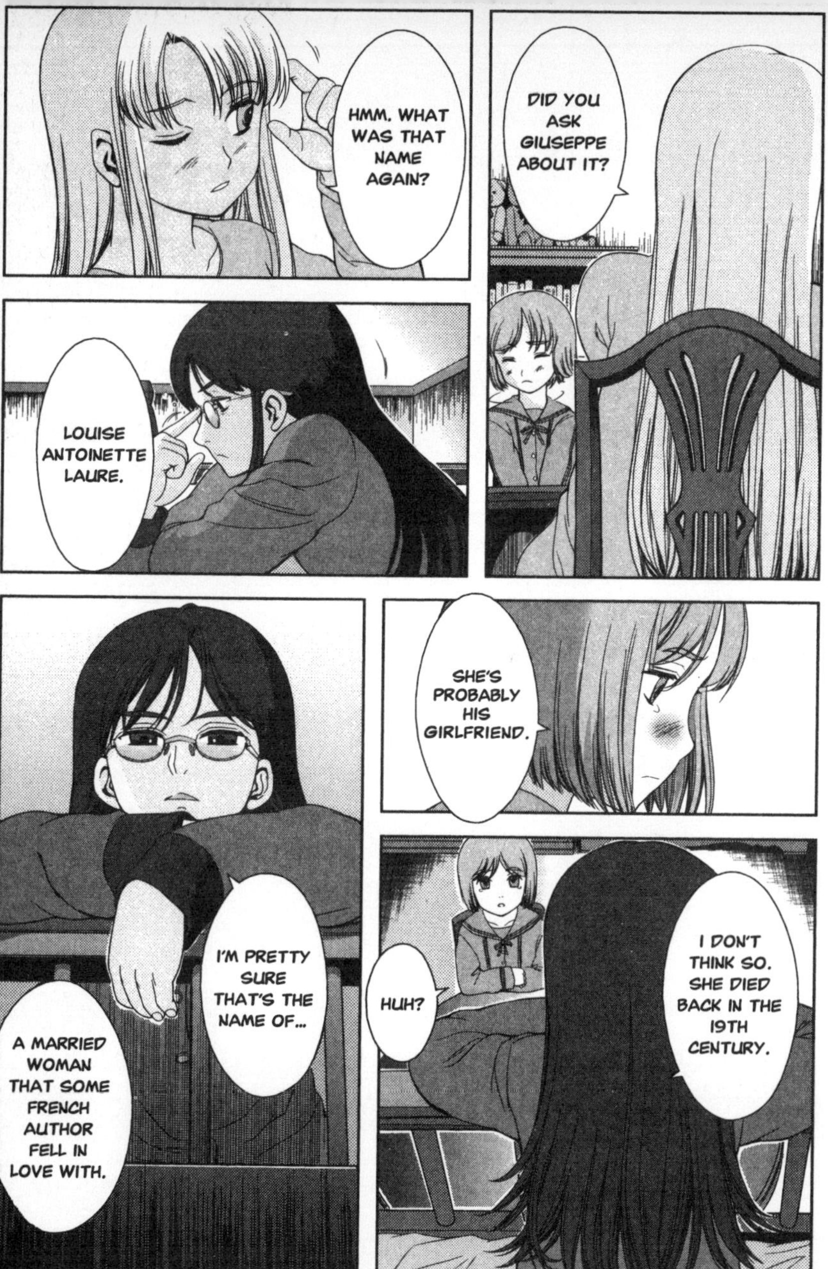
HMM. WHAT WAS THAT NAME AGAIN?
DID YOU ASK GIUSEPPE ABOUT IT?
LOUISE ANTOINETTE LAURE.
I'M PRETTY SURE THAT'S THE NAME OF...
A MARRIED WOMAN THAT SOME FRENCH AUTHOR FELL IN LOVE WITH.
SHE'S PROBABLY HIS GIRLFRIEND.
HUH?
I DON'T THINK SO. SHE DIED BACK IN THE 19TH CENTURY.

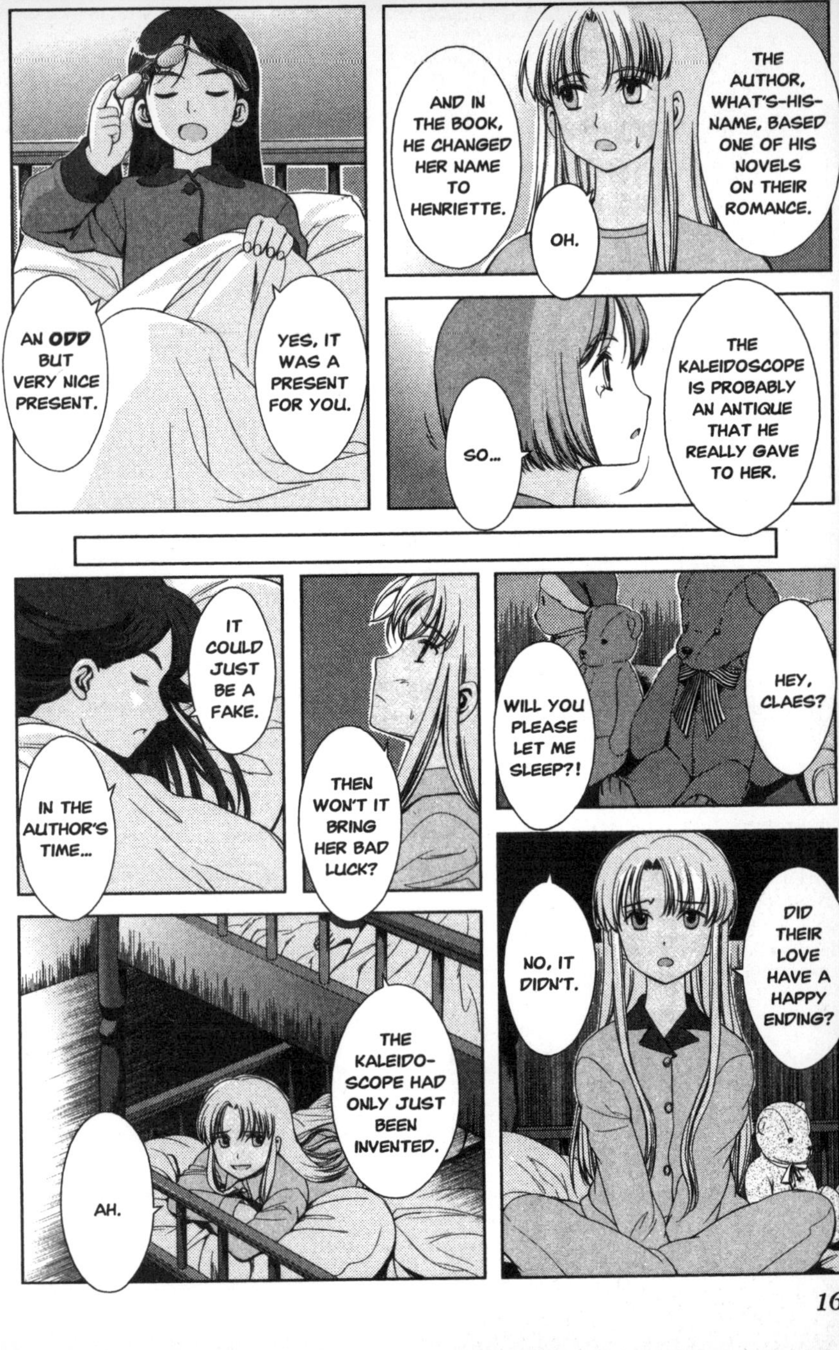
THE AUTHOR, WHAT'S-HIS-NAME, BASED ONE OF HIS NOVELS ON THEIR ROMANCE.
AND IN THE BOOK, HE CHANGED HER NAME TO HENRIETTE.
OH.
YES, IT WAS A PRESENT FOR YOU.
AN ODD BUT VERY NICE PRESENT.
THE KALEIDOSCOPE IS PROBABLY AN ANTIQUE THAT HE REALLY GAVE TO HER.
SO...
HEY, CLAES?
WILL YOU PLEASE LET ME SLEEP?!
DID THEIR LOVE HAVE A HAPPY ENDING?
NO, IT DIDN'T.
THEN WON'T IT BRING HER BAD LUCK?
IT COULD JUST BE A FAKE.
IN THE AUTHOR'S TIME...
THE KALEIDOSCOPE HAD ONLY JUST BEEN INVENTED.
AH.

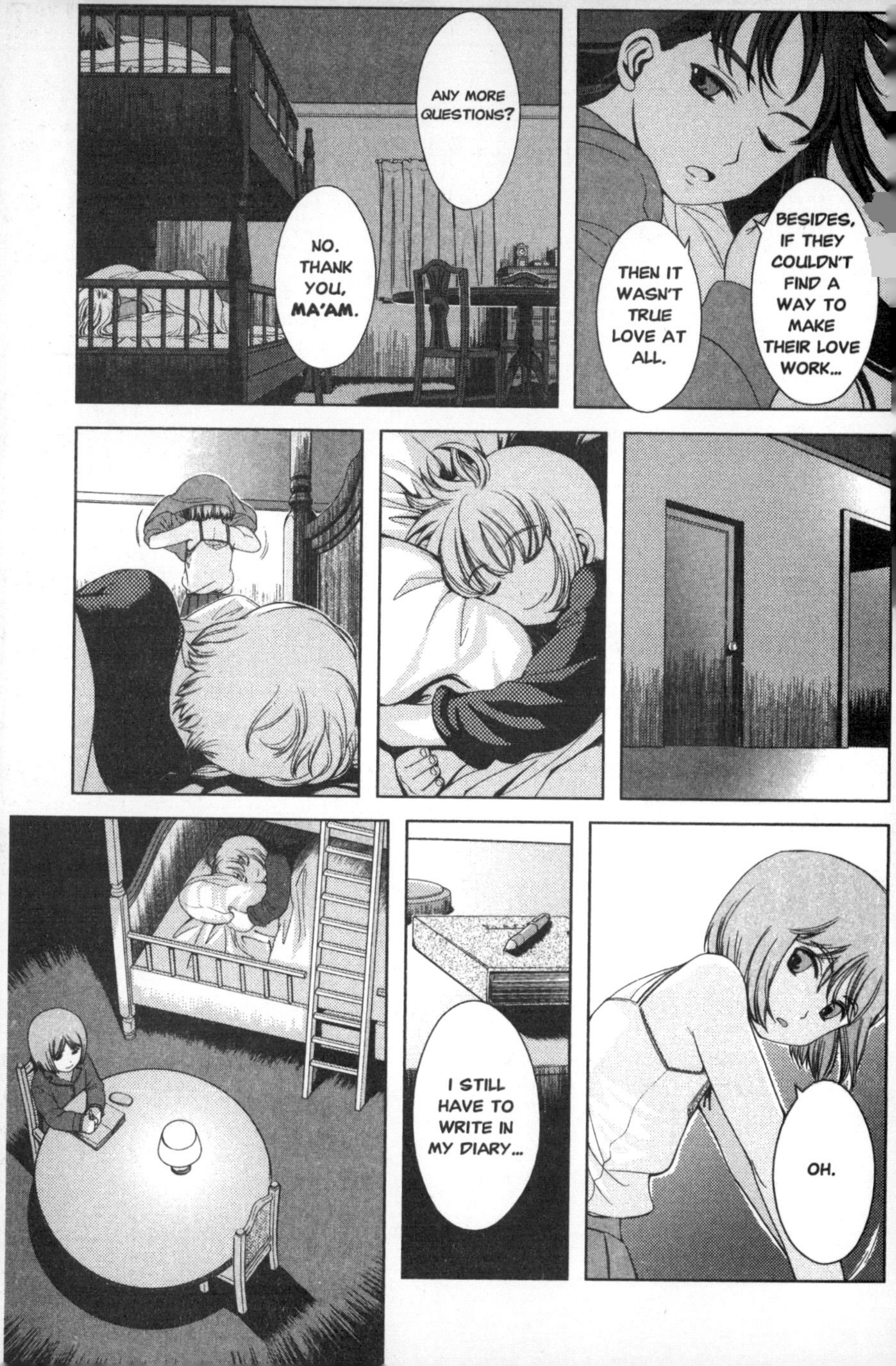
BESIDES, IF THEY COULDN'T FIND A WAY TO MAKE THEIR LOVE WORK...
THEN IT WASN'T TRUE LOVE AT ALL.
ANY MORE QUESTIONS?
NO. THANK YOU, MA'AM.
OH.
I STILL HAVE TO WRITE IN MY DIARY...

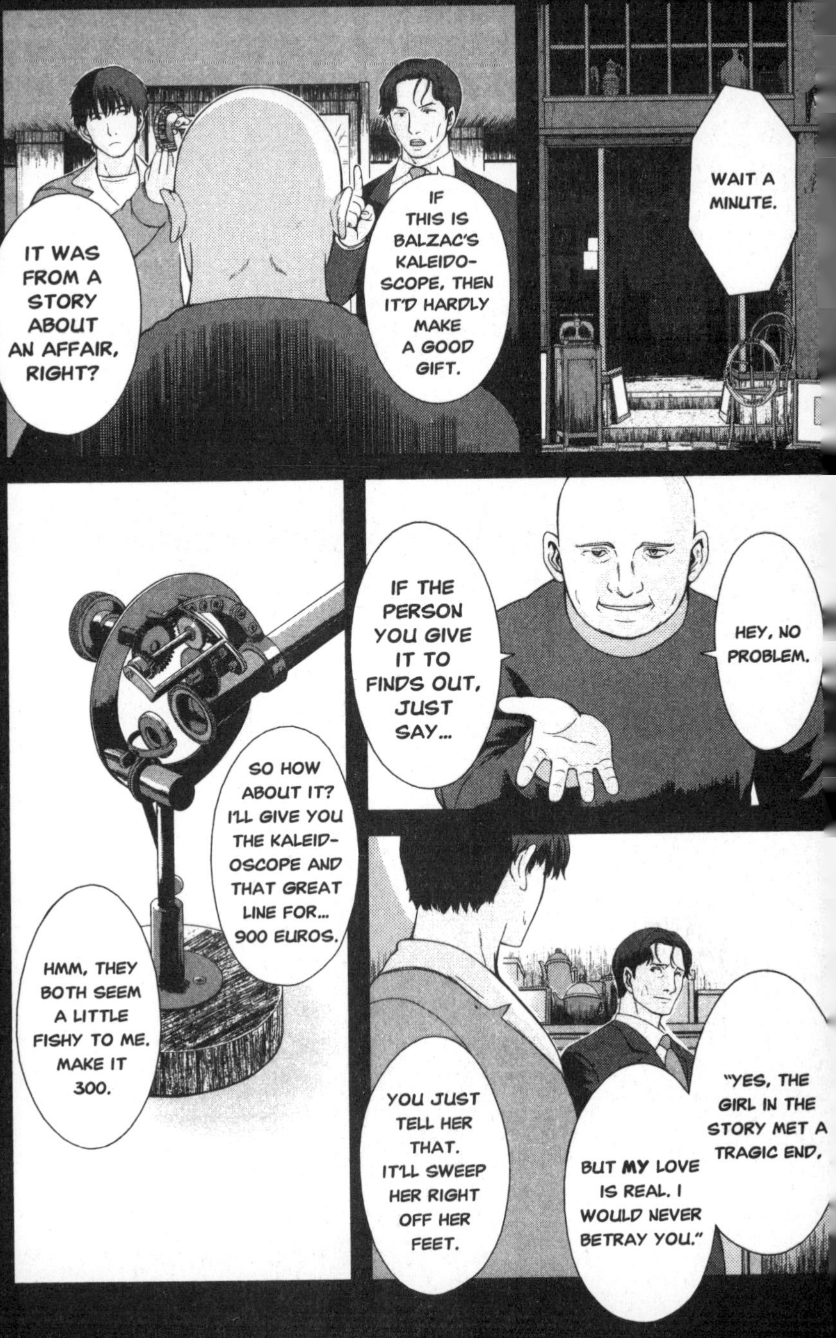
IT WAS FROM A STORY ABOUT AN AFFAIR, RIGHT?
IF THIS IS BALZAC'S KALEIDO-SCOPE, THEN IT'D HARDLY MAKE A GOOD GIFT.
WAIT A MINUTE.
HEY, NO PROBLEM.
IF THE PERSON YOU GIVE IT TO FINDS OUT, JUST SAY...
"YES, THE GIRL IN THE STORY MET A TRAGIC END,
BUT MY LOVE IS REAL. I WOULD NEVER BETRAY YOU."
YOU JUST TELL HER THAT. IT'LL SWEEP HER RIGHT OFF HER FEET.
SO HOW ABOUT IT? I'LL GIVE YOU THE KALEID-OSCOPE AND THAT GREAT LINE FOR... 900 EUROS.
HMM, THEY BOTH SEEM A LITTLE FISHY TO ME. MAKE IT 300.

GUNSLINGERGIRL.

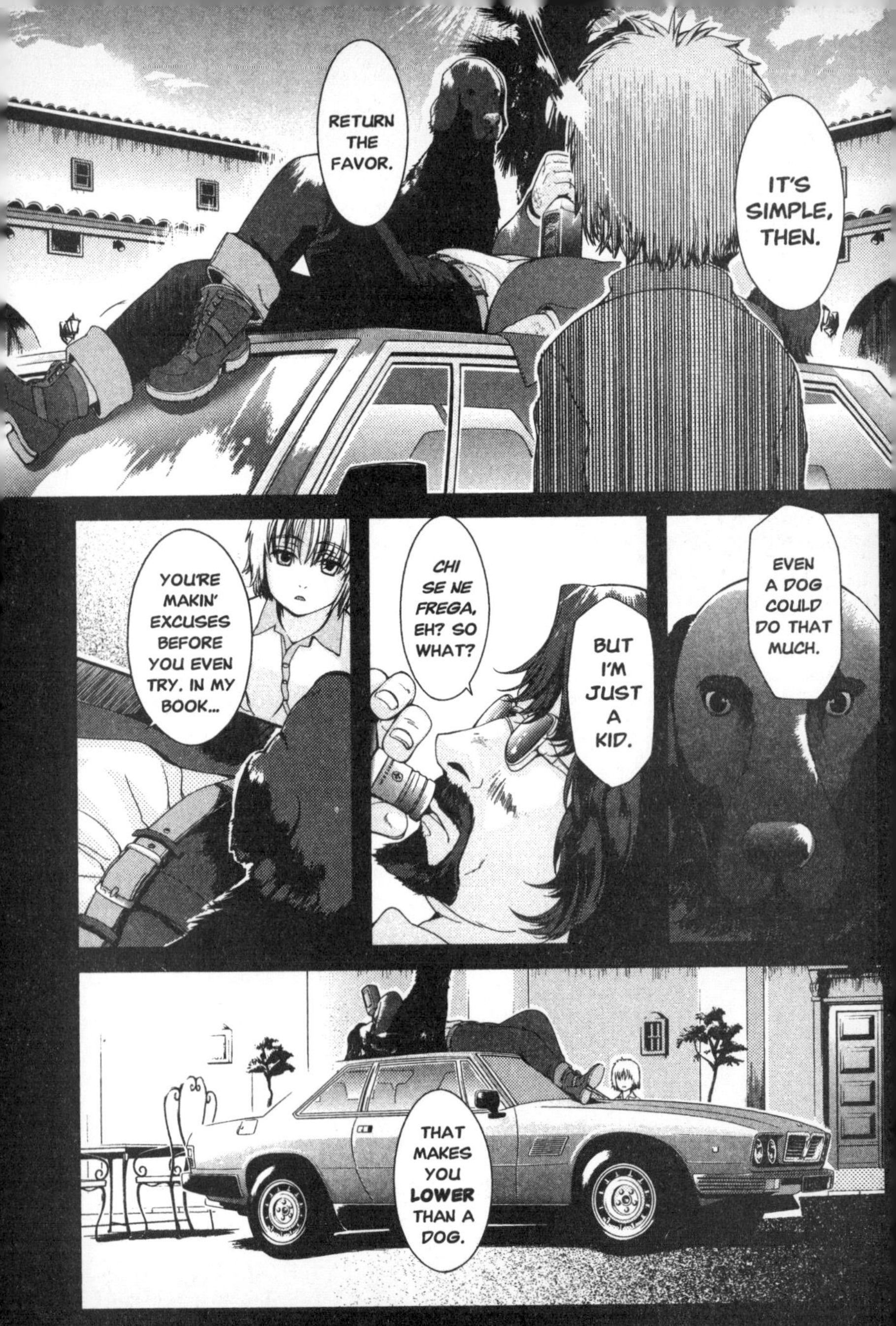

IT'S SIMPLE, THEN.
RETURN THE FAVOR.
EVEN A DOG COULD DO THAT MUCH.
BUT I'M JUST A KID.
CHI SE NE FREGA, EH? SO WHAT?
YOU'RE MAKIN' EXCUSES BEFORE YOU EVEN TRY. IN MY BOOK...
THAT MAKES YOU LOWER THAN A DOG.

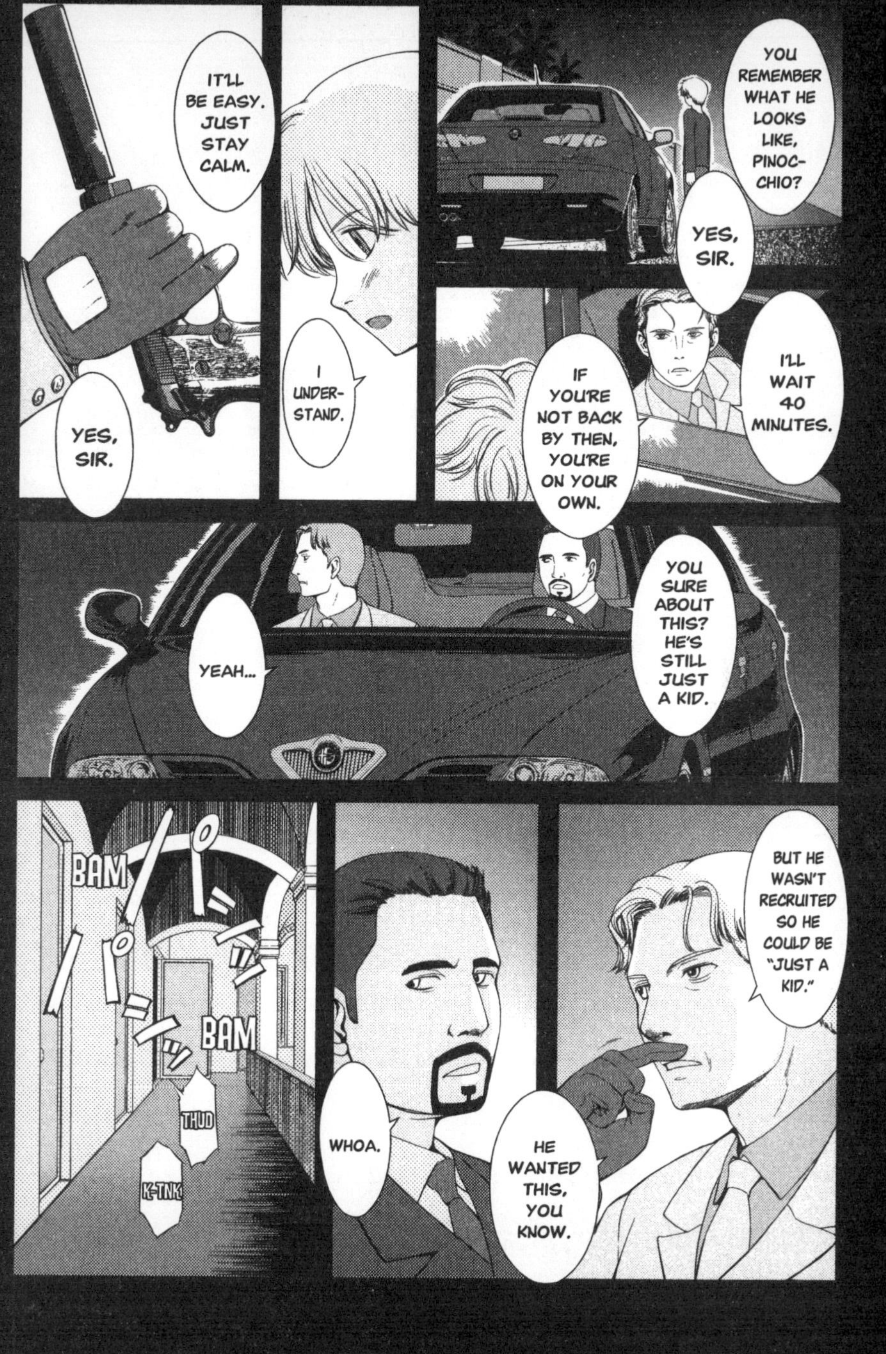
YOU REMEMBER WHAT HE LOOKS LIKE, PINOCCHIO?
YES, SIR.
I'LL WAIT 40 MINUTES.
IF YOU'RE NOT BACK BY THEN, YOU'RE ON YOUR OWN.
I UNDERSTAND.
IT'LL BE EASY. JUST STAY CALM.
YES, SIR.
YOU SURE ABOUT THIS? HE'S STILL JUST A KID.
YEAH...
BUT HE WASN'T RECRUITED SO HE COULD BE "JUST A KID."
HE WANTED THIS, YOU KNOW.
WHOA.
BAM
BAM
THUD
K-TNK

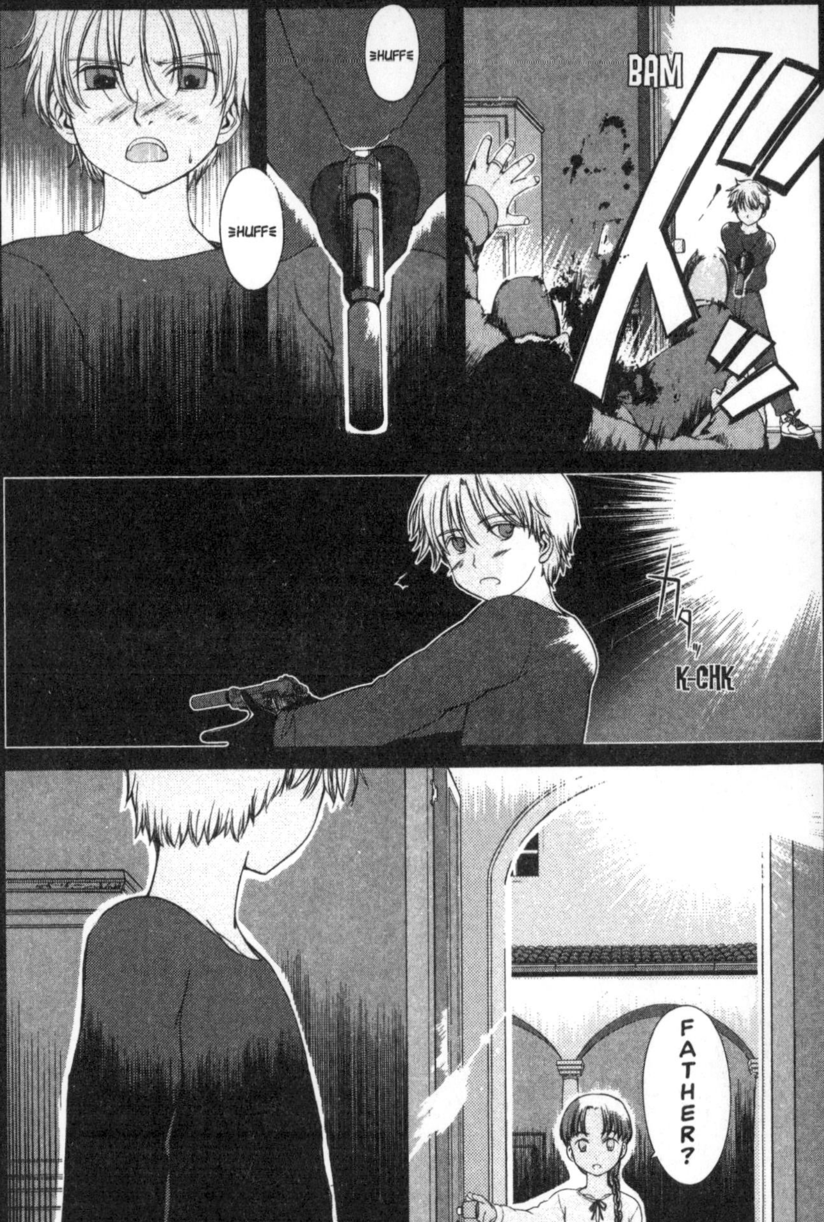
HUFF
HUFF
BAM
K-CHK
FATHER?

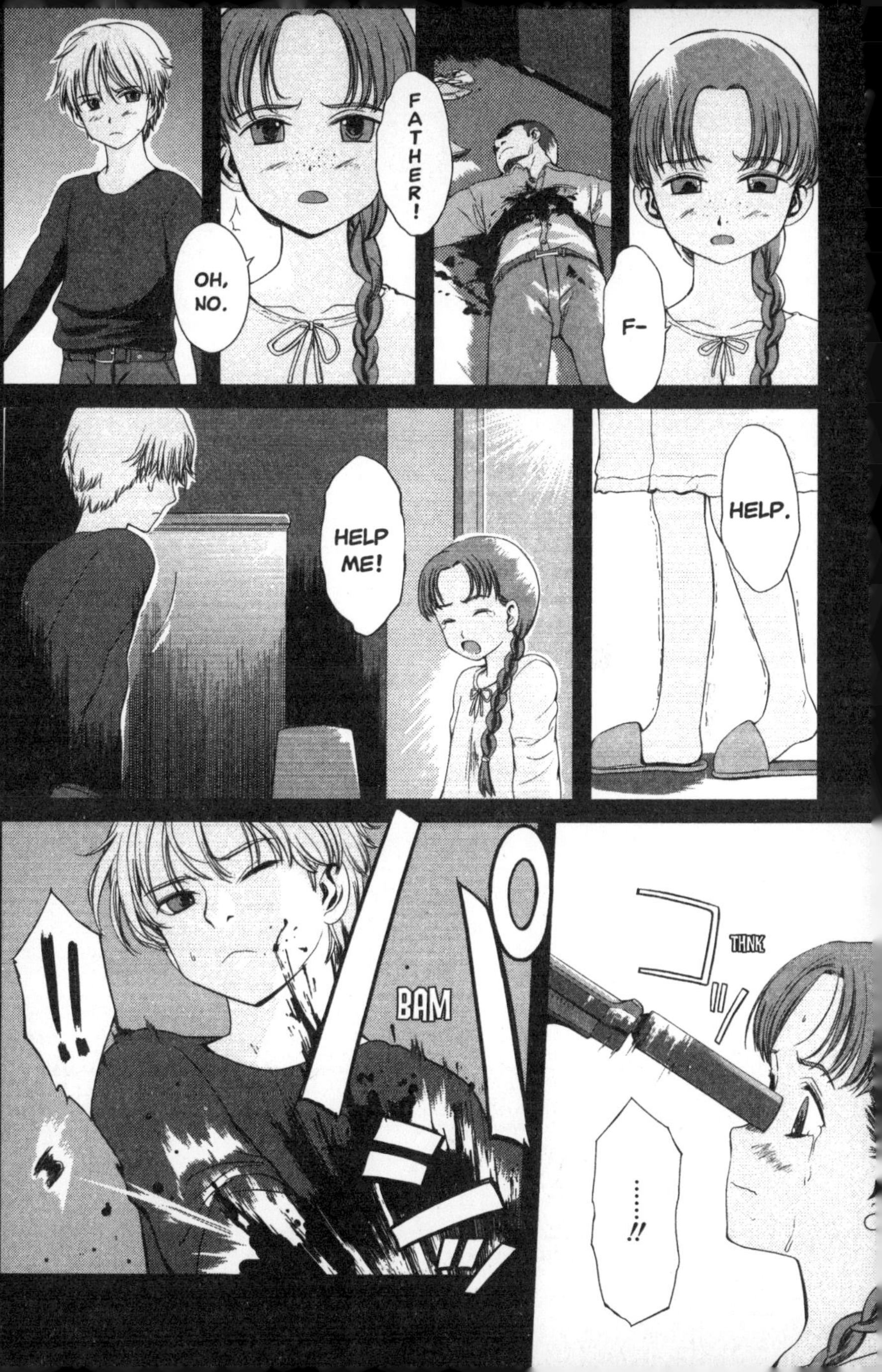
F-
FATHER!
OH, NO.
HELP.
HELP ME!
THNK
……!!
BAM
!!

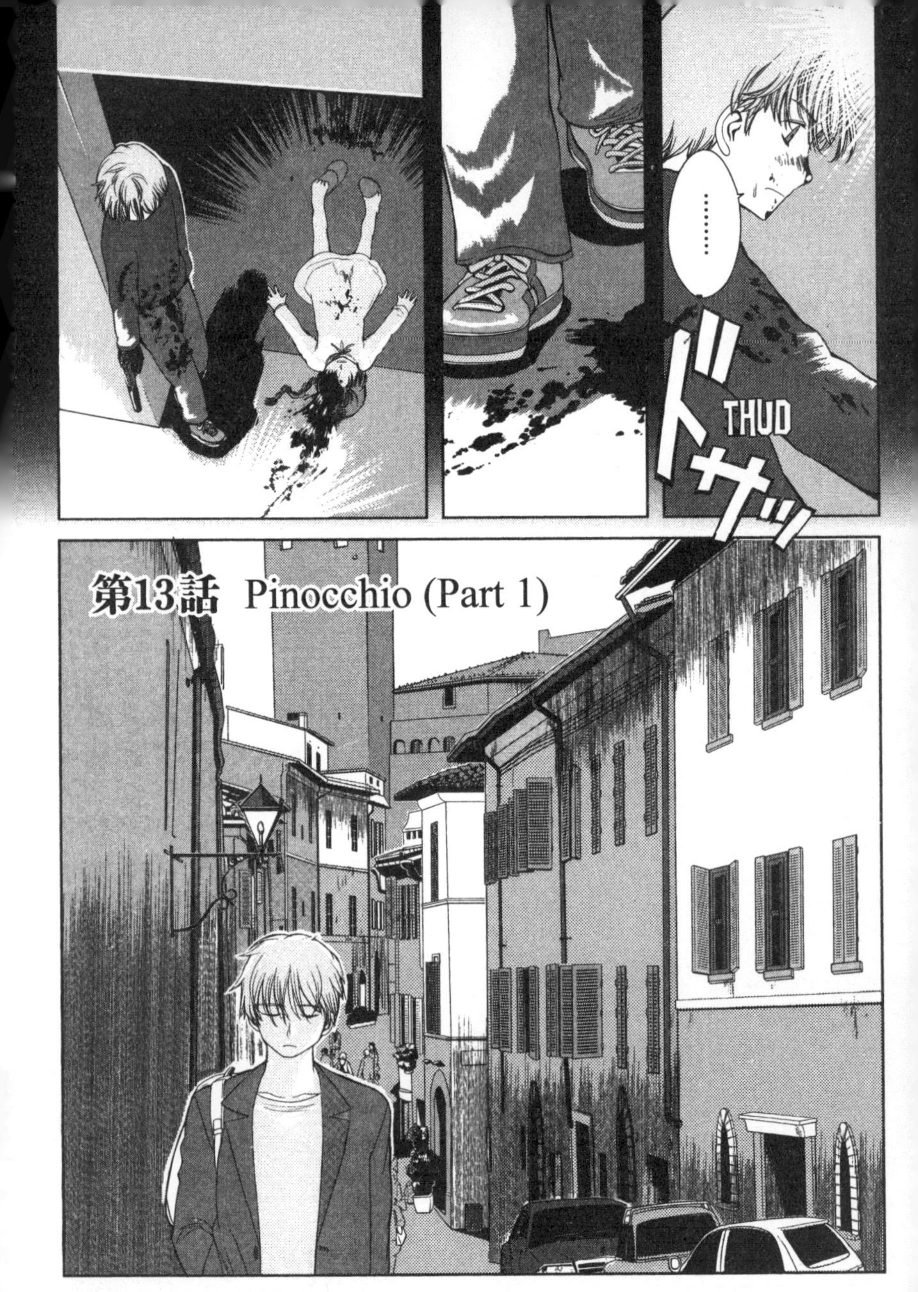
……
ドサッ
THUD
第13話 Pinocchio (Part 1)

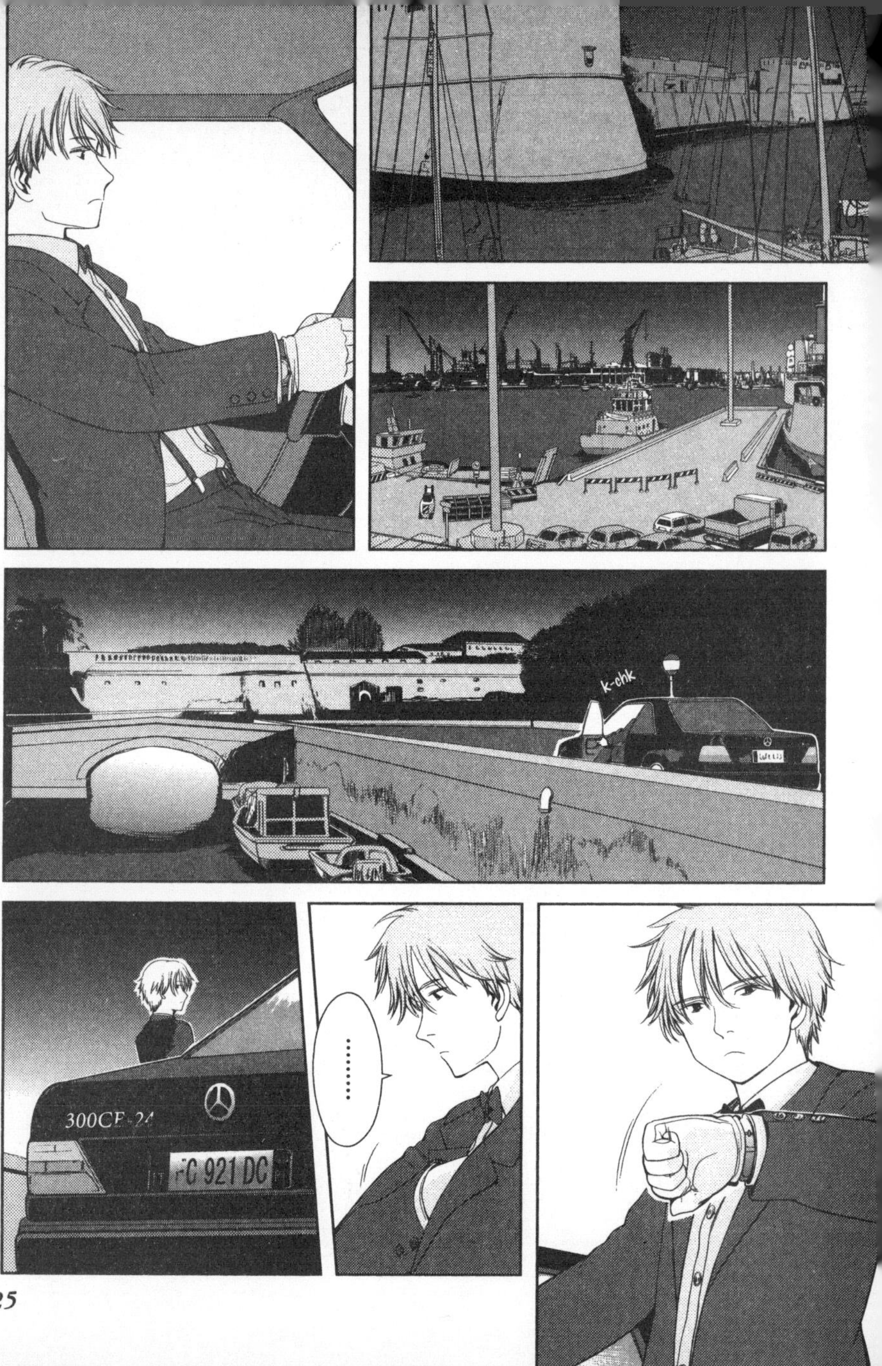
k-chk
300CE-24
FC 921 DC
....

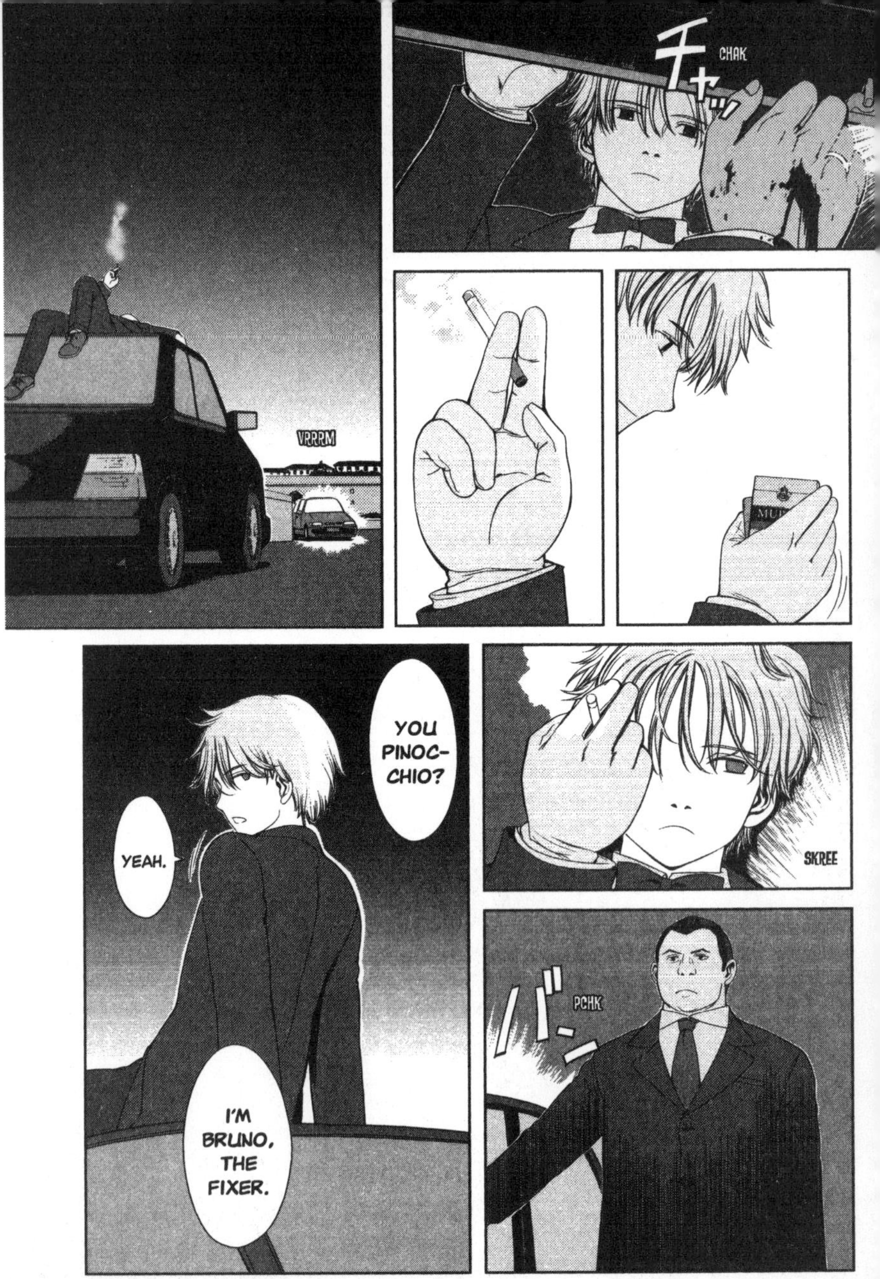
チャッ
CHAK
VRRRM
SKREE
PCHK
YOU PINOCCHIO?
YEAH.
I'M BRUNO, THE FIXER.

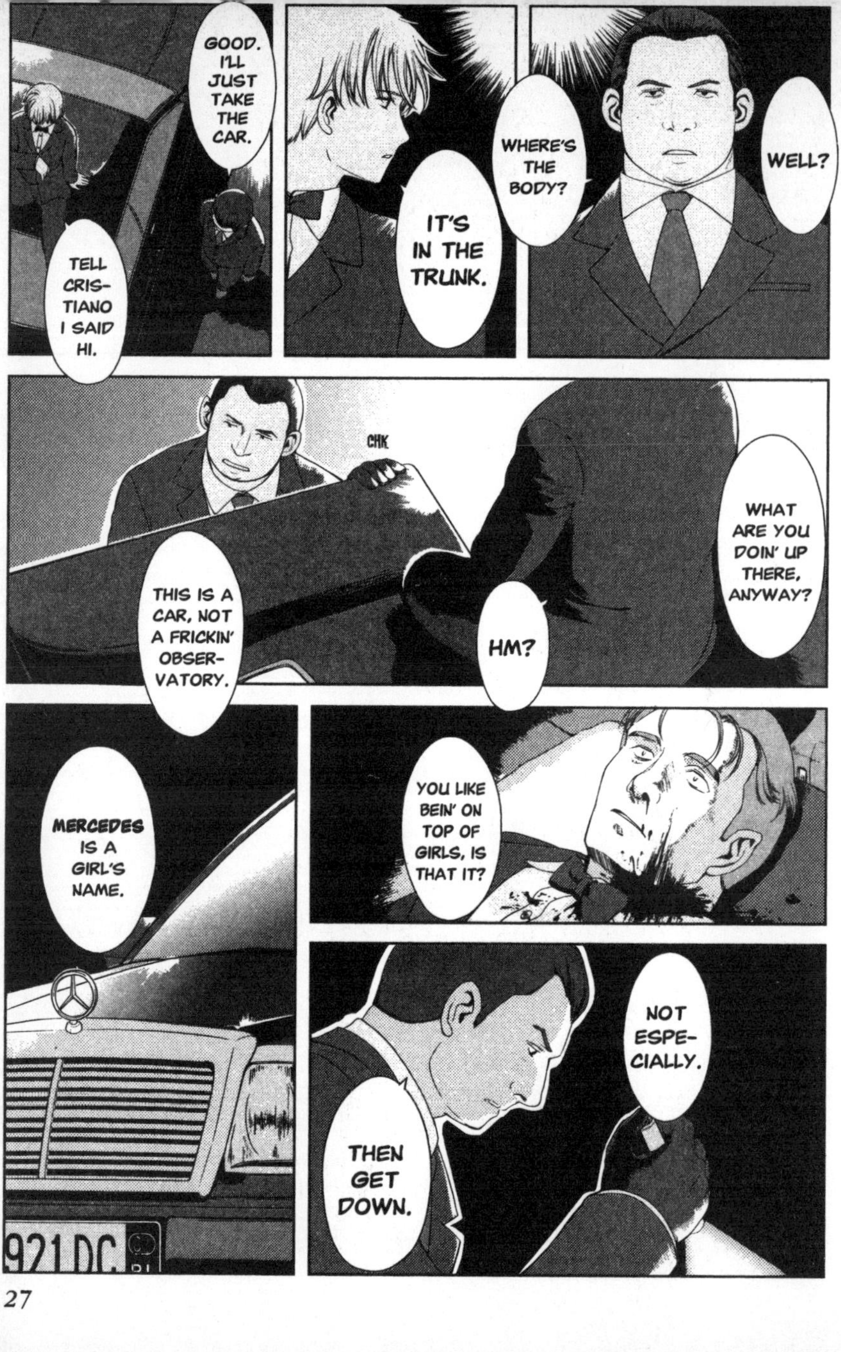
WELL?
WHERE'S THE BODY?
IT'S IN THE TRUNK.
GOOD. I'LL JUST TAKE THE CAR.
TELL CRIS-TIANO I SAID HI.
CHK
WHAT ARE YOU DOIN' UP THERE, ANYWAY?
HM?
THIS IS A CAR, NOT A FRICKIN' OBSER-VATORY.
MERCEDES IS A GIRL'S NAME.
YOU LIKE BEIN' ON TOP OF GIRLS, IS THAT IT?
NOT ESPE-CIALLY.
THEN GET DOWN.
921 DC

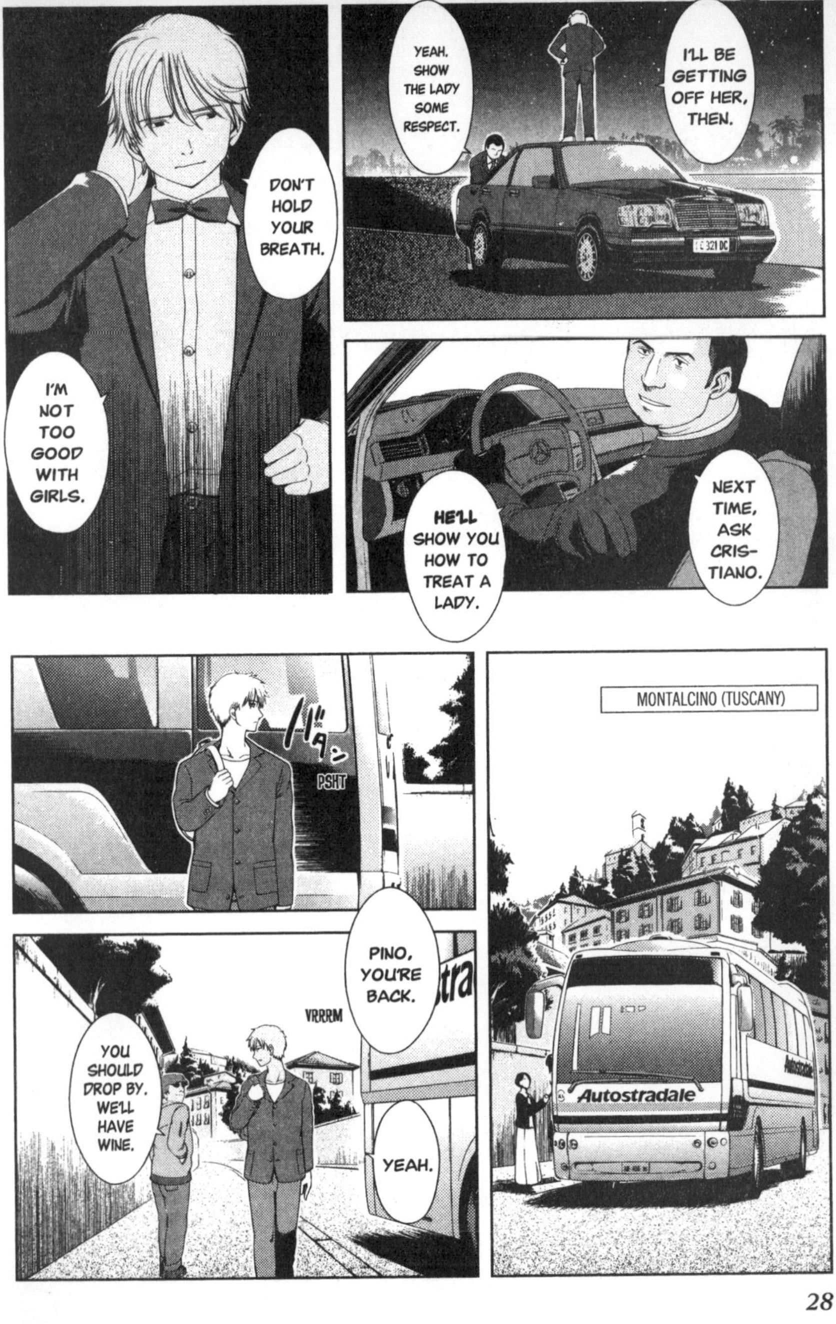

I'LL BE GETTING OFF HER, THEN.
YEAH. SHOW THE LADY SOME RESPECT.
NEXT TIME, ASK CRIS-TIANO.
HE'LL SHOW YOU HOW TO TREAT A LADY.
DON'T HOLD YOUR BREATH.
I'M NOT TOO GOOD WITH GIRLS.
MONTALCINO (TUSCANY)
Autostradale
バタン
PSHT
PINO, YOU'RE BACK.
VRRRM
YEAH.
YOU SHOULD DROP BY. WE'LL HAVE WINE.

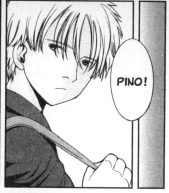

PINO!
HI, AURORA.
ARE YOU HEADING BACK?
YOUR WORK MUST BE DONE THEN, HUH?
YEAH.
MY MOM KNEW YOU'D BE BACK SOON, SO SHE WENT TO BUY SOME MEAT.
I TOLD HER SHE DIDN'T HAVE TO.
WE'RE JUST NEIGHBORS...
BUT YOU'RE REALLY COOL!
AND GOOD THINGS HAPPEN TO COOL PEOPLE!
SAY, UM...
WHAT KIND OF WORK DO YOU DO?

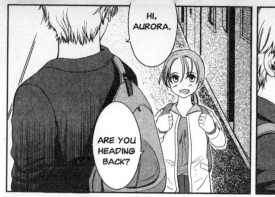

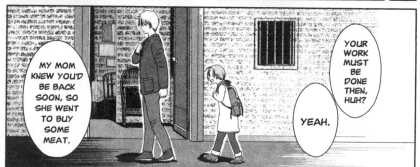

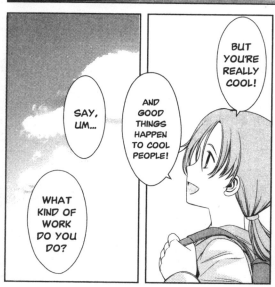

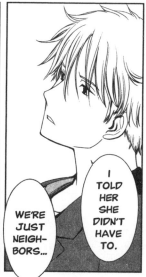

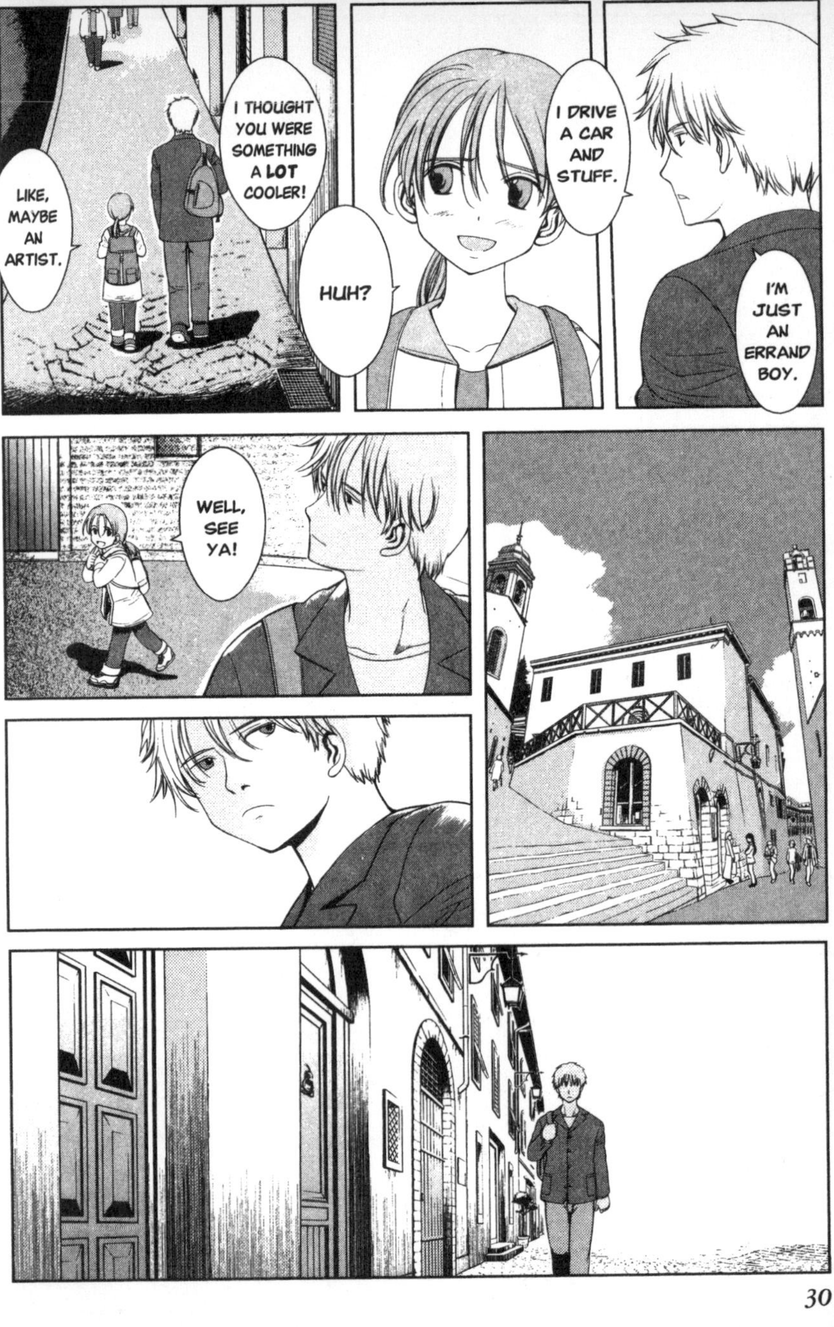
I DRIVE A CAR AND STUFF.
I'M JUST AN ERRAND BOY.
HUH?
I THOUGHT YOU WERE SOMETHING A LOT COOLER!
LIKE, MAYBE AN ARTIST.
WELL, SEE YA!

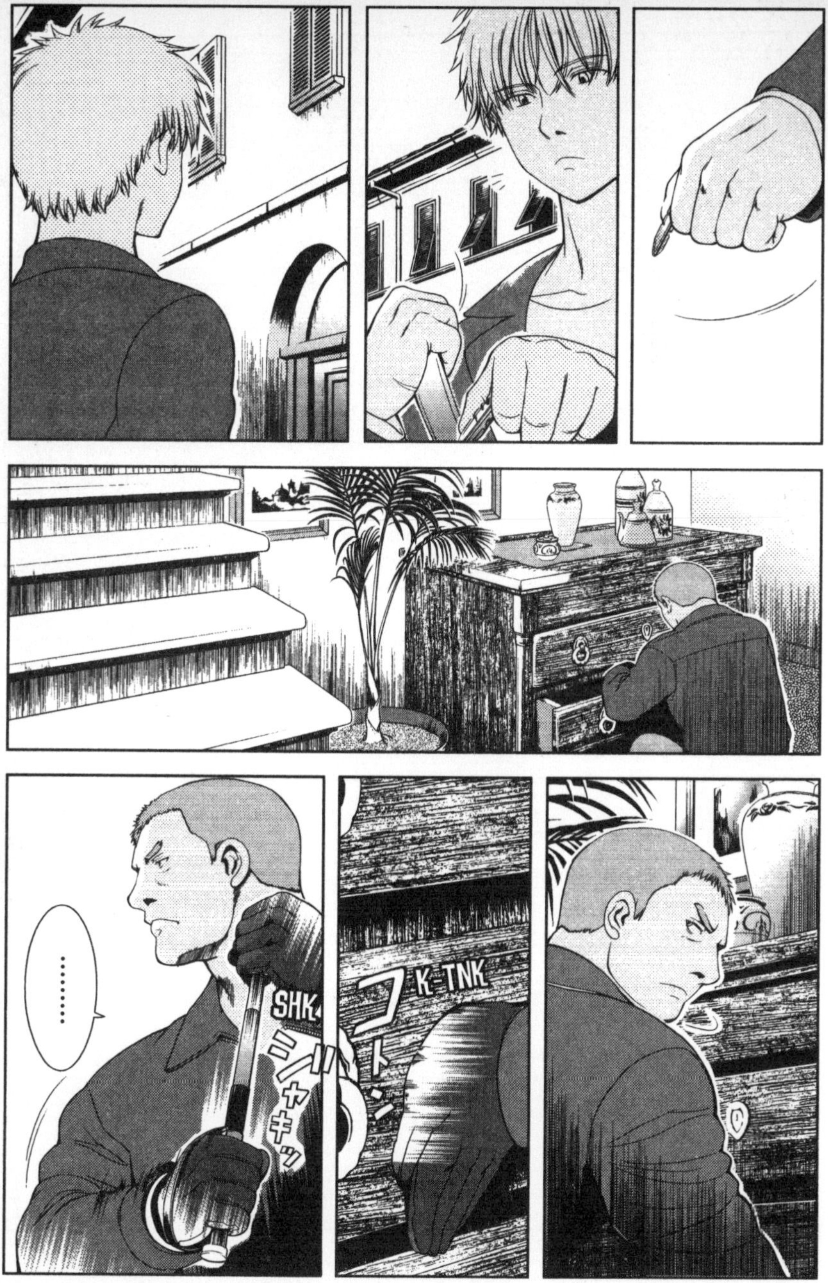
K-TNK
コトン
SHK
シャキッ
……

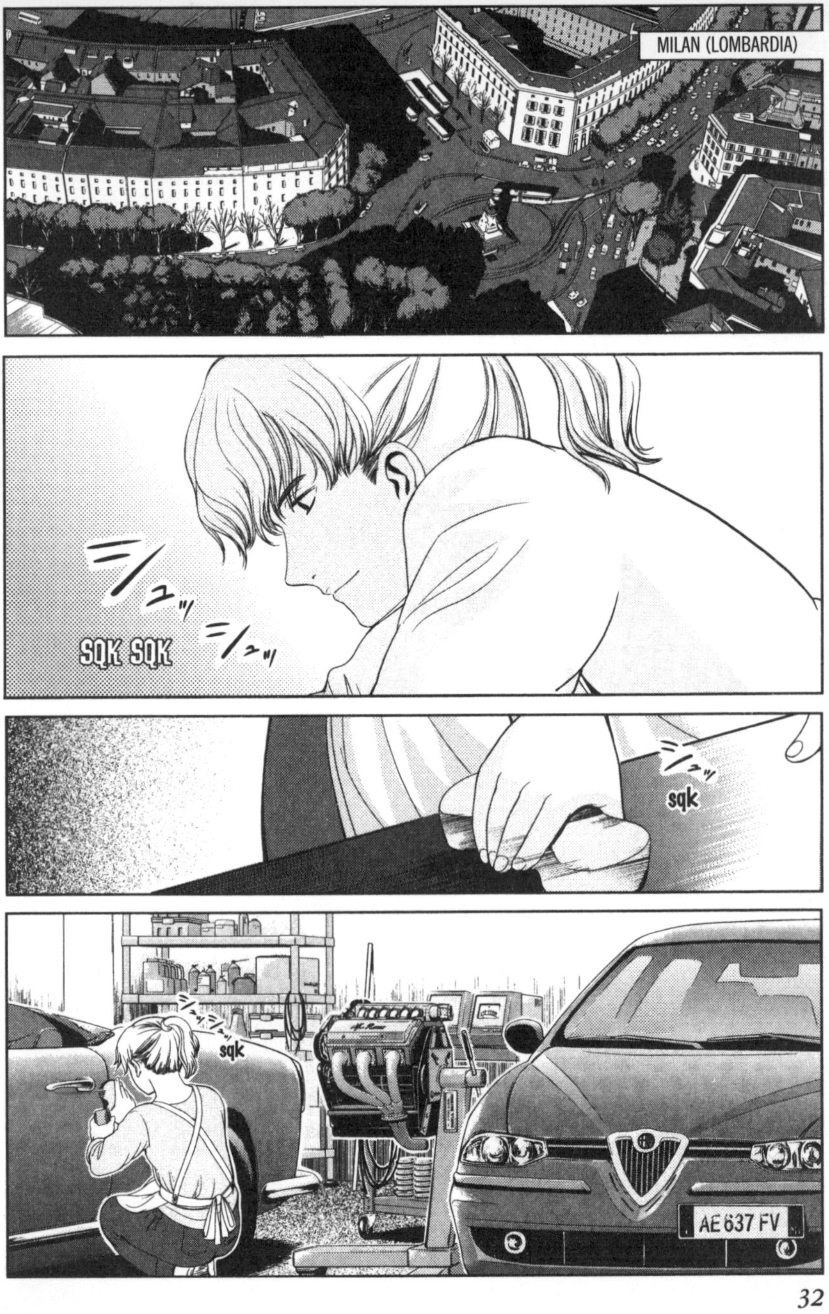
MILAN (LOMBARDIA)
SQK SQK
sqk
sqk
AE 637 FV

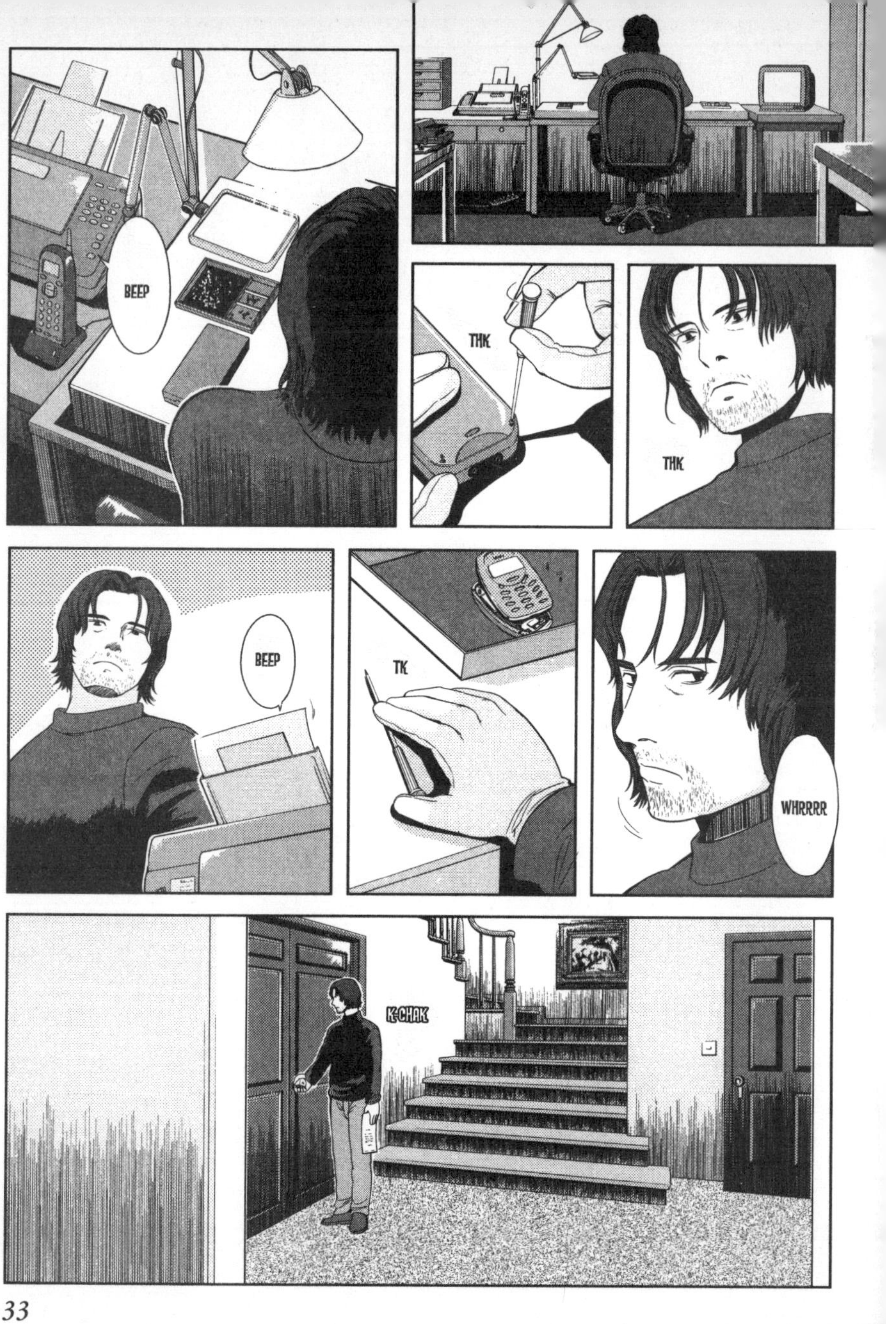
BEEP
THK
THK
BEEP
TK
WHRRRR
K-CHAK

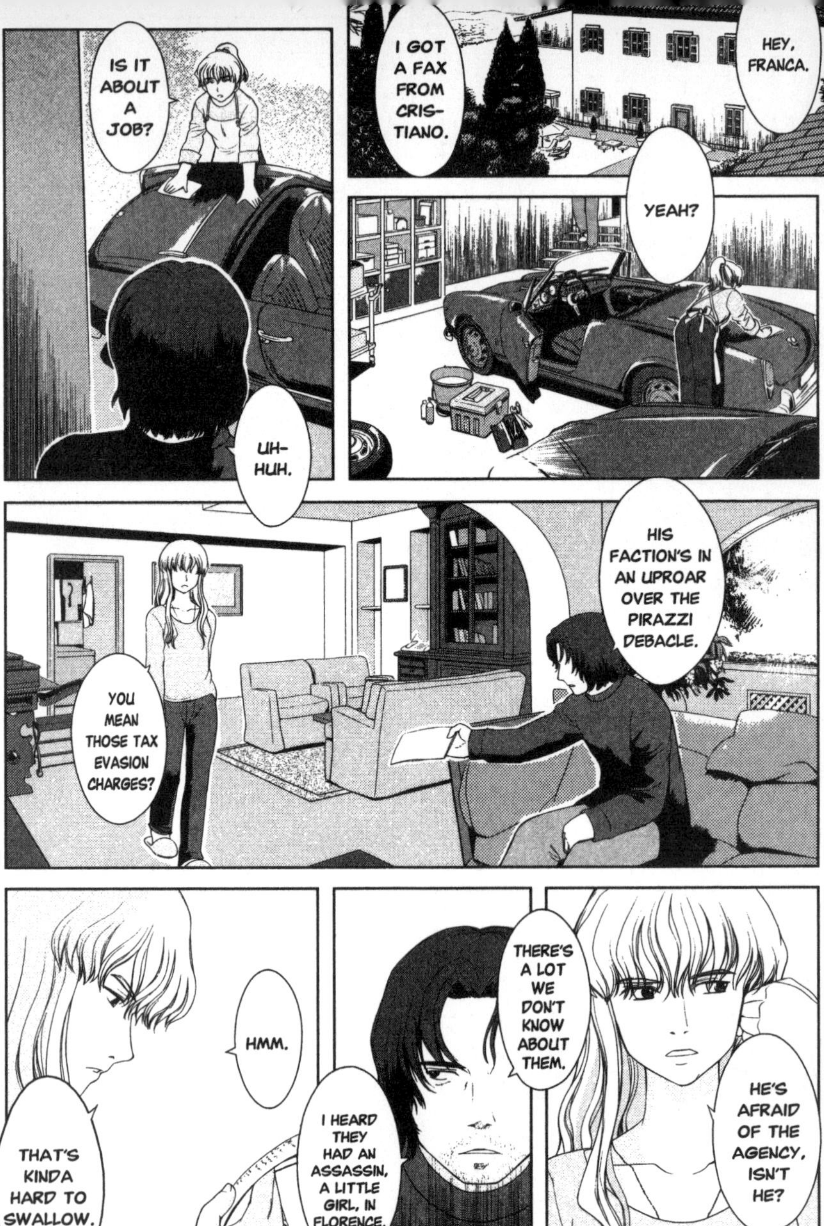
HEY, FRANCA.
I GOT A FAX FROM CRIS-TIANO.
YEAH?
IS IT ABOUT A JOB?
UH-HUH.
HIS FACTION'S IN AN UPROAR OVER THE PIRAZZI DEBACLE.
YOU MEAN THOSE TAX EVASION CHARGES?
HE'S AFRAID OF THE AGENCY, ISN'T HE?
THERE'S A LOT WE DON'T KNOW ABOUT THEM.
I HEARD THEY HAD AN ASSASSIN, A LITTLE GIRL, IN FLORENCE.
HMM.
THAT'S KINDA HARD TO SWALLOW.

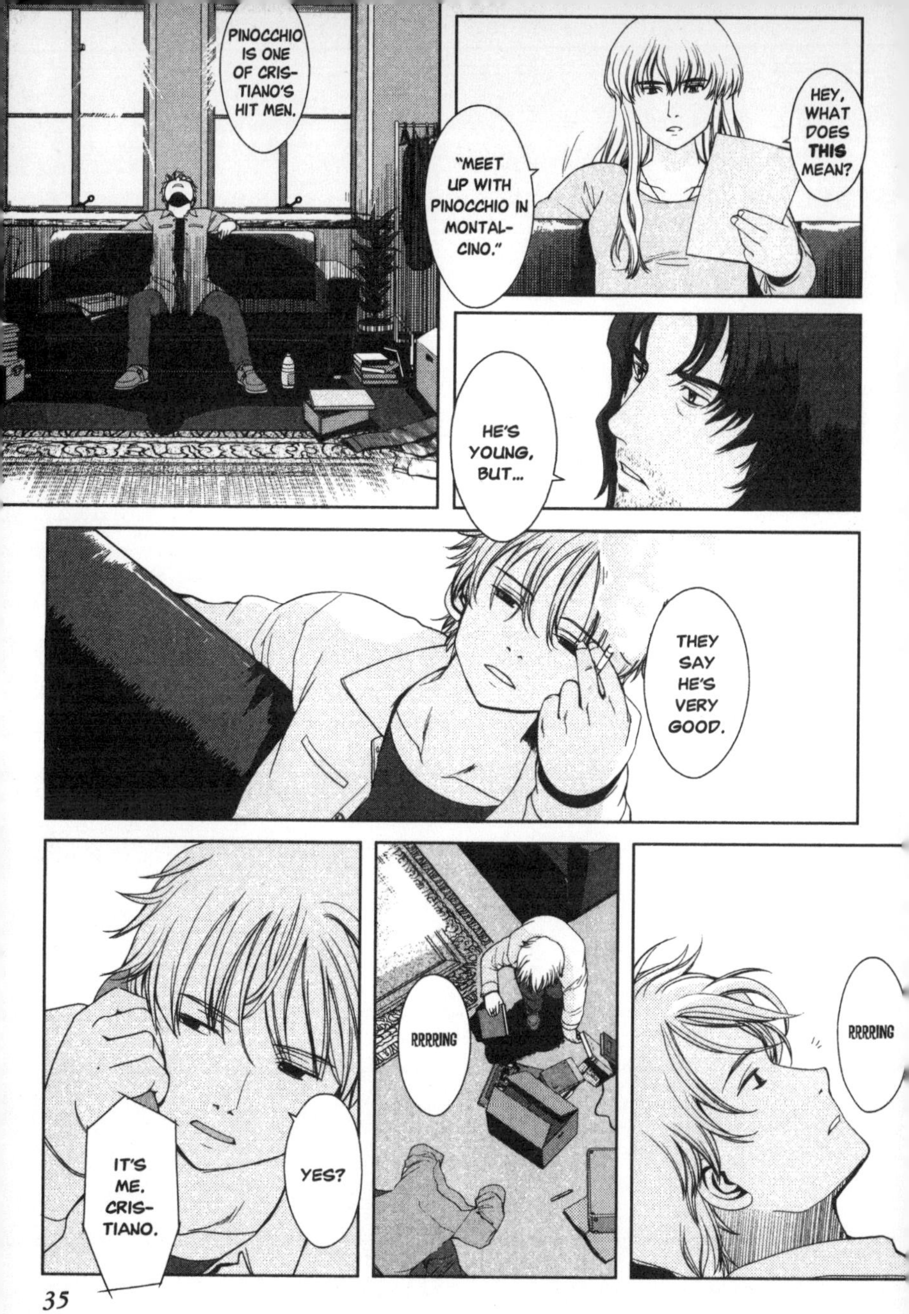
HEY, WHAT DOES THIS MEAN?
"MEET UP WITH PINOCCHIO IN MONTAL-CINO."
PINOCCHIO IS ONE OF CRIS-TIANO'S HIT MEN.
HE'S YOUNG, BUT...
THEY SAY HE'S VERY GOOD.
RRRRING
RRRRING
YES?
IT'S ME. CRIS-TIANO.

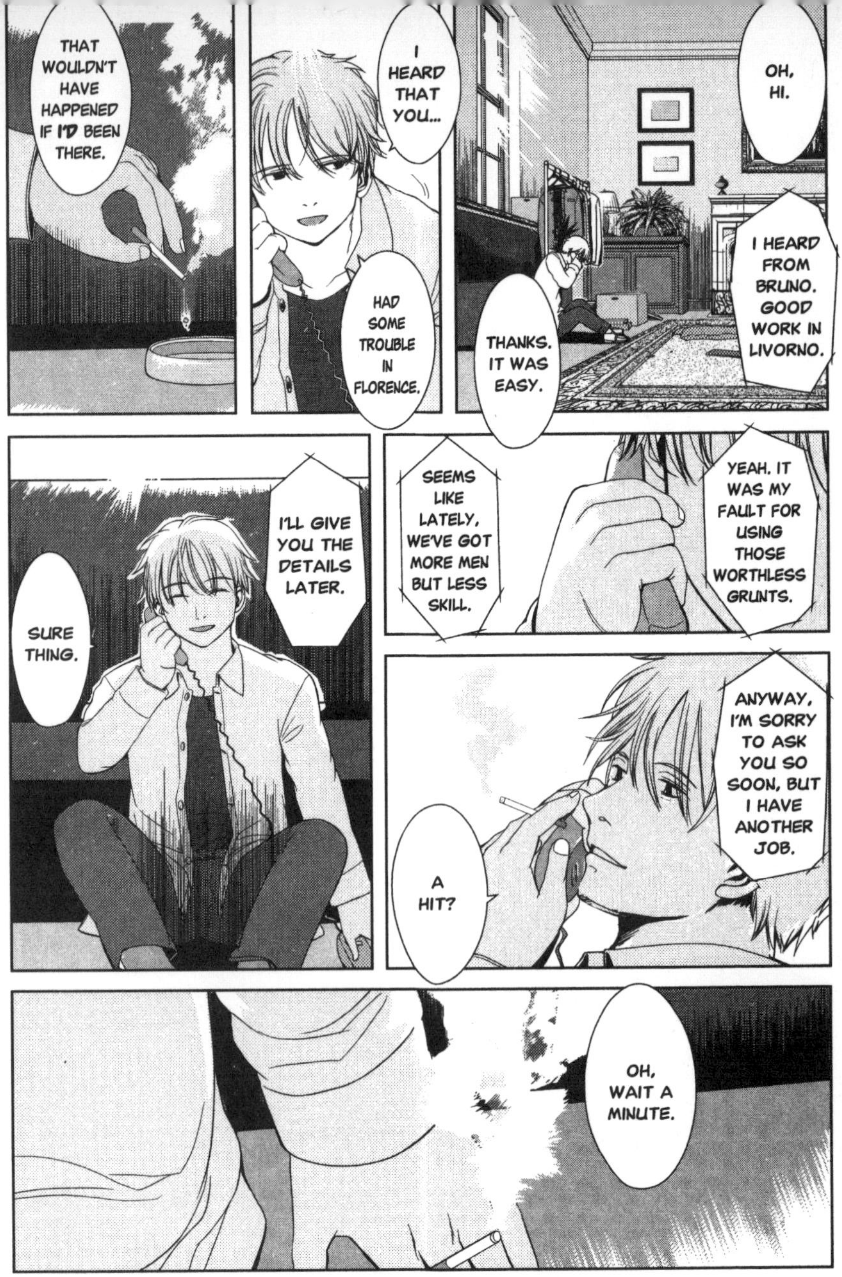
OH, HI.
I HEARD FROM BRUNO. GOOD WORK IN LIVORNO.
THANKS. IT WAS EASY.
I HEARD THAT YOU...
HAD SOME TROUBLE IN FLORENCE.
THAT WOULDN'T HAVE HAPPENED IF I'D BEEN THERE.
YEAH. IT WAS MY FAULT FOR USING THOSE WORTHLESS GRUNTS.
SEEMS LIKE LATELY, WE'VE GOT MORE MEN BUT LESS SKILL.
ANYWAY, I'M SORRY TO ASK YOU SO SOON, BUT I HAVE ANOTHER JOB.
A HIT?
I'LL GIVE YOU THE DETAILS LATER.
SURE THING.
OH, WAIT A MINUTE.

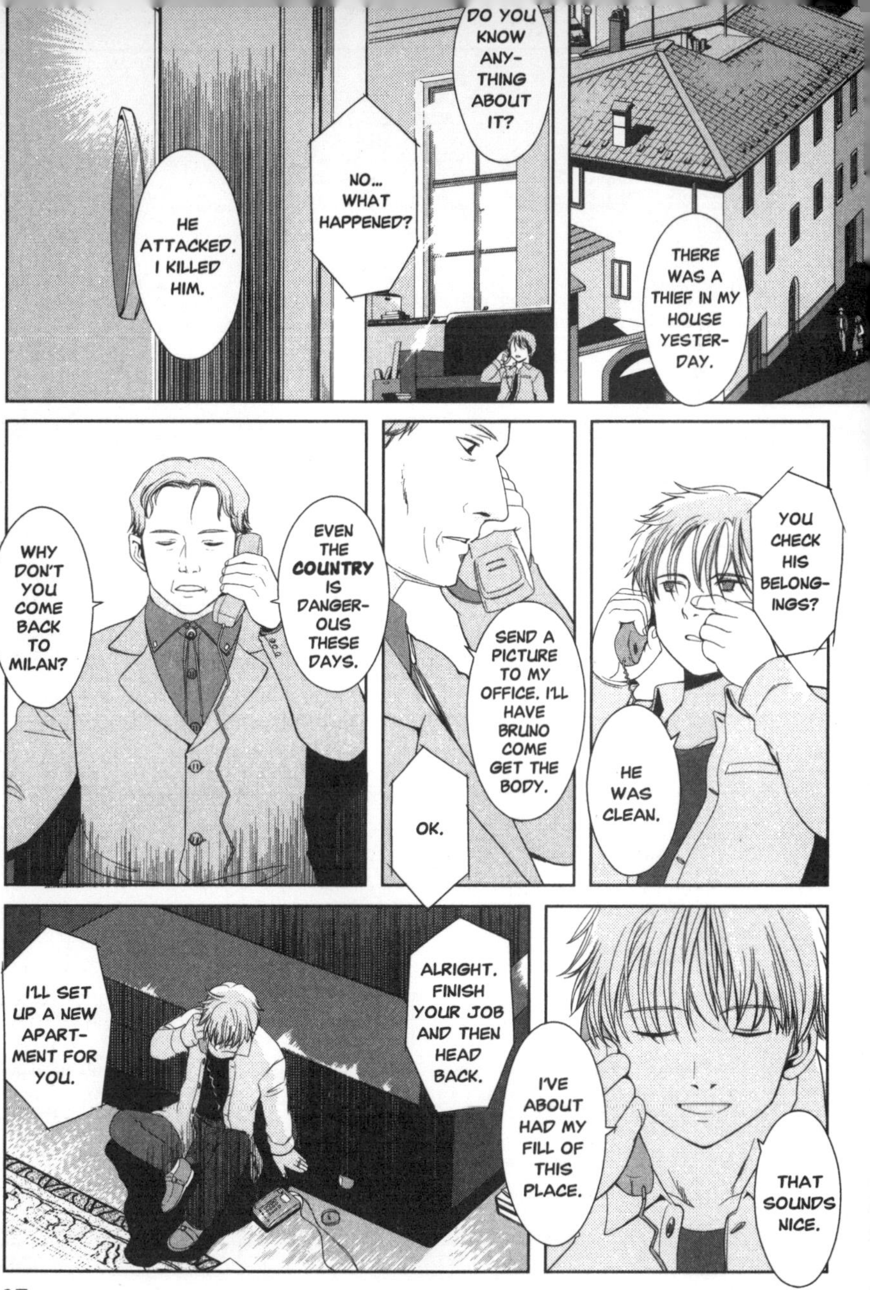
THERE WAS A THIEF IN MY HOUSE YESTER-DAY.
DO YOU KNOW ANY-THING ABOUT IT?
NO... WHAT HAPPENED?
HE ATTACKED. I KILLED HIM.
YOU CHECK HIS BELONG-INGS?
HE WAS CLEAN.
SEND A PICTURE TO MY OFFICE. I'LL HAVE BRUNO COME GET THE BODY.
OK.
EVEN THE **COUNTRY** IS DANGER-OUS THESE DAYS.
WHY DON'T YOU COME BACK TO MILAN?
I'VE ABOUT HAD MY FILL OF THIS PLACE.
THAT SOUNDS NICE.
ALRIGHT. FINISH YOUR JOB AND THEN HEAD BACK.
I'LL SET UP A NEW APART-MENT FOR YOU.

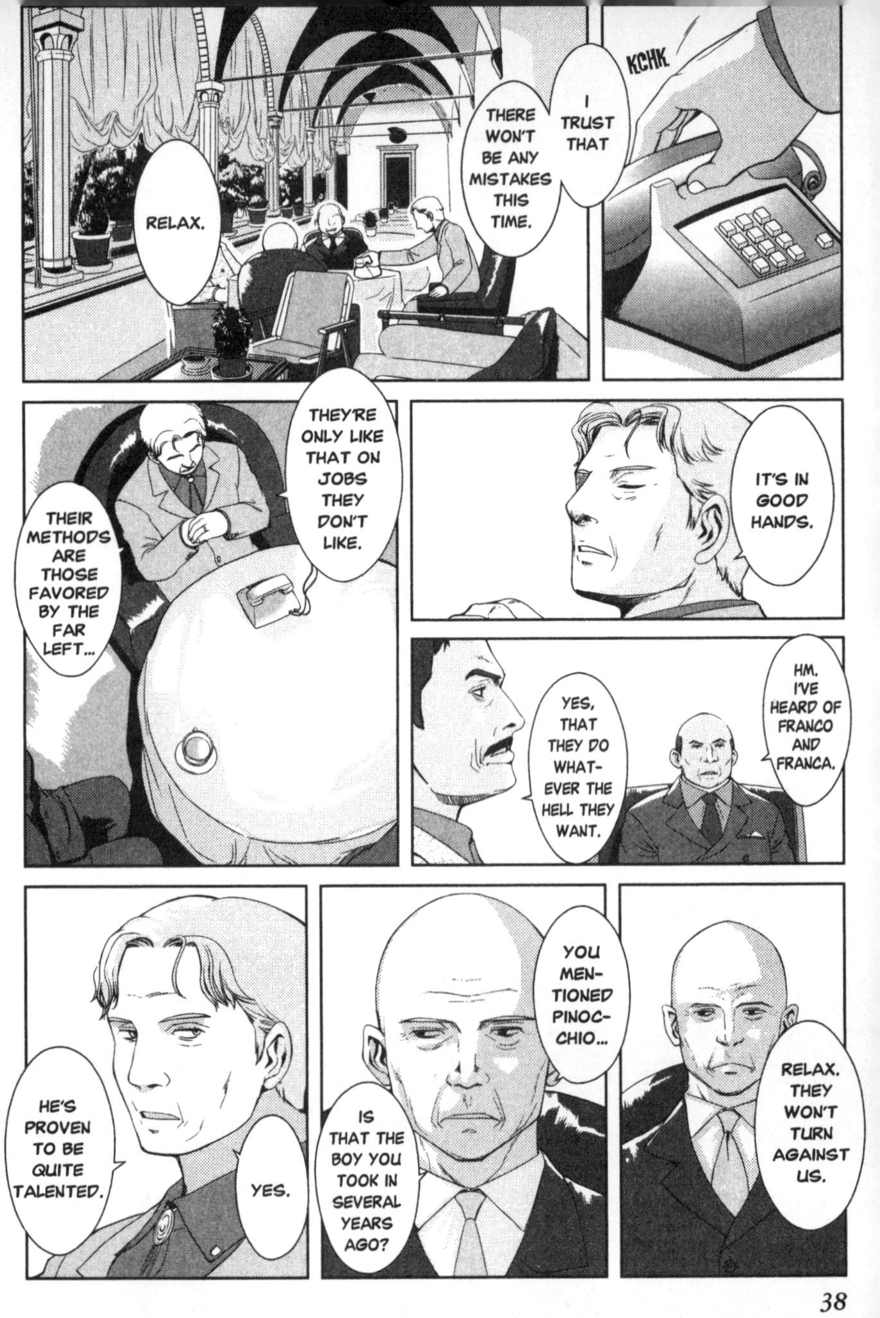
KCHK
I TRUST THAT
THERE WON'T BE ANY MISTAKES THIS TIME.
RELAX.
IT'S IN GOOD HANDS.
HM. I'VE HEARD OF FRANCO AND FRANCA.
YES, THAT THEY DO WHAT-EVER THE HELL THEY WANT.
THEIR METHODS ARE THOSE FAVORED BY THE FAR LEFT...
THEY'RE ONLY LIKE THAT ON JOBS THEY DON'T LIKE.
RELAX. THEY WON'T TURN AGAINST US.
YOU MEN-TIONED PINOC-CHIO...
IS THAT THE BOY YOU TOOK IN SEVERAL YEARS AGO?
YES.
HE'S PROVEN TO BE QUITE TALENTED.

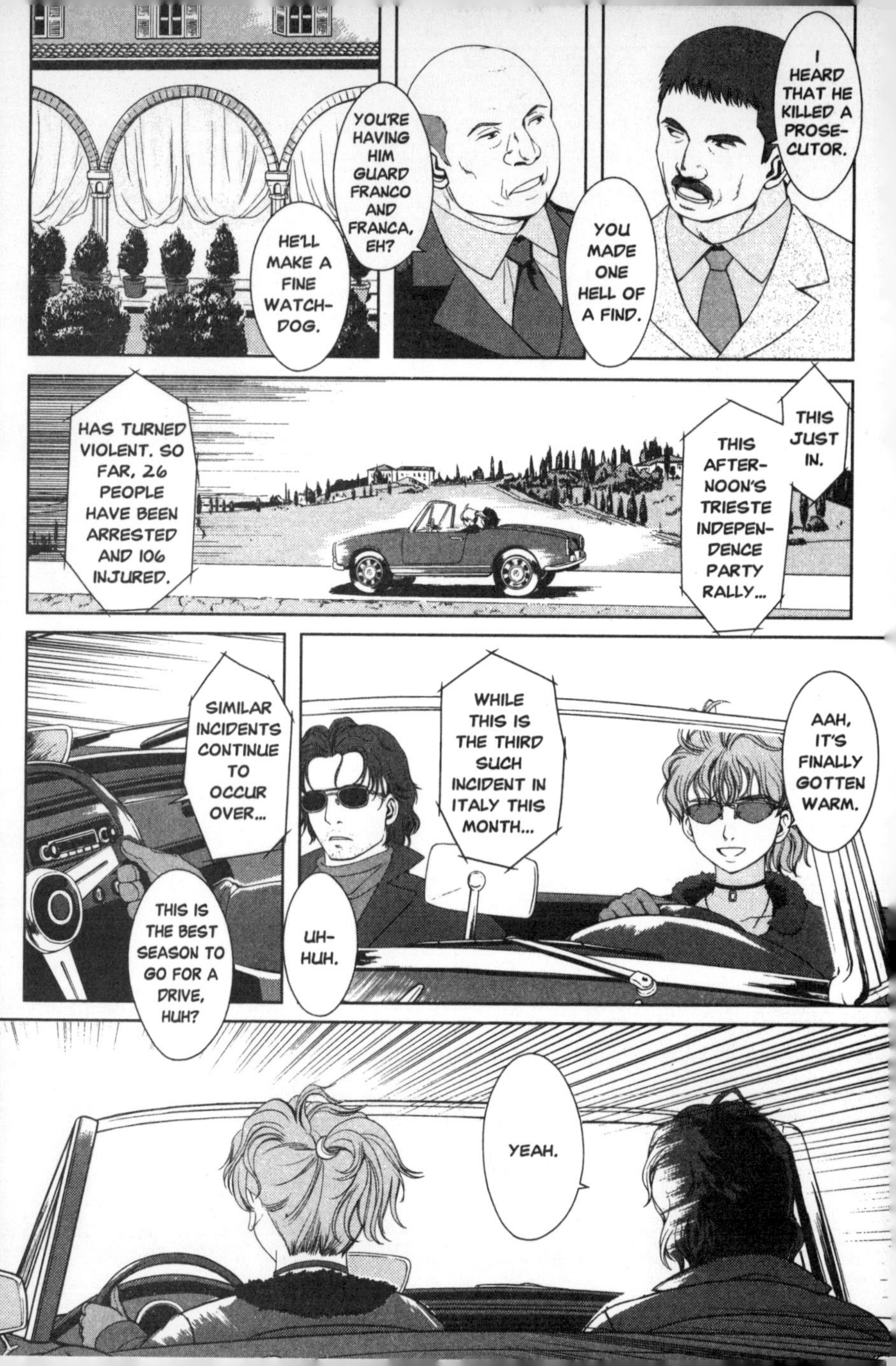
I HEARD THAT HE KILLED A PROSECUTOR.
YOU MADE ONE HELL OF A FIND.
YOU'RE HAVING HIM GUARD FRANCO AND FRANCA, EH?
HE'LL MAKE A FINE WATCHDOG.
THIS JUST IN.
THIS AFTERNOON'S TRIESTE INDEPENDENCE PARTY RALLY...
HAS TURNED VIOLENT. SO FAR, 26 PEOPLE HAVE BEEN ARRESTED AND 106 INJURED.
AAH, IT'S FINALLY GOTTEN WARM.
WHILE THIS IS THE THIRD SUCH INCIDENT IN ITALY THIS MONTH...
UH-HUH.
SIMILAR INCIDENTS CONTINUE TO OCCUR OVER...
THIS IS THE BEST SEASON TO GO FOR A DRIVE, HUH?
YEAH.

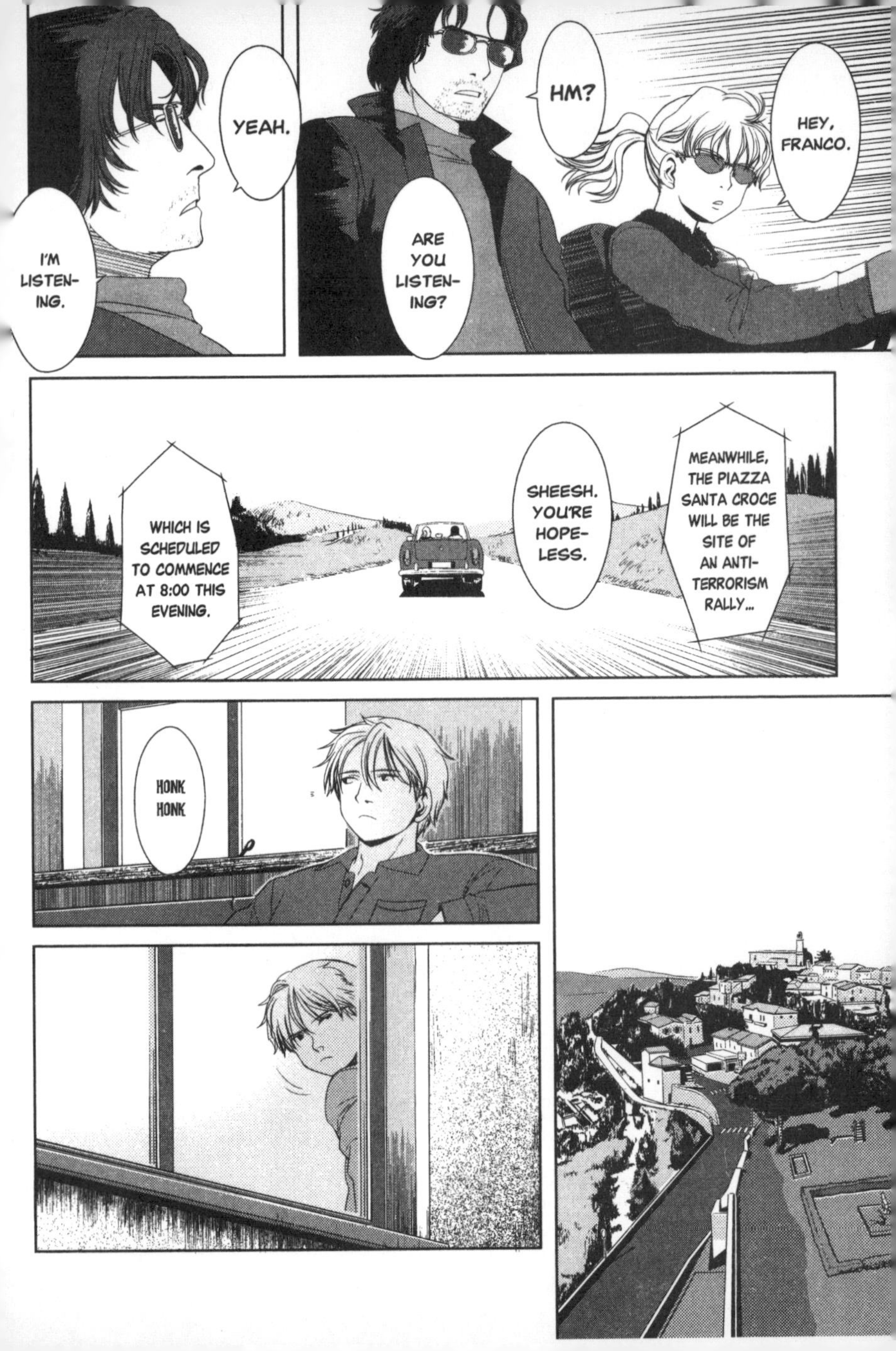
HEY, FRANCO.
HM?
ARE YOU LISTENING?
YEAH.
I'M LISTENING.
MEANWHILE, THE PIAZZA SANTA CROCE WILL BE THE SITE OF AN ANTI-TERRORISM RALLY...
SHEESH. YOU'RE HOPELESS.
WHICH IS SCHEDULED TO COMMENCE AT 8:00 THIS EVENING.
HONK HONK

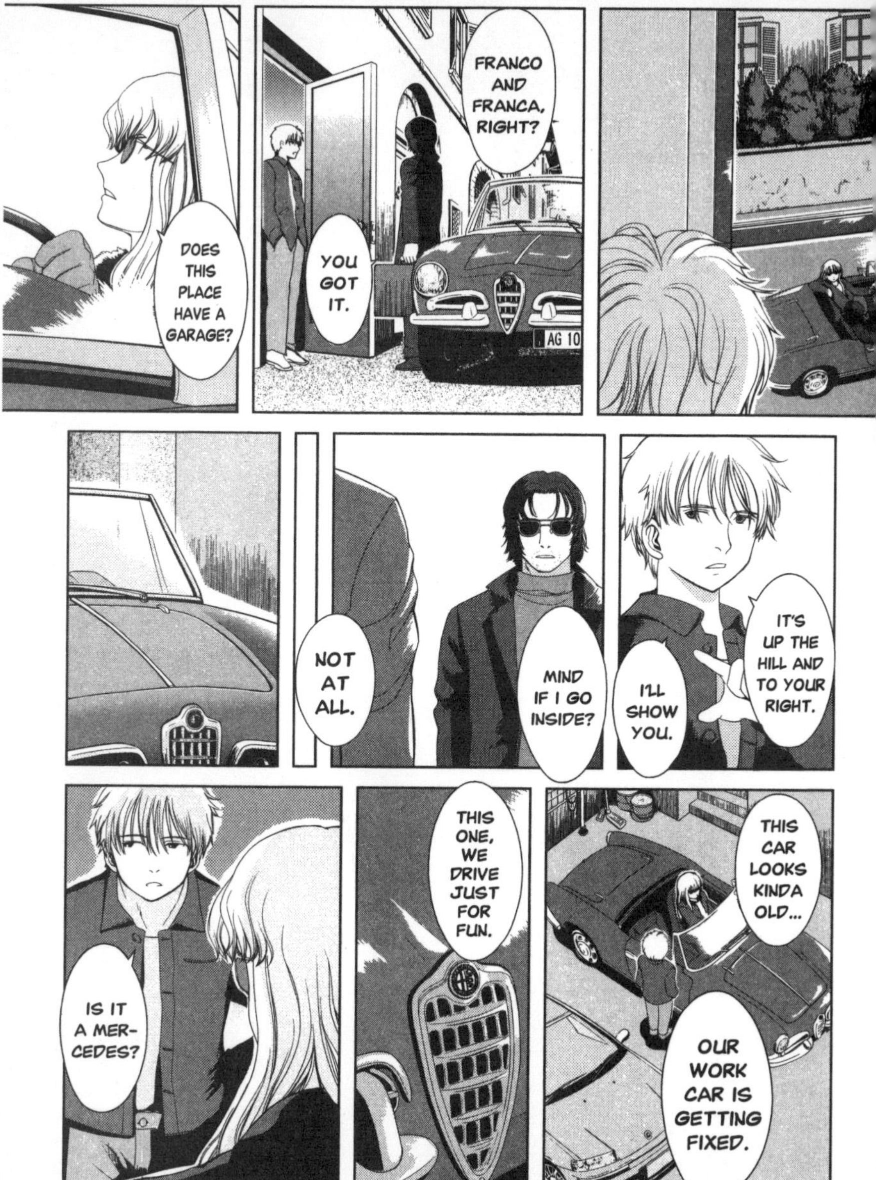
FRANCO AND FRANCA, RIGHT?
YOU GOT IT.
DOES THIS PLACE HAVE A GARAGE?
IT'S UP THE HILL AND TO YOUR RIGHT.
I'LL SHOW YOU.
MIND IF I GO INSIDE?
NOT AT ALL.
THIS CAR LOOKS KINDA OLD...
OUR WORK CAR IS GETTING FIXED.
THIS ONE, WE DRIVE JUST FOR FUN.
IS IT A MER-CEDES?

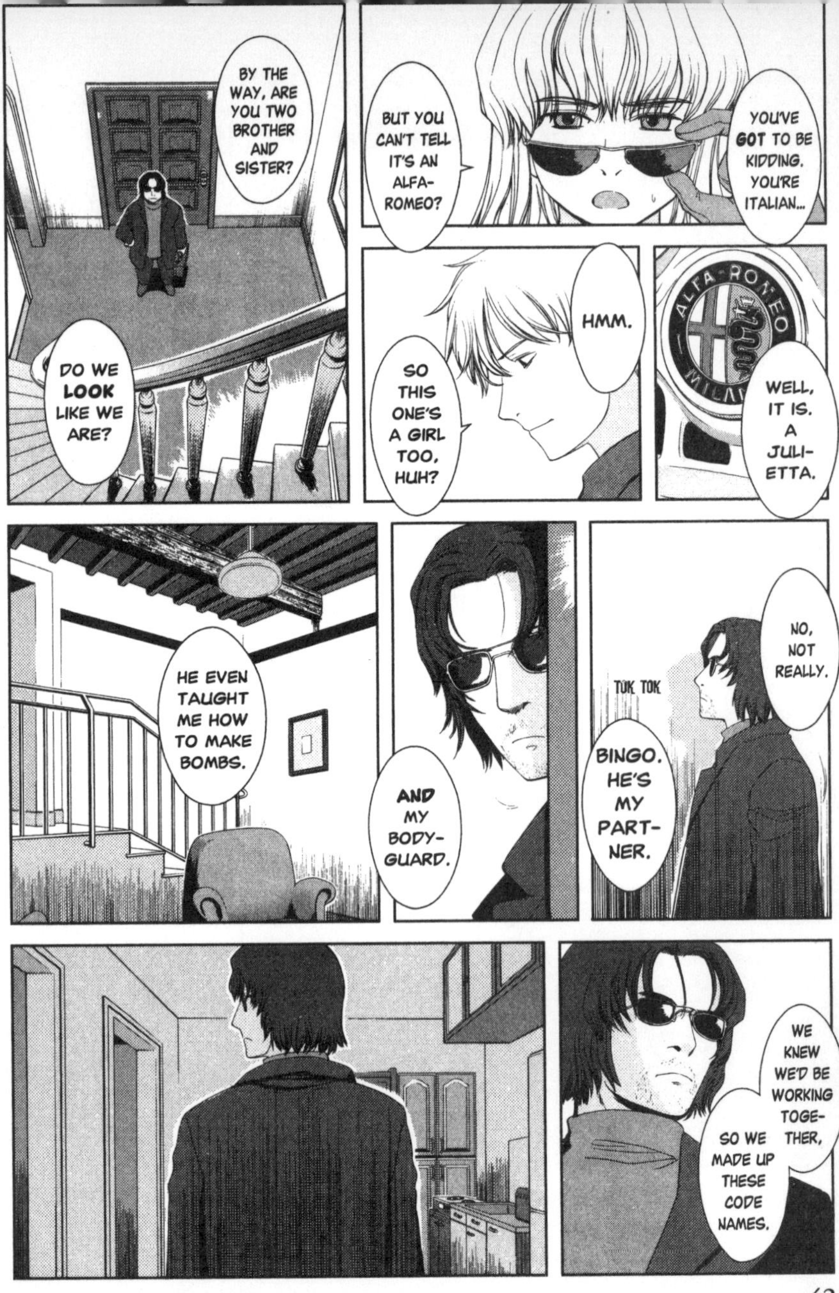
BY THE WAY, ARE YOU TWO BROTHER AND SISTER?
DO WE LOOK LIKE WE ARE?
BUT YOU CAN'T TELL IT'S AN ALFA-ROMEO?
YOU'VE GOT TO BE KIDDING. YOU'RE ITALIAN...
HMM.
SO THIS ONE'S A GIRL TOO, HUH?
ALFA-ROMEO
WELL, IT IS. A JULI-ETTA.
HE EVEN TAUGHT ME HOW TO MAKE BOMBS.
AND MY BODY-GUARD.
TOK TOK
NO, NOT REALLY.
BINGO. HE'S MY PART-NER.
WE KNEW WE'D BE WORKING TOGE-THER,
SO WE MADE UP THESE CODE NAMES.

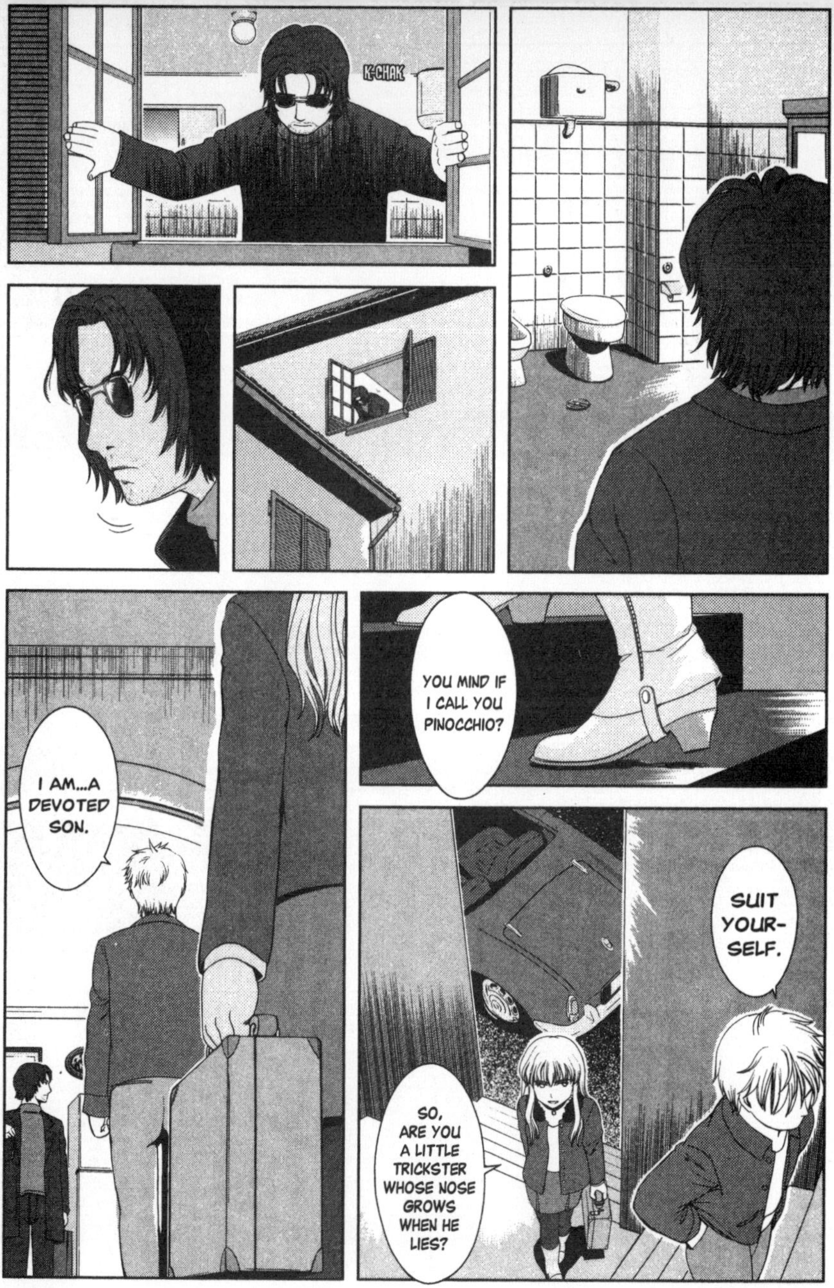
K-CHAK
YOU MIND IF I CALL YOU PINOCCHIO?
I AM...A DEVOTED SON.
SUIT YOUR-SELF.
SO, ARE YOU A LITTLE TRICKSTER WHOSE NOSE GROWS WHEN HE LIES?

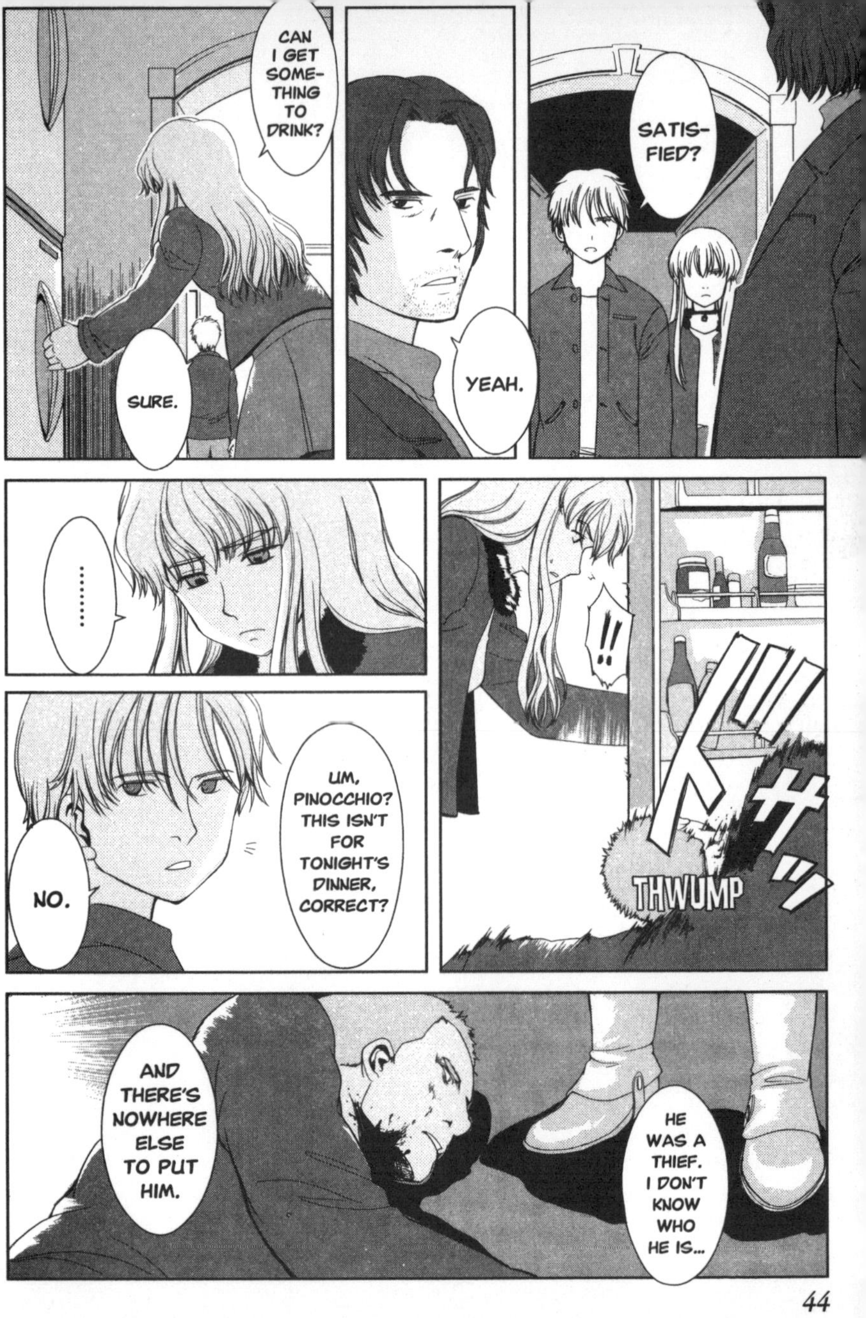
CAN I GET SOME-THING TO DRINK?
SURE.
YEAH.
SATIS-FIED?
......
!!
ドサッ
THWUMP
UM, PINOCCHIO? THIS ISN'T FOR TONIGHT'S DINNER, CORRECT?
NO.
AND THERE'S NOWHERE ELSE TO PUT HIM.
HE WAS A THIEF. I DON'T KNOW WHO HE IS...

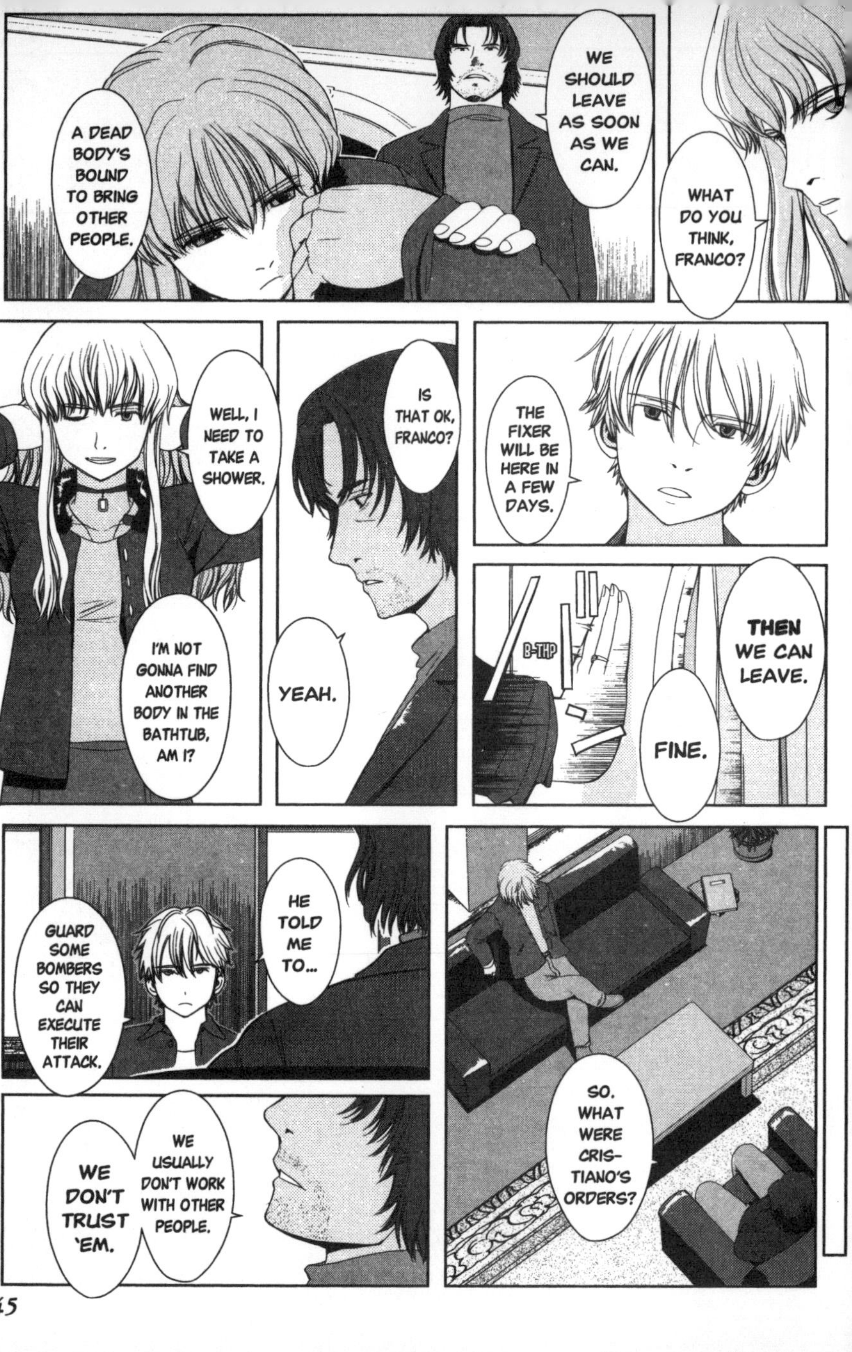
WHAT DO YOU THINK, FRANCO?
WE SHOULD LEAVE AS SOON AS WE CAN.
A DEAD BODY'S BOUND TO BRING OTHER PEOPLE.
THE FIXER WILL BE HERE IN A FEW DAYS.
THEN WE CAN LEAVE.
B-THP
FINE.
IS THAT OK, FRANCO?
YEAH.
WELL, I NEED TO TAKE A SHOWER.
I'M NOT GONNA FIND ANOTHER BODY IN THE BATHTUB, AM I?
SO. WHAT WERE CRIS-TIANO'S ORDERS?
HE TOLD ME TO...
GUARD SOME BOMBERS SO THEY CAN EXECUTE THEIR ATTACK.
WE USUALLY DON'T WORK WITH OTHER PEOPLE.
WE DON'T TRUST 'EM.

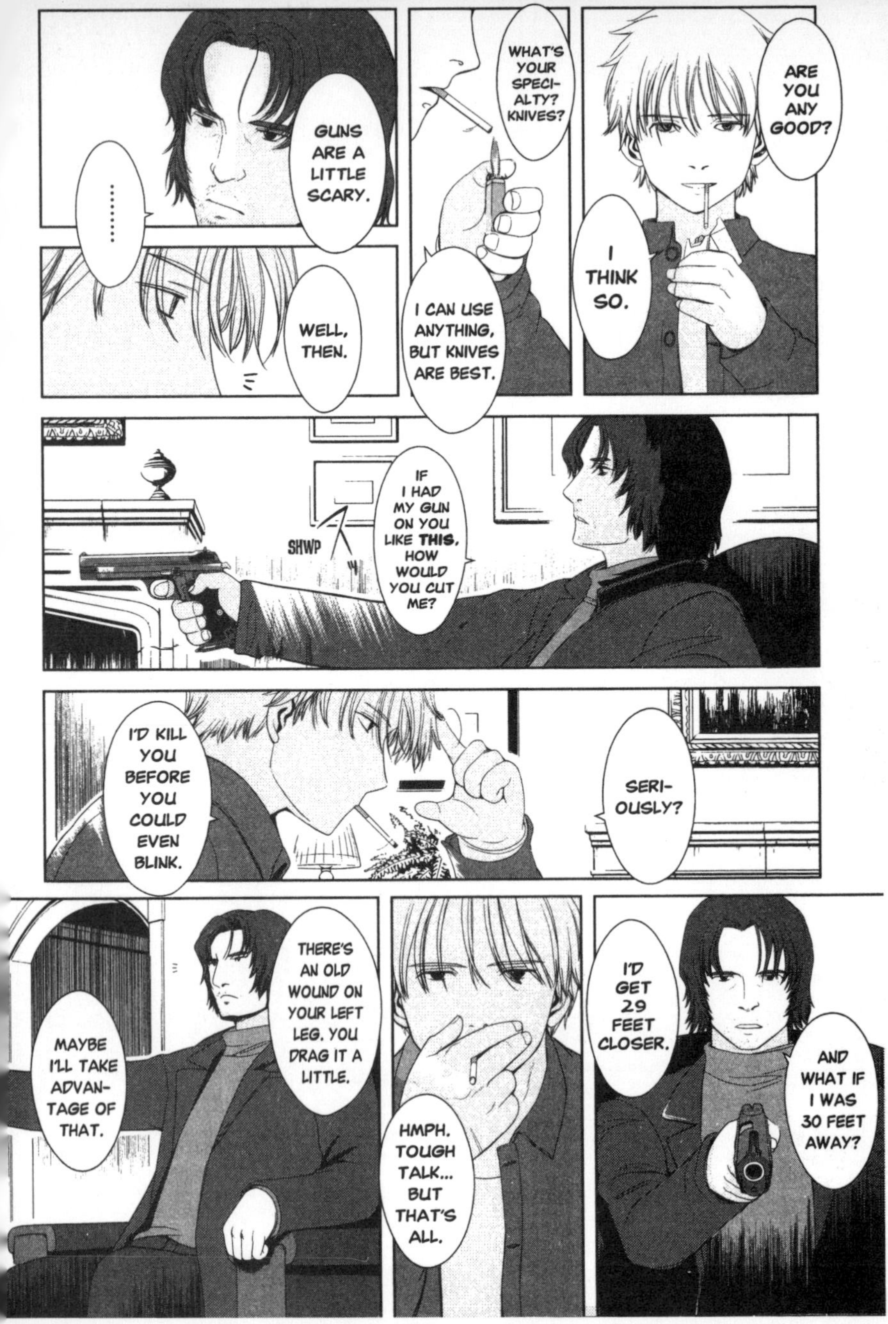
ARE YOU ANY GOOD?
I THINK SO.
WHAT'S YOUR SPECI-ALTY? KNIVES?
I CAN USE ANYTHING, BUT KNIVES ARE BEST.
GUNS ARE A LITTLE SCARY.
......
WELL, THEN.
SHWP
IF I HAD MY GUN ON YOU LIKE **THIS**, HOW WOULD YOU CUT ME?
SERI-OUSLY?
I'D KILL YOU BEFORE YOU COULD EVEN BLINK.
AND WHAT IF I WAS 30 FEET AWAY?
I'D GET 29 FEET CLOSER.
HMPH. TOUGH TALK... BUT THAT'S ALL.
THERE'S AN OLD WOUND ON YOUR LEFT LEG. YOU DRAG IT A LITTLE.
MAYBE I'LL TAKE ADVAN-TAGE OF THAT.

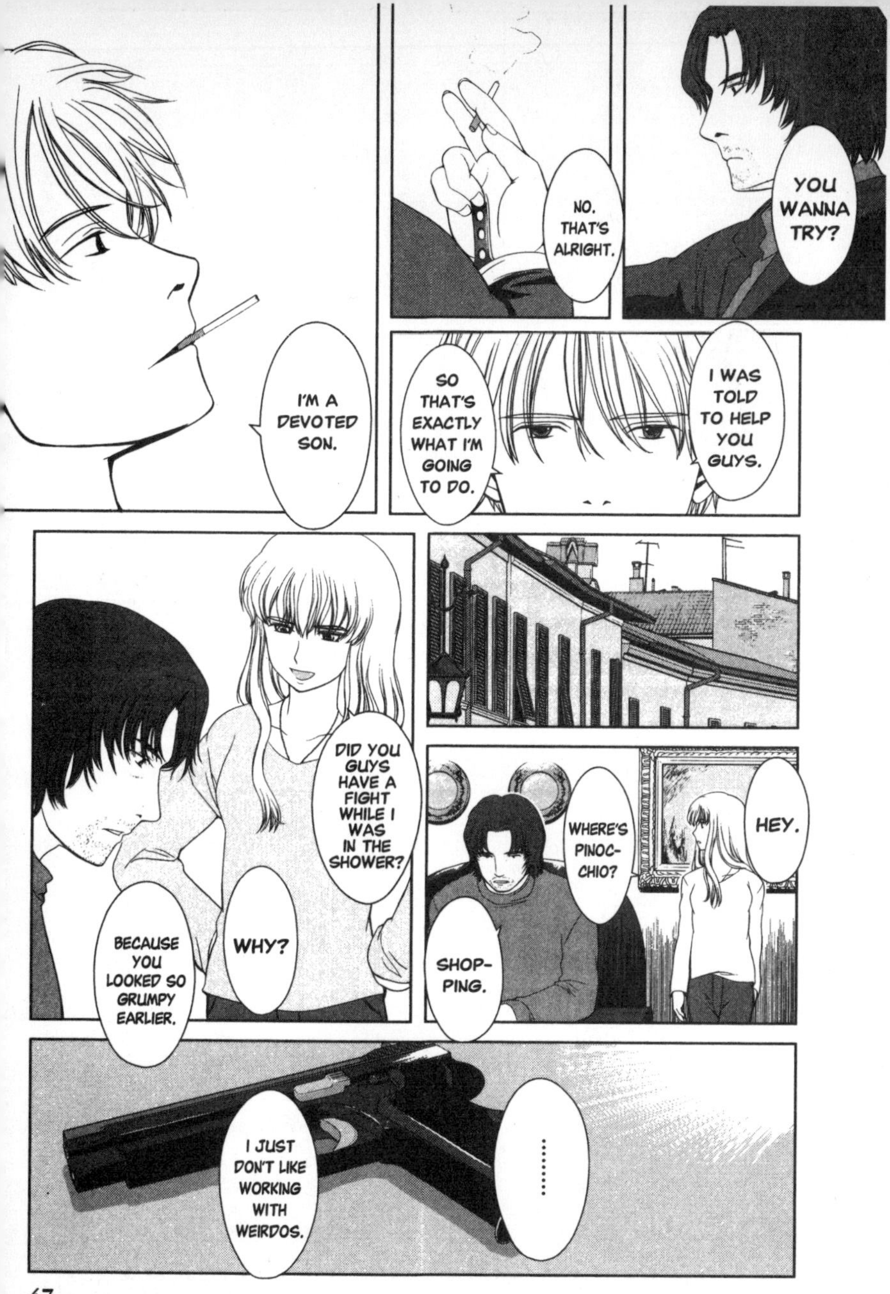
YOU WANNA TRY?
NO. THAT'S ALRIGHT.
I WAS TOLD TO HELP YOU GUYS.
SO THAT'S EXACTLY WHAT I'M GOING TO DO.
I'M A DEVOTED SON.
HEY.
WHERE'S PINOCCHIO?
SHOP-PING.
DID YOU GUYS HAVE A FIGHT WHILE I WAS IN THE SHOWER?
WHY?
BECAUSE YOU LOOKED SO GRUMPY EARLIER.
....
I JUST DON'T LIKE WORKING WITH WEIRDOS.

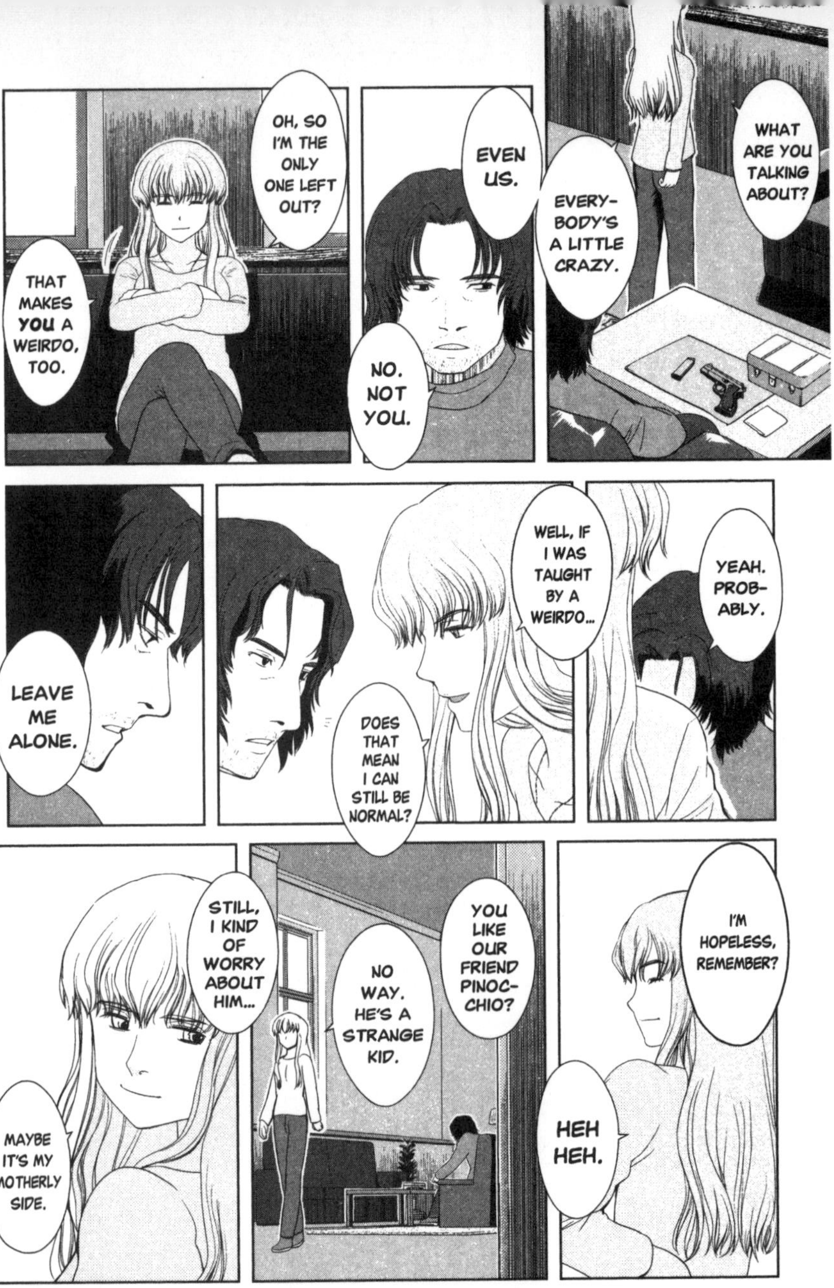
WHAT ARE YOU TALKING ABOUT?
EVERY-BODY'S A LITTLE CRAZY.
EVEN US.
NO. NOT YOU.
OH, SO I'M THE ONLY ONE LEFT OUT?
THAT MAKES **YOU** A WEIRDO, TOO.
YEAH. PROB-ABLY.
WELL, IF I WAS TAUGHT BY A WEIRDO...
DOES THAT MEAN I CAN STILL BE NORMAL?
LEAVE ME ALONE.
I'M HOPELESS, REMEMBER?
HEH HEH.
YOU LIKE OUR FRIEND PINOCC-CHIO?
NO WAY. HE'S A STRANGE KID.
STILL, I KIND OF WORRY ABOUT HIM...
MAYBE IT'S MY MOTHERLY SIDE.

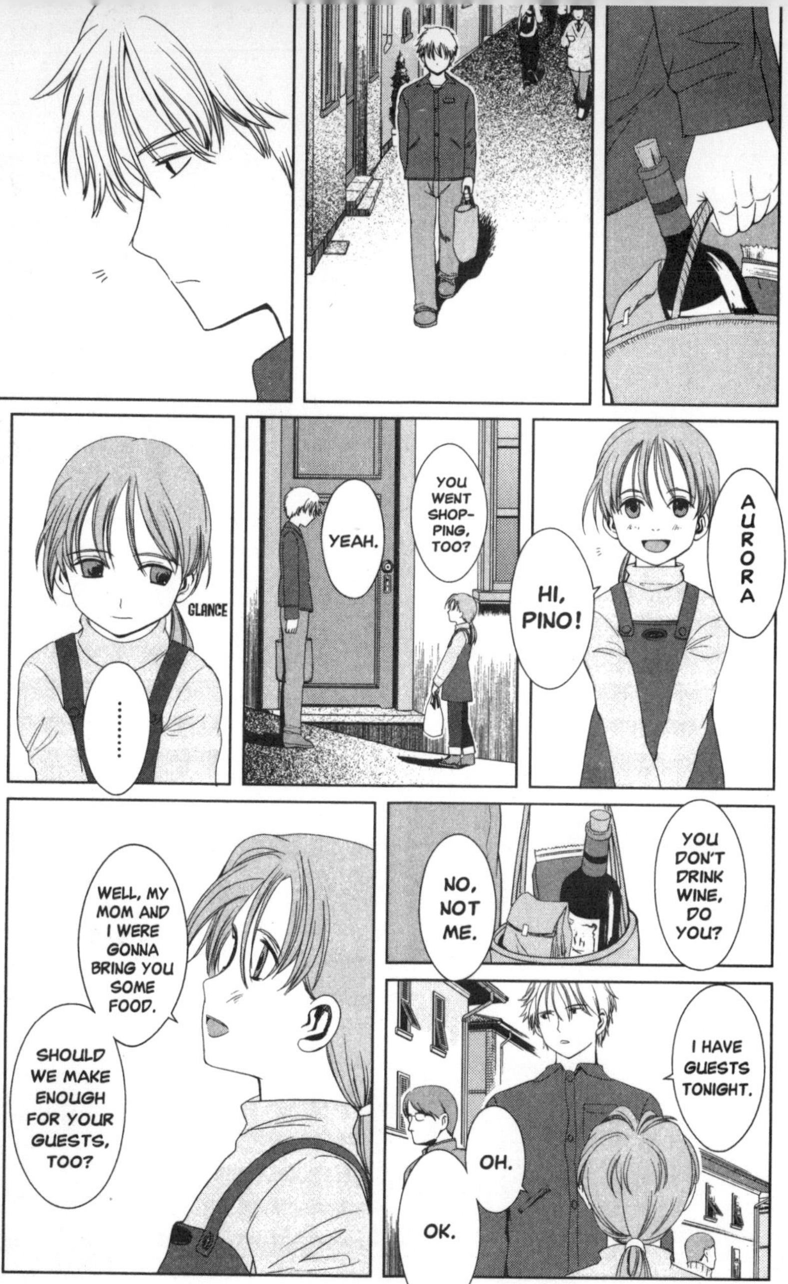
AURORA
HI, PINO!
YOU WENT SHOP-PING, TOO?
YEAH.
GLANCE
....
YOU DON'T DRINK WINE, DO YOU?
NO, NOT ME.
I HAVE GUESTS TONIGHT.
OH.
OK.
WELL, MY MOM AND I WERE GONNA BRING YOU SOME FOOD.
SHOULD WE MAKE ENOUGH FOR YOUR GUESTS, TOO?

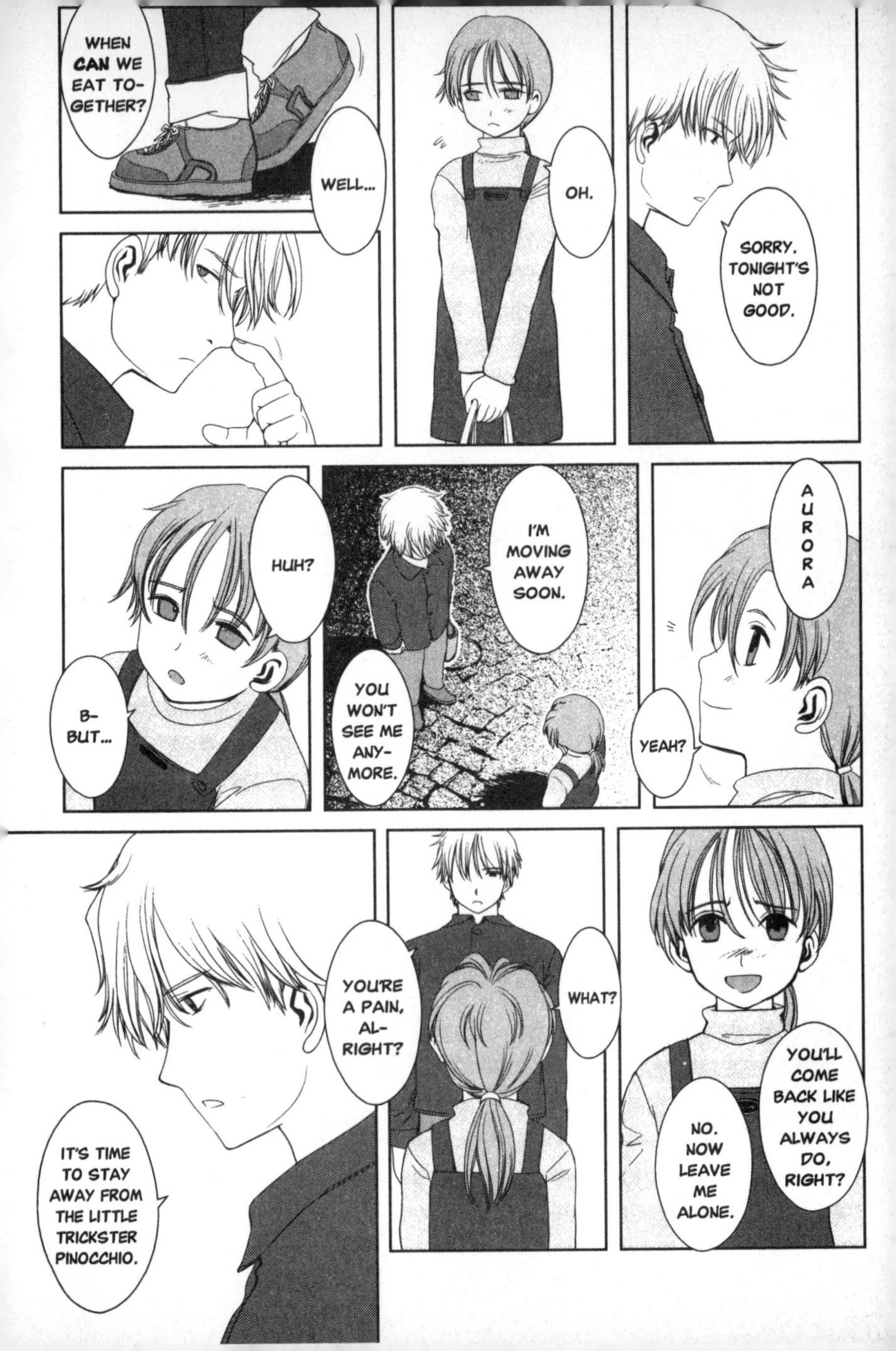

SORRY. TONIGHT'S NOT GOOD.
OH.
WHEN CAN WE EAT TO-GETHER?
WELL...
AURORA
YEAH?
I'M MOVING AWAY SOON.
YOU WON'T SEE ME ANY-MORE.
HUH?
B-BUT...
YOU'LL COME BACK LIKE YOU ALWAYS DO, RIGHT?
NO. NOW LEAVE ME ALONE.
WHAT?
YOU'RE A PAIN, AL-RIGHT?
IT'S TIME TO STAY AWAY FROM THE LITTLE TRICKSTER PINOCCHIO.

GUNSLINGERGIRL.

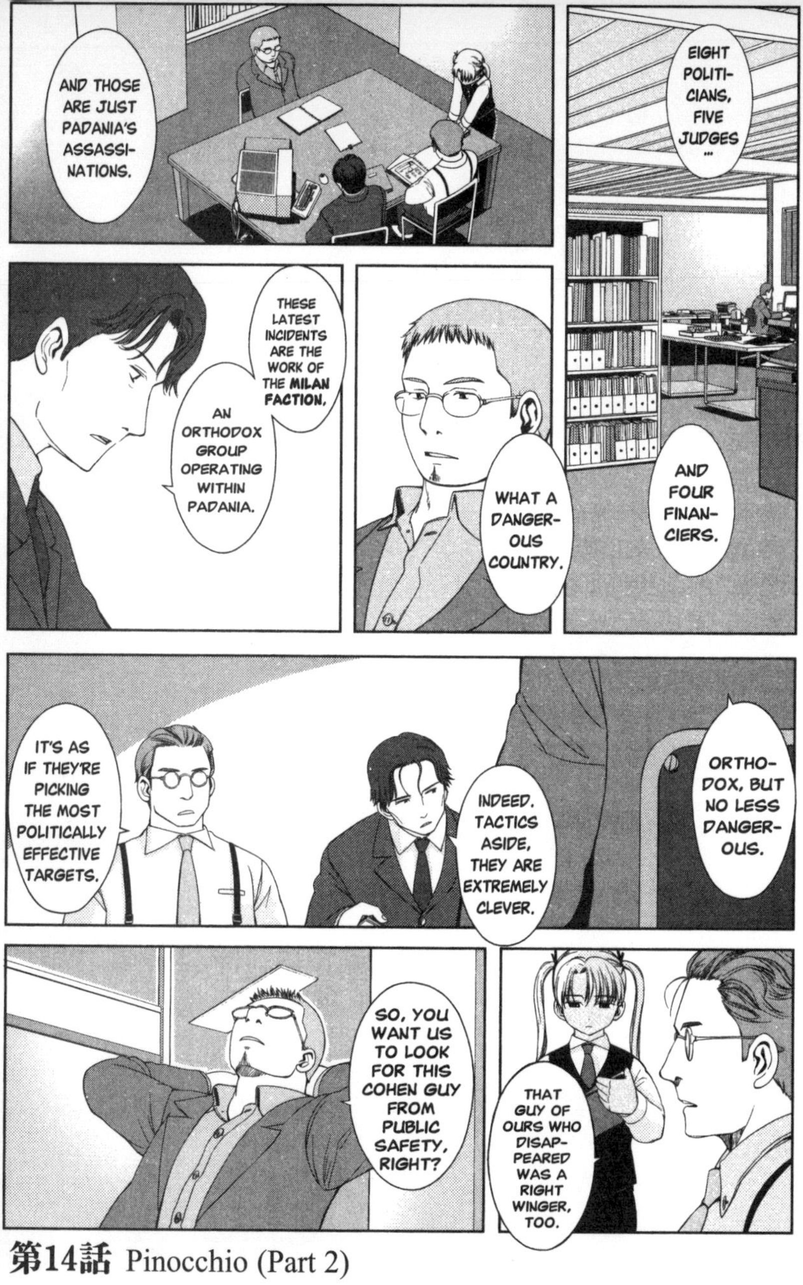
EIGHT POLITI- CIANS, FIVE JUDGES ...
AND FOUR FINAN- CIERS.
AND THOSE ARE JUST PADANIA'S ASSASSI- NATIONS.
WHAT A DANGER- OUS COUNTRY.
THESE LATEST INCIDENTS ARE THE WORK OF THE **MILAN FACTION**,
AN ORTHODOX GROUP OPERATING WITHIN PADANIA.
ORTHO- DOX, BUT NO LESS DANGER- OUS.
INDEED. TACTICS ASIDE, THEY ARE EXTREMELY CLEVER.
IT'S AS IF THEY'RE PICKING THE MOST POLITICALLY EFFECTIVE TARGETS.
THAT GUY OF OURS WHO DISAP- PEARED WAS A RIGHT WINGER, TOO.
SO, YOU WANT US TO LOOK FOR THIS COHEN GUY FROM PUBLIC SAFETY, RIGHT?

第14話 Pinocchio (Part 2)

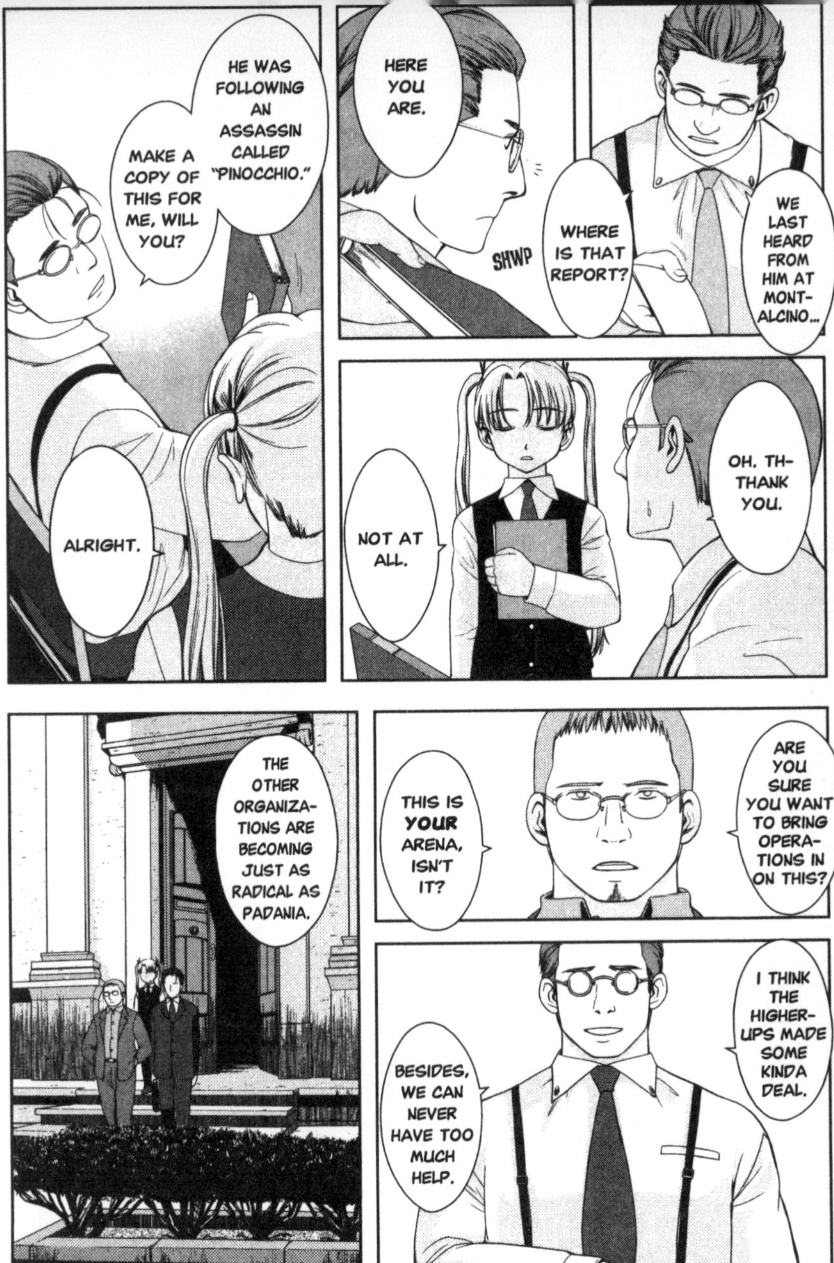
WE LAST HEARD FROM HIM AT MONT-ALCINO...
WHERE IS THAT REPORT?
SHWP
HERE YOU ARE.
HE WAS FOLLOWING AN ASSASSIN CALLED "PINOCCHIO."
MAKE A COPY OF THIS FOR ME, WILL YOU?
ALRIGHT.
OH. TH-THANK YOU.
NOT AT ALL.
ARE YOU SURE YOU WANT TO BRING OPERA-TIONS IN ON THIS?
THIS IS **YOUR** ARENA, ISN'T IT?
I THINK THE HIGHER-UPS MADE SOME KINDA DEAL.
BESIDES, WE CAN NEVER HAVE TOO MUCH HELP.
THE OTHER ORGANIZA-TIONS ARE BECOMING JUST AS RADICAL AS PADANIA.

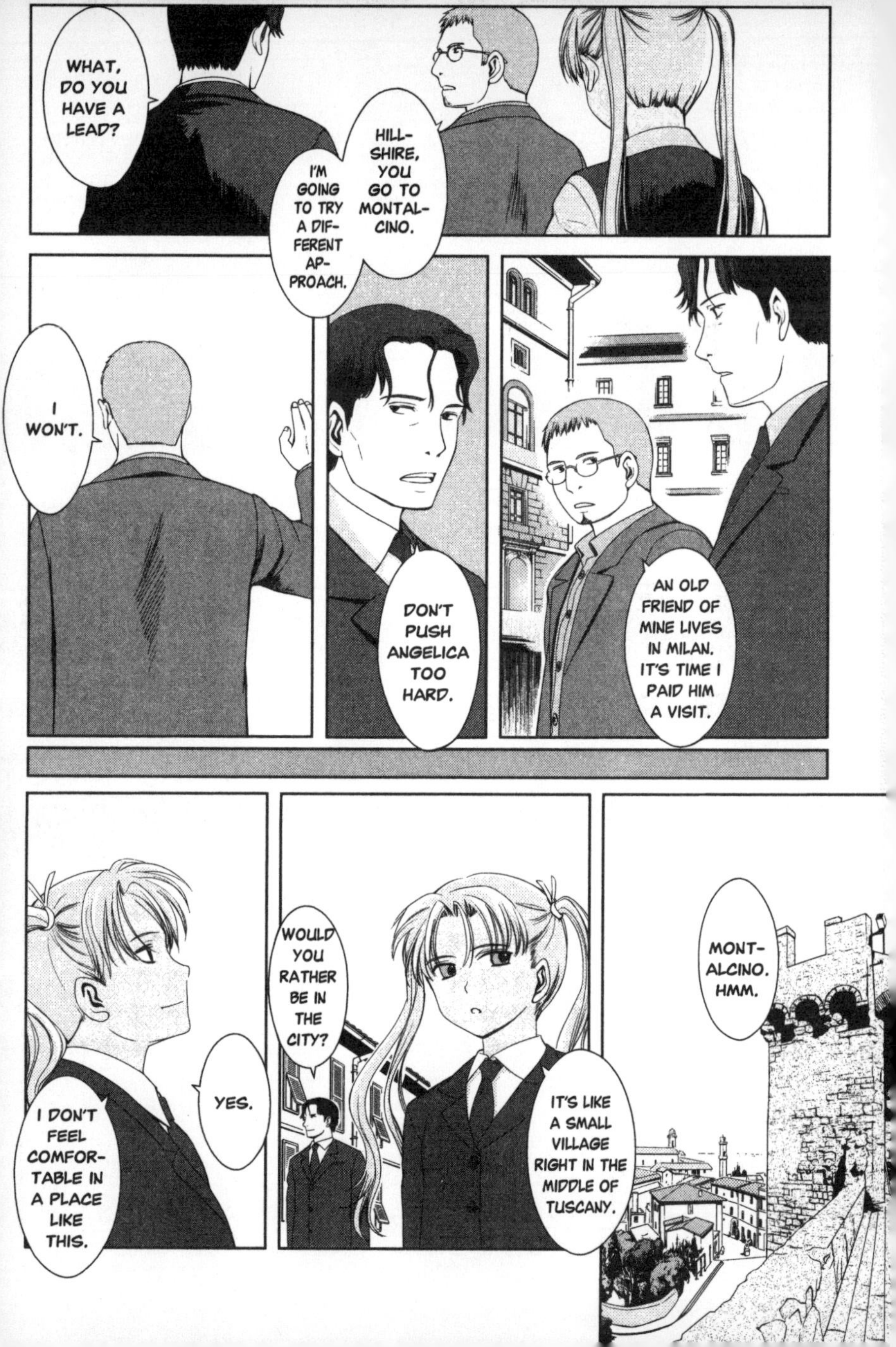
HILLSHIRE, YOU GO TO MONTALCINO.
I'M GOING TO TRY A DIFFERENT APPROACH.
WHAT, DO YOU HAVE A LEAD?
AN OLD FRIEND OF MINE LIVES IN MILAN. IT'S TIME I PAID HIM A VISIT.
DON'T PUSH ANGELICA TOO HARD.
I WON'T.
MONTALCINO. HMM.
IT'S LIKE A SMALL VILLAGE RIGHT IN THE MIDDLE OF TUSCANY.
WOULD YOU RATHER BE IN THE CITY?
YES.
I DON'T FEEL COMFORTABLE IN A PLACE LIKE THIS.

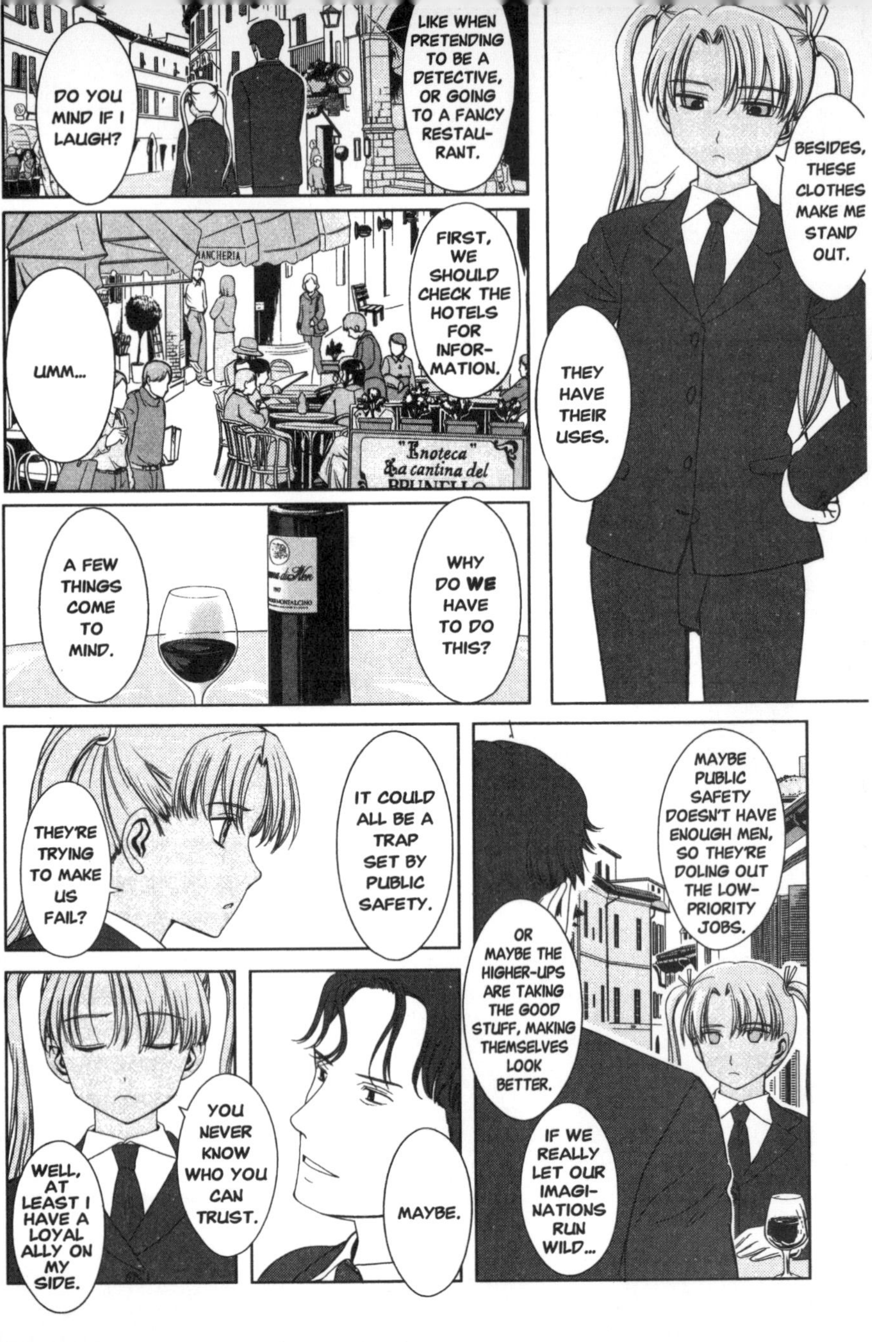
BESIDES, THESE CLOTHES MAKE ME STAND OUT.
THEY HAVE THEIR USES.
LIKE WHEN PRETENDING TO BE A DETECTIVE, OR GOING TO A FANCY RESTAURANT.
DO YOU MIND IF I LAUGH?
FIRST, WE SHOULD CHECK THE HOTELS FOR INFORMATION.
UMM...
"Enoteca"
La cantina del
WHY DO **WE** HAVE TO DO THIS?
A FEW THINGS COME TO MIND.
MAYBE PUBLIC SAFETY DOESN'T HAVE ENOUGH MEN, SO THEY'RE DOLING OUT THE LOW-PRIORITY JOBS.
OR MAYBE THE HIGHER-UPS ARE TAKING THE GOOD STUFF, MAKING THEMSELVES LOOK BETTER.
IF WE REALLY LET OUR IMAGINATIONS RUN WILD...
IT COULD ALL BE A TRAP SET BY PUBLIC SAFETY.
THEY'RE TRYING TO MAKE US FAIL?
MAYBE.
YOU NEVER KNOW WHO YOU CAN TRUST.
WELL, AT LEAST I HAVE A LOYAL ALLY ON MY SIDE.

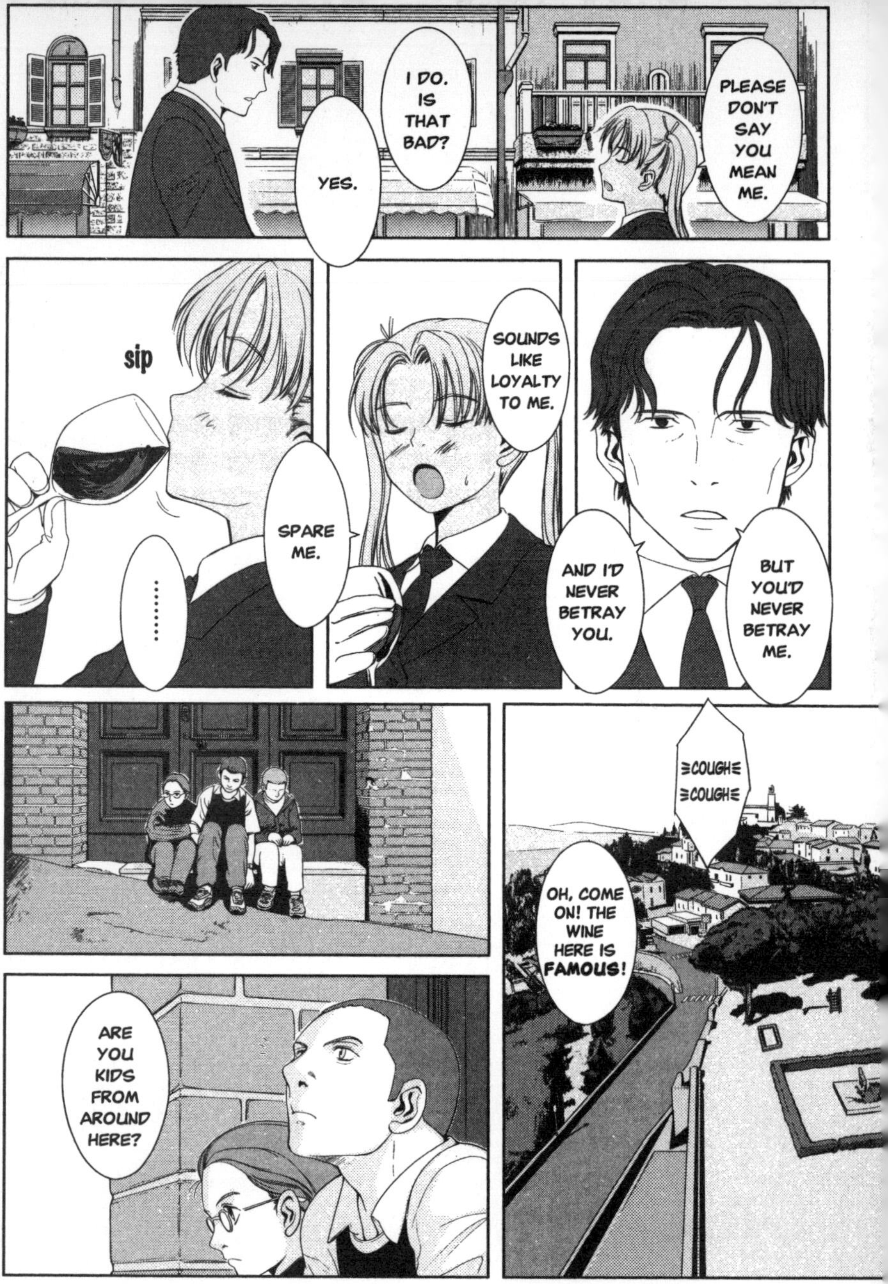
PLEASE DON'T SAY YOU MEAN ME.
I DO. IS THAT BAD?
YES.
BUT YOU'D NEVER BETRAY ME.
AND I'D NEVER BETRAY YOU.
SOUNDS LIKE LOYALTY TO ME.
SPARE ME.
sip
....
≡COUGH≡ ≡COUGH≡
OH, COME ON! THE WINE HERE IS FAMOUS!
ARE YOU KIDS FROM AROUND HERE?

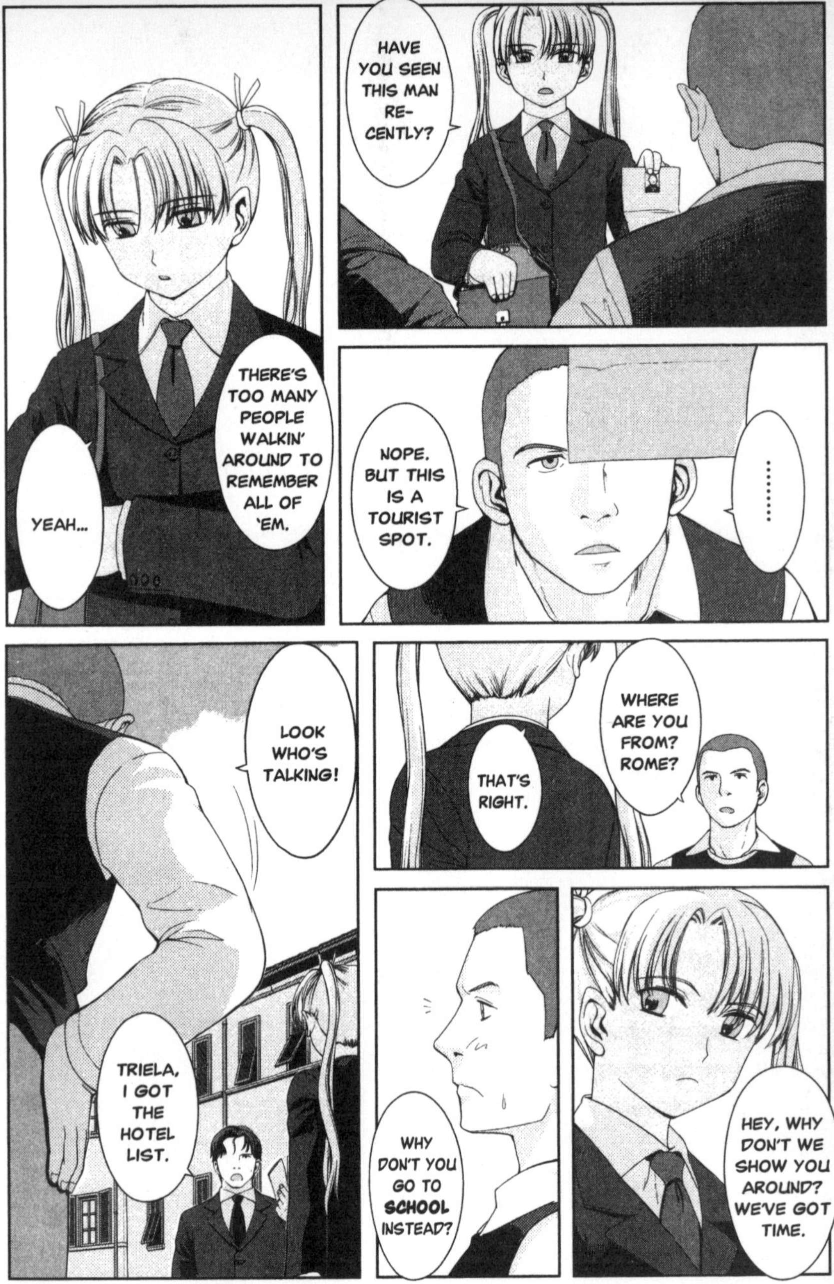

HAVE YOU SEEN THIS MAN RE-CENTLY?
NOPE. BUT THIS IS A TOURIST SPOT.
......
THERE'S TOO MANY PEOPLE WALKIN' AROUND TO REMEMBER ALL OF 'EM.
YEAH...
WHERE ARE YOU FROM? ROME?
THAT'S RIGHT.
HEY, WHY DON'T WE SHOW YOU AROUND? WE'VE GOT TIME.
WHY DON'T YOU GO TO **SCHOOL** INSTEAD?
LOOK WHO'S TALKING!
TRIELA, I GOT THE HOTEL LIST.

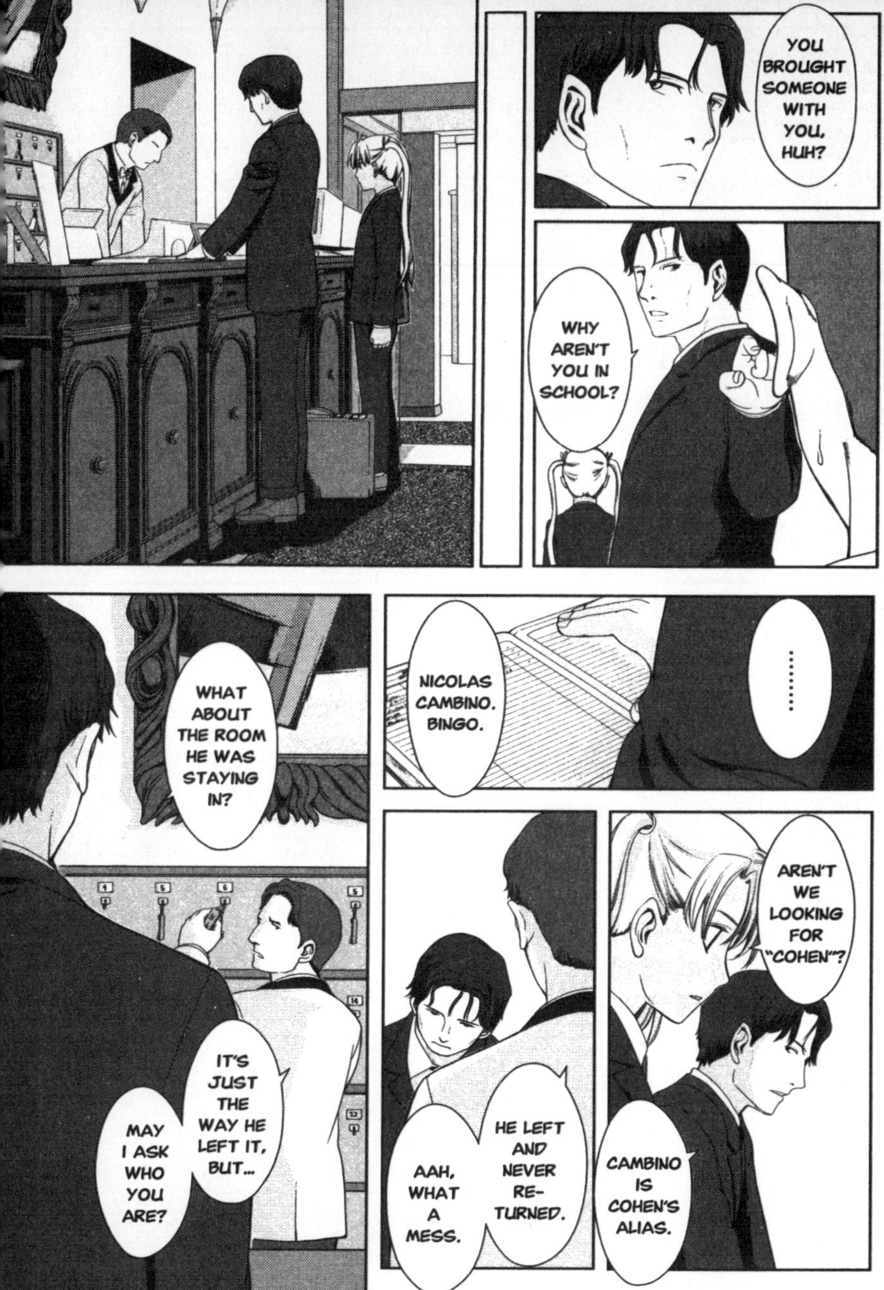
YOU BROUGHT SOMEONE WITH YOU, HUH?
WHY AREN'T YOU IN SCHOOL?
......
NICOLAS CAMBINO. BINGO.
AREN'T WE LOOKING FOR "COHEN"?
CAMBINO IS COHEN'S ALIAS.
HE LEFT AND NEVER RE-TURNED.
AAH, WHAT A MESS.
WHAT ABOUT THE ROOM HE WAS STAYING IN?
IT'S JUST THE WAY HE LEFT IT, BUT...
MAY I ASK WHO YOU ARE?

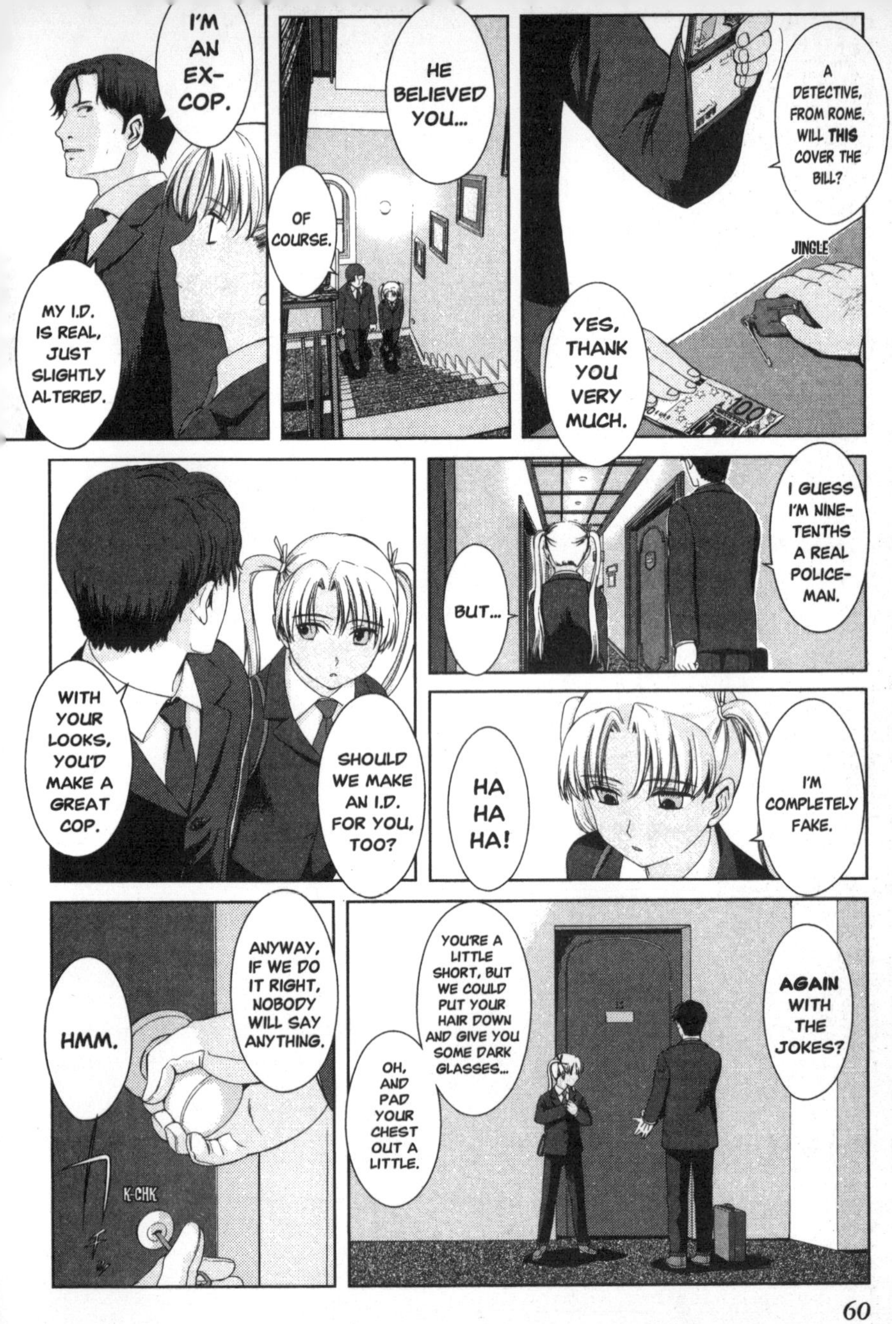
A DETECTIVE, FROM ROME. WILL THIS COVER THE BILL?
JINGLE
YES, THANK YOU VERY MUCH.
HE BELIEVED YOU...
OF COURSE.
I'M AN EX-COP.
MY I.D. IS REAL, JUST SLIGHTLY ALTERED.
I GUESS I'M NINE-TENTHS A REAL POLICE-MAN.
BUT...
I'M COMPLETELY FAKE.
HA HA HA!
SHOULD WE MAKE AN I.D. FOR YOU, TOO?
WITH YOUR LOOKS, YOU'D MAKE A GREAT COP.
AGAIN WITH THE JOKES?
YOU'RE A LITTLE SHORT, BUT WE COULD PUT YOUR HAIR DOWN AND GIVE YOU SOME DARK GLASSES...
OH, AND PAD YOUR CHEST OUT A LITTLE.
ANYWAY, IF WE DO IT RIGHT, NOBODY WILL SAY ANYTHING.
HMM.
K-CHK

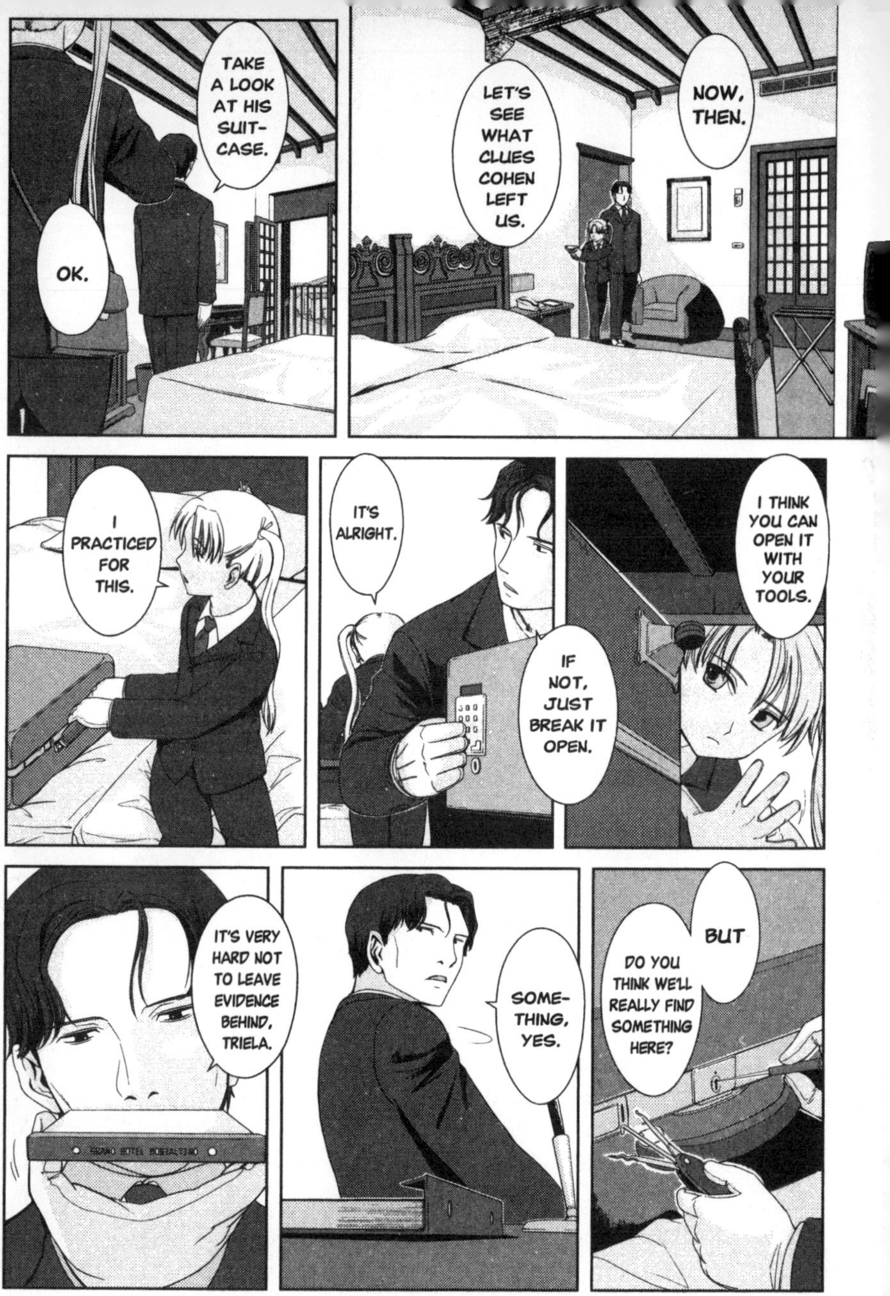
NOW, THEN.
LET'S SEE WHAT CLUES COHEN LEFT US.
TAKE A LOOK AT HIS SUIT-CASE.
OK.
I THINK YOU CAN OPEN IT WITH YOUR TOOLS.
IF NOT, JUST BREAK IT OPEN.
IT'S ALRIGHT.
I PRACTICED FOR THIS.
BUT
DO YOU THINK WE'LL REALLY FIND SOMETHING HERE?
SOME-THING, YES.
IT'S VERY HARD NOT TO LEAVE EVIDENCE BEHIND, TRIELA.

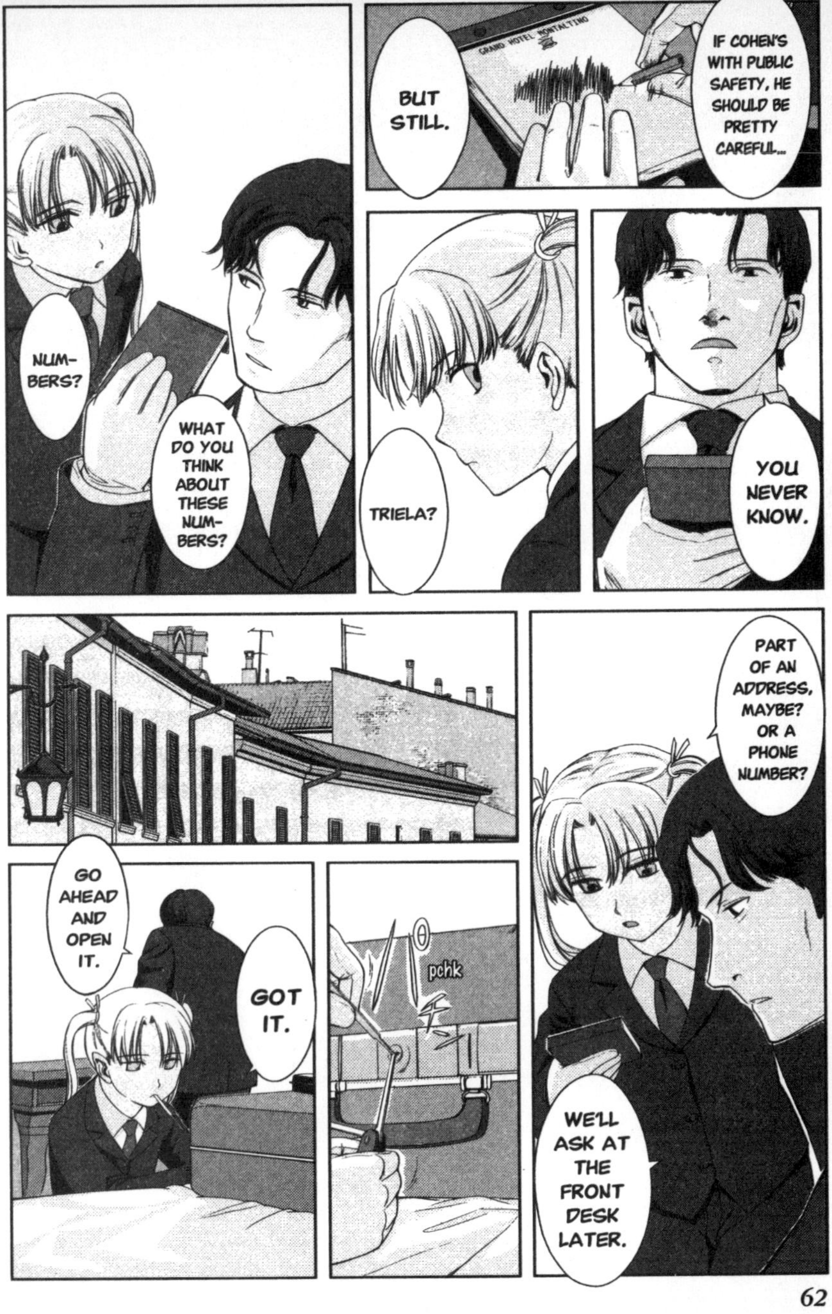
GRAND HOTEL MONTALTINO
IF COHEN'S WITH PUBLIC SAFETY, HE SHOULD BE PRETTY CAREFUL...
BUT STILL.
YOU NEVER KNOW.
TRIELA?
WHAT DO YOU THINK ABOUT THESE NUM-BERS?
NUM-BERS?
PART OF AN ADDRESS, MAYBE? OR A PHONE NUMBER?
WE'LL ASK AT THE FRONT DESK LATER.
pchk
GO AHEAD AND OPEN IT.
GOT IT.

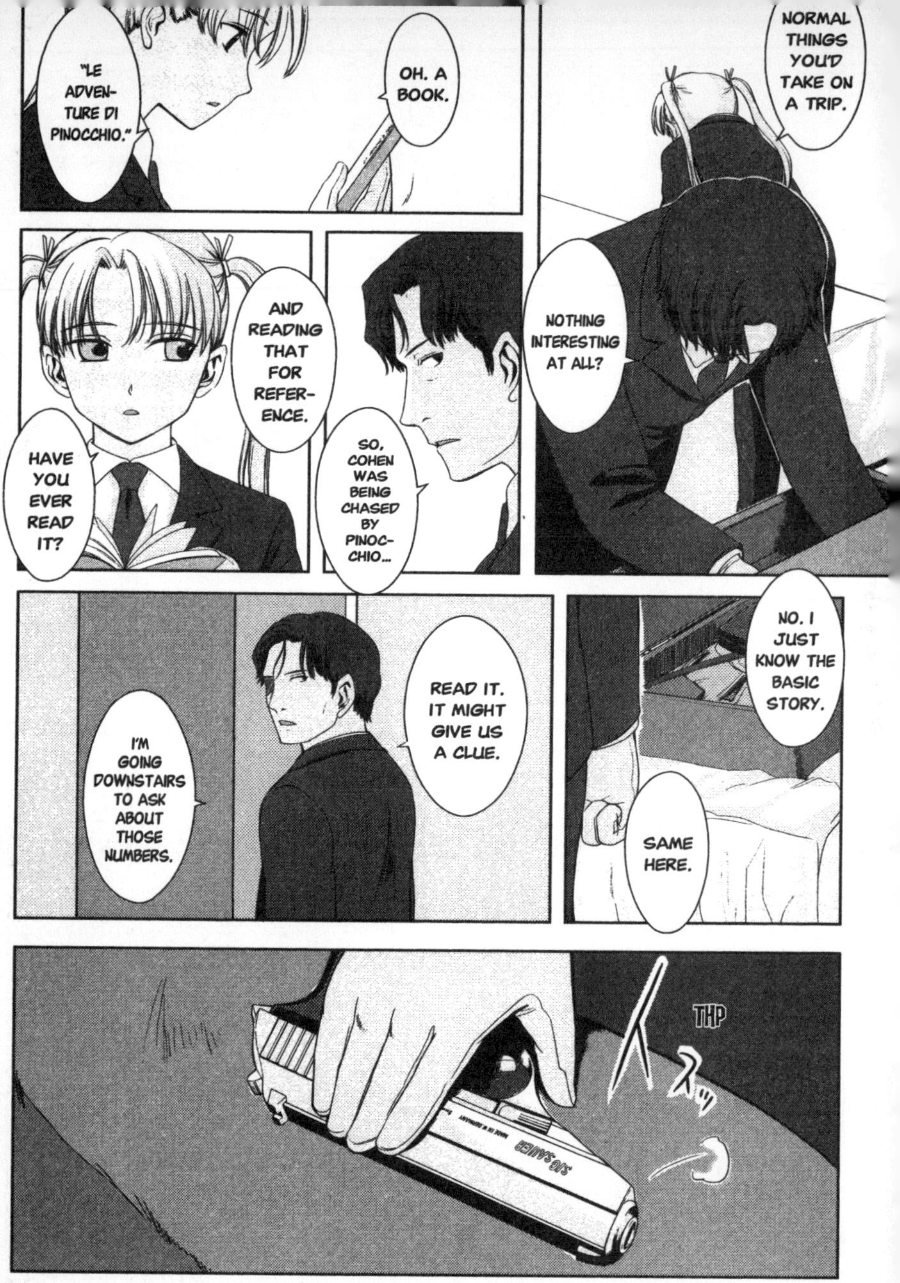
NORMAL THINGS YOU'D TAKE ON A TRIP.
NOTHING INTERESTING AT ALL?
OH. A BOOK.
"LE ADVENTURE DI PINOCCHIO."
SO, COHEN WAS BEING CHASED BY PINOCCHIO...
AND READING THAT FOR REFERENCE.
HAVE YOU EVER READ IT?
NO. I JUST KNOW THE BASIC STORY.
SAME HERE.
READ IT. IT MIGHT GIVE US A CLUE.
I'M GOING DOWNSTAIRS TO ASK ABOUT THOSE NUMBERS.
THP
スッ
SIG SAUER

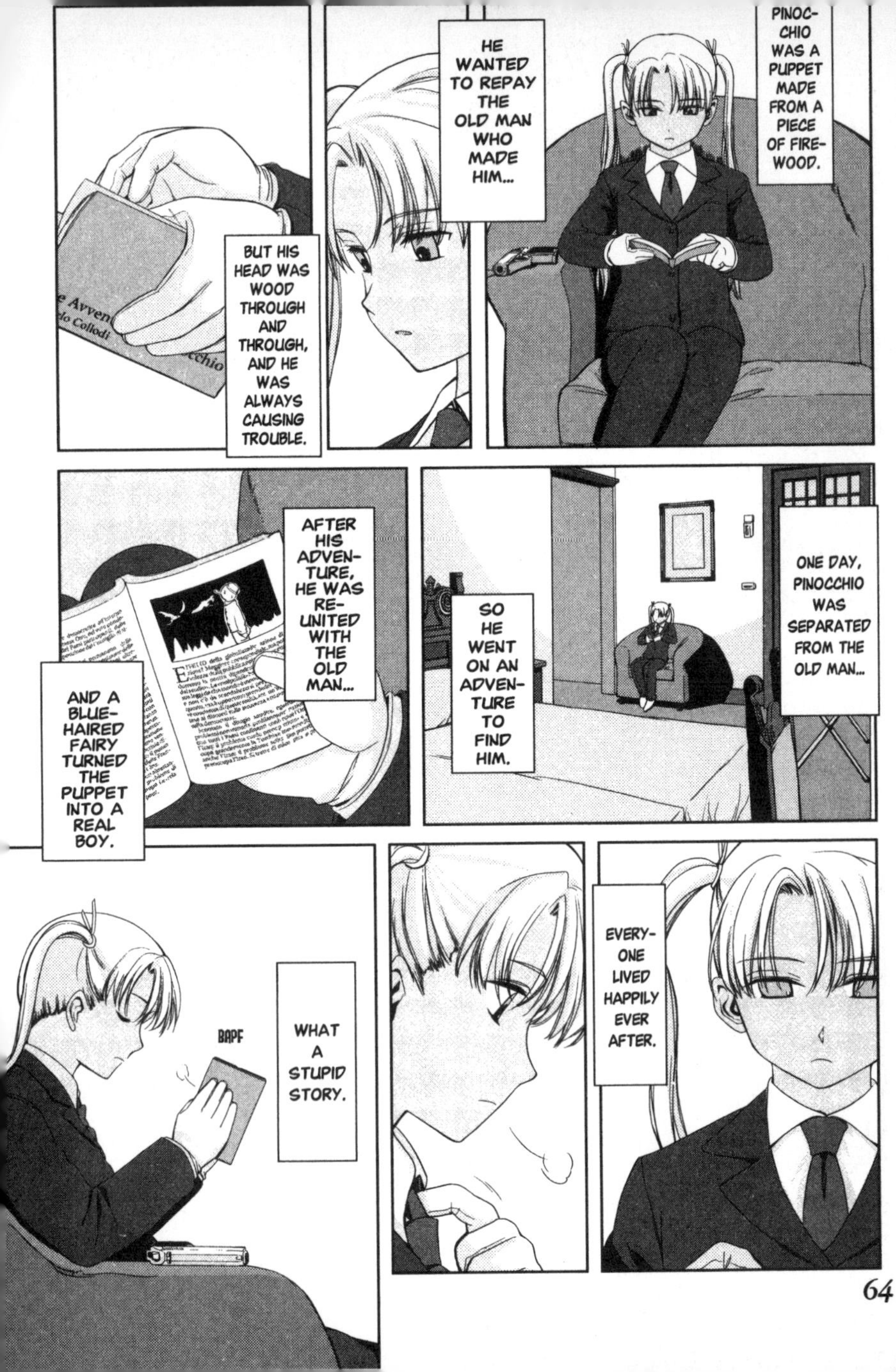
PINOCCHIO WAS A PUPPET MADE FROM A PIECE OF FIREWOOD.
HE WANTED TO REPAY THE OLD MAN WHO MADE HIM...
BUT HIS HEAD WAS WOOD THROUGH AND THROUGH, AND HE WAS ALWAYS CAUSING TROUBLE.
ONE DAY, PINOCCHIO WAS SEPARATED FROM THE OLD MAN...
SO HE WENT ON AN ADVENTURE TO FIND HIM.
AFTER HIS ADVENTURE, HE WAS REUNITED WITH THE OLD MAN...
AND A BLUE-HAIRED FAIRY TURNED THE PUPPET INTO A REAL BOY.
EVERYONE LIVED HAPPILY EVER AFTER.
BAPF
WHAT A STUPID STORY.

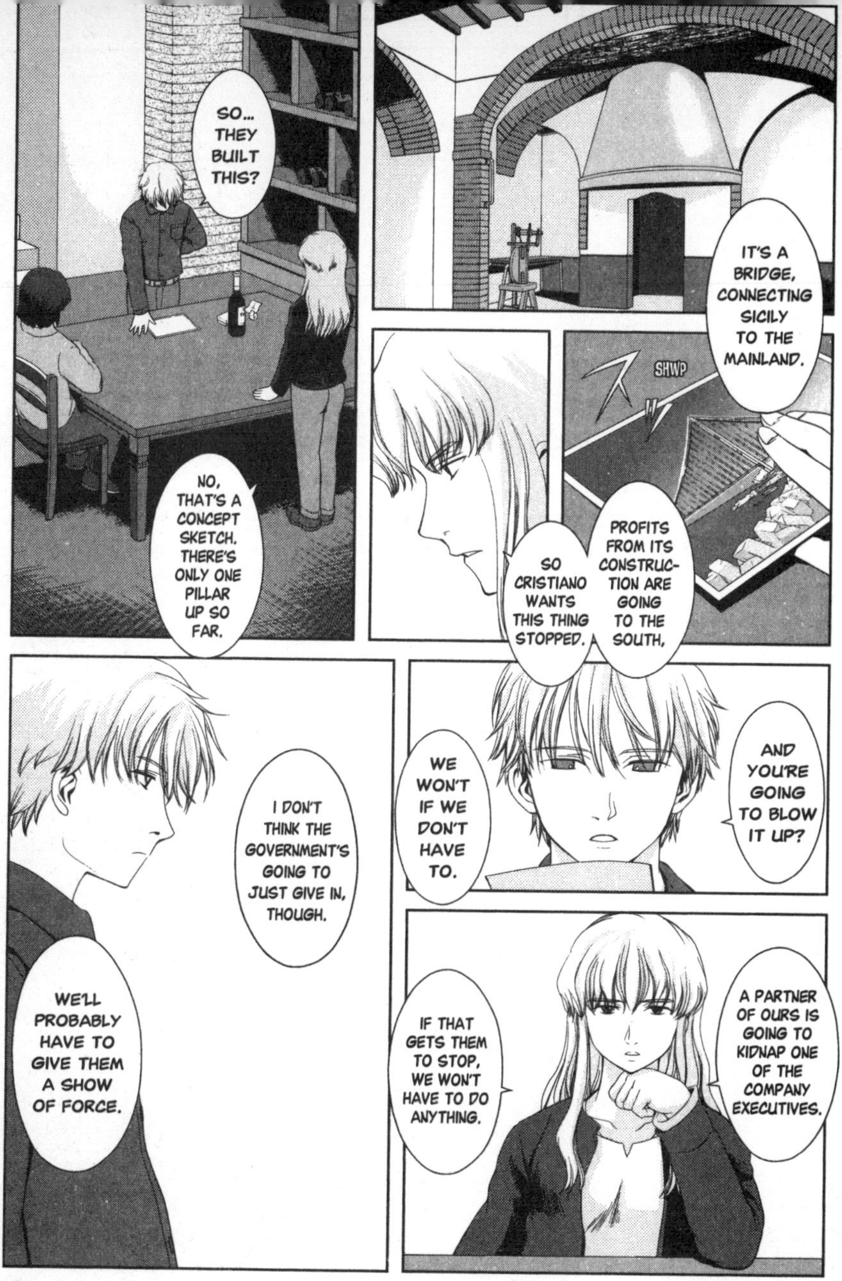
IT'S A BRIDGE, CONNECTING SICILY TO THE MAINLAND.
SO... THEY BUILT THIS?
NO, THAT'S A CONCEPT SKETCH. THERE'S ONLY ONE PILLAR UP SO FAR.
SHWP
PROFITS FROM ITS CONSTRUCTION ARE GOING TO THE SOUTH,
SO CRISTIANO WANTS THIS THING STOPPED.
AND YOU'RE GOING TO BLOW IT UP?
WE WON'T IF WE DON'T HAVE TO.
A PARTNER OF OURS IS GOING TO KIDNAP ONE OF THE COMPANY EXECUTIVES.
IF THAT GETS THEM TO STOP, WE WON'T HAVE TO DO ANYTHING.
I DON'T THINK THE GOVERNMENT'S GOING TO JUST GIVE IN, THOUGH.
WE'LL PROBABLY HAVE TO GIVE THEM A SHOW OF FORCE.

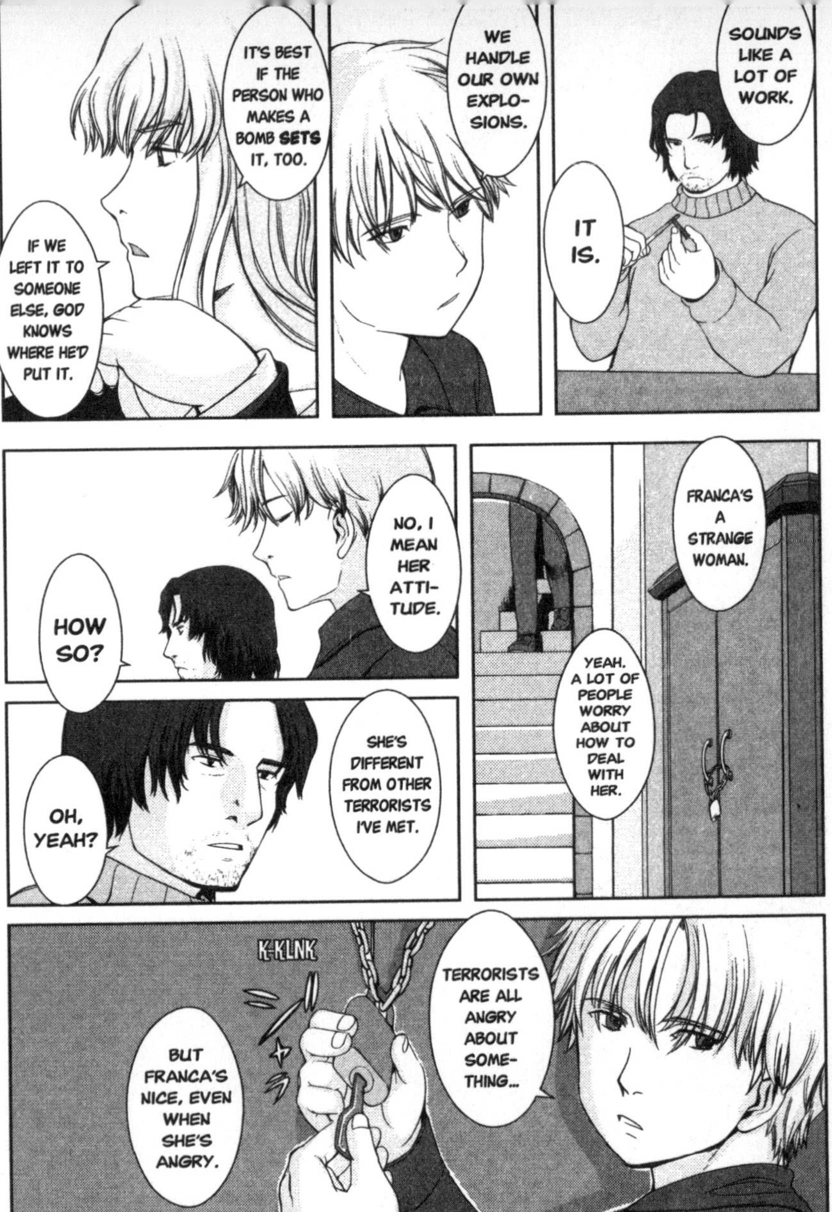
SOUNDS LIKE A LOT OF WORK.
IT IS.
WE HANDLE OUR OWN EXPLOSIONS.
IT'S BEST IF THE PERSON WHO MAKES A BOMB **SETS** IT, TOO.
IF WE LEFT IT TO SOMEONE ELSE, GOD KNOWS WHERE HE'D PUT IT.
FRANCA'S A STRANGE WOMAN.
YEAH. A LOT OF PEOPLE WORRY ABOUT HOW TO DEAL WITH HER.
NO, I MEAN HER ATTITUDE.
HOW SO?
SHE'S DIFFERENT FROM OTHER TERRORISTS I'VE MET.
OH, YEAH?
K-KLNK
TERRORISTS ARE ALL ANGRY ABOUT SOMETHING...
BUT FRANCA'S NICE, EVEN WHEN SHE'S ANGRY.

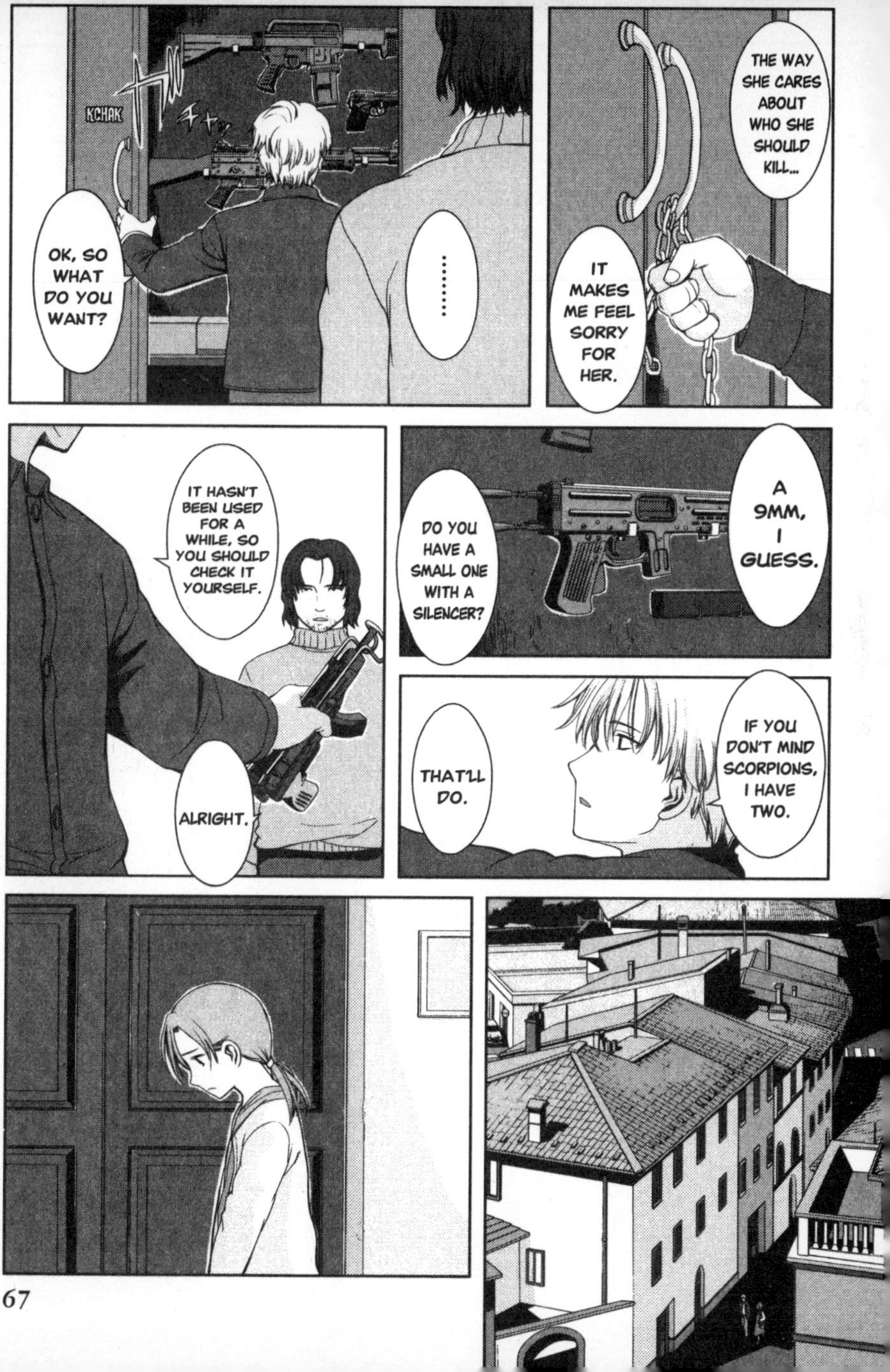
THE WAY SHE CARES ABOUT WHO SHE SHOULD KILL...
IT MAKES ME FEEL SORRY FOR HER.
KCHAK
OK, SO WHAT DO YOU WANT?
....
A 9MM, I GUESS.
DO YOU HAVE A SMALL ONE WITH A SILENCER?
IF YOU DON'T MIND SCORPIONS, I HAVE TWO.
THAT'LL DO.
IT HASN'T BEEN USED FOR A WHILE, SO YOU SHOULD CHECK IT YOURSELF.
ALRIGHT.

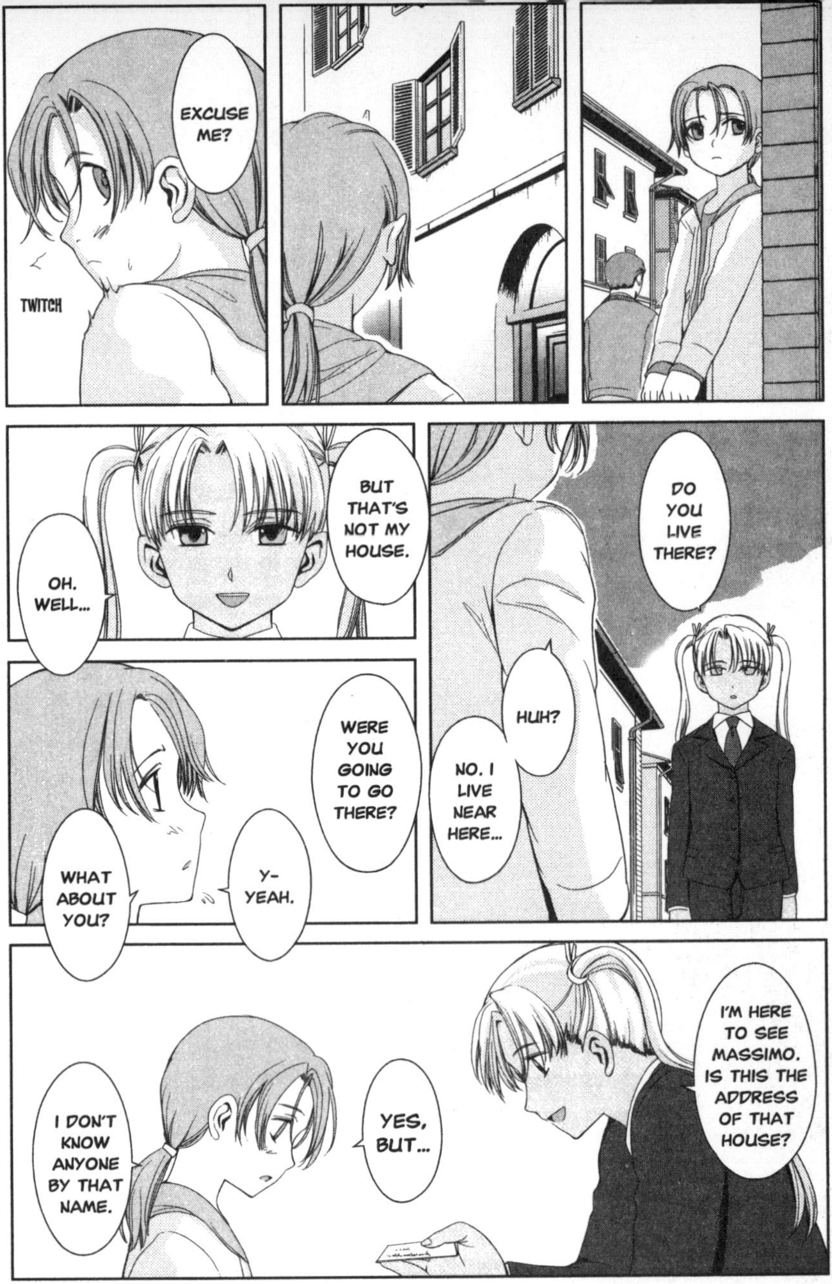
EXCUSE ME?
TWITCH
DO YOU LIVE THERE?
HUH?
NO. I LIVE NEAR HERE...
BUT THAT'S NOT MY HOUSE.
OH. WELL...
WERE YOU GOING TO GO THERE?
Y-YEAH.
WHAT ABOUT YOU?
I'M HERE TO SEE MASSIMO. IS THIS THE ADDRESS OF THAT HOUSE?
YES, BUT...
I DON'T KNOW ANYONE BY THAT NAME.

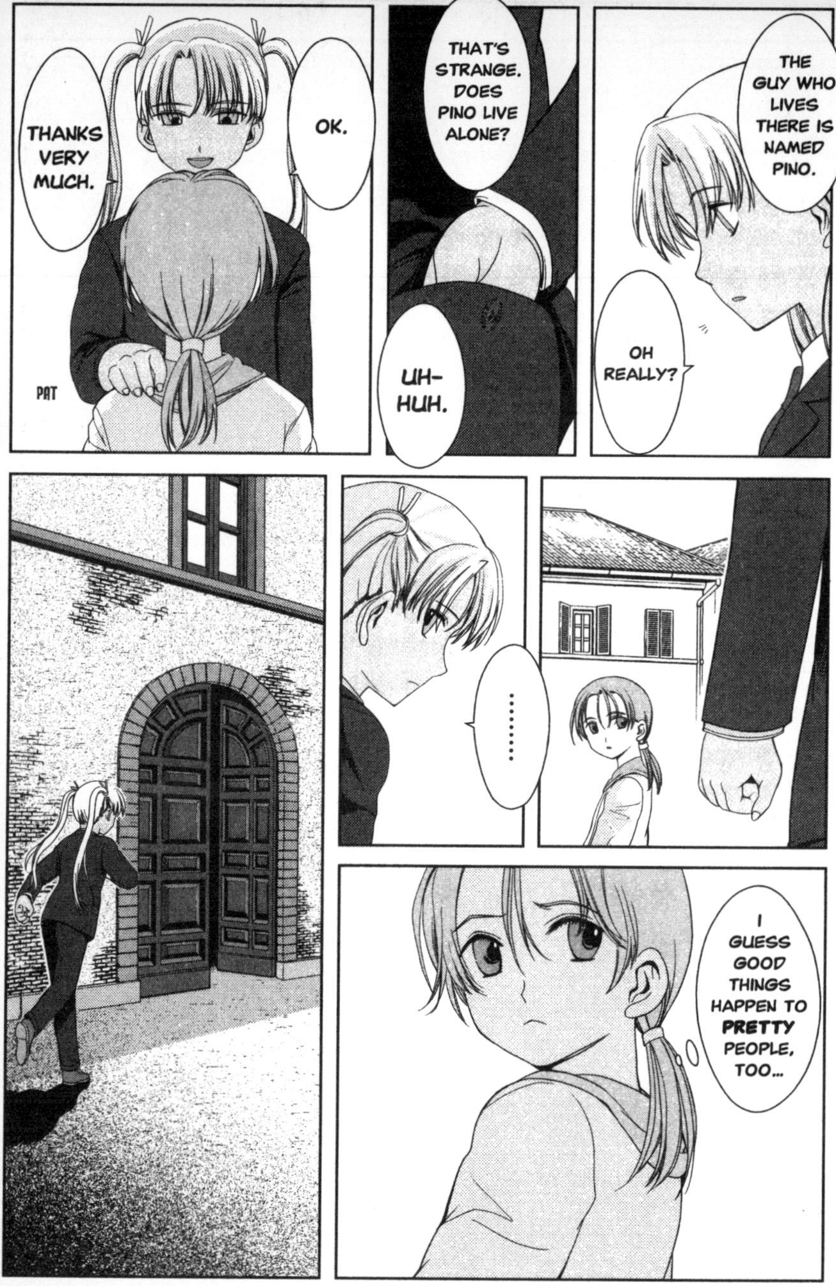
THE GUY WHO LIVES THERE IS NAMED PINO.
OH REALLY?
THAT'S STRANGE. DOES PINO LIVE ALONE?
UH-HUH.
OK.
THANKS VERY MUCH.
PAT
....
I GUESS GOOD THINGS HAPPEN TO **PRETTY** PEOPLE, TOO...

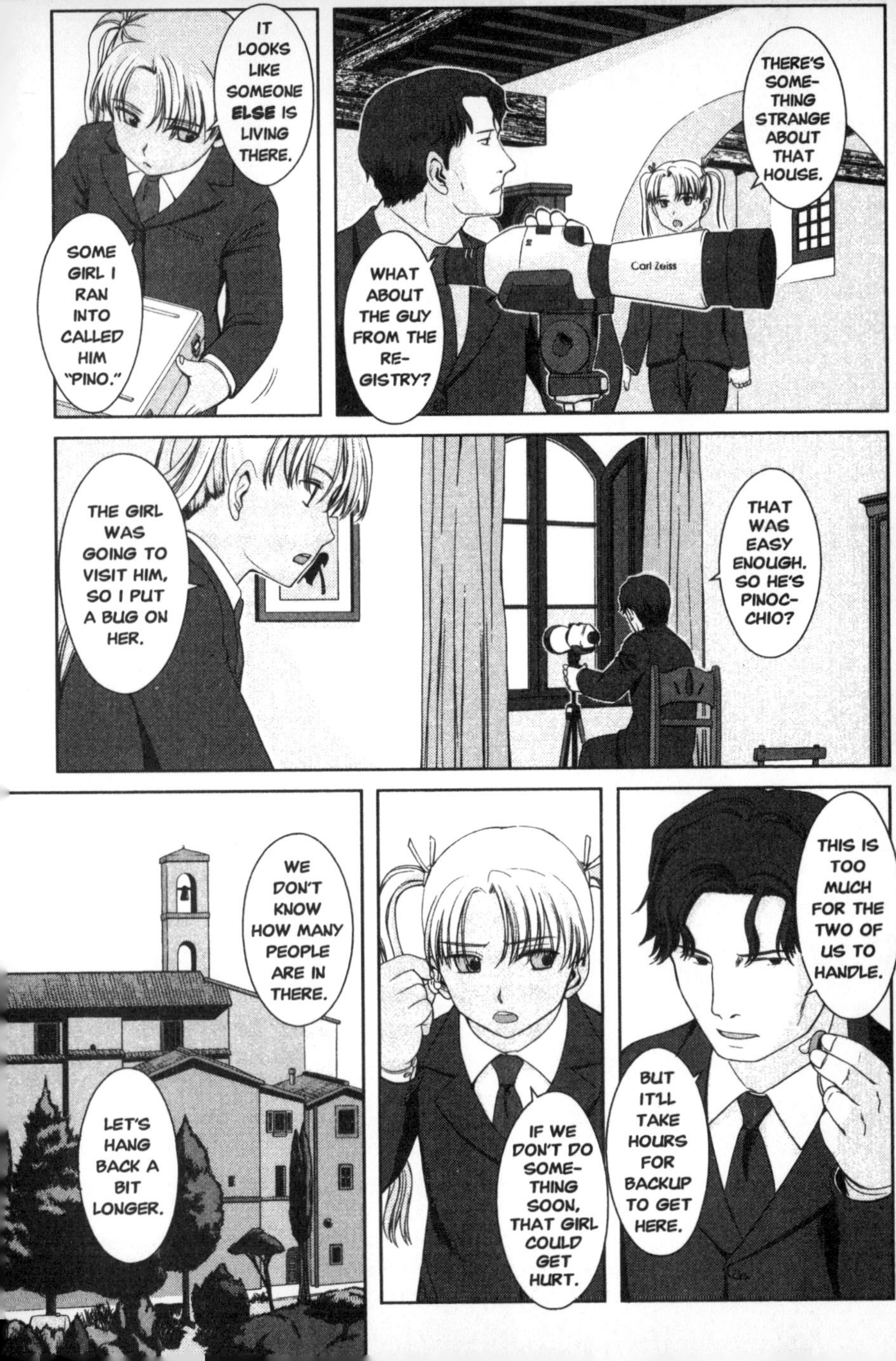
THERE'S SOME-THING STRANGE ABOUT THAT HOUSE.
WHAT ABOUT THE GUY FROM THE RE-GISTRY?
IT LOOKS LIKE SOMEONE **ELSE** IS LIVING THERE.
SOME GIRL I RAN INTO CALLED HIM "PINO."
Carl Zeiss
THAT WAS EASY ENOUGH. SO HE'S PINOC-CHIO?
THE GIRL WAS GOING TO VISIT HIM, SO I PUT A BUG ON HER.
THIS IS TOO MUCH FOR THE TWO OF US TO HANDLE.
BUT IT'LL TAKE HOURS FOR BACKUP TO GET HERE.
IF WE DON'T DO SOME-THING SOON, THAT GIRL COULD GET HURT.
WE DON'T KNOW HOW MANY PEOPLE ARE IN THERE.
LET'S HANG BACK A BIT LONGER.

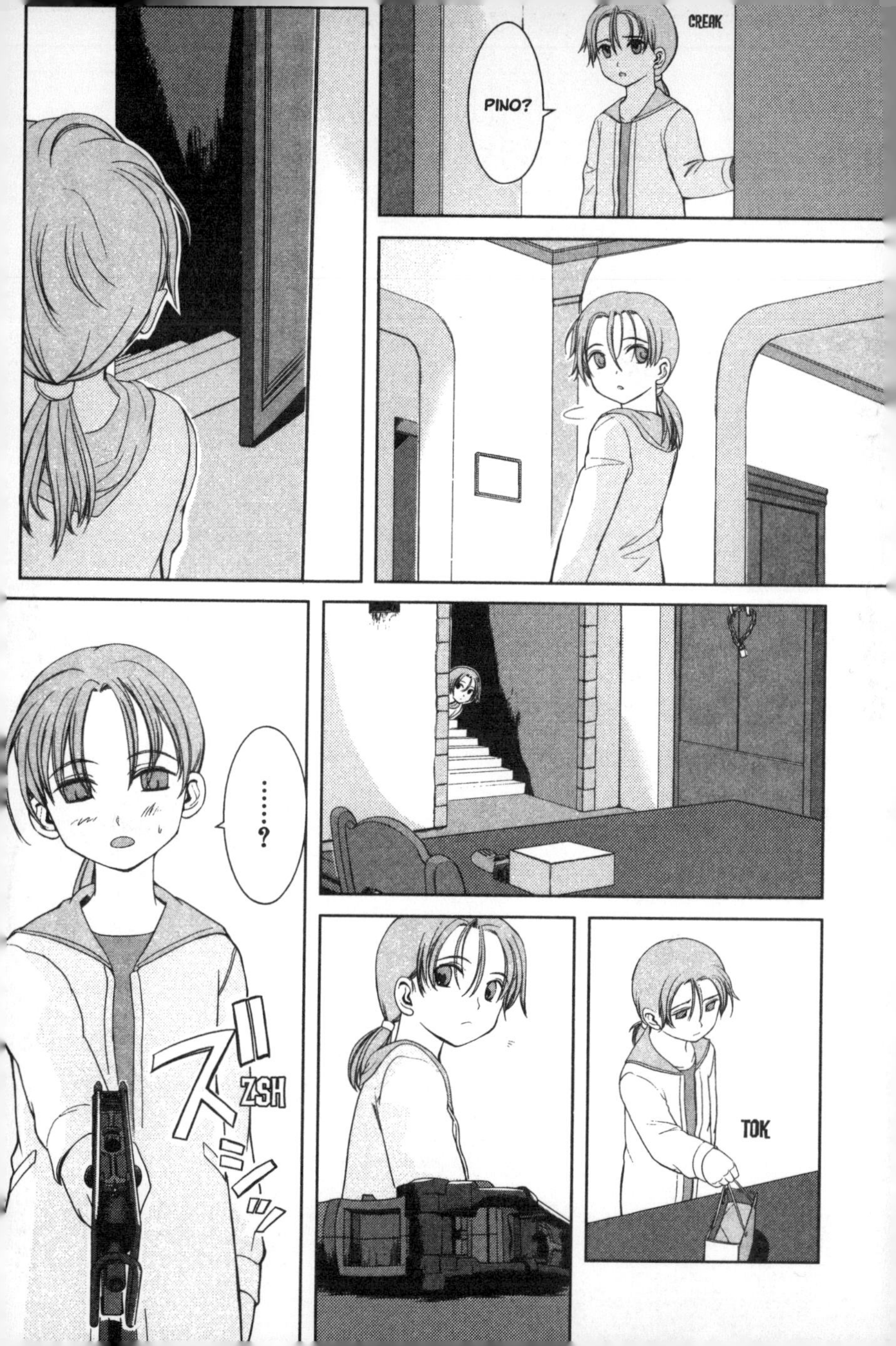
CREAK
PINO?
TOK
......?
ZSH

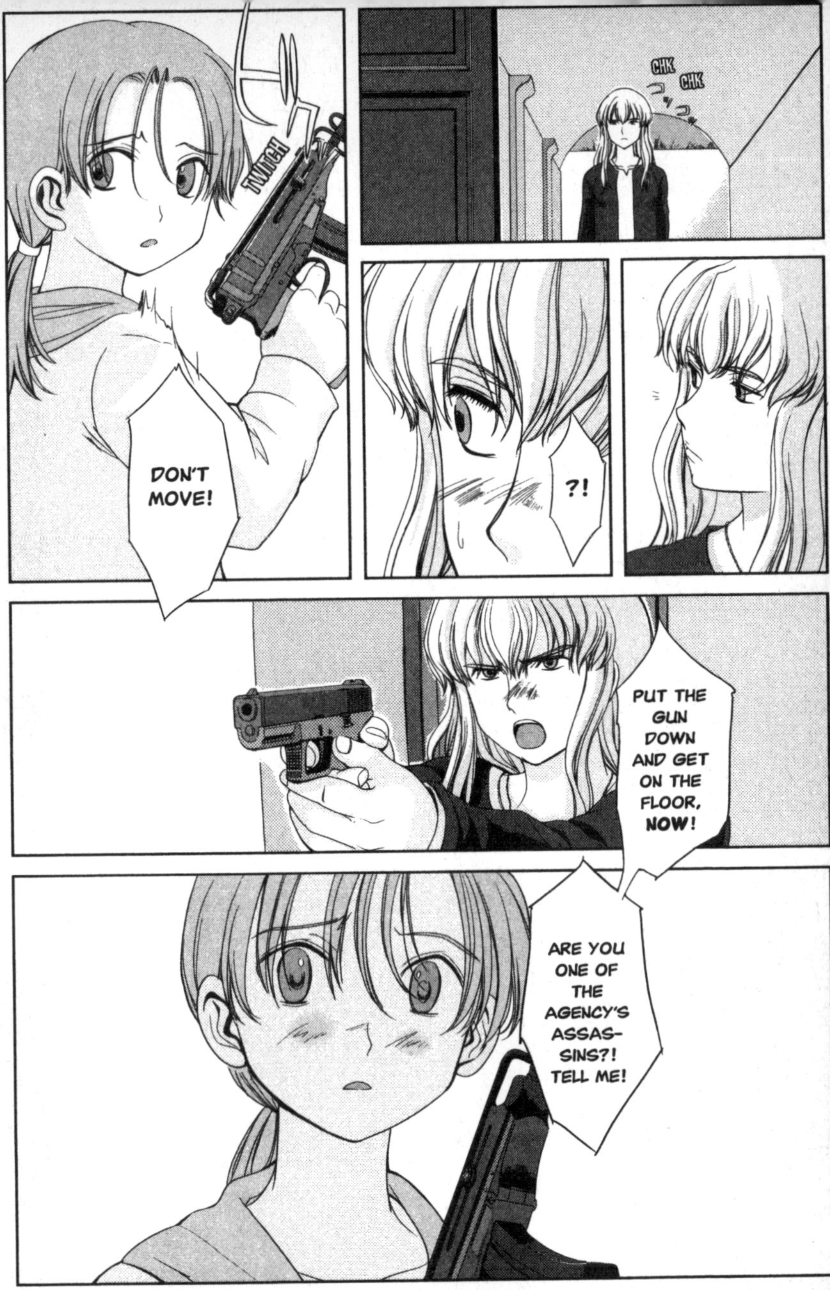
TWITCH
DON'T MOVE!
CHK CHK
?!
PUT THE GUN DOWN AND GET ON THE FLOOR, **NOW**!
ARE YOU ONE OF THE AGENCY'S ASSAS-SINS?! TELL ME!

GUNSLINGERGIRL.

第15話 Pinocchio (Part 3)

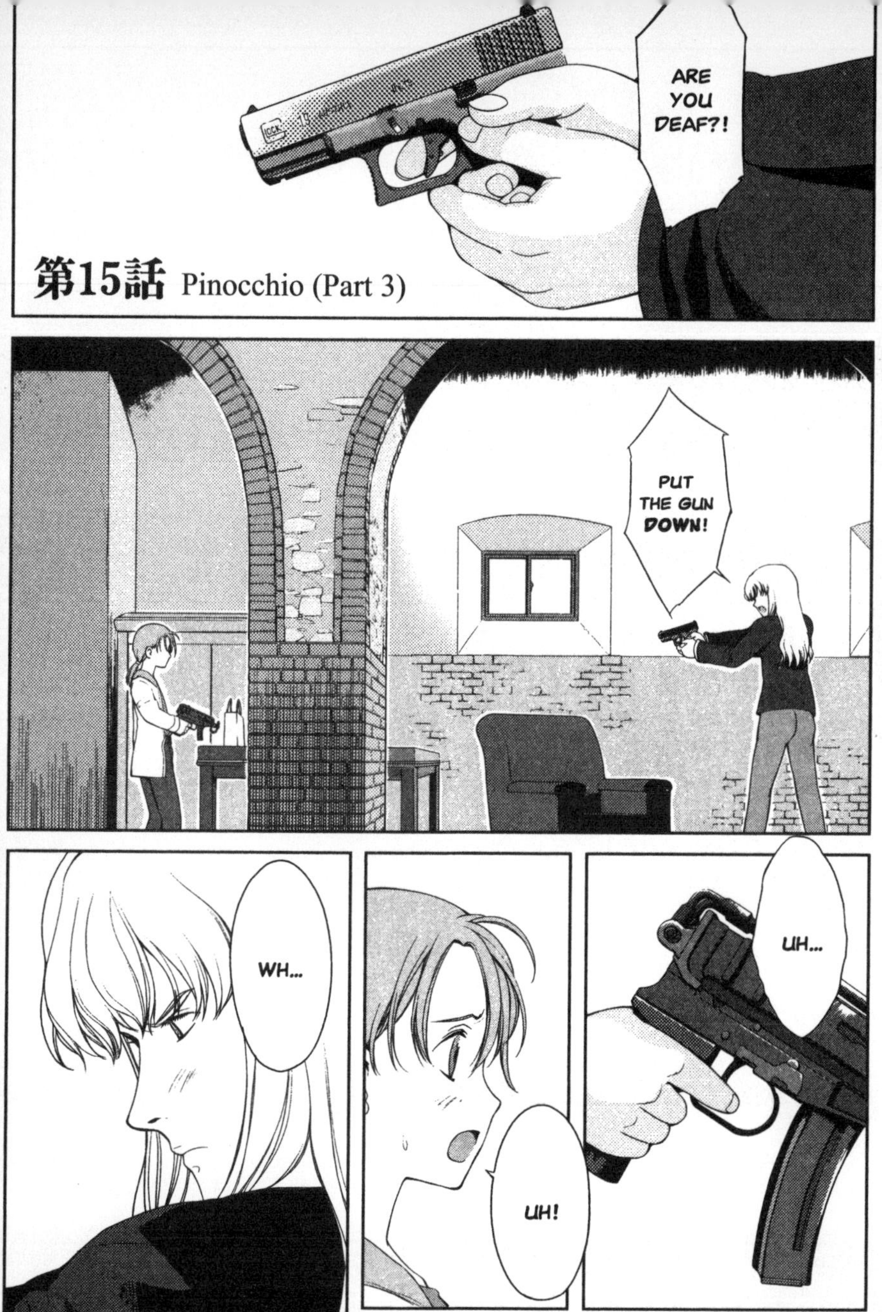
ARE YOU DEAF?!
PUT THE GUN DOWN!
UH...
UH!
WH...

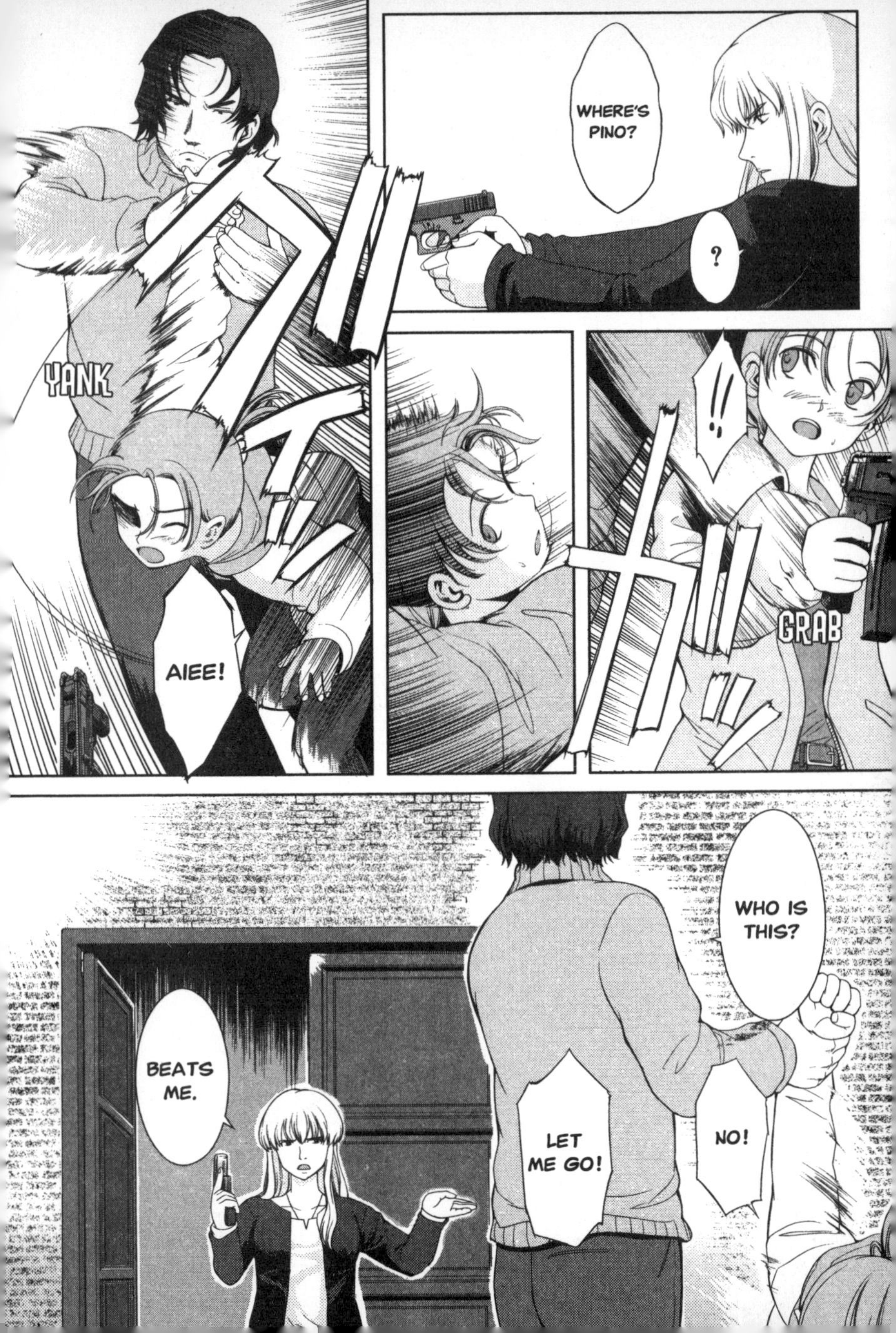
WHERE'S PINO?
?
YANK
AIEE!
!!
GRAB
WHO IS THIS?
NO!
LET ME GO!
BEATS ME.

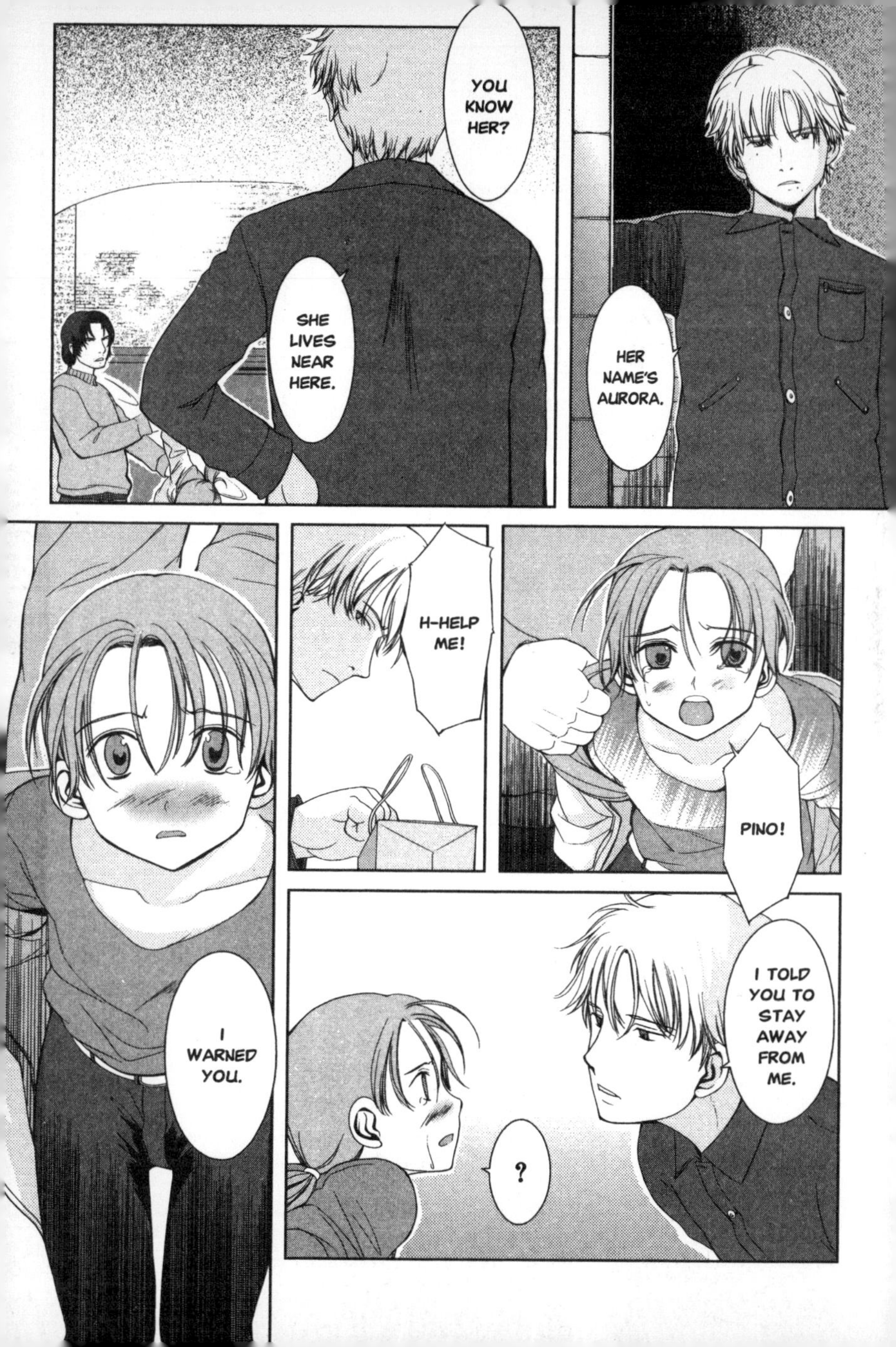
YOU KNOW HER?
SHE LIVES NEAR HERE.
HER NAME'S AURORA.
I WARNED YOU.
H-HELP ME!
PINO!
I TOLD YOU TO STAY AWAY FROM ME.
?

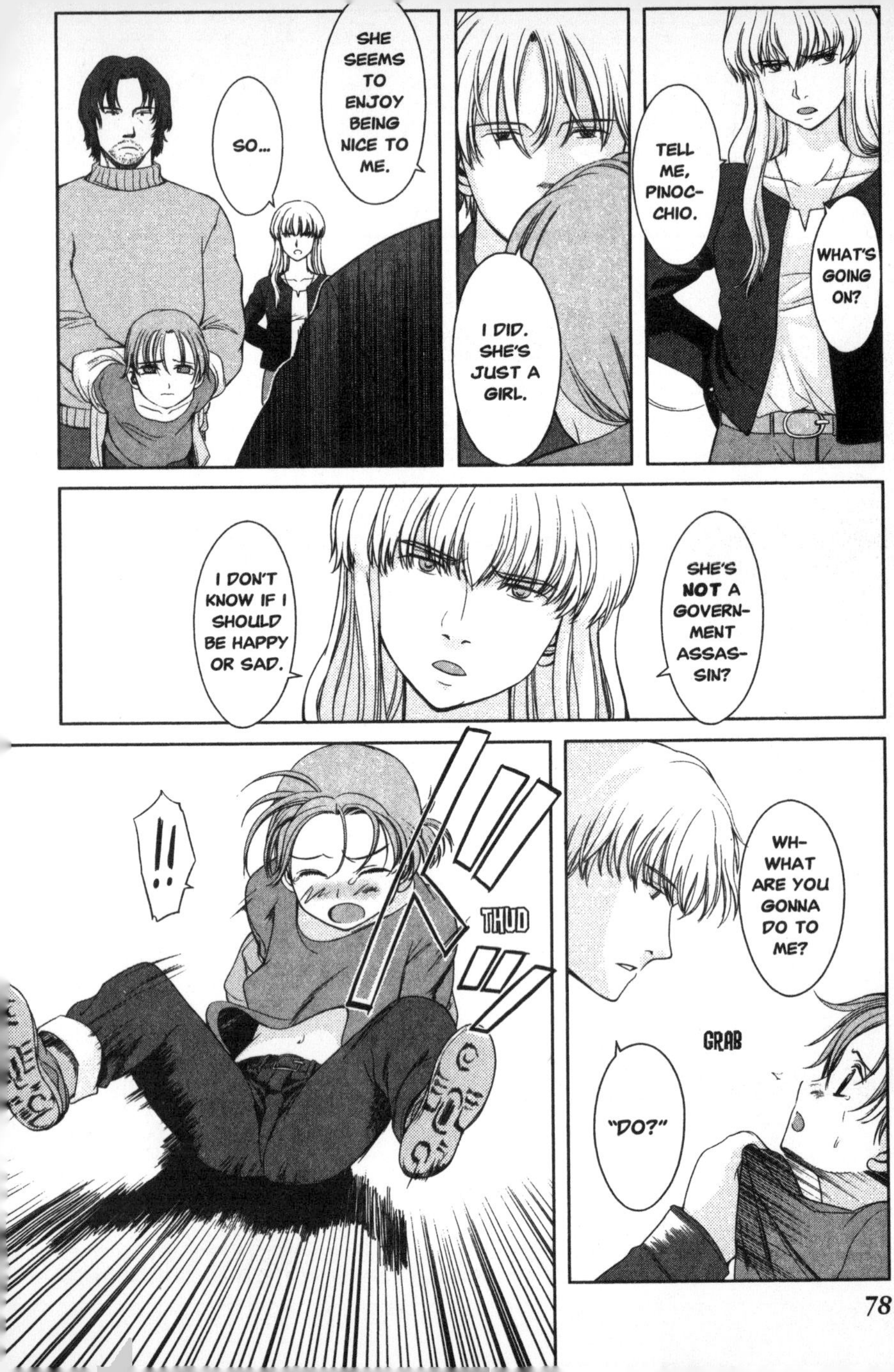
WHAT'S GOING ON?
TELL ME, PINOCCHIO.
I DID. SHE'S JUST A GIRL.
SHE SEEMS TO ENJOY BEING NICE TO ME.
SO...
SHE'S **NOT** A GOVERNMENT ASSASSIN?
I DON'T KNOW IF I SHOULD BE HAPPY OR SAD.
WH-WHAT ARE YOU GONNA DO TO ME?
GRAB
"DO?"
THUD
!!

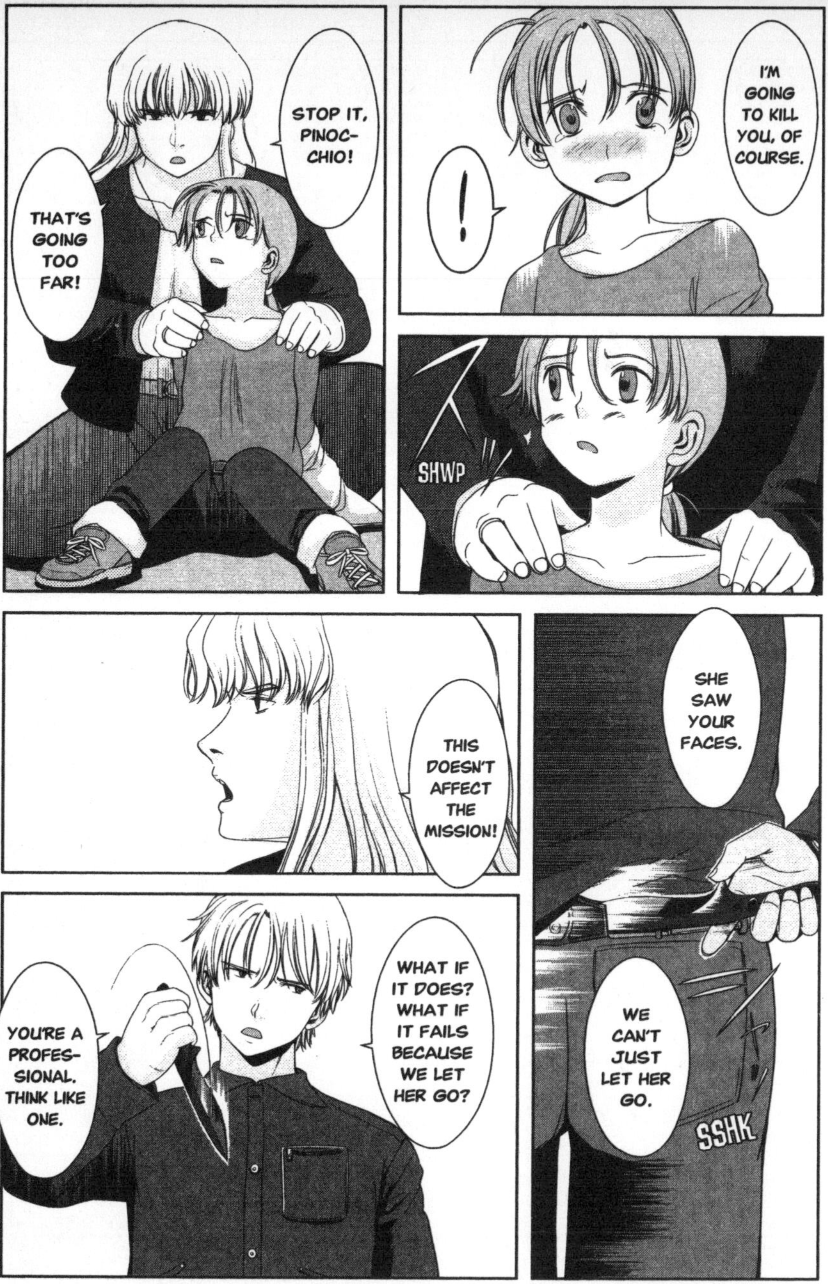
I'M GOING TO KILL YOU, OF COURSE.
!
SHWP
STOP IT, PINOCCHIO!
THAT'S GOING TOO FAR!
SHE SAW YOUR FACES.
WE CAN'T JUST LET HER GO.
SSHK
THIS DOESN'T AFFECT THE MISSION!
WHAT IF IT DOES? WHAT IF IT FAILS BECAUSE WE LET HER GO?
YOU'RE A PROFESSIONAL. THINK LIKE ONE.

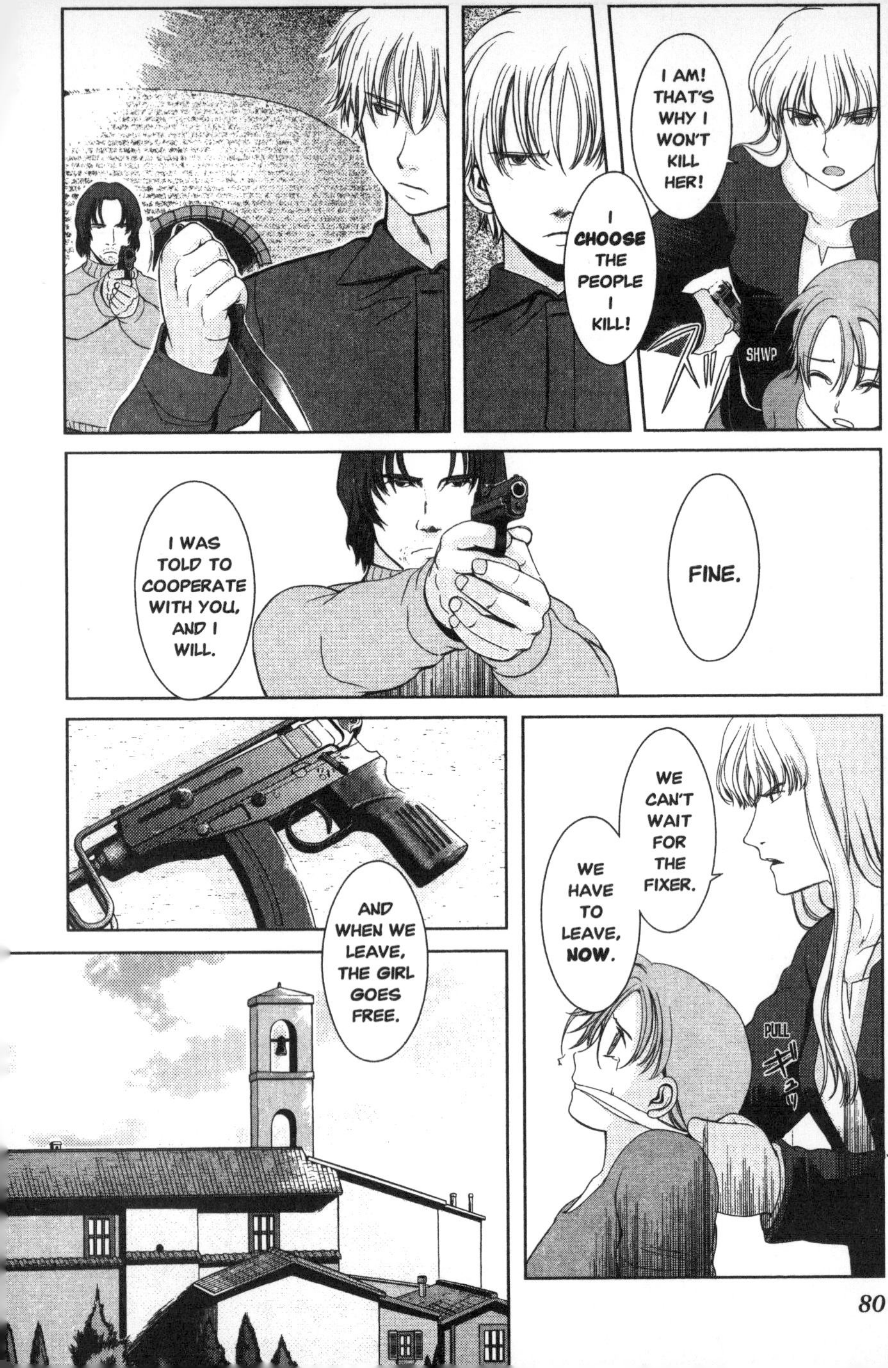
I AM! THAT'S WHY I WON'T KILL HER!
SHWP
I **CHOOSE** THE PEOPLE I KILL!
FINE.
I WAS TOLD TO COOPERATE WITH YOU, AND I WILL.
WE CAN'T WAIT FOR THE FIXER.
WE HAVE TO LEAVE, **NOW**.
PULL
AND WHEN WE LEAVE, THE GIRL GOES FREE.

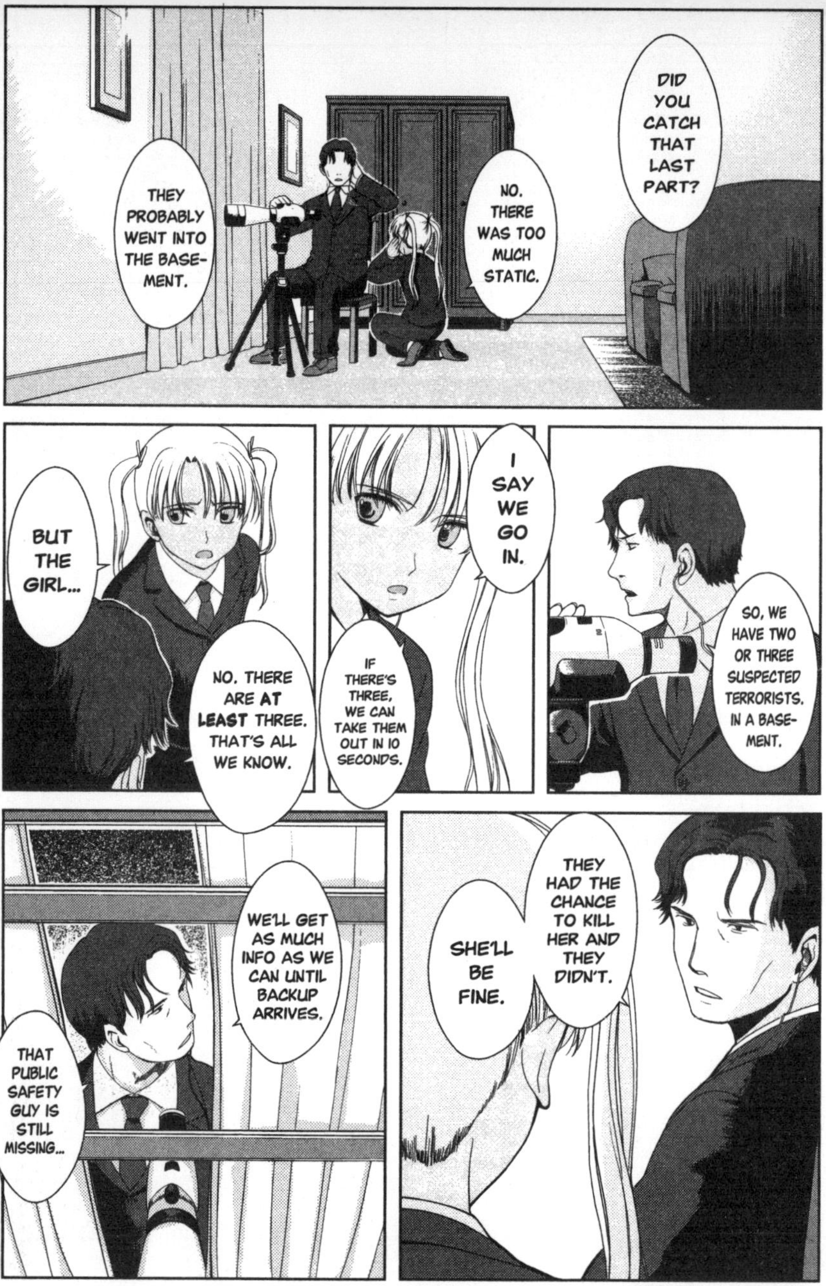
DID YOU CATCH THAT LAST PART?
NO. THERE WAS TOO MUCH STATIC.
THEY PROBABLY WENT INTO THE BASE-MENT.
SO, WE HAVE TWO OR THREE SUSPECTED TERRORISTS. IN A BASE-MENT.
I SAY WE GO IN.
IF THERE'S THREE, WE CAN TAKE THEM OUT IN 10 SECONDS.
BUT THE GIRL...
NO. THERE ARE **AT LEAST** THREE. THAT'S ALL WE KNOW.
THEY HAD THE CHANCE TO KILL HER AND THEY DIDN'T.
SHE'LL BE FINE.
WE'LL GET AS MUCH INFO AS WE CAN UNTIL BACKUP ARRIVES.
THAT PUBLIC SAFETY GUY IS STILL MISSING...

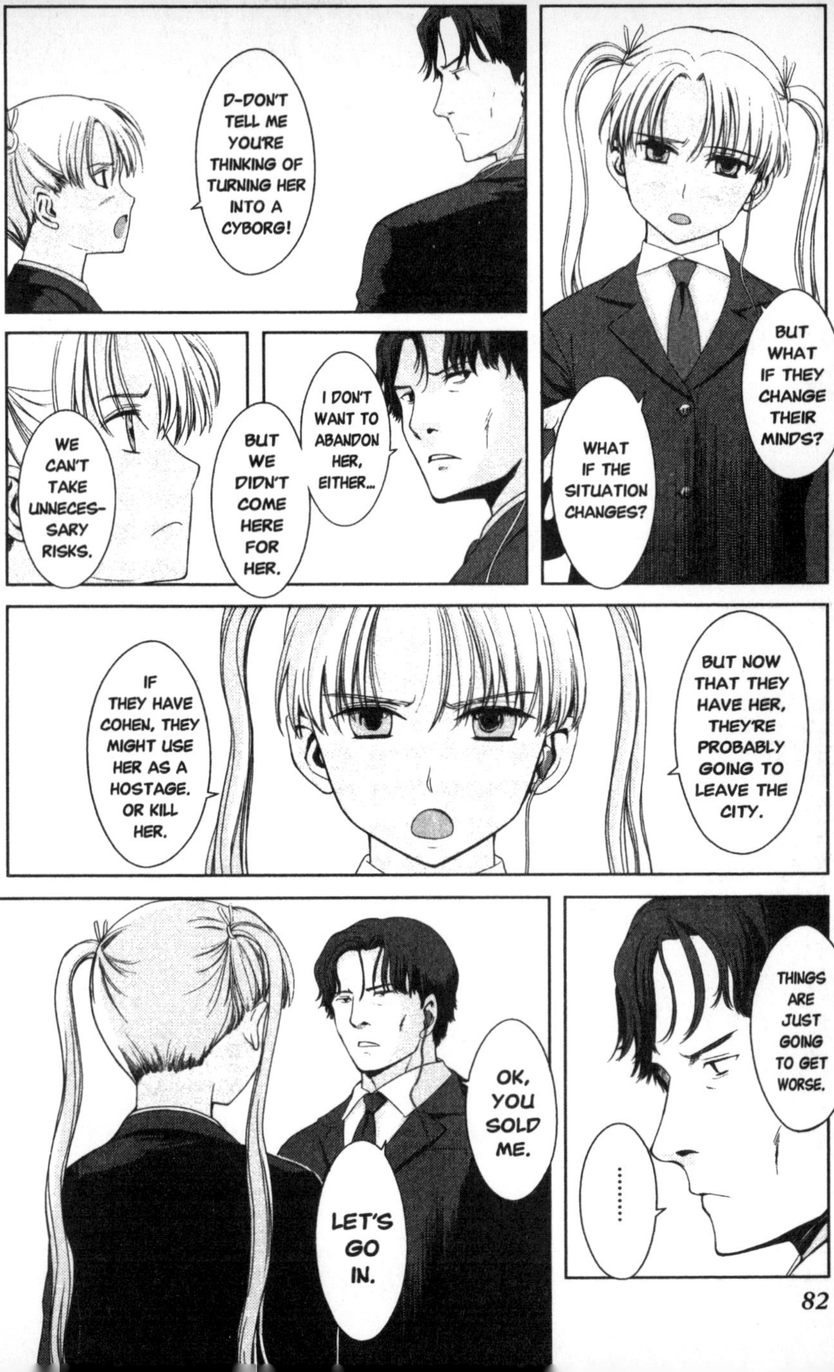
D-DON'T TELL ME YOU'RE THINKING OF TURNING HER INTO A CYBORG!
BUT WHAT IF THEY CHANGE THEIR MINDS?
WHAT IF THE SITUATION CHANGES?
I DON'T WANT TO ABANDON HER, EITHER...
BUT WE DIDN'T COME HERE FOR HER.
WE CAN'T TAKE UNNECES-SARY RISKS.
IF THEY HAVE COHEN, THEY MIGHT USE HER AS A HOSTAGE. OR KILL HER.
BUT NOW THAT THEY HAVE HER, THEY'RE PROBABLY GOING TO LEAVE THE CITY.
THINGS ARE JUST GOING TO GET WORSE.
......
OK, YOU SOLD ME.
LET'S GO IN.

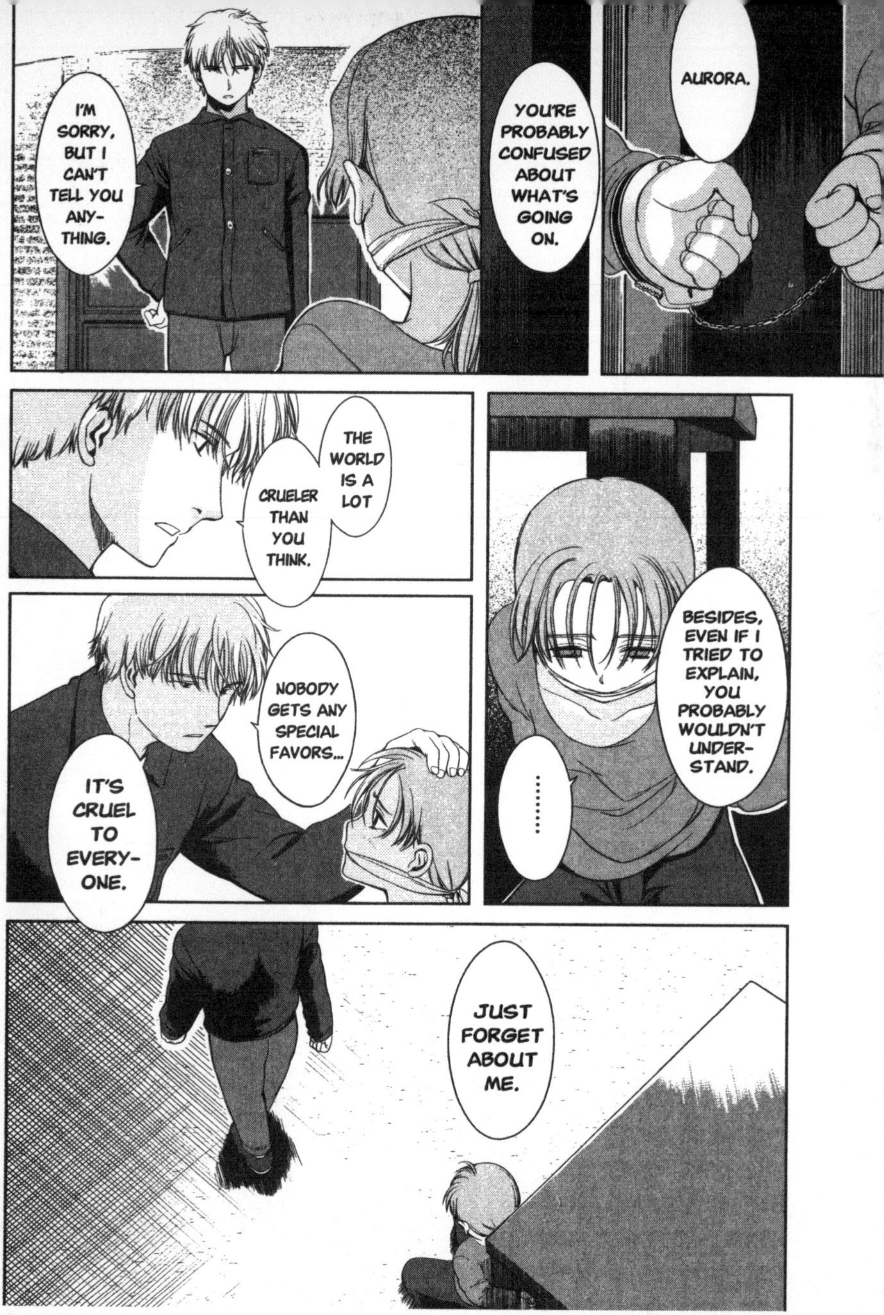
AURORA.
YOU'RE PROBABLY CONFUSED ABOUT WHAT'S GOING ON.
I'M SORRY, BUT I CAN'T TELL YOU ANY-THING.
BESIDES, EVEN IF I TRIED TO EXPLAIN, YOU PROBABLY WOULDN'T UNDER-STAND.
....
THE WORLD IS A LOT
CRUELER THAN YOU THINK.
NOBODY GETS ANY SPECIAL FAVORS...
IT'S CRUEL TO EVERY-ONE.
JUST FORGET ABOUT ME.

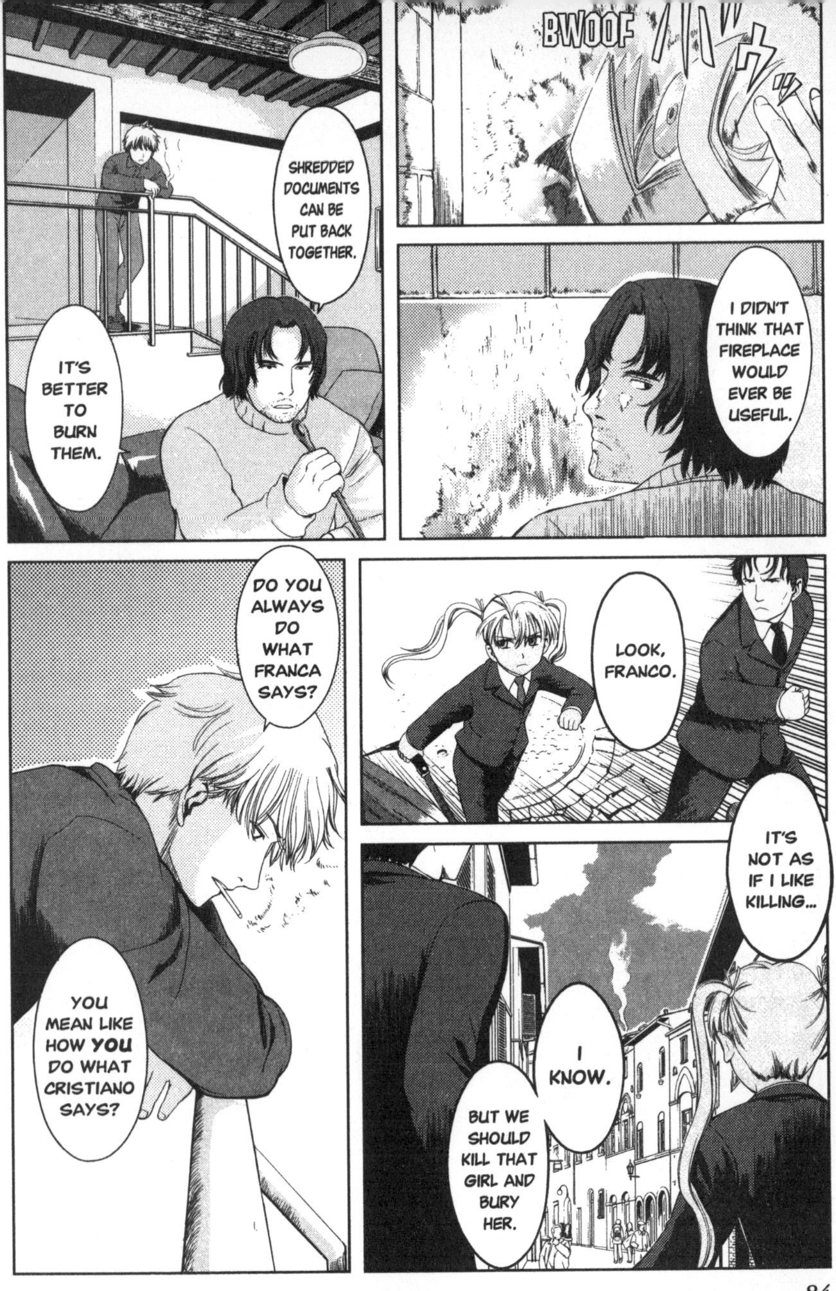
BWOOF
I DIDN'T THINK THAT FIREPLACE WOULD EVER BE USEFUL.
SHREDDED DOCUMENTS CAN BE PUT BACK TOGETHER.
IT'S BETTER TO BURN THEM.
LOOK, FRANCO.
IT'S NOT AS IF I LIKE KILLING...
I KNOW.
BUT WE SHOULD KILL THAT GIRL AND BURY HER.
DO YOU ALWAYS DO WHAT FRANCA SAYS?
YOU MEAN LIKE HOW **YOU** DO WHAT CRISTIANO SAYS?

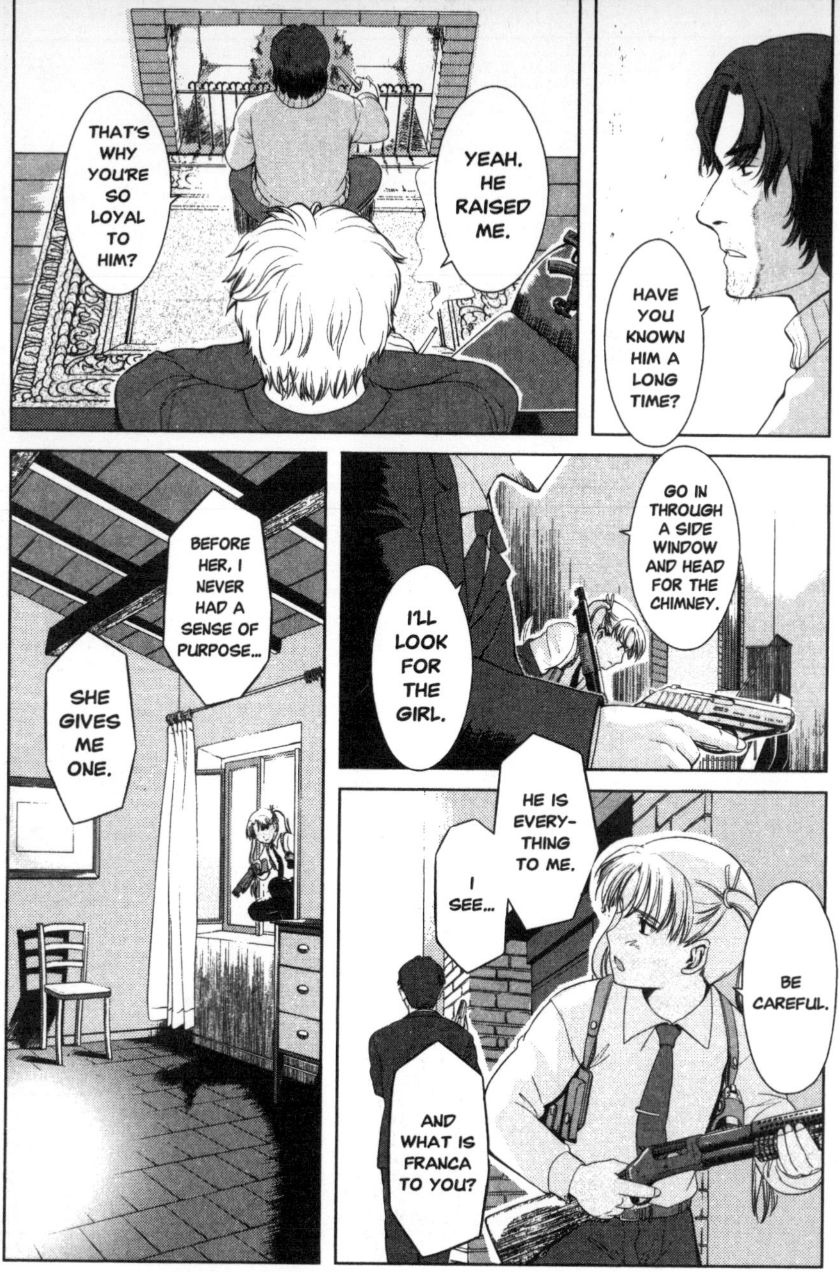
HAVE YOU KNOWN HIM A LONG TIME?
YEAH. HE RAISED ME.
THAT'S WHY YOU'RE SO LOYAL TO HIM?
GO IN THROUGH A SIDE WINDOW AND HEAD FOR THE CHIMNEY.
I'LL LOOK FOR THE GIRL.
BE CAREFUL.
HE IS EVERYTHING TO ME.
I SEE...
AND WHAT IS FRANCA TO YOU?
BEFORE HER, I NEVER HAD A SENSE OF PURPOSE...
SHE GIVES ME ONE.

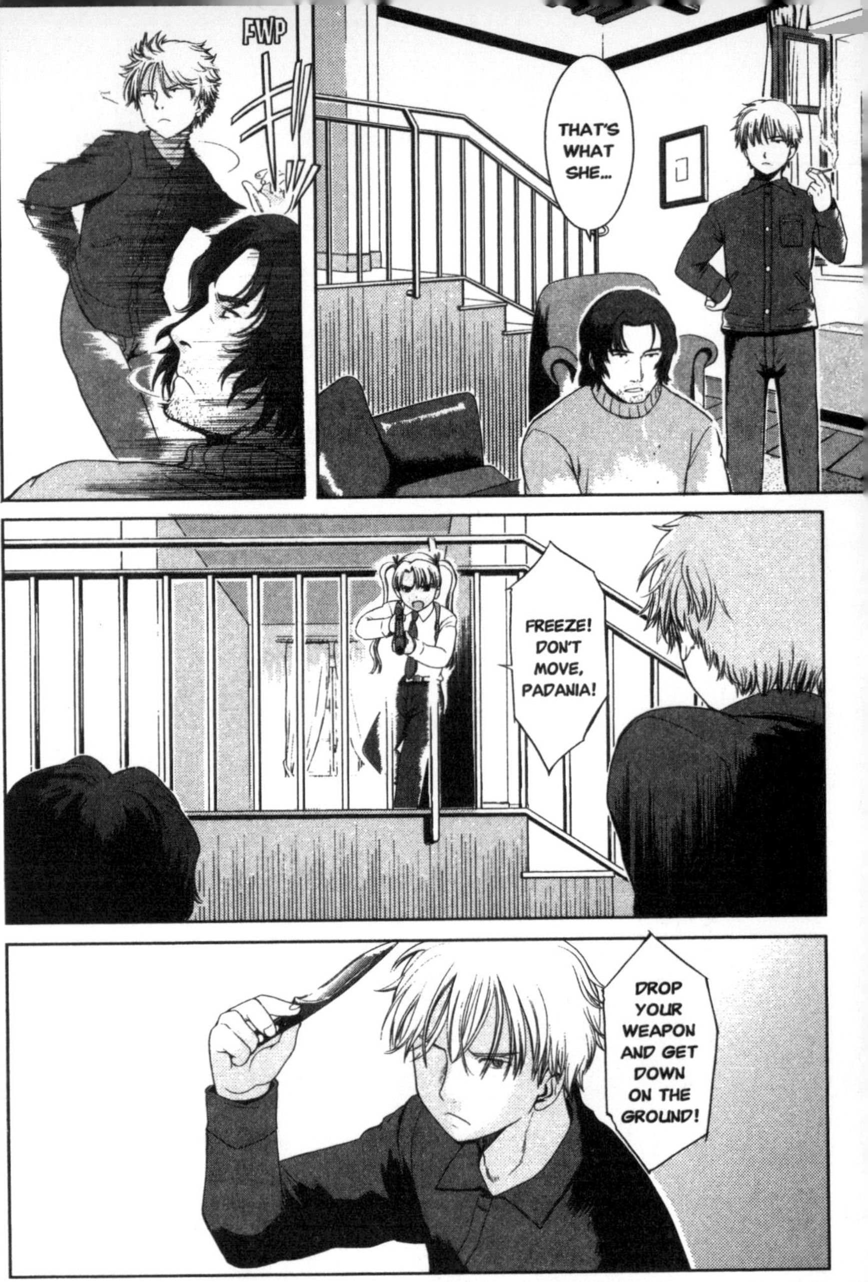
THAT'S WHAT SHE...
FWP
FREEZE! DON'T MOVE, PADANIA!
DROP YOUR WEAPON AND GET DOWN ON THE GROUND!

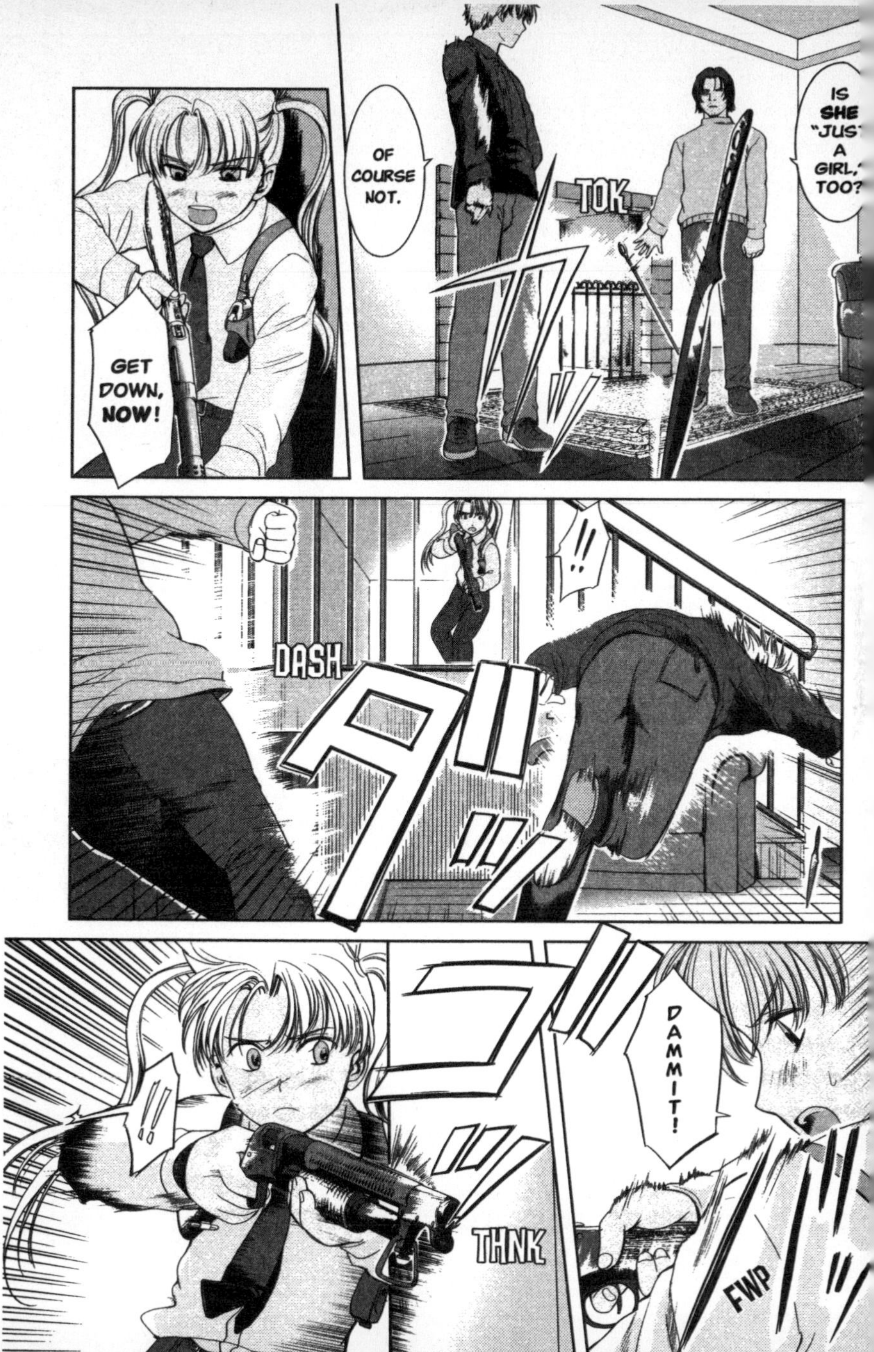
IS SHE "JUST A GIRL," TOO?
OF COURSE NOT.
TOK
GET DOWN, NOW!
!!
DASH
DAMMIT!
!!
THNK
FWP

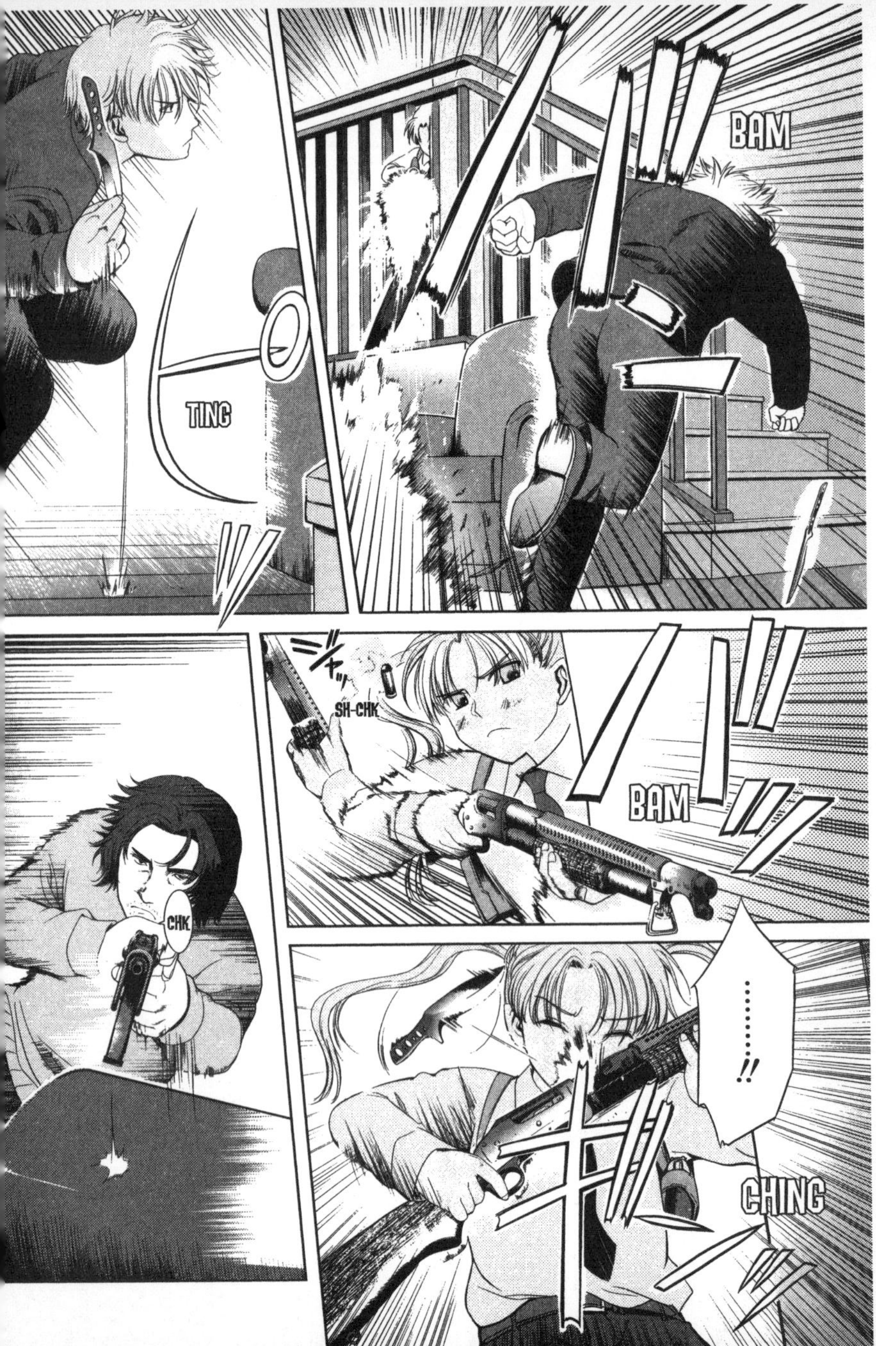
BAM
TING
SH-CHK
BAM
CHK
......!!
CHING

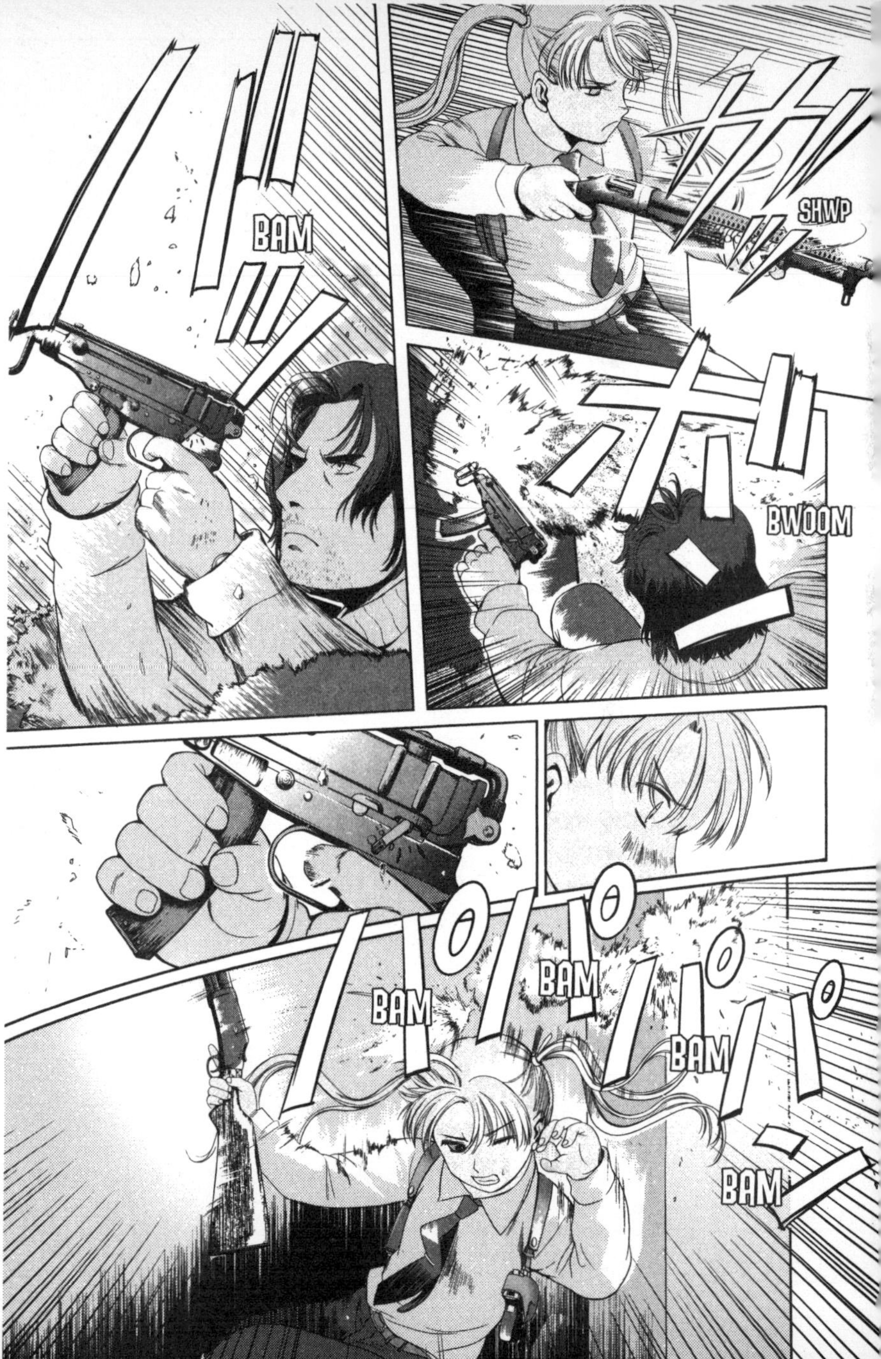
SHWP
BWOOM
BAM
BAM
BAM
BAM
BAM

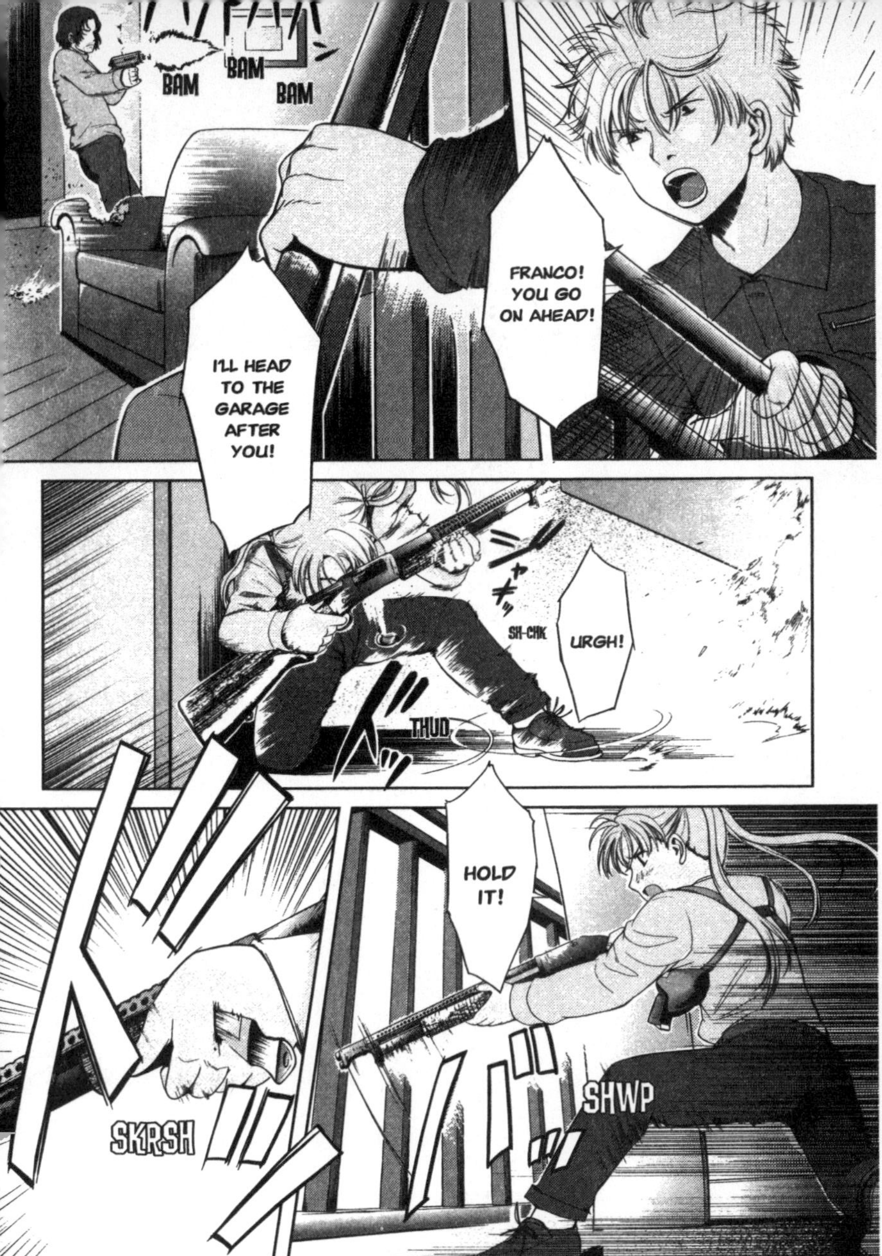
BAM
BAM
BAM
FRANCO! YOU GO ON AHEAD!
I'LL HEAD TO THE GARAGE AFTER YOU!
SH-CHK
URGH!
THUD
HOLD IT!
SKRSH
SHWP

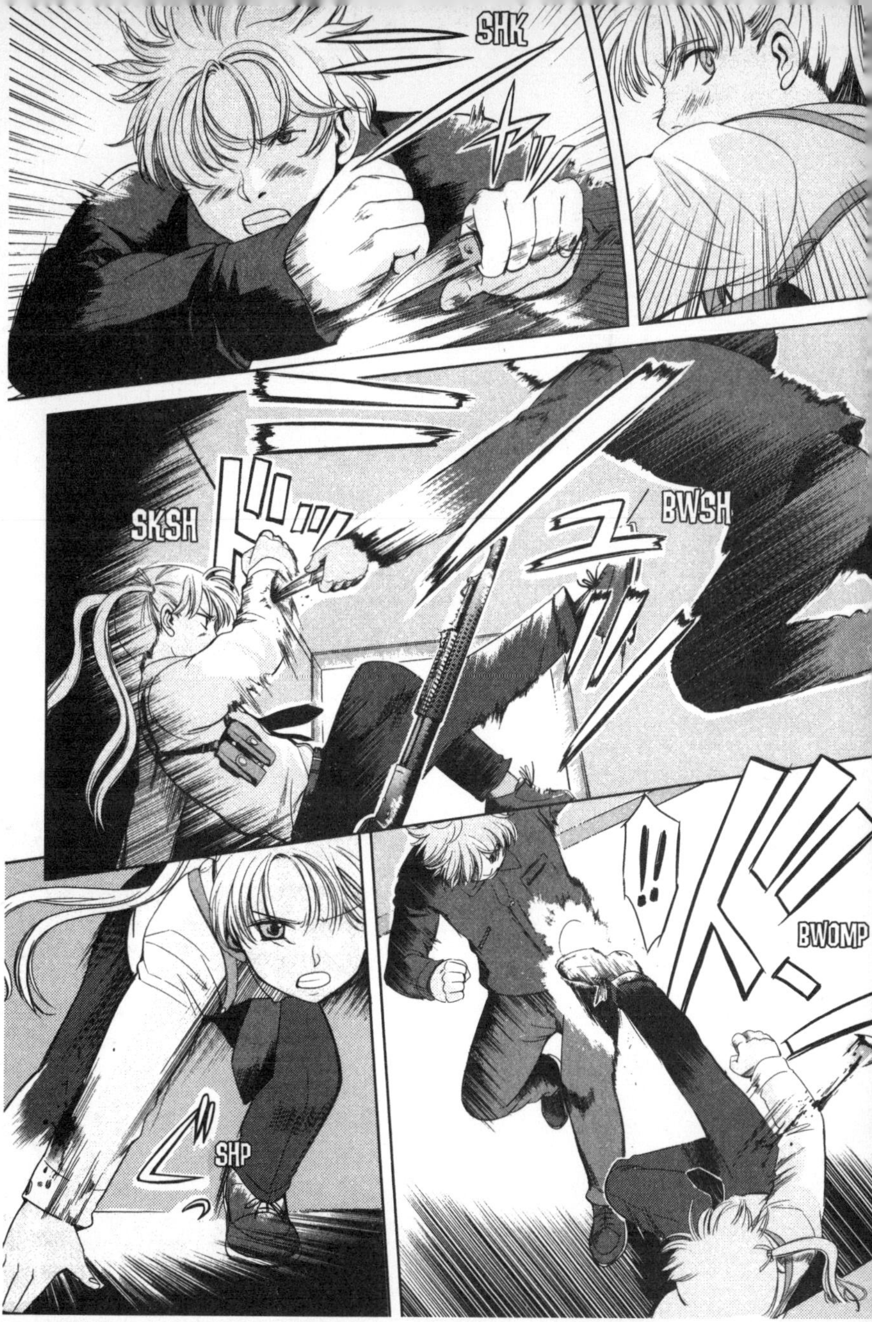
SHK
BWSH
SKSH
BWOMP
!!
SHP

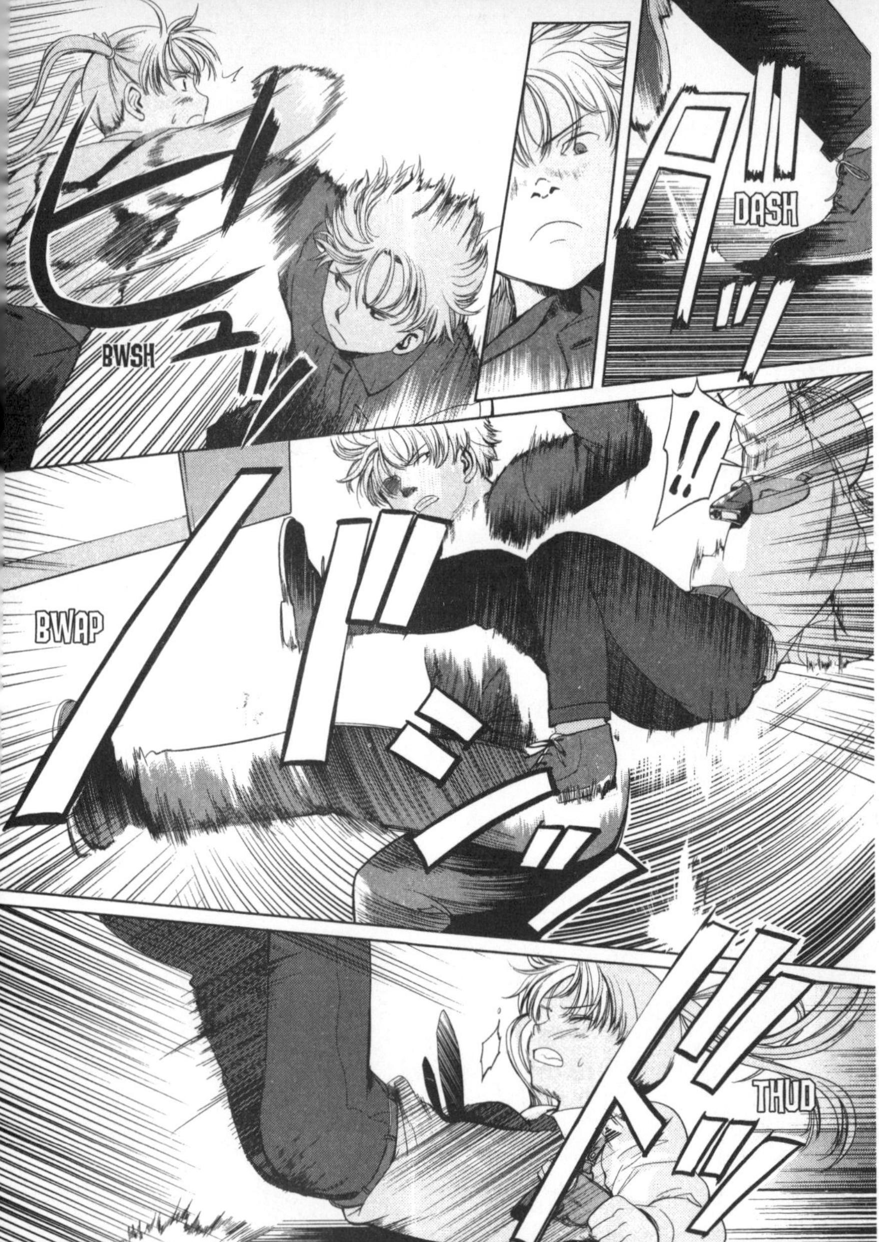
DASH
BWSH
!!
BWAP
THUD

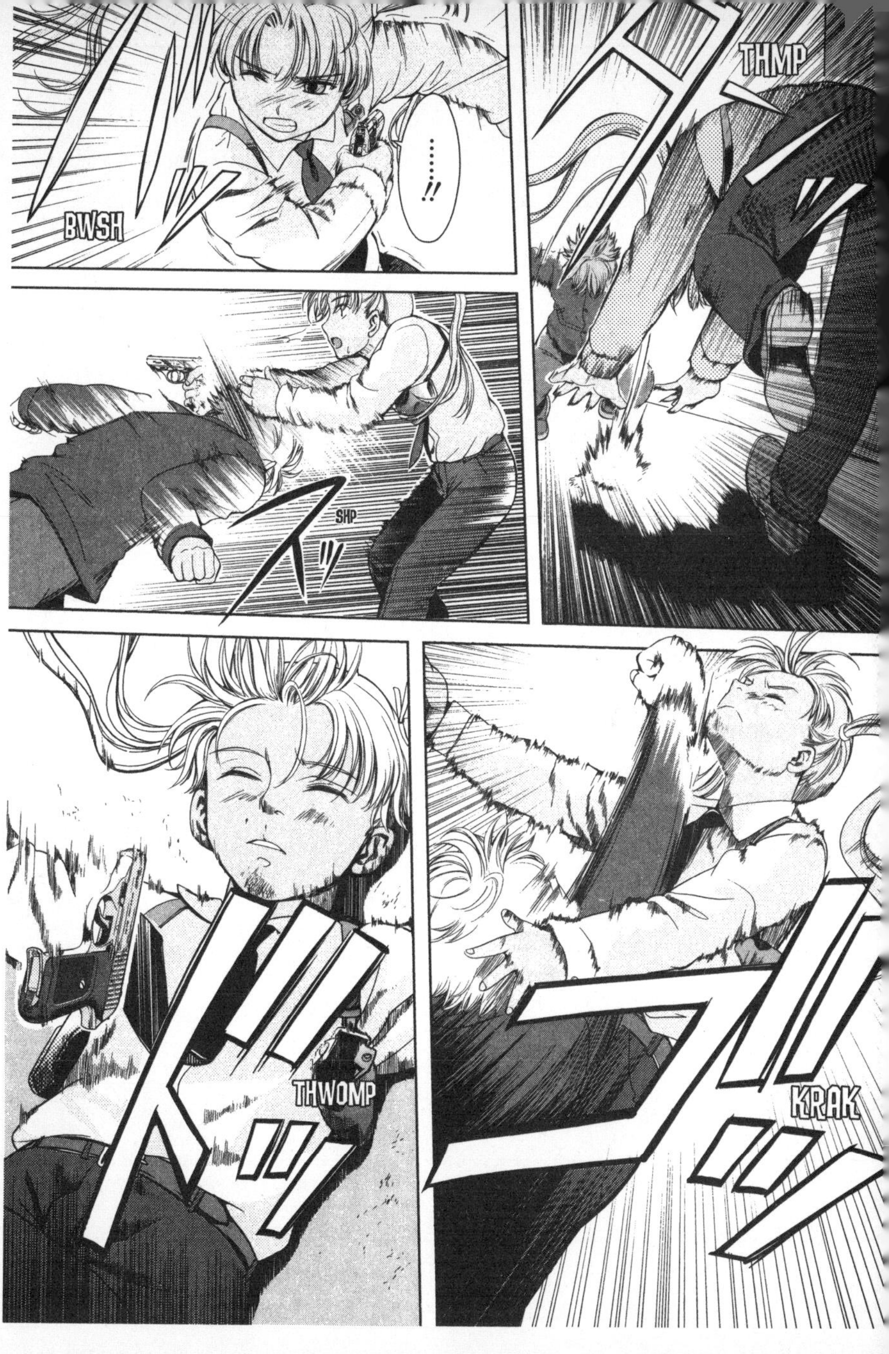
THMP
......!!
BWSH
SHP
KRAK
THWOMP

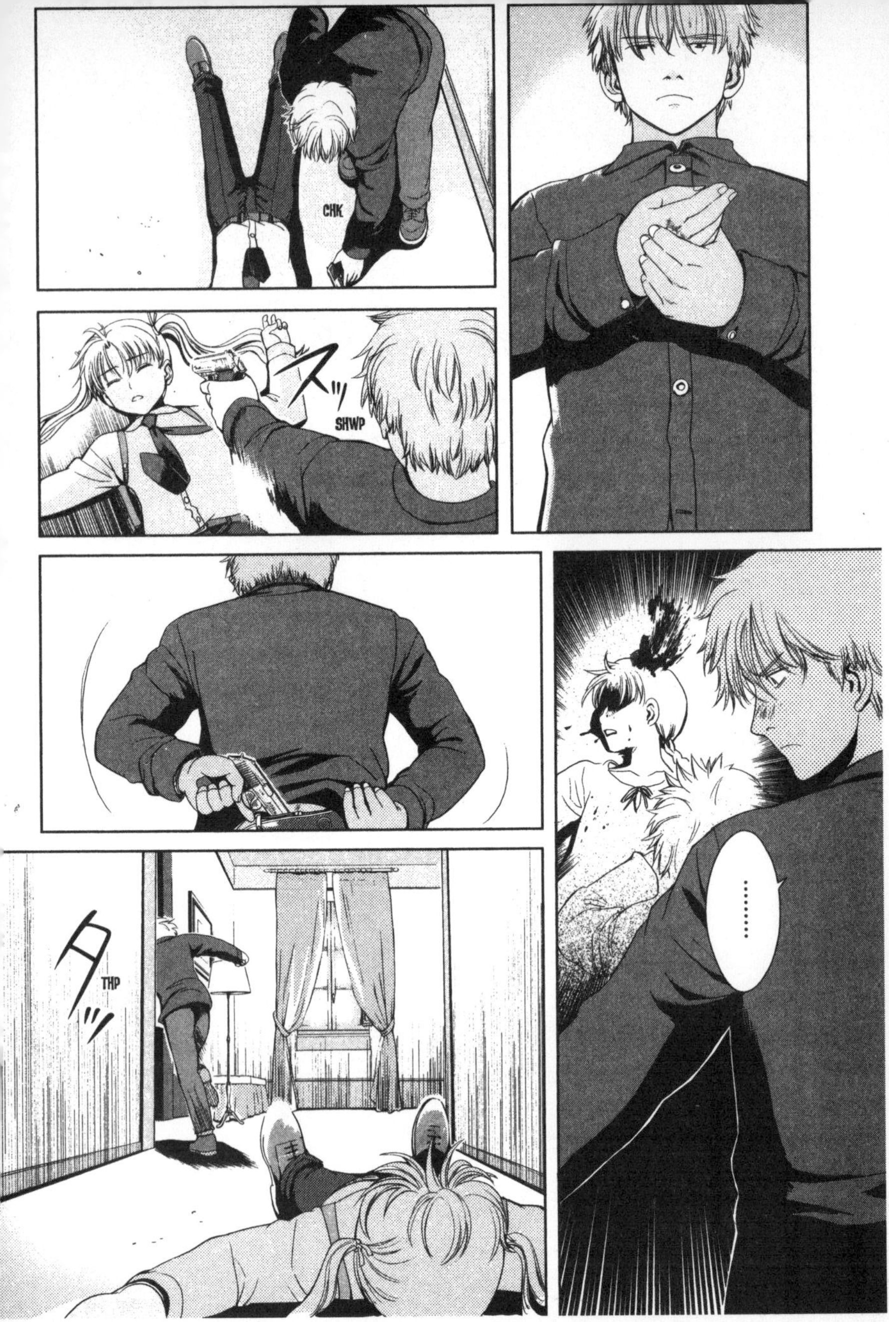CHK
スッ
SHWP
………
タッ
THP

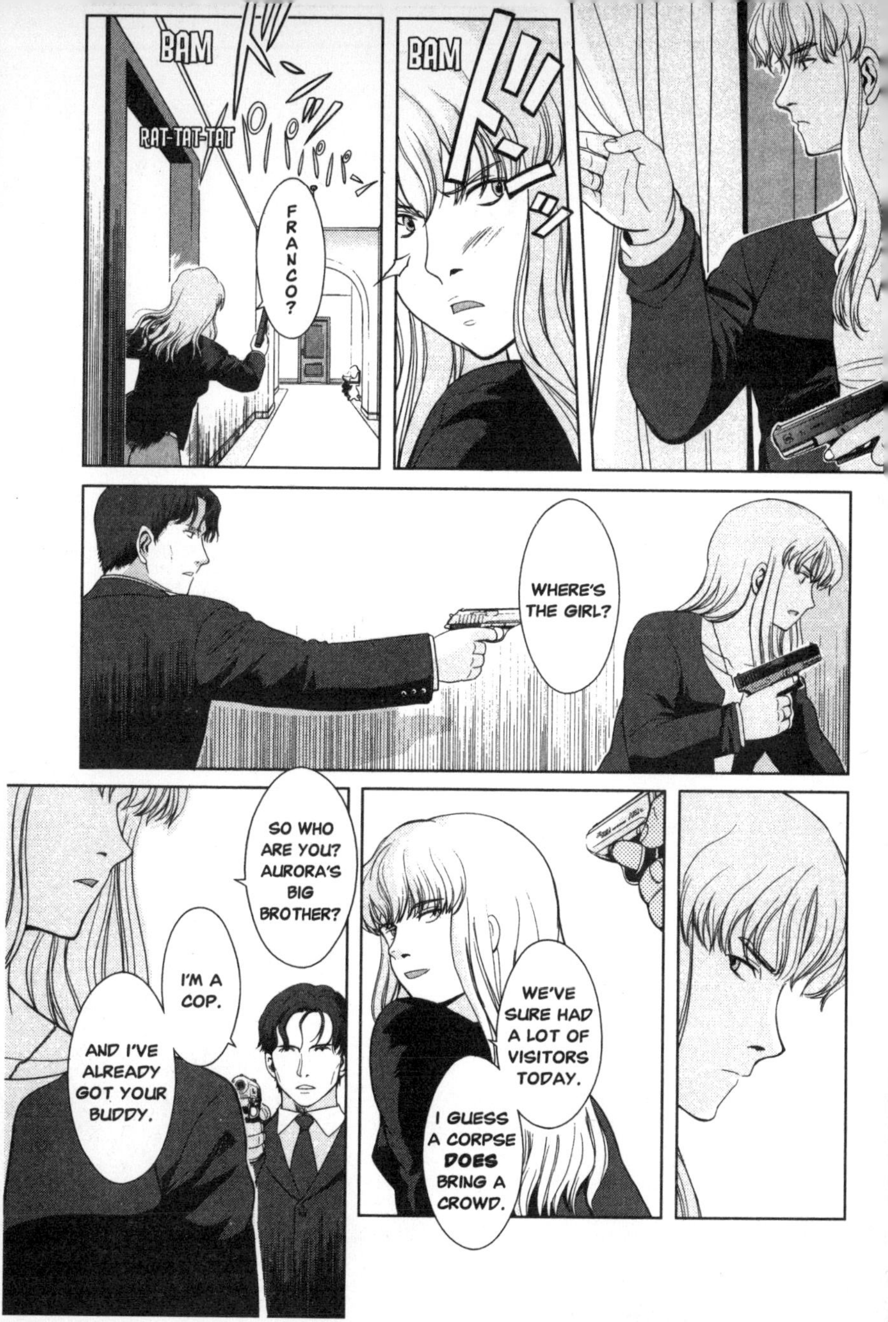

BAM
RAT-TAT-TAT
FRANCO?
BAM
WHERE'S THE GIRL?
SO WHO ARE YOU? AURORA'S BIG BROTHER?
I'M A COP.
AND I'VE ALREADY GOT YOUR BUDDY.
WE'VE SURE HAD A LOT OF VISITORS TODAY.
I GUESS A CORPSE **DOES** BRING A CROWD.

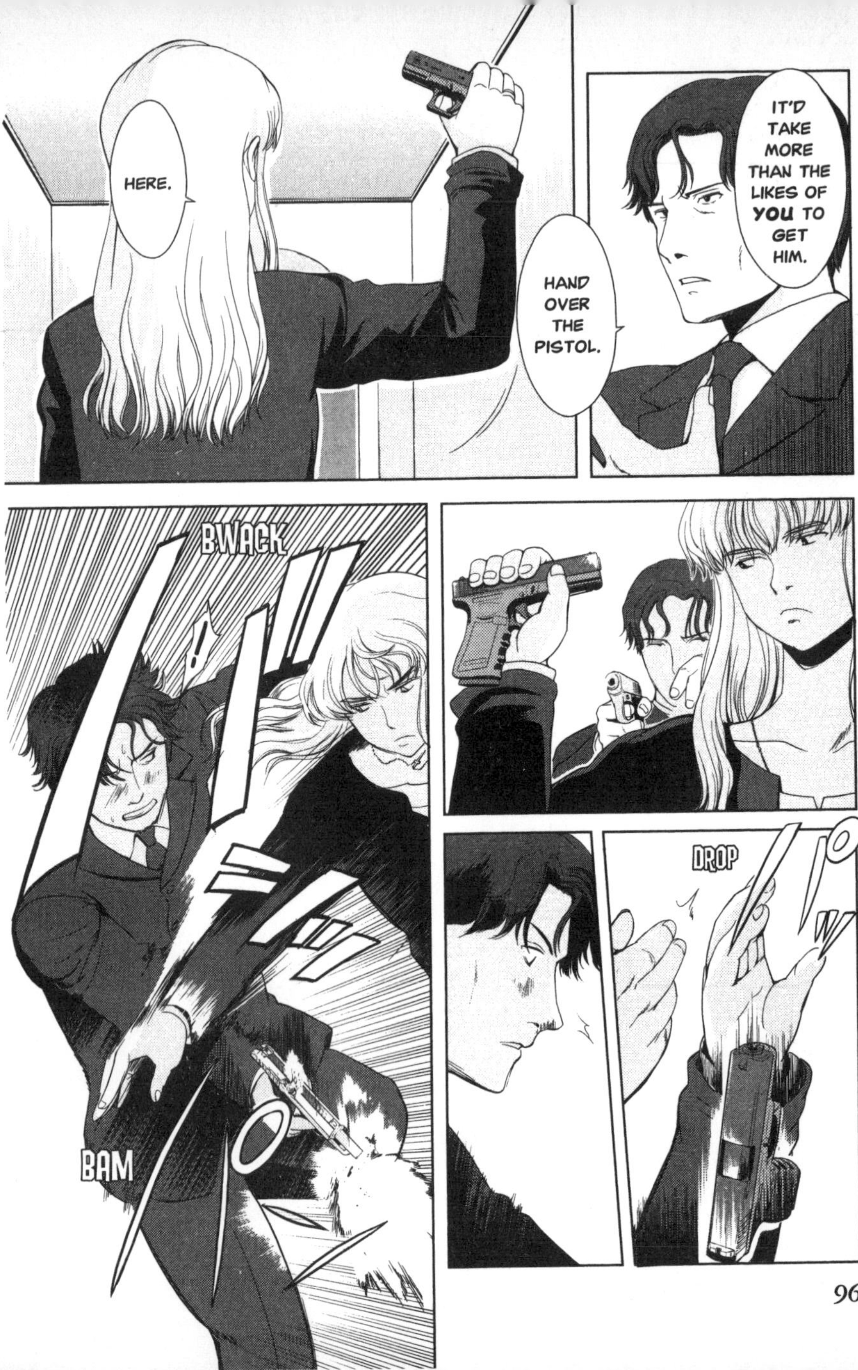
IT'D TAKE MORE THAN THE LIKES OF YOU TO GET HIM.
HAND OVER THE PISTOL.
HERE.
!
BWACK
BAM
DROP

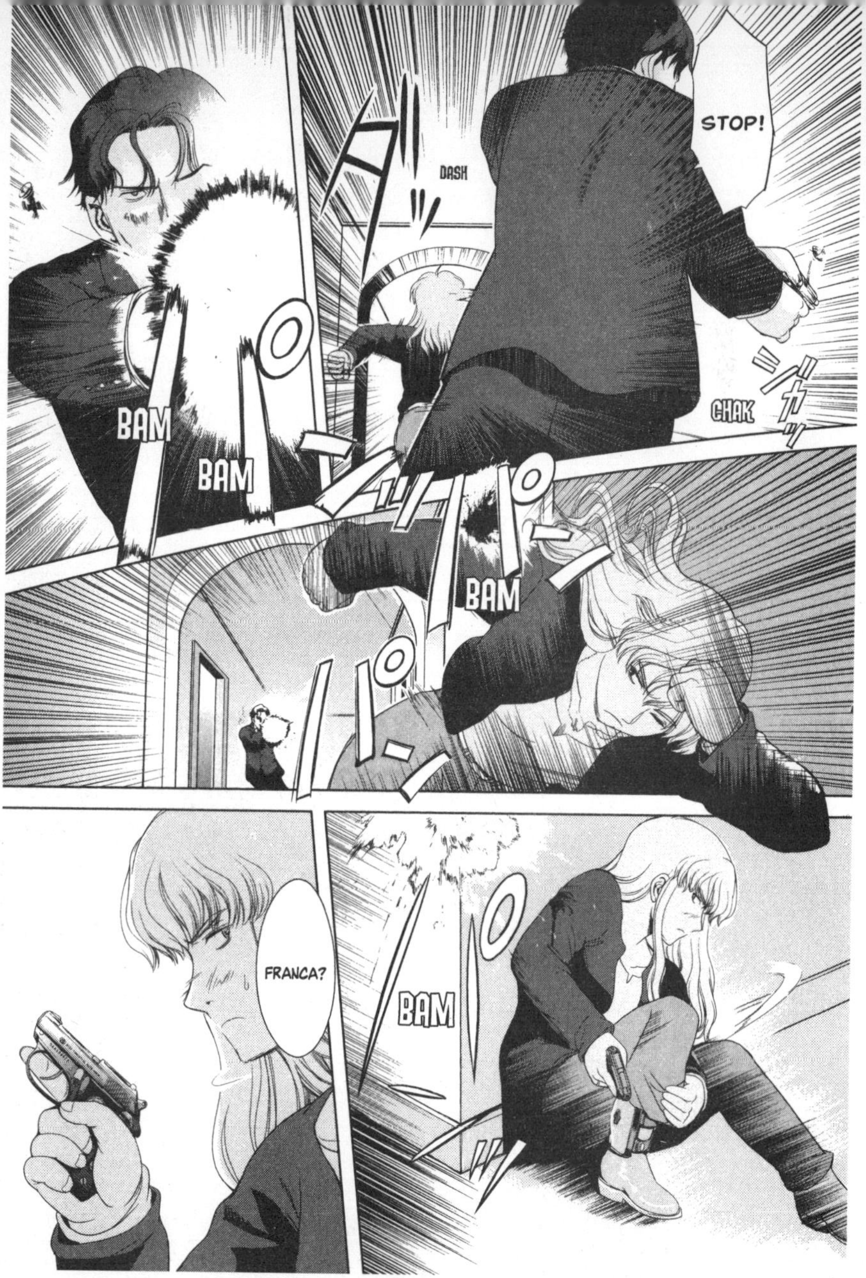
STOP!
DASH
CHAK
BAM
BAM
BAM
BAM
FRANCA?

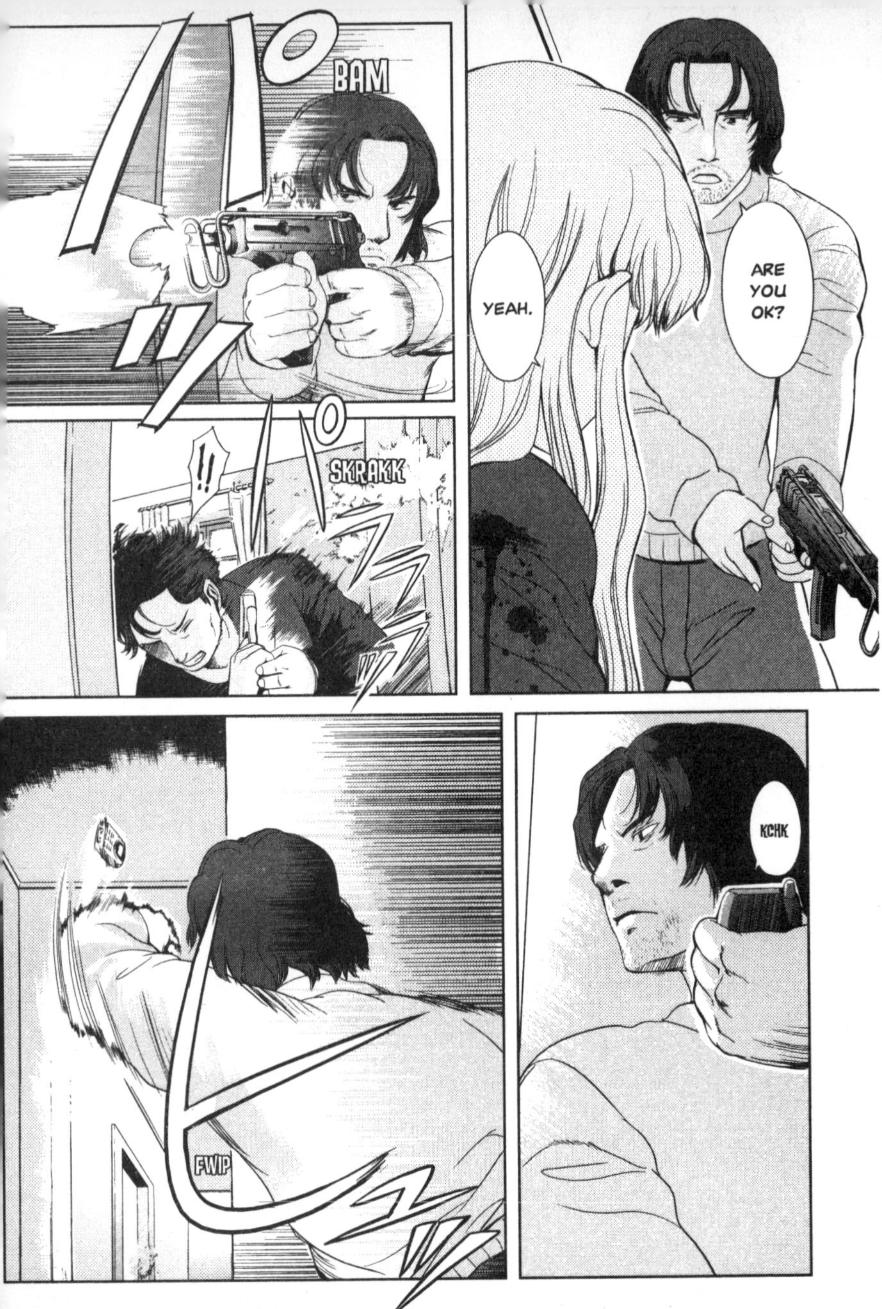
BAM
!!
SKRAKK
ARE YOU OK?
YEAH.
FWIP
KCHK

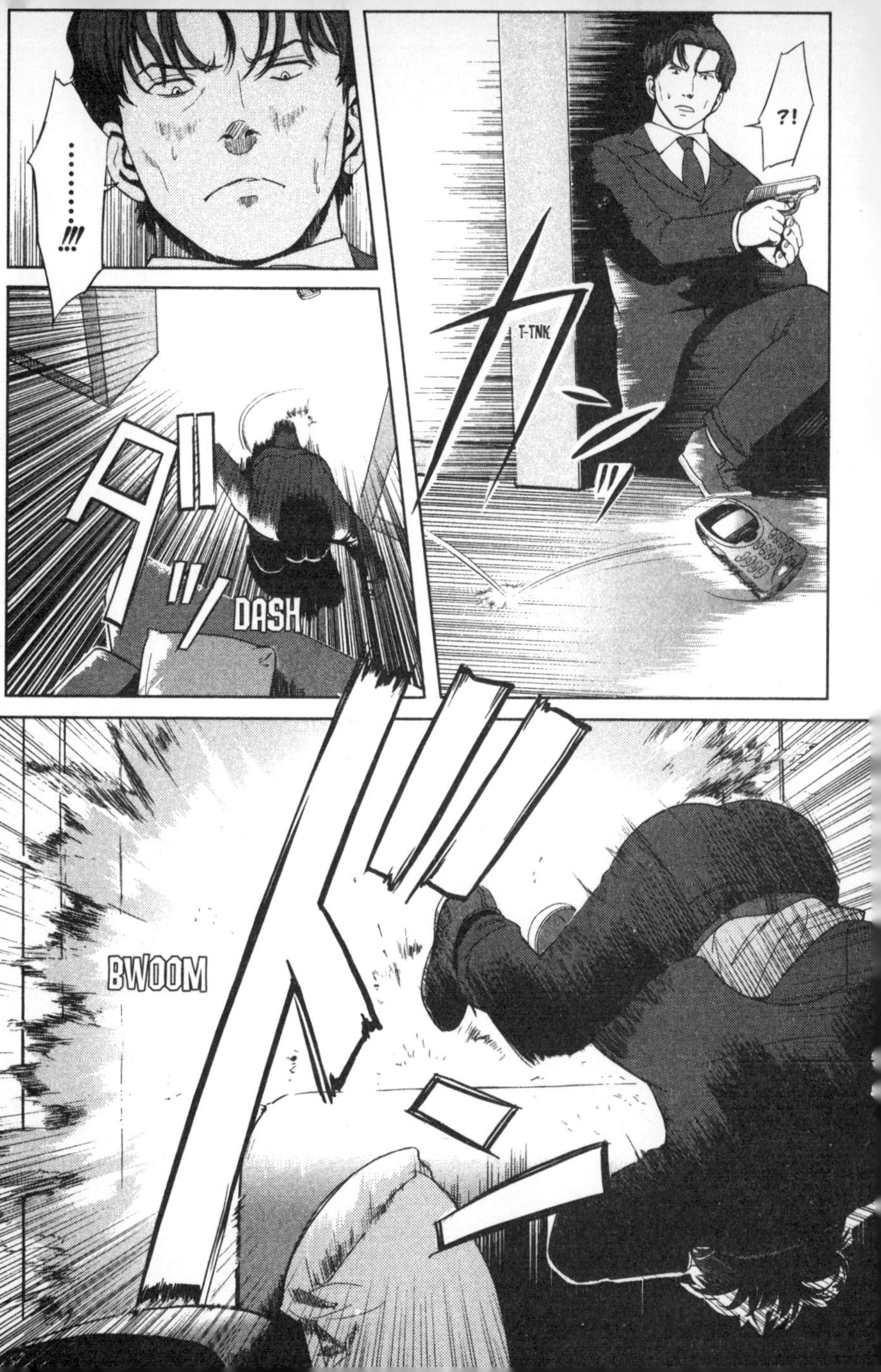
?!
T-TNK
......!!!
DASH
BWOOM

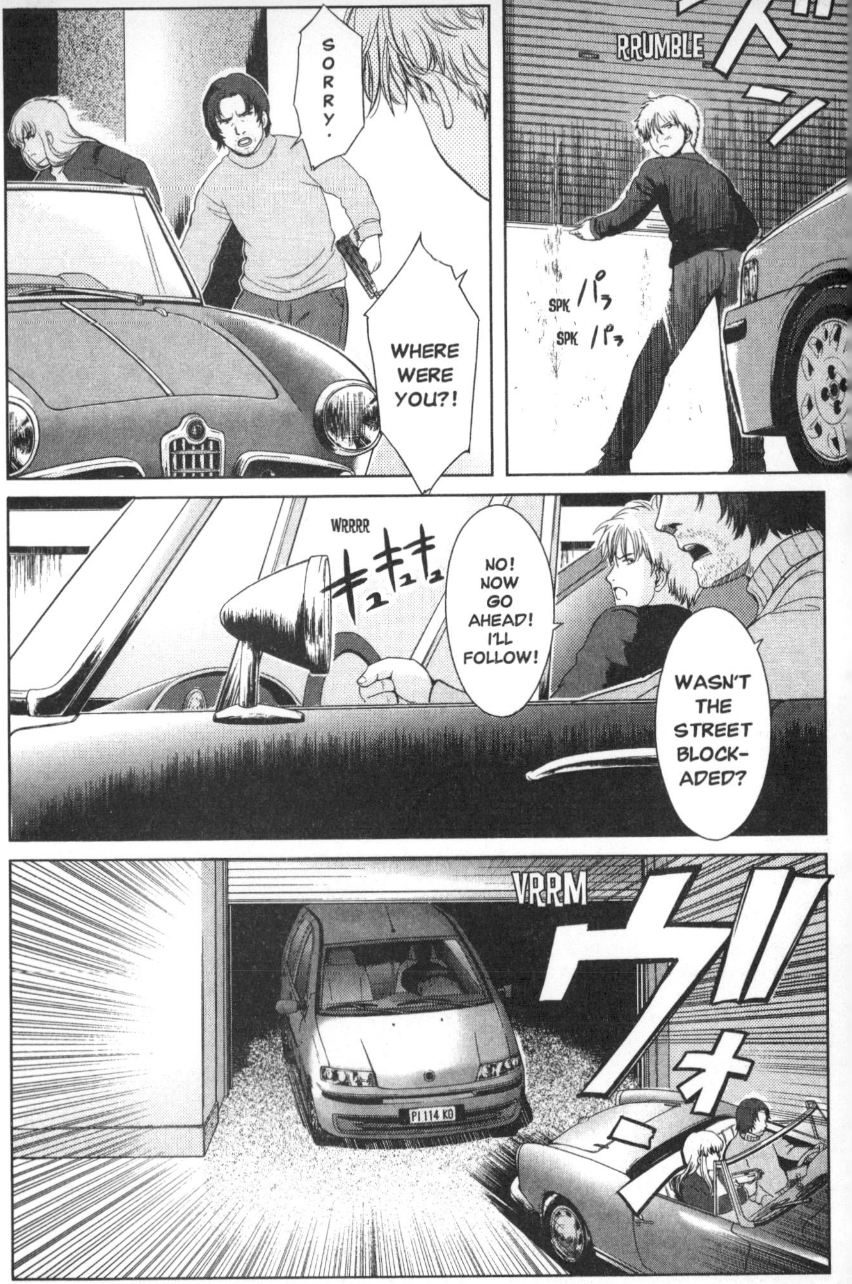
RRUMBLE
SPK
SPK
SORRY.
WHERE WERE YOU?!
WASN'T THE STREET BLOCKADED?
NO! NOW GO AHEAD! I'LL FOLLOW!
WRRRR
VRRM
PI 114 KO

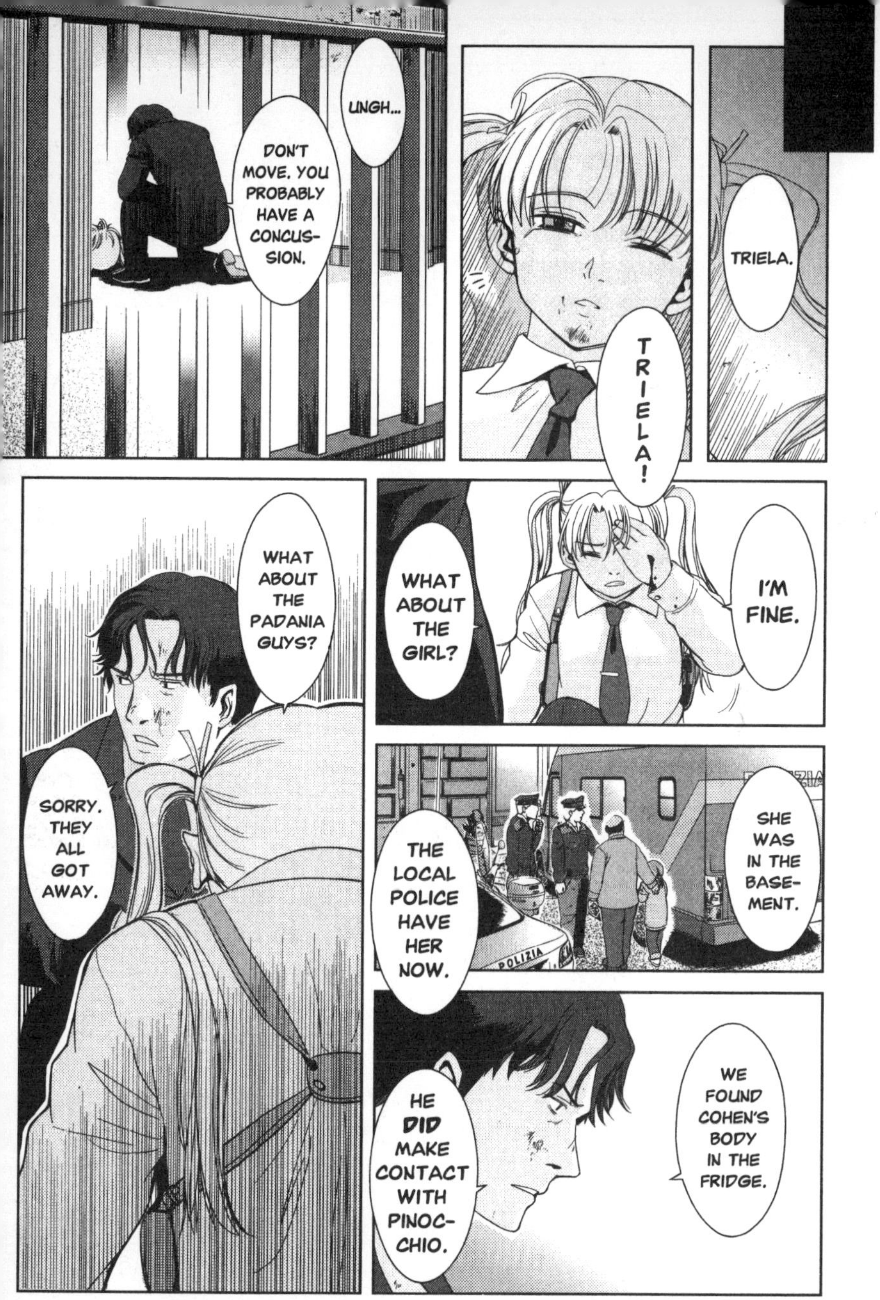

TRIELA.
TRIELA!
UNGH...
DON'T MOVE. YOU PROBABLY HAVE A CONCUSSION.
I'M FINE.
WHAT ABOUT THE GIRL?
SHE WAS IN THE BASEMENT.
THE LOCAL POLICE HAVE HER NOW.
POLIZIA
WHAT ABOUT THE PADANIA GUYS?
SORRY. THEY ALL GOT AWAY.
WE FOUND COHEN'S BODY IN THE FRIDGE.
HE **DID** MAKE CONTACT WITH PINOCCHIO.

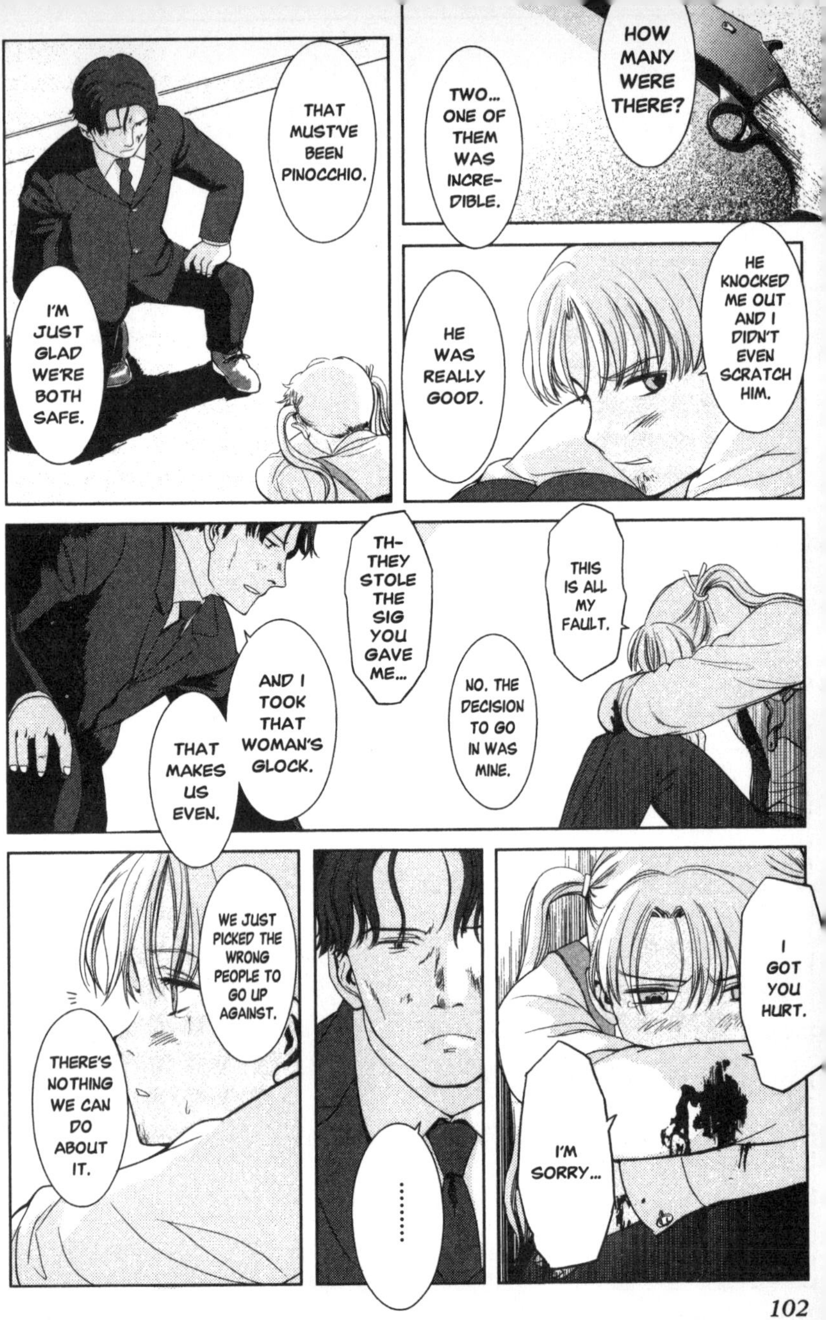
HOW MANY WERE THERE?
TWO... ONE OF THEM WAS INCREDIBLE.
THAT MUST'VE BEEN PINOCCHIO.
I'M JUST GLAD WE'RE BOTH SAFE.
HE KNOCKED ME OUT AND I DIDN'T EVEN SCRATCH HIM.
HE WAS REALLY GOOD.
THIS IS ALL MY FAULT.
NO. THE DECISION TO GO IN WAS MINE.
TH-THEY STOLE THE SIG YOU GAVE ME...
AND I TOOK THAT WOMAN'S GLOCK.
THAT MAKES US EVEN.
I GOT YOU HURT.
I'M SORRY...
....
WE JUST PICKED THE WRONG PEOPLE TO GO UP AGAINST.
THERE'S NOTHING WE CAN DO ABOUT IT.

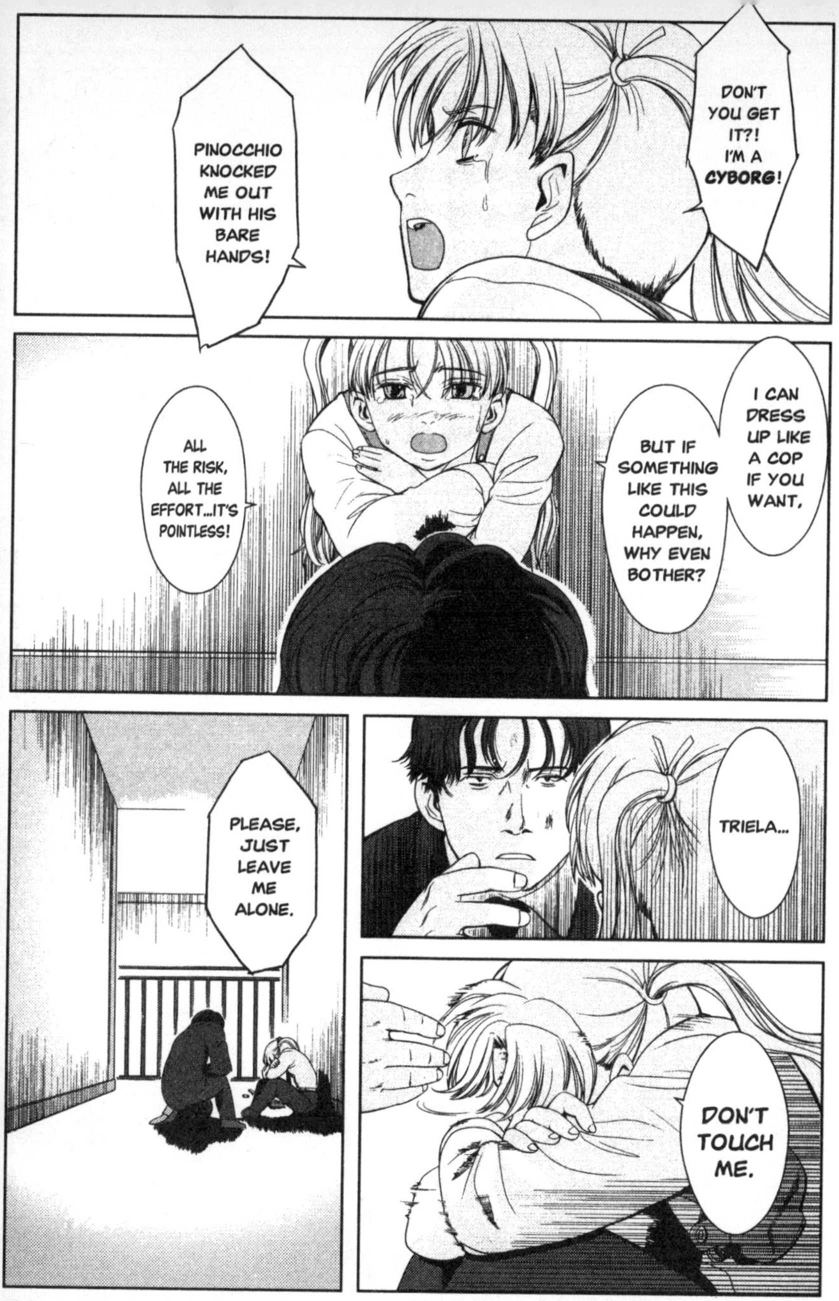
DON'T YOU GET IT?! I'M A CYBORG!
PINOCCHIO KNOCKED ME OUT WITH HIS BARE HANDS!
I CAN DRESS UP LIKE A COP IF YOU WANT,
BUT IF SOMETHING LIKE THIS COULD HAPPEN, WHY EVEN BOTHER?
ALL THE RISK, ALL THE EFFORT...IT'S POINTLESS!
TRIELA...
DON'T TOUCH ME.
PLEASE, JUST LEAVE ME ALONE.

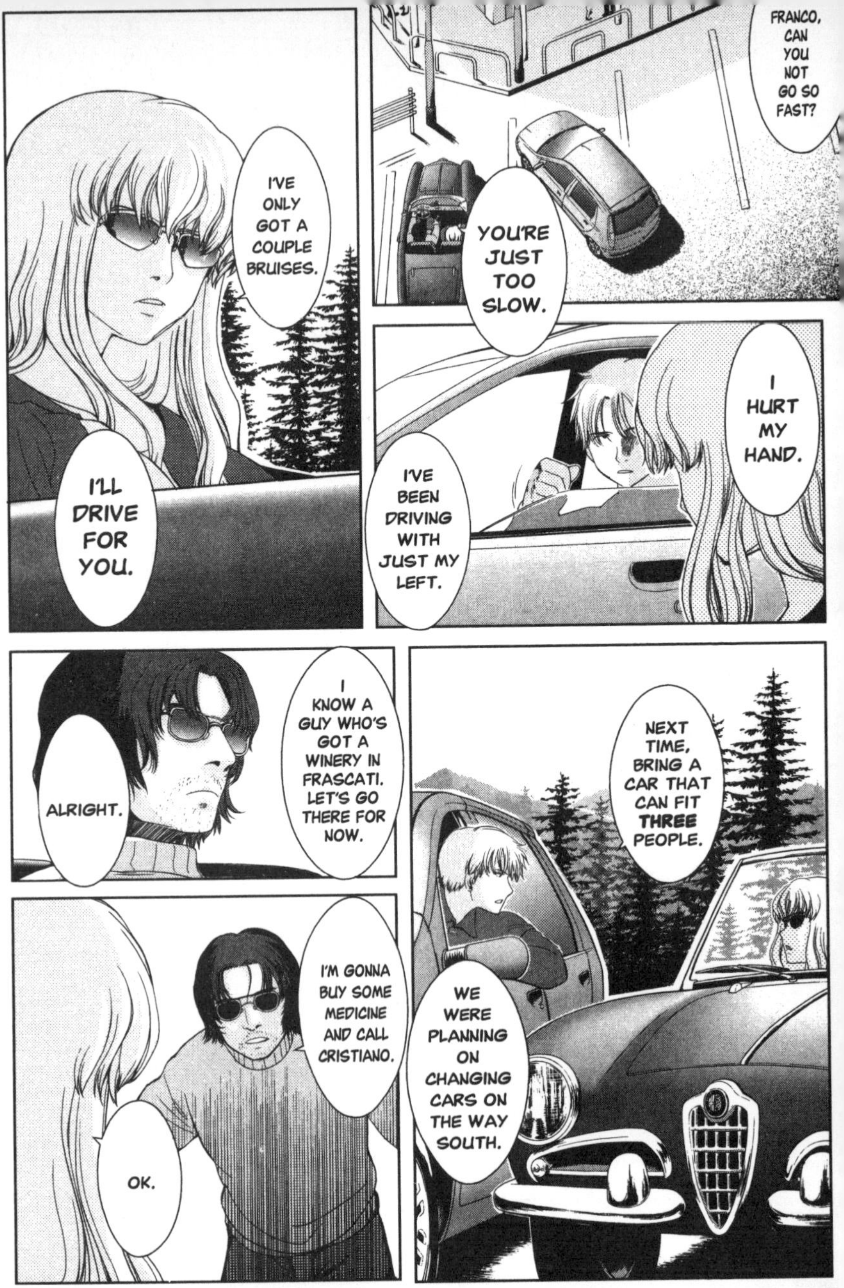
FRANCO, CAN YOU NOT GO SO FAST?
YOU'RE JUST TOO SLOW.
I HURT MY HAND.
I'VE BEEN DRIVING WITH JUST MY LEFT.
I'VE ONLY GOT A COUPLE BRUISES.
I'LL DRIVE FOR YOU.
NEXT TIME, BRING A CAR THAT CAN FIT **THREE** PEOPLE.
WE WERE PLANNING ON CHANGING CARS ON THE WAY SOUTH.
I KNOW A GUY WHO'S GOT A WINERY IN FRASCATI. LET'S GO THERE FOR NOW.
ALRIGHT.
I'M GONNA BUY SOME MEDICINE AND CALL CRISTIANO.
OK.

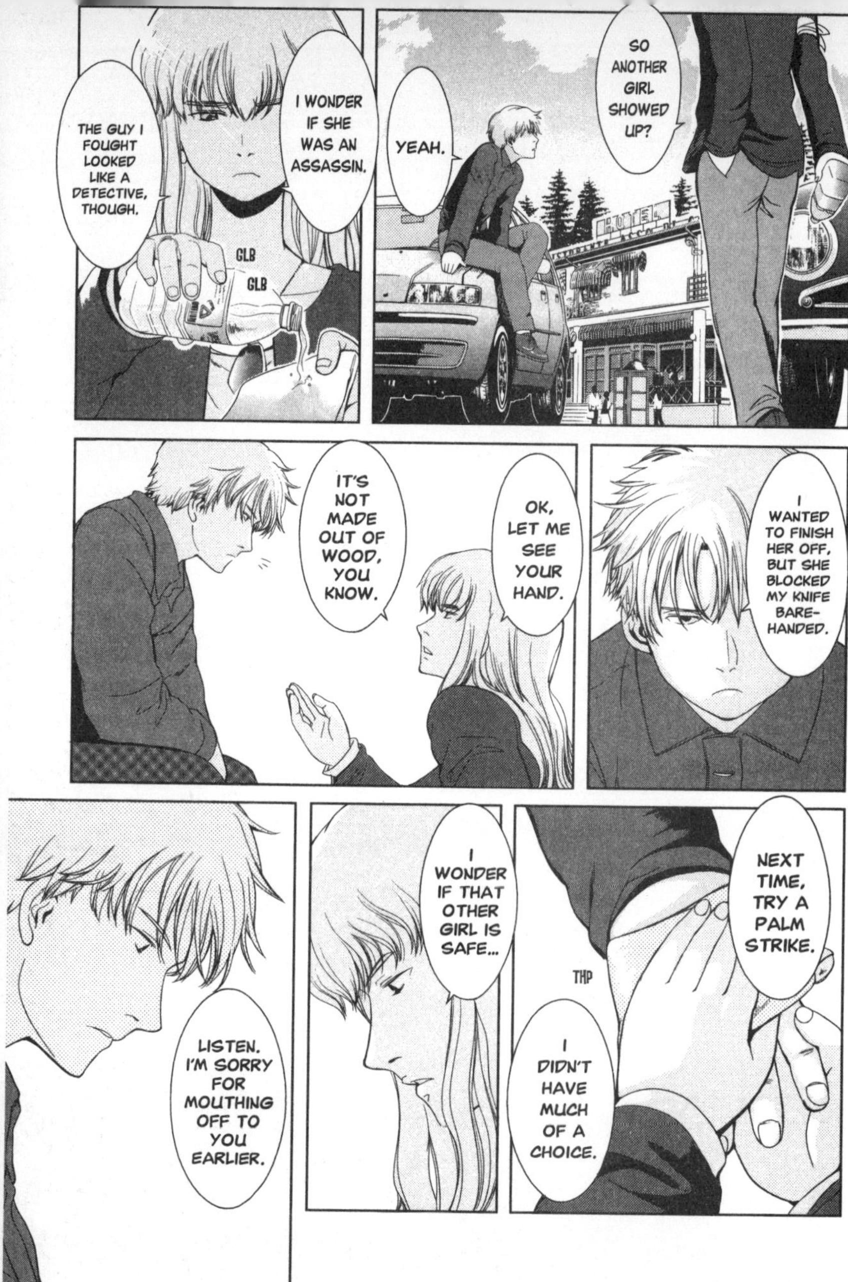
SO ANOTHER GIRL SHOWED UP?
YEAH.
I WONDER IF SHE WAS AN ASSASSIN.
THE GUY I FOUGHT LOOKED LIKE A DETECTIVE, THOUGH.
GLB
GLB
I WANTED TO FINISH HER OFF, BUT SHE BLOCKED MY KNIFE BARE-HANDED.
OK, LET ME SEE YOUR HAND.
IT'S NOT MADE OUT OF WOOD, YOU KNOW.
NEXT TIME, TRY A PALM STRIKE.
THP
I DIDN'T HAVE MUCH OF A CHOICE.
I WONDER IF THAT OTHER GIRL IS SAFE...
LISTEN. I'M SORRY FOR MOUTHING OFF TO YOU EARLIER.

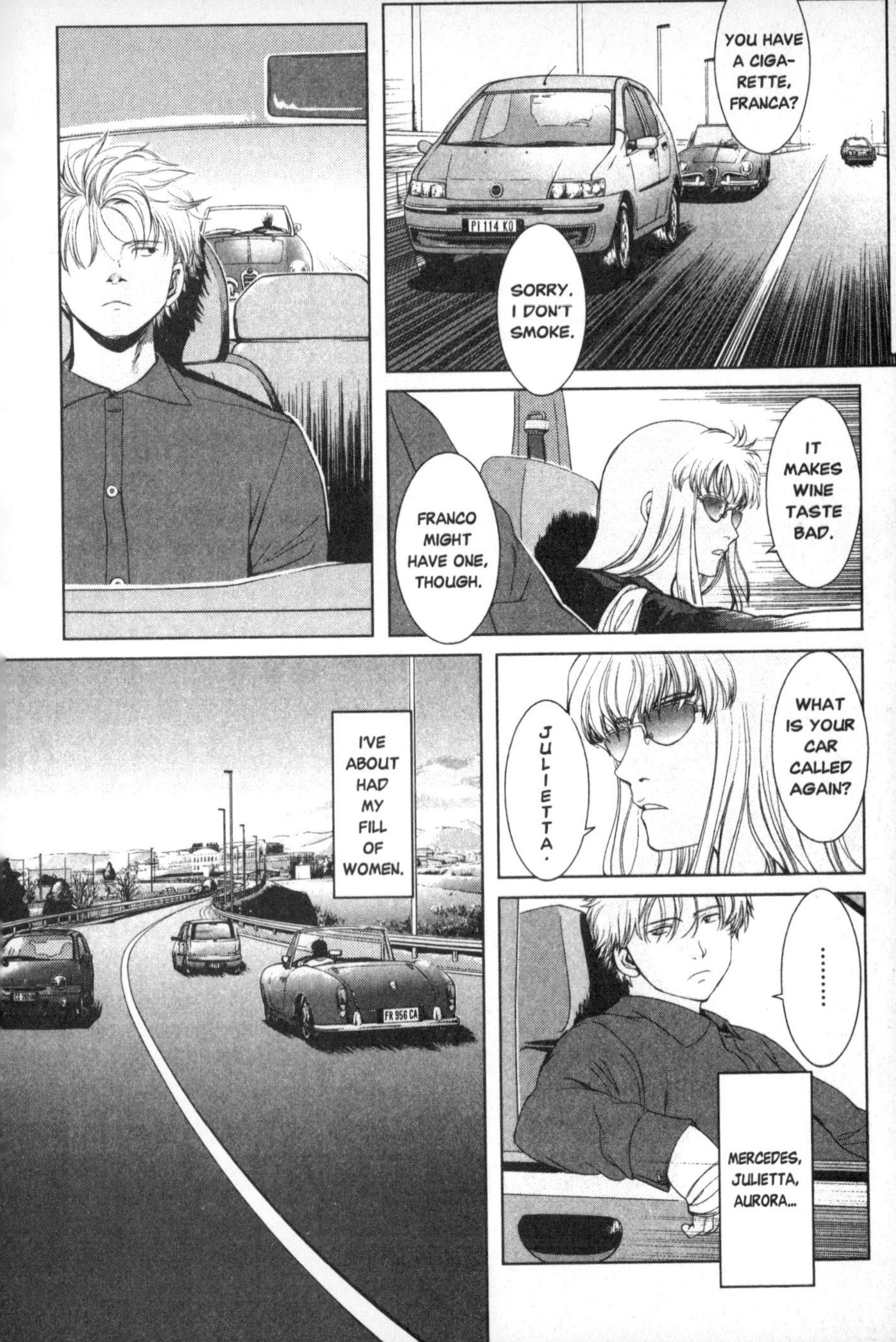
YOU HAVE A CIGARETTE, FRANCA?
PI 114 KO
SORRY. I DON'T SMOKE.
IT MAKES WINE TASTE BAD.
FRANCO MIGHT HAVE ONE, THOUGH.
WHAT IS YOUR CAR CALLED AGAIN?
JULIETTA.
....
MERCEDES, JULIETTA, AURORA...
I'VE ABOUT HAD MY FILL OF WOMEN.
FR 956 CA

GUNSLINGERGIRL.

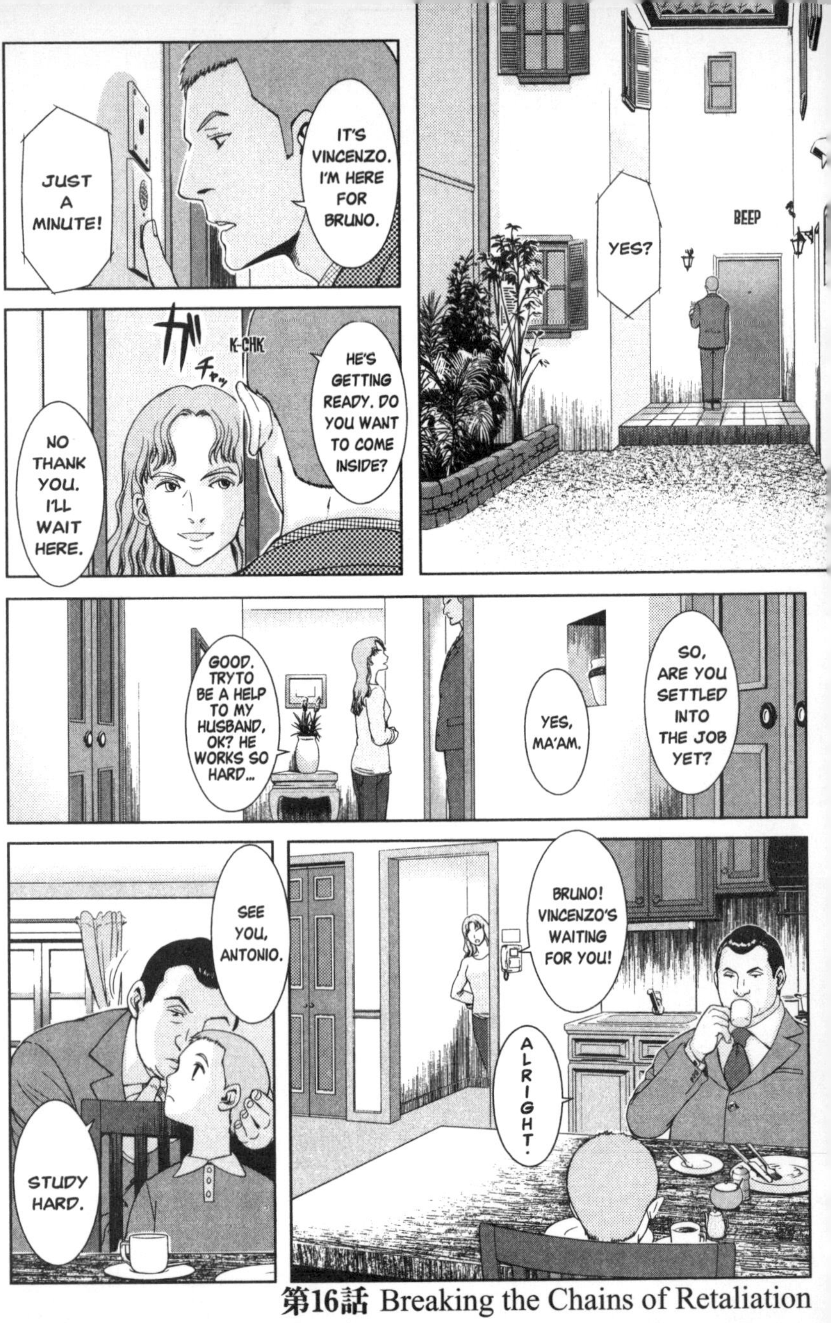
BEEP
YES?
IT'S VINCENZO. I'M HERE FOR BRUNO.
JUST A MINUTE!
K-CHK
HE'S GETTING READY. DO YOU WANT TO COME INSIDE?
NO THANK YOU. I'LL WAIT HERE.
SO, ARE YOU SETTLED INTO THE JOB YET?
YES, MA'AM.
GOOD. TRYTO BE A HELP TO MY HUSBAND, OK? HE WORKS SO HARD...
BRUNO! VINCENZO'S WAITING FOR YOU!
ALRIGHT.
SEE YOU, ANTONIO.
STUDY HARD.

第16話 Breaking the Chains of Retaliation

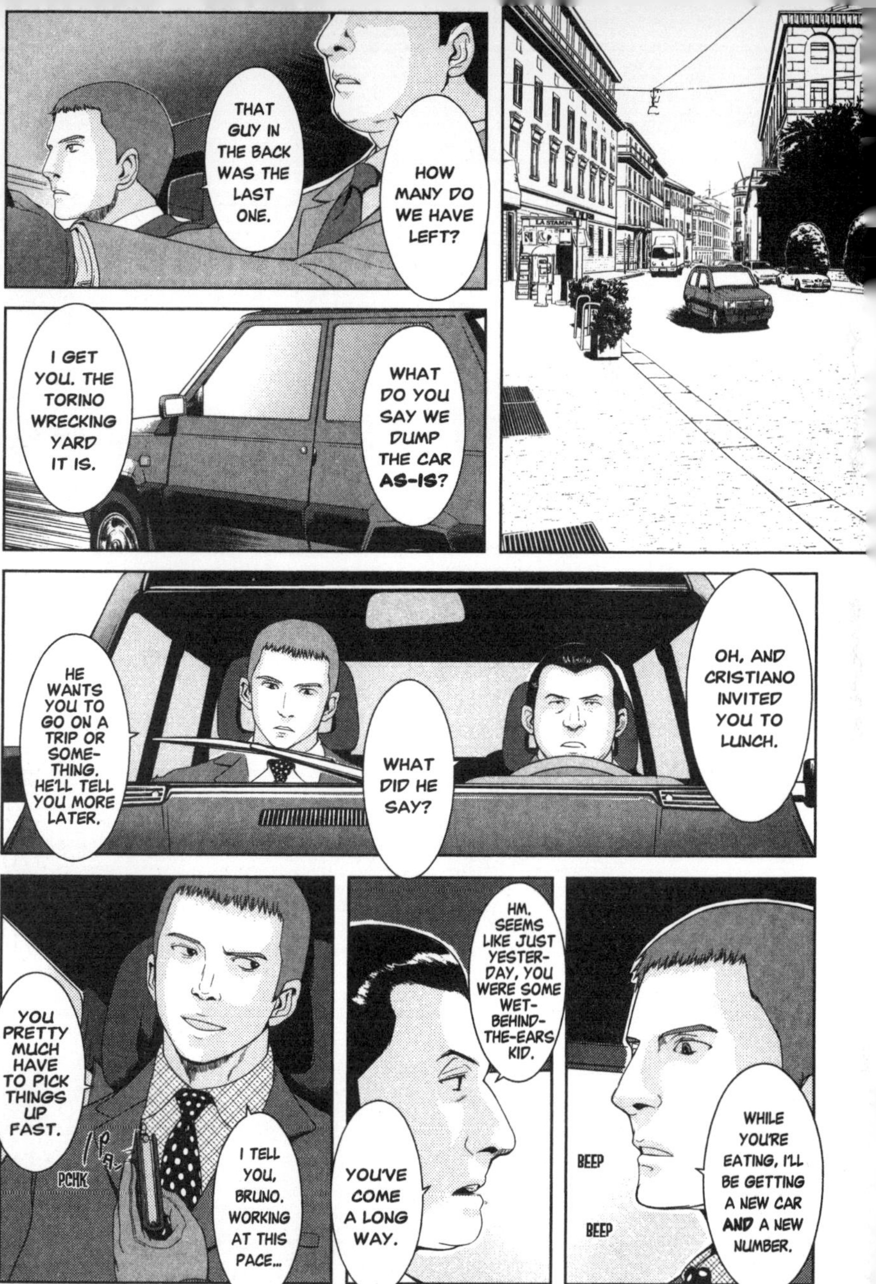
HOW MANY DO WE HAVE LEFT?
THAT GUY IN THE BACK WAS THE LAST ONE.
LA STAMPA
WHAT DO YOU SAY WE DUMP THE CAR AS-IS?
I GET YOU. THE TORINO WRECKING YARD IT IS.
OH, AND CRISTIANO INVITED YOU TO LUNCH.
WHAT DID HE SAY?
HE WANTS YOU TO GO ON A TRIP OR SOME-THING. HE'LL TELL YOU MORE LATER.
WHILE YOU'RE EATING, I'LL BE GETTING A NEW CAR AND A NEW NUMBER.
BEEP
BEEP
HM. SEEMS LIKE JUST YESTER-DAY, YOU WERE SOME WET-BEHIND-THE-EARS KID.
YOU'VE COME A LONG WAY.
I TELL YOU, BRUNO. WORKING AT THIS PACE...
YOU PRETTY MUCH HAVE TO PICK THINGS UP FAST.
PCHK

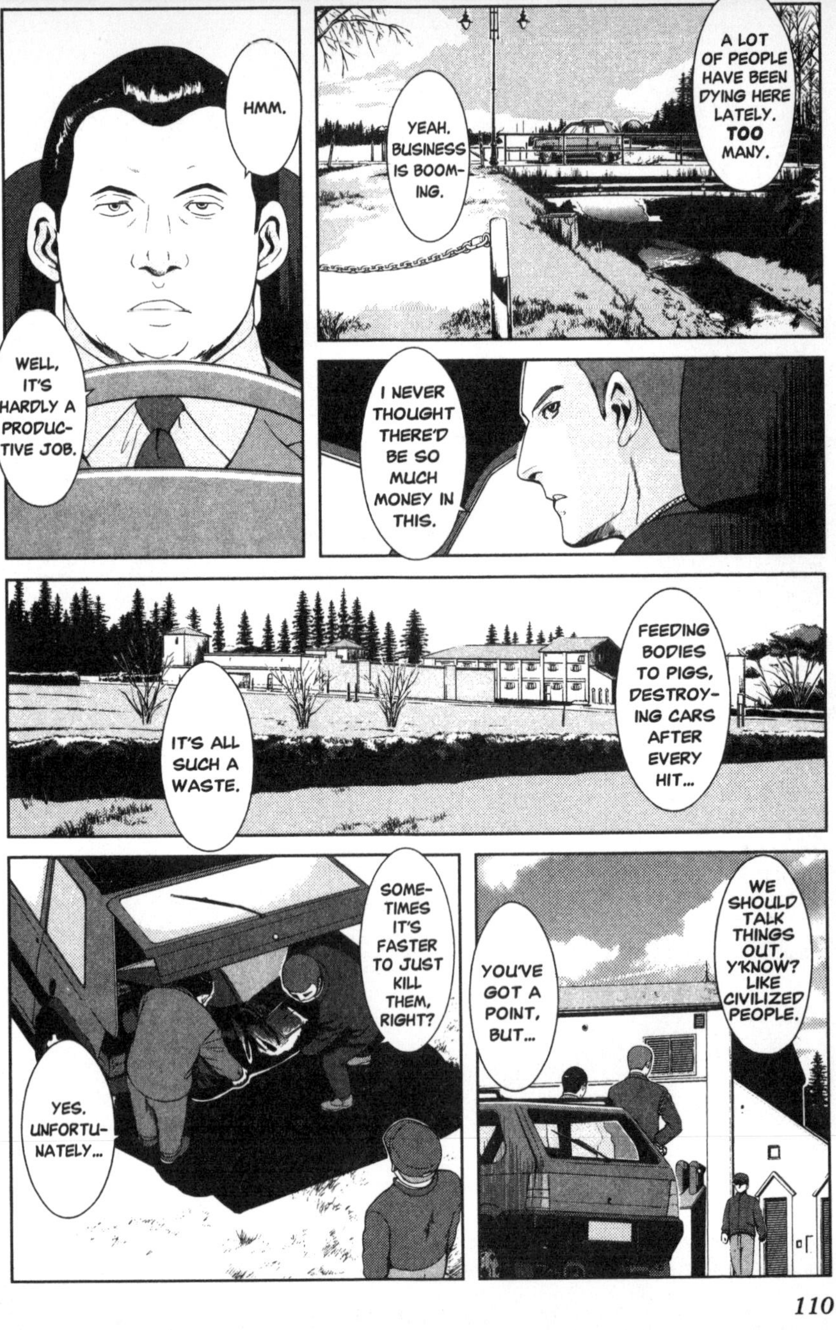
A LOT OF PEOPLE HAVE BEEN DYING HERE LATELY. **TOO** MANY.
YEAH. BUSINESS IS BOOM-ING.
HMM.
WELL, IT'S HARDLY A PRODUC-TIVE JOB.
I NEVER THOUGHT THERE'D BE SO MUCH MONEY IN THIS.
FEEDING BODIES TO PIGS, DESTROY-ING CARS AFTER EVERY HIT...
IT'S ALL SUCH A WASTE.
WE SHOULD TALK THINGS OUT, Y'KNOW? LIKE CIVILIZED PEOPLE.
YOU'VE GOT A POINT, BUT...
SOME-TIMES IT'S FASTER TO JUST KILL THEM, RIGHT?
YES. UNFORTU-NATELY...

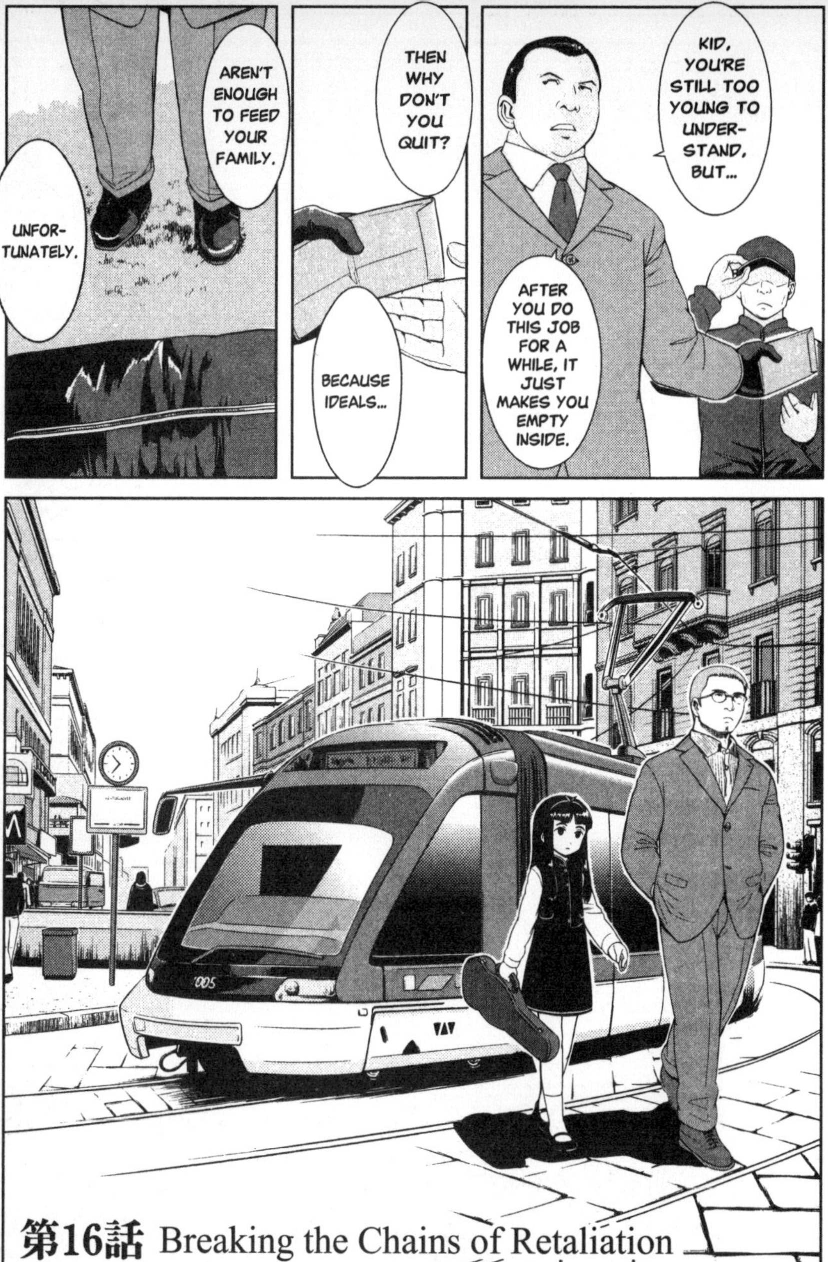
KID, YOU'RE STILL TOO YOUNG TO UNDER-STAND, BUT...
AFTER YOU DO THIS JOB FOR A WHILE, IT JUST MAKES YOU EMPTY INSIDE.
THEN WHY DON'T YOU QUIT?
BECAUSE IDEALS...
AREN'T ENOUGH TO FEED YOUR FAMILY.
UNFOR-TUNATELY.

第16話 Breaking the Chains of Retaliation

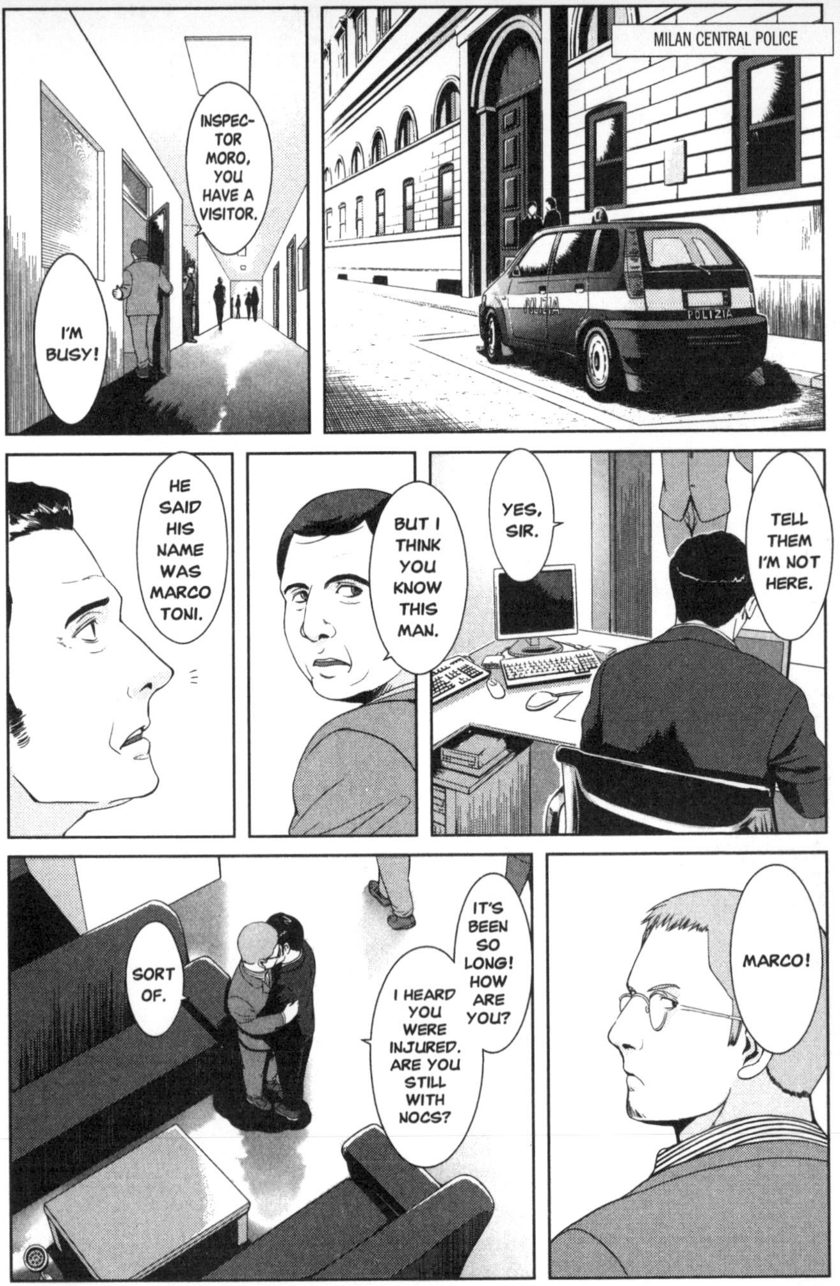
MILAN CENTRAL POLICE
POLIZIA
POLIZIA
INSPECTOR MORO, YOU HAVE A VISITOR.
I'M BUSY!
TELL THEM I'M NOT HERE.
YES, SIR.
BUT I THINK YOU KNOW THIS MAN.
HE SAID HIS NAME WAS MARCO TONI.
MARCO!
IT'S BEEN SO LONG! HOW ARE YOU?
I HEARD YOU WERE INJURED. ARE YOU STILL WITH NOCS?
SORT OF.

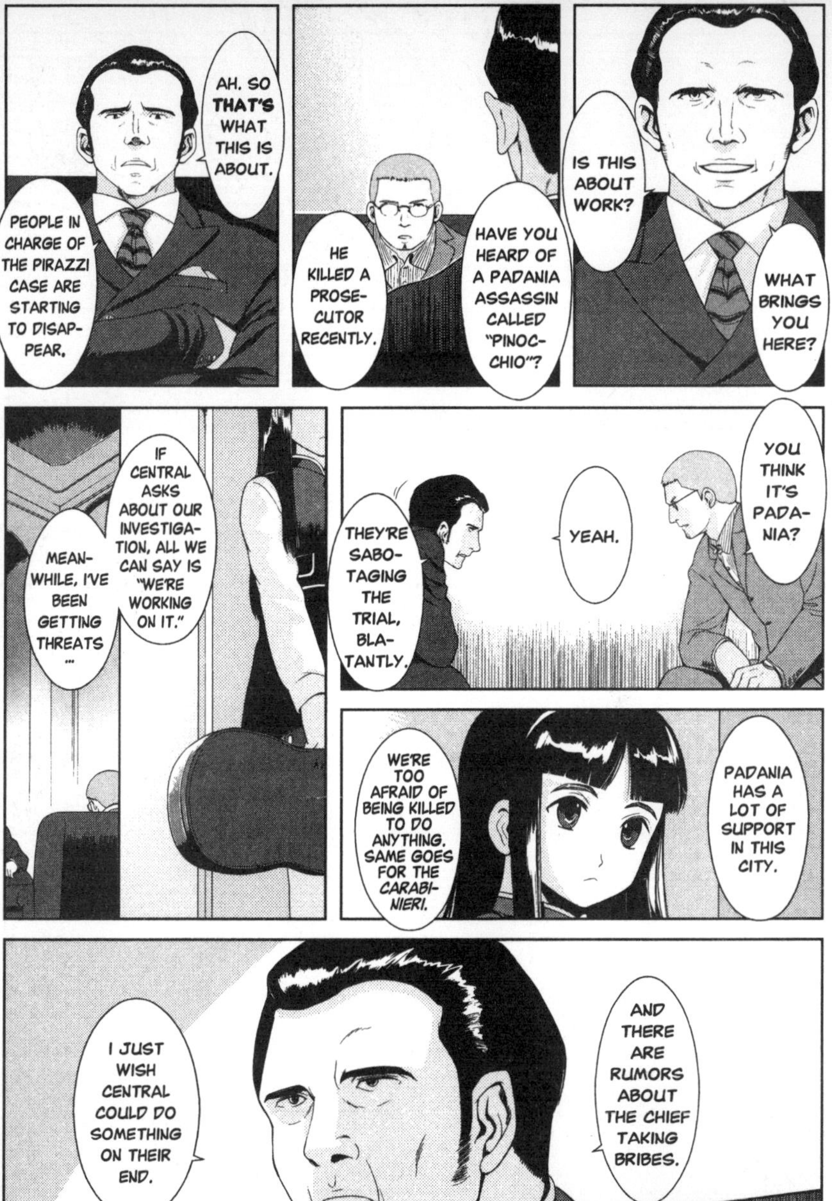
WHAT BRINGS YOU HERE?
IS THIS ABOUT WORK?
HAVE YOU HEARD OF A PADANIA ASSASSIN CALLED "PINOCCHIO"?
HE KILLED A PROSECUTOR RECENTLY.
AH. SO **THAT'S** WHAT THIS IS ABOUT.
PEOPLE IN CHARGE OF THE PIRAZZI CASE ARE STARTING TO DISAPPEAR.
YOU THINK IT'S PADANIA?
YEAH.
THEY'RE SABOTAGING THE TRIAL, BLATANTLY.
PADANIA HAS A LOT OF SUPPORT IN THIS CITY.
WE'RE TOO AFRAID OF BEING KILLED TO DO ANYTHING. SAME GOES FOR THE *CARABINIERI.*
IF CENTRAL ASKS ABOUT OUR INVESTIGATION, ALL WE CAN SAY IS "WE'RE WORKING ON IT."
MEANWHILE, I'VE BEEN GETTING THREATS...
AND THERE ARE RUMORS ABOUT THE CHIEF TAKING BRIBES.
I JUST WISH CENTRAL COULD DO SOMETHING ON THEIR END.

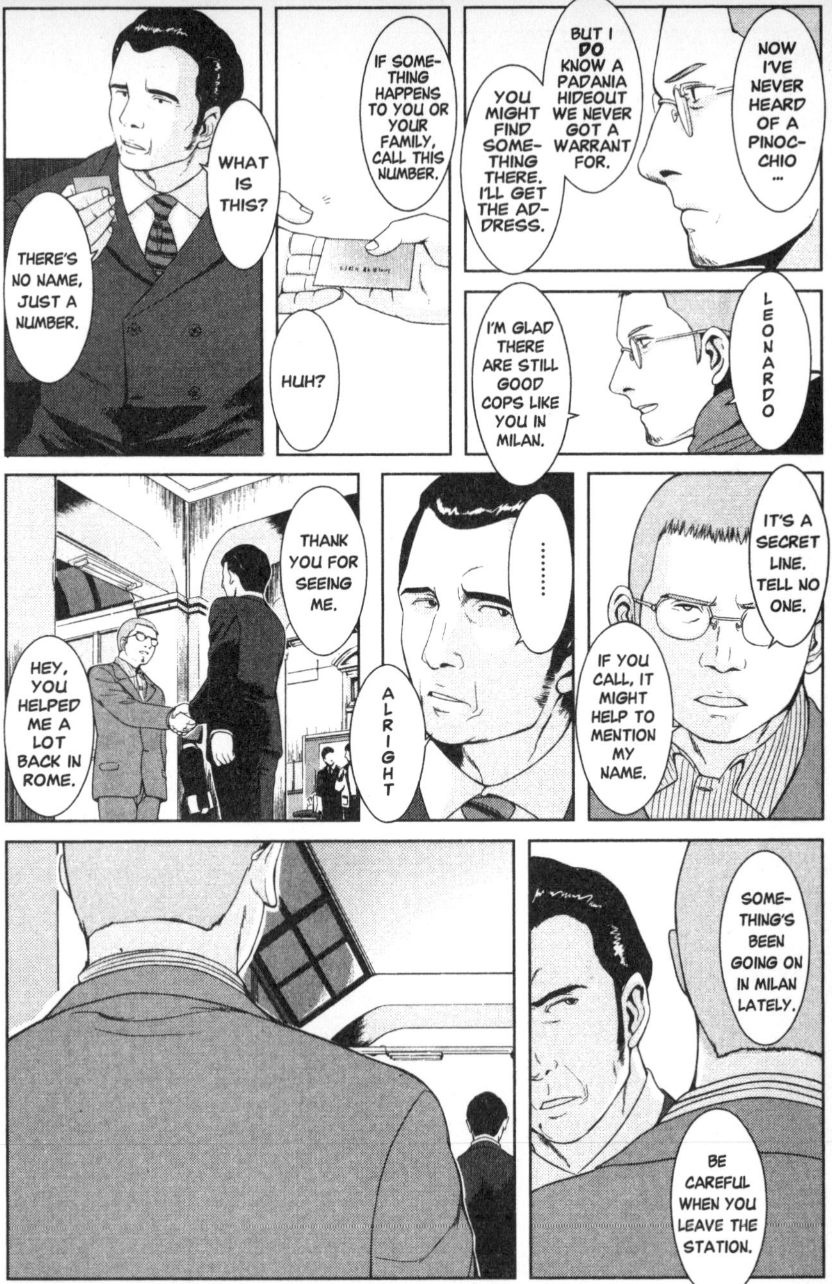
NOW I'VE NEVER HEARD OF A PINOCCHIO ...
BUT I DO KNOW A PADANIA HIDEOUT WE NEVER GOT A WARRANT FOR.
YOU MIGHT FIND SOMETHING THERE. I'LL GET THE ADDRESS.
LEONARDO
I'M GLAD THERE ARE STILL GOOD COPS LIKE YOU IN MILAN.
IF SOMETHING HAPPENS TO YOU OR YOUR FAMILY, CALL THIS NUMBER.
HUH?
WHAT IS THIS?
THERE'S NO NAME, JUST A NUMBER.
IT'S A SECRET LINE. TELL NO ONE.
IF YOU CALL, IT MIGHT HELP TO MENTION MY NAME.
....
ALRIGHT
THANK YOU FOR SEEING ME.
HEY, YOU HELPED ME A LOT BACK IN ROME.
SOMETHING'S BEEN GOING ON IN MILAN LATELY.
BE CAREFUL WHEN YOU LEAVE THE STATION.

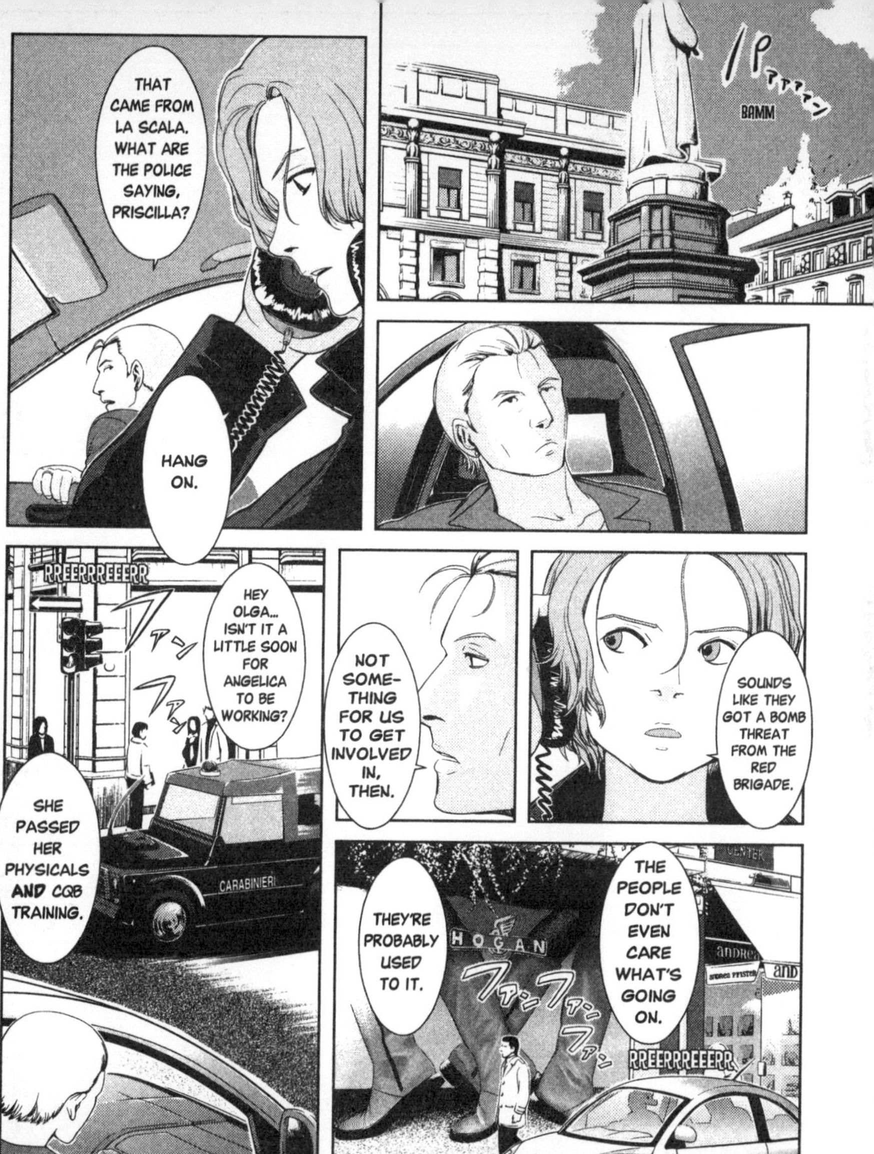
BAMM
THAT CAME FROM LA SCALA. WHAT ARE THE POLICE SAYING, PRISCILLA?
HANG ON.
SOUNDS LIKE THEY GOT A BOMB THREAT FROM THE RED BRIGADE.
NOT SOMETHING FOR US TO GET INVOLVED IN, THEN.
HEY OLGA... ISN'T IT A LITTLE SOON FOR ANGELICA TO BE WORKING?
RREERRREEERR
CARABINIERI
SHE PASSED HER PHYSICALS AND CQB TRAINING.
THE PEOPLE DON'T EVEN CARE WHAT'S GOING ON.
THEY'RE PROBABLY USED TO IT.
HOGAN
RREERRREEERR

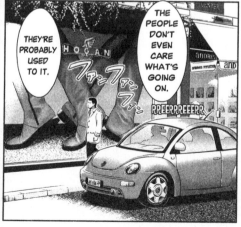

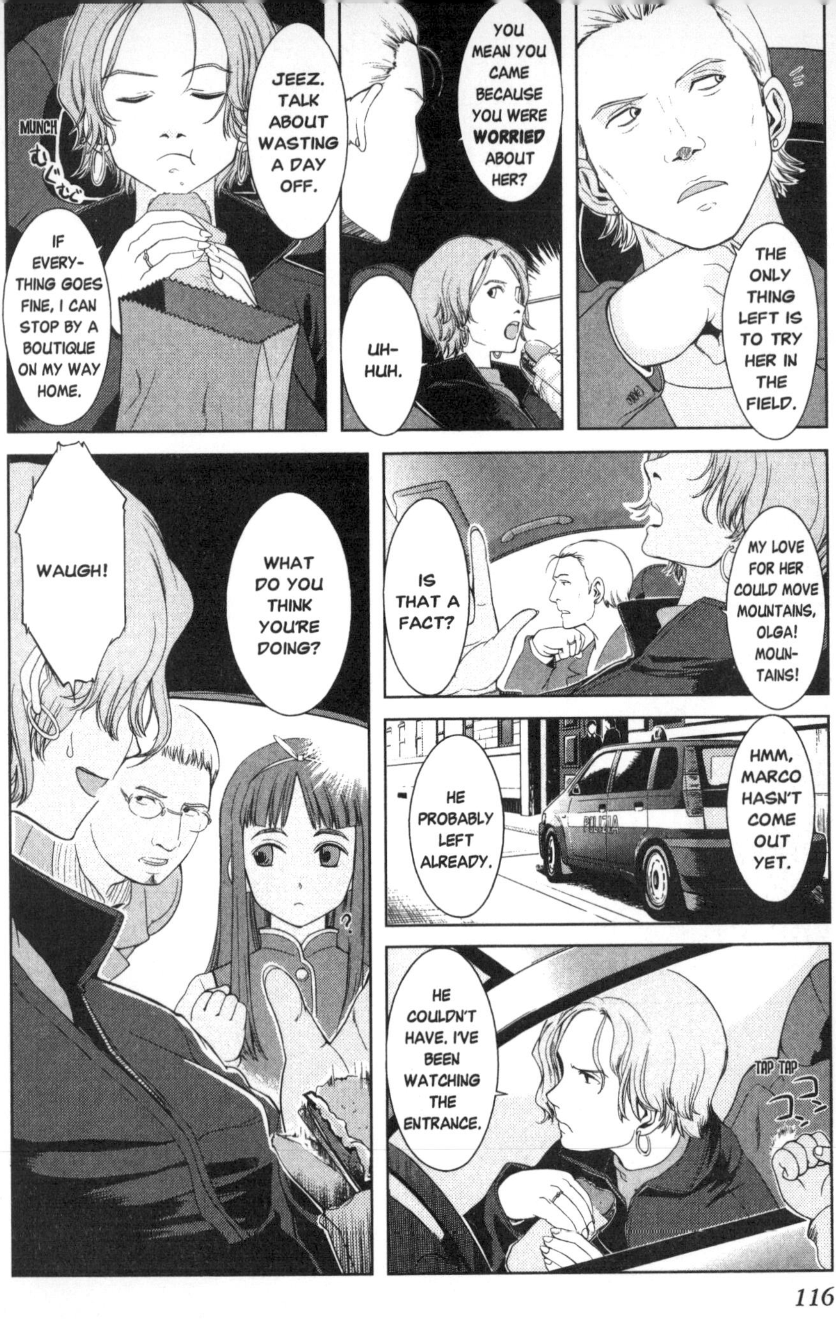
THE ONLY THING LEFT IS TO TRY HER IN THE FIELD.
YOU MEAN YOU CAME BECAUSE YOU WERE **WORRIED** ABOUT HER?
UH-HUH.
JEEZ. TALK ABOUT WASTING A DAY OFF.
MUNCH
IF EVERYTHING GOES FINE, I CAN STOP BY A BOUTIQUE ON MY WAY HOME.
MY LOVE FOR HER COULD MOVE MOUNTAINS, OLGA! MOUNTAINS!
IS THAT A FACT?
HMM, MARCO HASN'T COME OUT YET.
HE PROBABLY LEFT ALREADY.
HE COULDN'T HAVE. I'VE BEEN WATCHING THE ENTRANCE.
TAP TAP
WAUGH!
WHAT DO YOU THINK YOU'RE DOING?

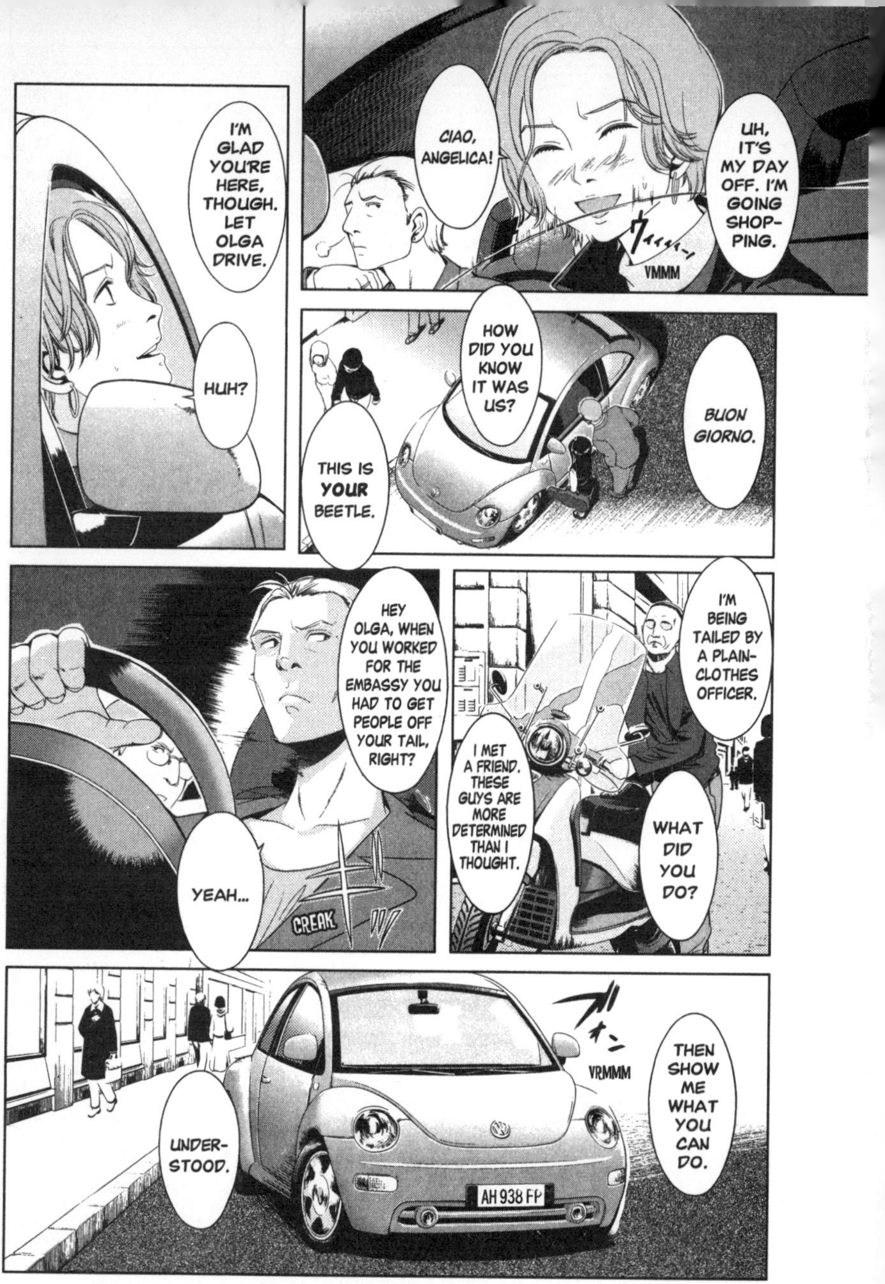
UH, IT'S MY DAY OFF. I'M GOING SHOP-PING.
VMMM
CIAO, ANGELICA!
I'M GLAD YOU'RE HERE, THOUGH. LET OLGA DRIVE.
HUH?
BUON GIORNO.
HOW DID YOU KNOW IT WAS US?
THIS IS YOUR BEETLE.
I'M BEING TAILED BY A PLAIN-CLOTHES OFFICER.
WHAT DID YOU DO?
I MET A FRIEND. THESE GUYS ARE MORE DETERMINED THAN I THOUGHT.
HEY OLGA, WHEN YOU WORKED FOR THE EMBASSY YOU HAD TO GET PEOPLE OFF YOUR TAIL, RIGHT?
YEAH...
CREAK
THEN SHOW ME WHAT YOU CAN DO.
VRMMM
UNDER-STOOD.
AH 938 FP

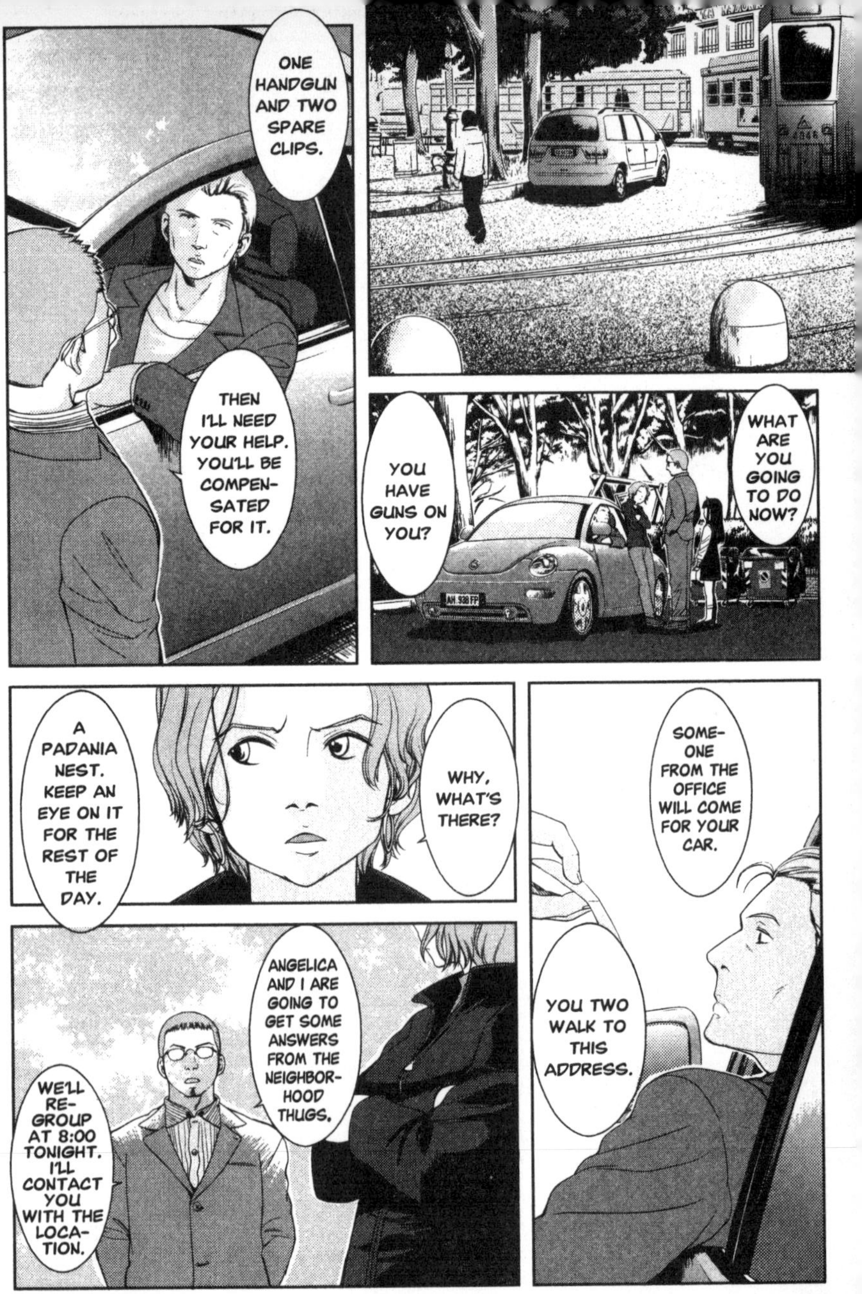
WHAT ARE YOU GOING TO DO NOW?
YOU HAVE GUNS ON YOU?
ONE HANDGUN AND TWO SPARE CLIPS.
THEN I'LL NEED YOUR HELP. YOU'LL BE COMPEN-SATED FOR IT.
SOME-ONE FROM THE OFFICE WILL COME FOR YOUR CAR.
YOU TWO WALK TO THIS ADDRESS.
WHY, WHAT'S THERE?
A PADANIA NEST. KEEP AN EYE ON IT FOR THE REST OF THE DAY.
ANGELICA AND I ARE GOING TO GET SOME ANSWERS FROM THE NEIGHBOR-HOOD THUGS.
WE'LL RE-GROUP AT 8:00 TONIGHT. I'LL CONTACT YOU WITH THE LOCA-TION.

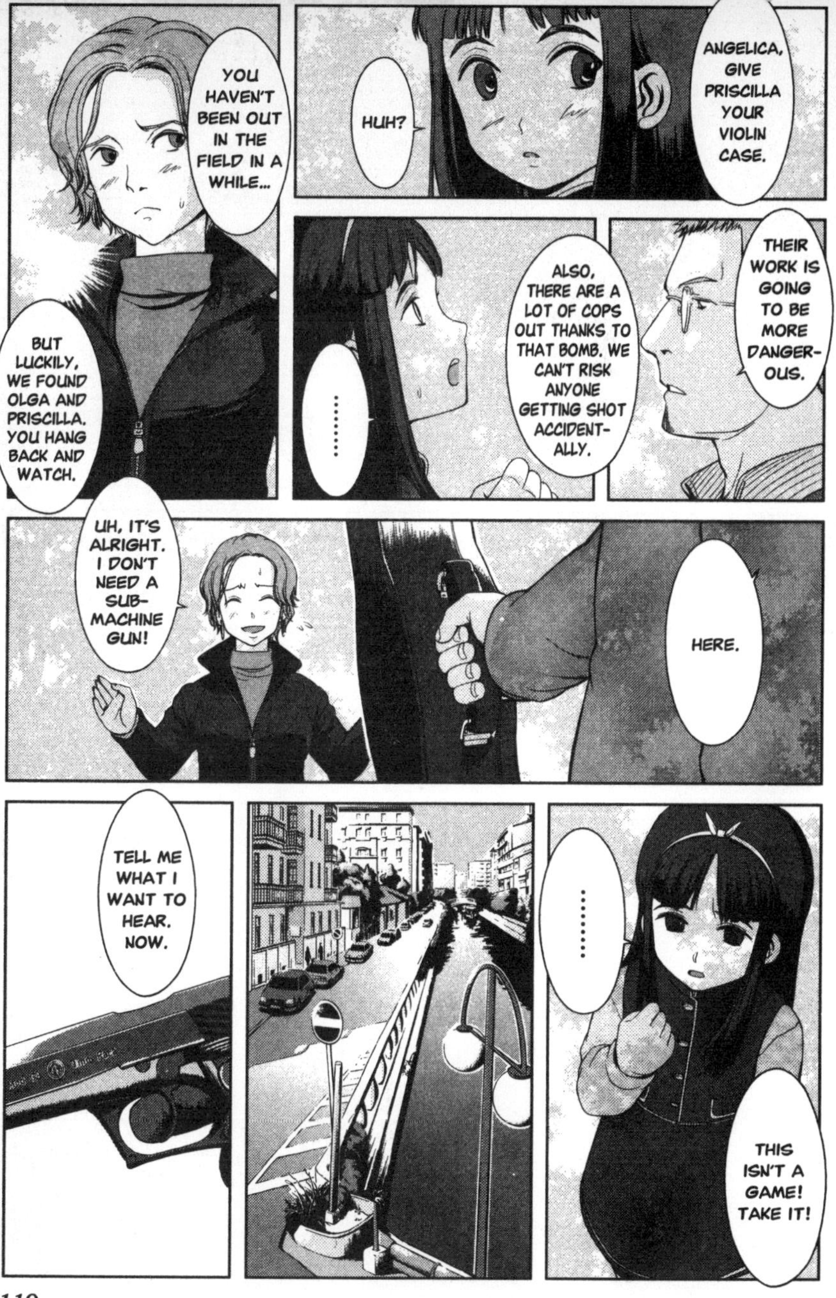
YOU HAVEN'T BEEN OUT IN THE FIELD IN A WHILE...
BUT LUCKILY, WE FOUND OLGA AND PRISCILLA. YOU HANG BACK AND WATCH.
ANGELICA, GIVE PRISCILLA YOUR VIOLIN CASE.
HUH?
THEIR WORK IS GOING TO BE MORE DANGER-OUS.
ALSO, THERE ARE A LOT OF COPS OUT THANKS TO THAT BOMB. WE CAN'T RISK ANYONE GETTING SHOT ACCIDENT-ALLY.
....
UH, IT'S ALRIGHT. I DON'T NEED A SUB-MACHINE GUN!
HERE.
TELL ME WHAT I WANT TO HEAR. NOW.
....
THIS ISN'T A GAME! TAKE IT!

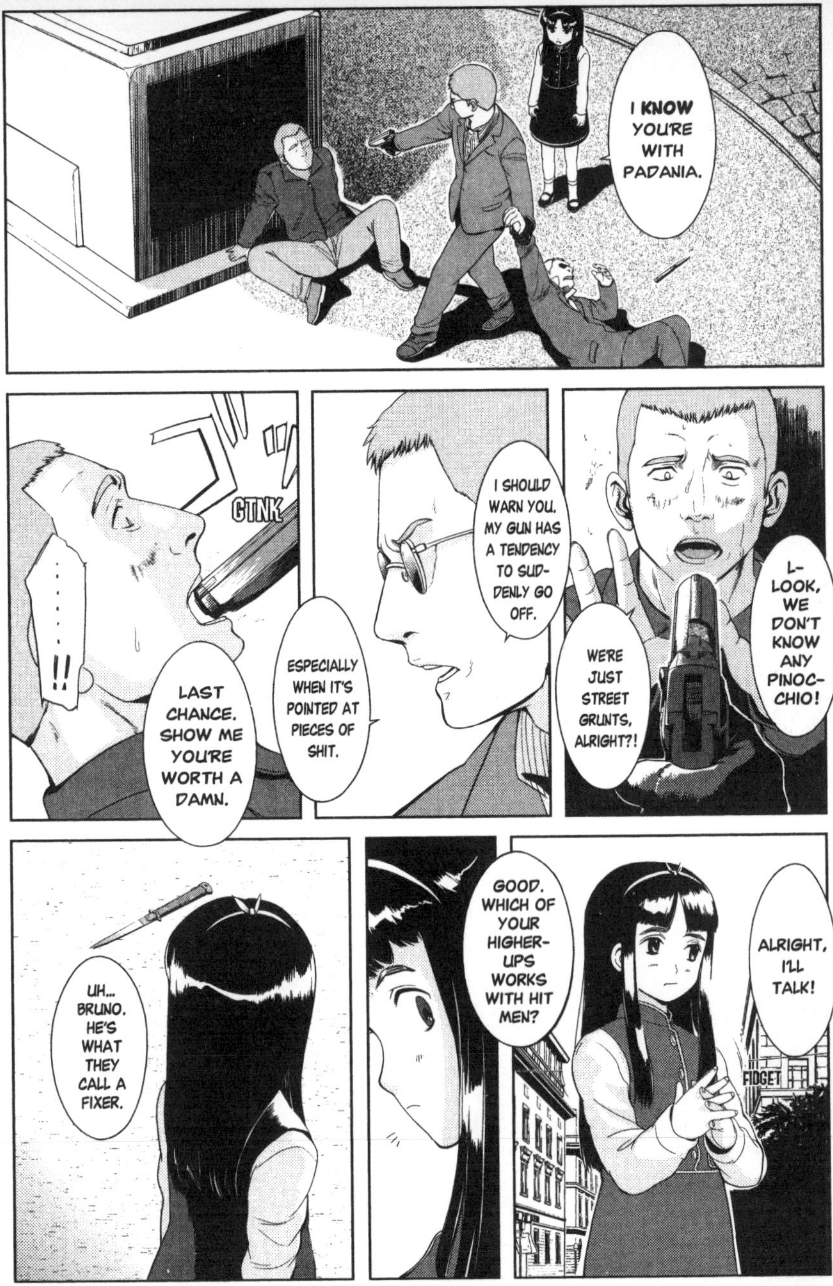
I KNOW YOU'RE WITH PADANIA.
L-LOOK, WE DON'T KNOW ANY PINOC-CHIO!
WE'RE JUST STREET GRUNTS, ALRIGHT?!
I SHOULD WARN YOU. MY GUN HAS A TENDENCY TO SUD-DENLY GO OFF.
ESPECIALLY WHEN IT'S POINTED AT PIECES OF SHIT.
GTNK
......!!
LAST CHANCE. SHOW ME YOU'RE WORTH A DAMN.
ALRIGHT, I'LL TALK!
FIDGET
GOOD. WHICH OF YOUR HIGHER-UPS WORKS WITH HIT MEN?
UH... BRUNO. HE'S WHAT THEY CALL A FIXER.

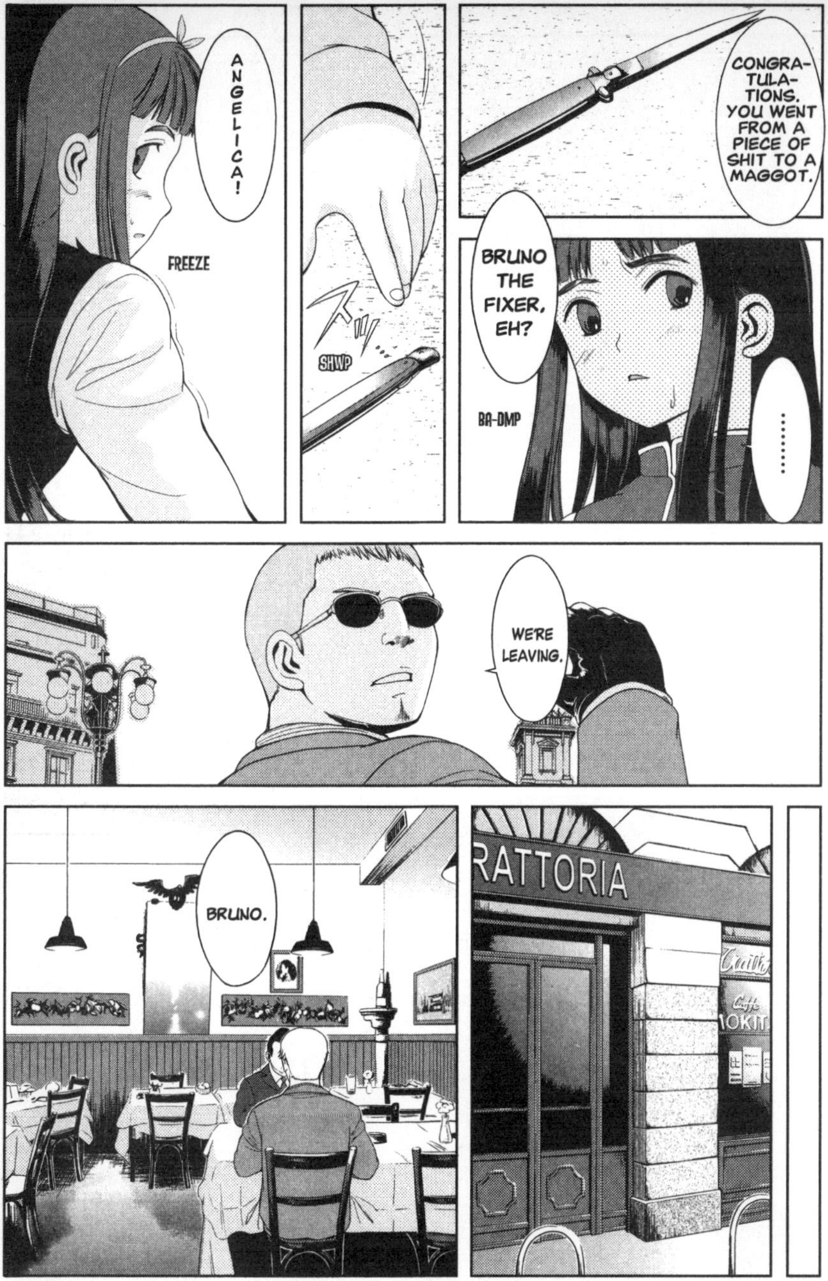
ANGELICA!
FREEZE
SHWP
CONGRATULATIONS. YOU WENT FROM A PIECE OF SHIT TO A MAGGOT.
BRUNO THE FIXER, EH?
BA-DMP
....
WE'RE LEAVING.
BRUNO.
RATTORIA
Caffe

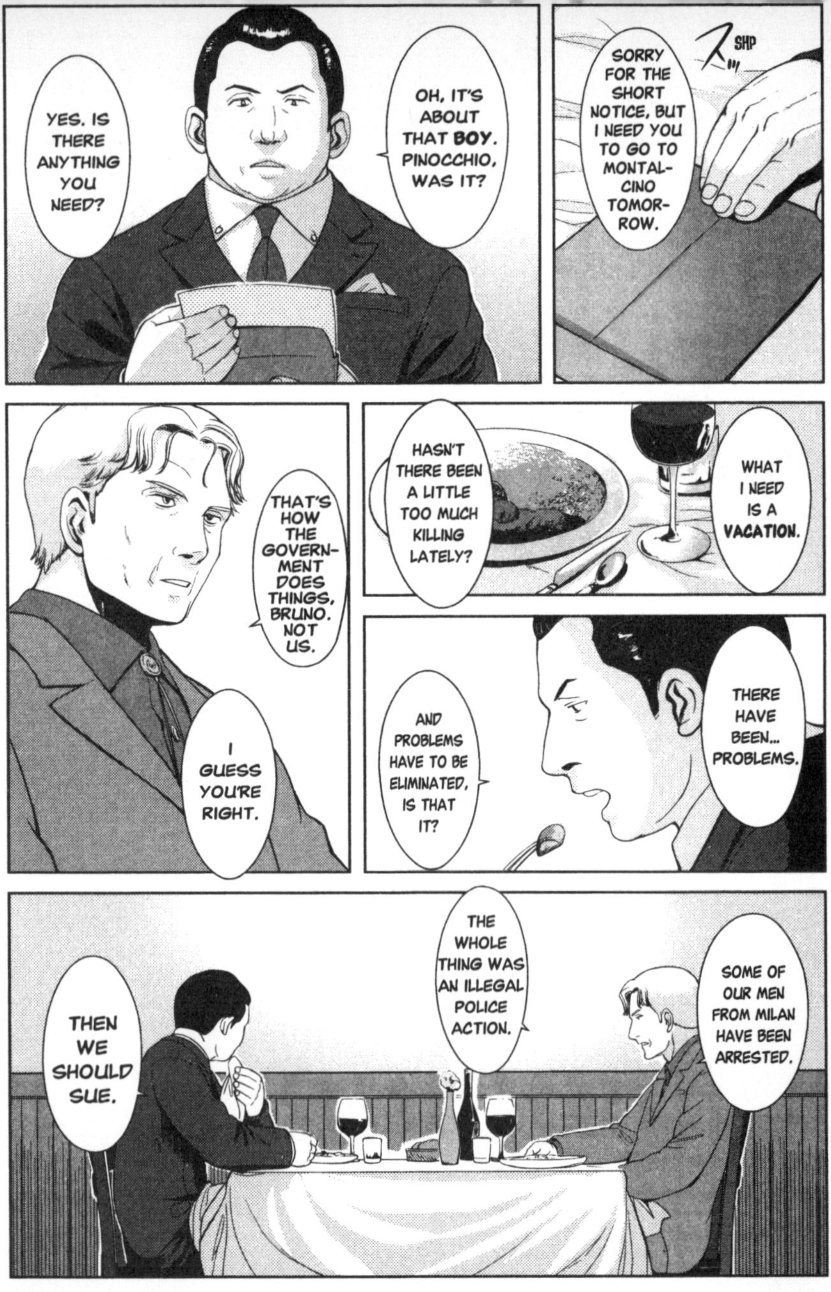
SHP
SORRY FOR THE SHORT NOTICE, BUT I NEED YOU TO GO TO MONTAL-CINO TOMOR-ROW.
YES. IS THERE ANYTHING YOU NEED?
OH, IT'S ABOUT THAT **BOY**. PINOCCHIO, WAS IT?
WHAT I NEED IS A **VACATION**.
HASN'T THERE BEEN A LITTLE TOO MUCH KILLING LATELY?
THAT'S HOW THE GOVERN-MENT DOES THINGS, BRUNO. NOT US.
THERE HAVE BEEN... PROBLEMS.
AND PROBLEMS HAVE TO BE ELIMINATED, IS THAT IT?
I GUESS YOU'RE RIGHT.
SOME OF OUR MEN FROM MILAN HAVE BEEN ARRESTED.
THE WHOLE THING WAS AN ILLEGAL POLICE ACTION.
THEN WE SHOULD SUE.

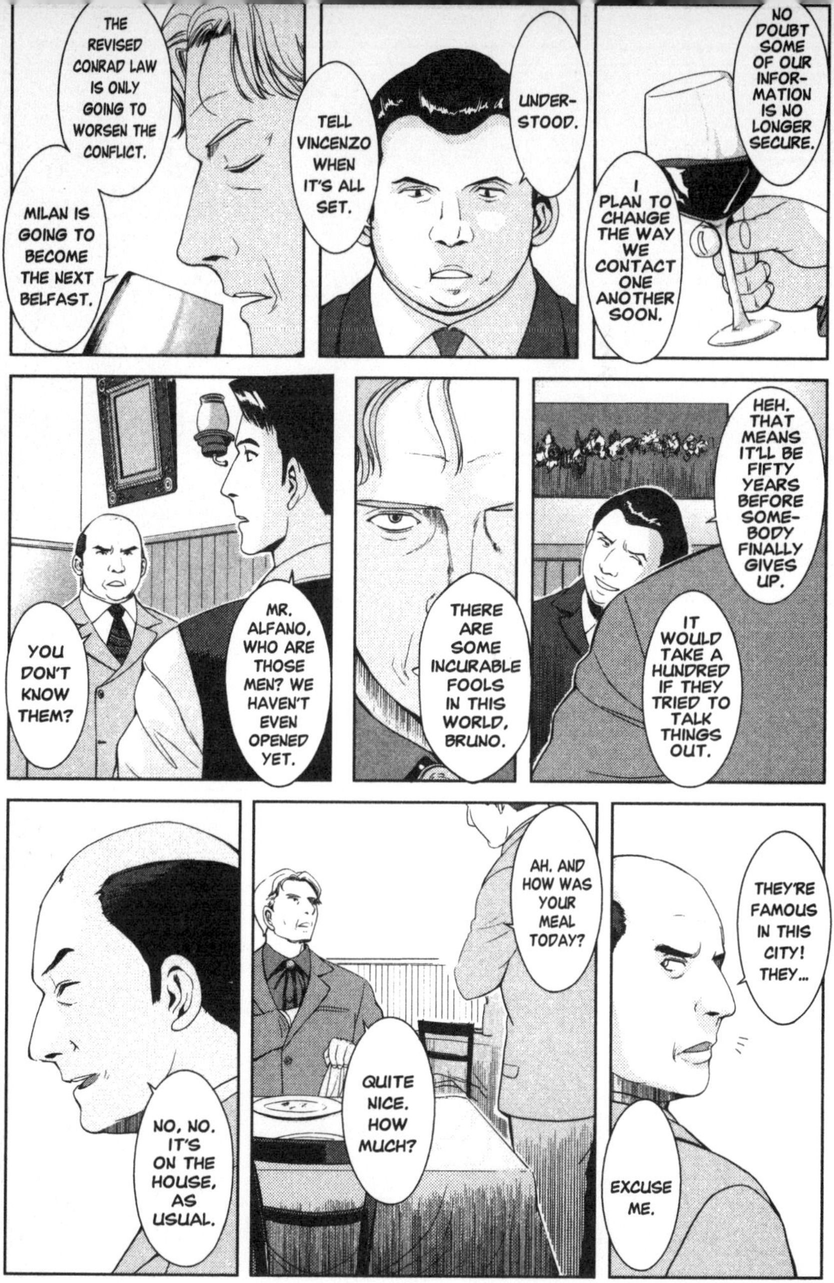
NO DOUBT SOME OF OUR INFORMATION IS NO LONGER SECURE.
I PLAN TO CHANGE THE WAY WE CONTACT ONE ANOTHER SOON.
UNDERSTOOD.
TELL VINCENZO WHEN IT'S ALL SET.
THE REVISED CONRAD LAW IS ONLY GOING TO WORSEN THE CONFLICT.
MILAN IS GOING TO BECOME THE NEXT BELFAST.
HEH. THAT MEANS IT'LL BE FIFTY YEARS BEFORE SOMEBODY FINALLY GIVES UP.
IT WOULD TAKE A HUNDRED IF THEY TRIED TO TALK THINGS OUT.
THERE ARE SOME INCURABLE FOOLS IN THIS WORLD, BRUNO.
MR. ALFANO, WHO ARE THOSE MEN? WE HAVEN'T EVEN OPENED YET.
YOU DON'T KNOW THEM?
THEY'RE FAMOUS IN THIS CITY! THEY...
EXCUSE ME.
AH. AND HOW WAS YOUR MEAL TODAY?
QUITE NICE. HOW MUCH?
NO, NO. IT'S ON THE HOUSE, AS USUAL.

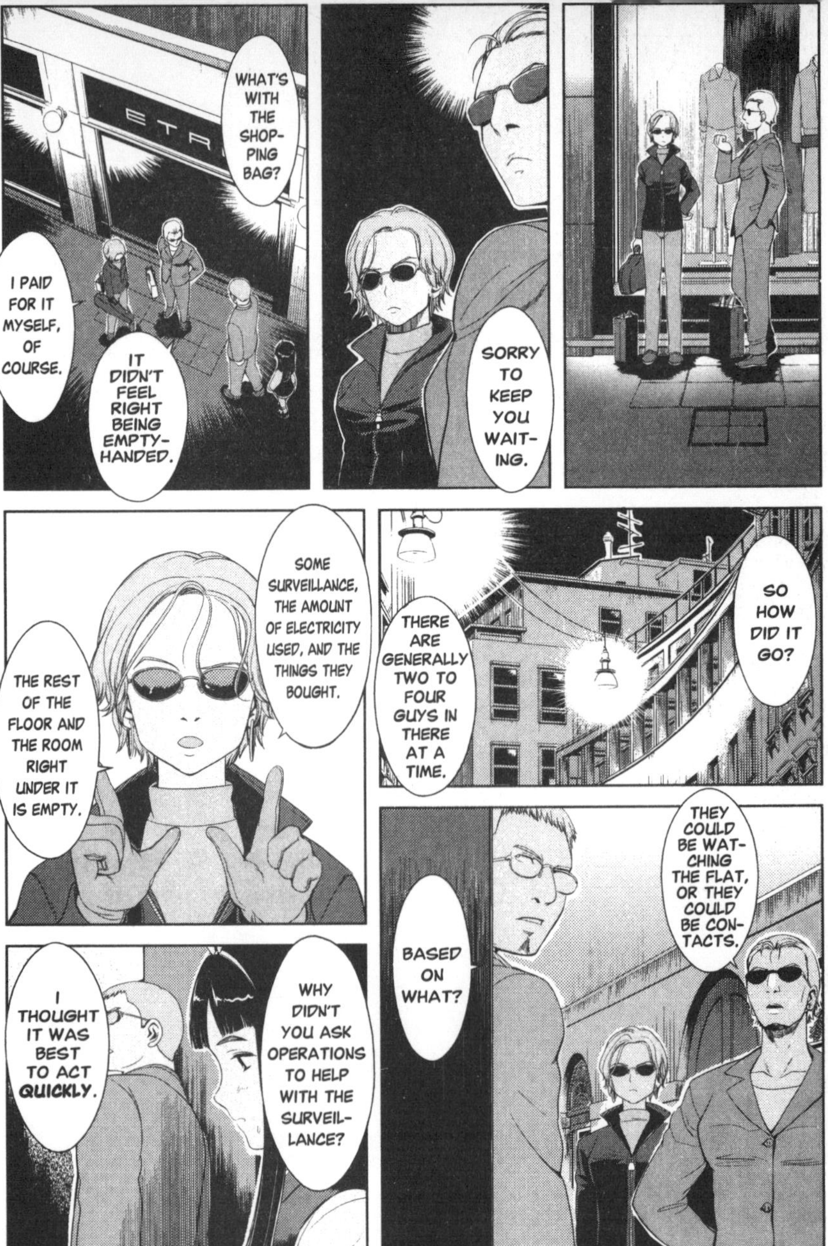
SORRY TO KEEP YOU WAIT-ING.
WHAT'S WITH THE SHOP-PING BAG?
I PAID FOR IT MYSELF, OF COURSE.
IT DIDN'T FEEL RIGHT BEING EMPTY-HANDED.
SO HOW DID IT GO?
THERE ARE GENERALLY TWO TO FOUR GUYS IN THERE AT A TIME.
SOME SURVEILLANCE, THE AMOUNT OF ELECTRICITY USED, AND THE THINGS THEY BOUGHT.
THE REST OF THE FLOOR AND THE ROOM RIGHT UNDER IT IS EMPTY.
THEY COULD BE WAT-CHING THE FLAT, OR THEY COULD BE CON-TACTS.
BASED ON WHAT?
WHY DIDN'T YOU ASK OPERATIONS TO HELP WITH THE SURVEIL-LANCE?
I THOUGHT IT WAS BEST TO ACT **QUICKLY**.

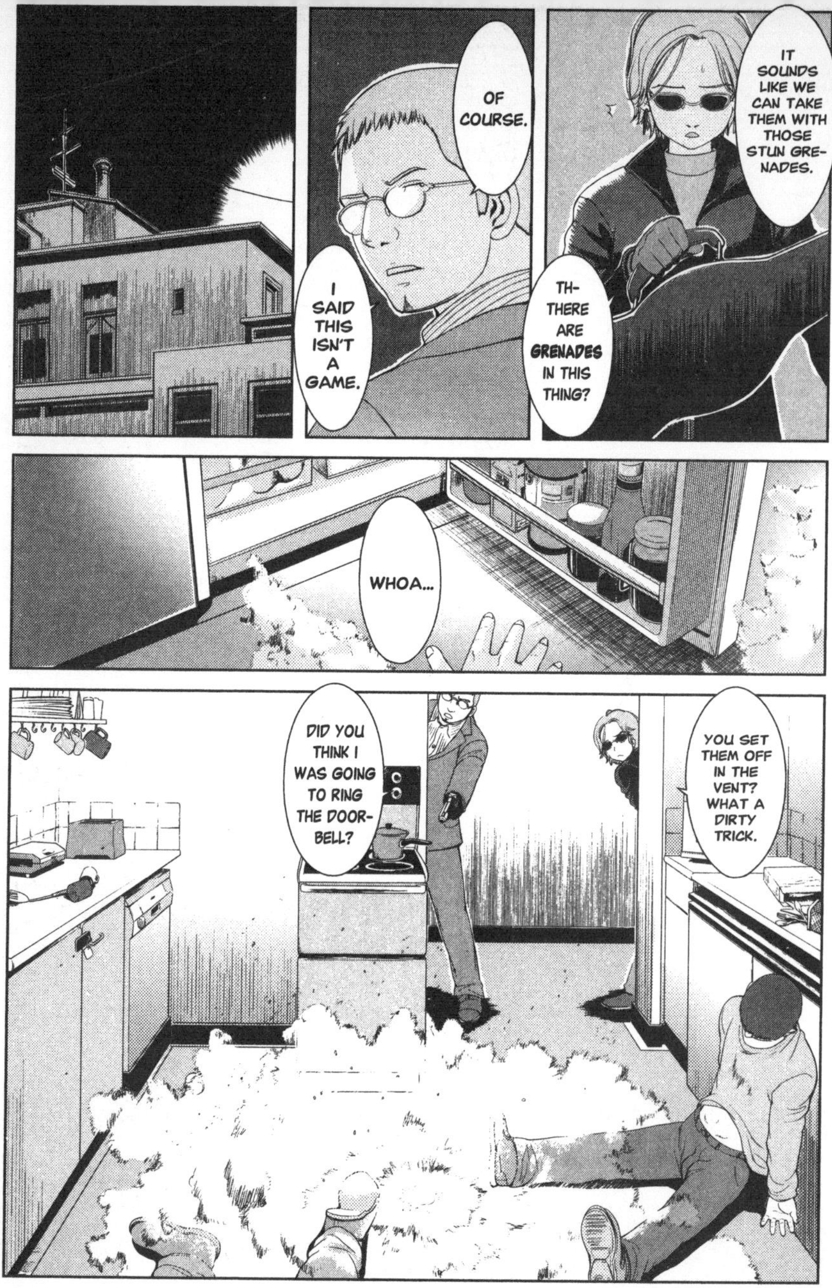
IT SOUNDS LIKE WE CAN TAKE THEM WITH THOSE STUN GRENADES.
TH-THERE ARE **GRENADES** IN THIS THING?
OF COURSE.
I SAID THIS ISN'T A GAME.
WHOA...
YOU SET THEM OFF IN THE VENT? WHAT A DIRTY TRICK.
DID YOU THINK I WAS GOING TO RING THE DOORBELL?

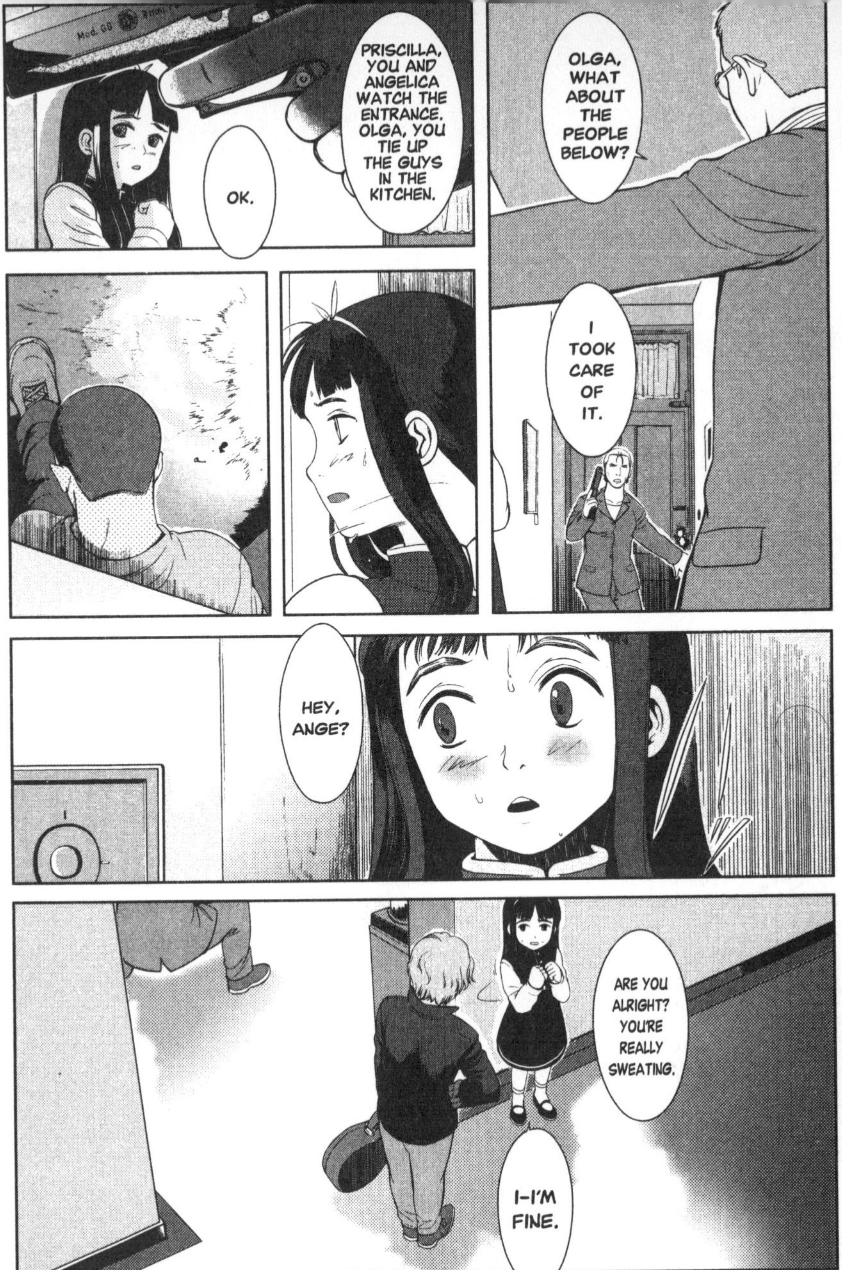
PRISCILLA, YOU AND ANGELICA WATCH THE ENTRANCE. OLGA, YOU TIE UP THE GUYS IN THE KITCHEN.
OK.
OLGA, WHAT ABOUT THE PEOPLE BELOW?
I TOOK CARE OF IT.
HEY, ANGE?
ARE YOU ALRIGHT? YOU'RE REALLY SWEATING.
I-I'M FINE.

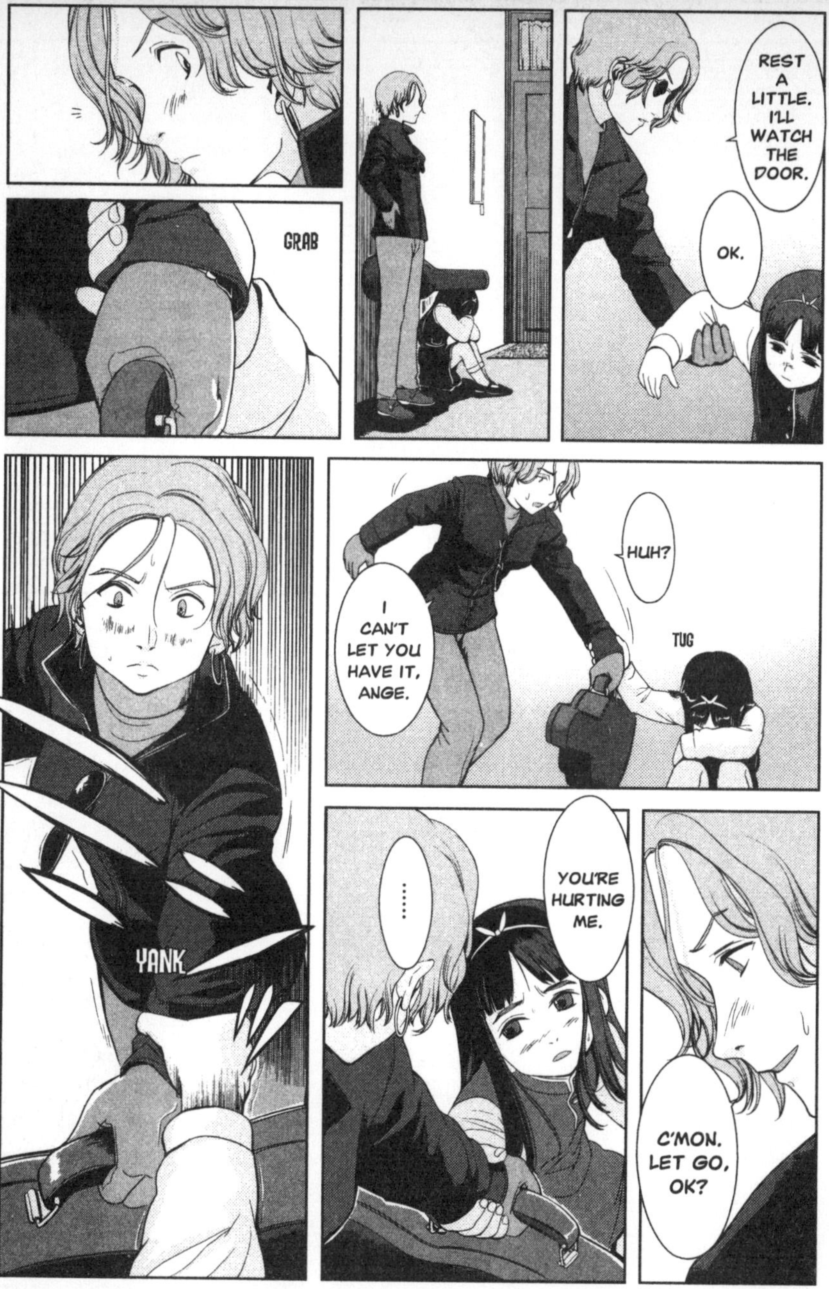
REST A LITTLE. I'LL WATCH THE DOOR.
OK.
GRAB
HUH?
I CAN'T LET YOU HAVE IT, ANGE.
TUG
C'MON. LET GO, OK?
YOU'RE HURTING ME.
......
YANK

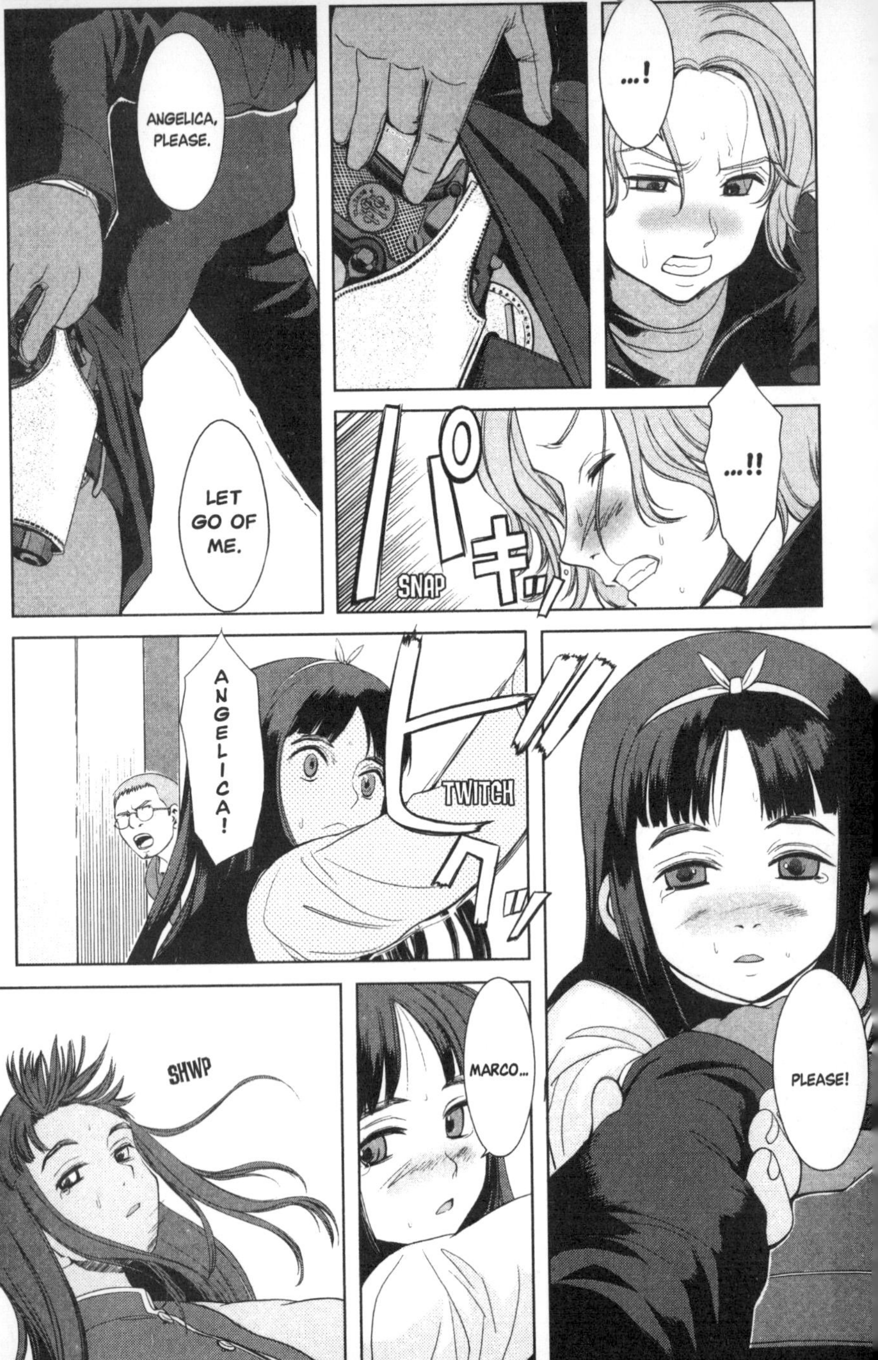

...!
ANGELICA, PLEASE.
LET GO OF ME.
...!!
SNAP
ANGELICA!
TWITCH
PLEASE!
MARCO...
SHWP

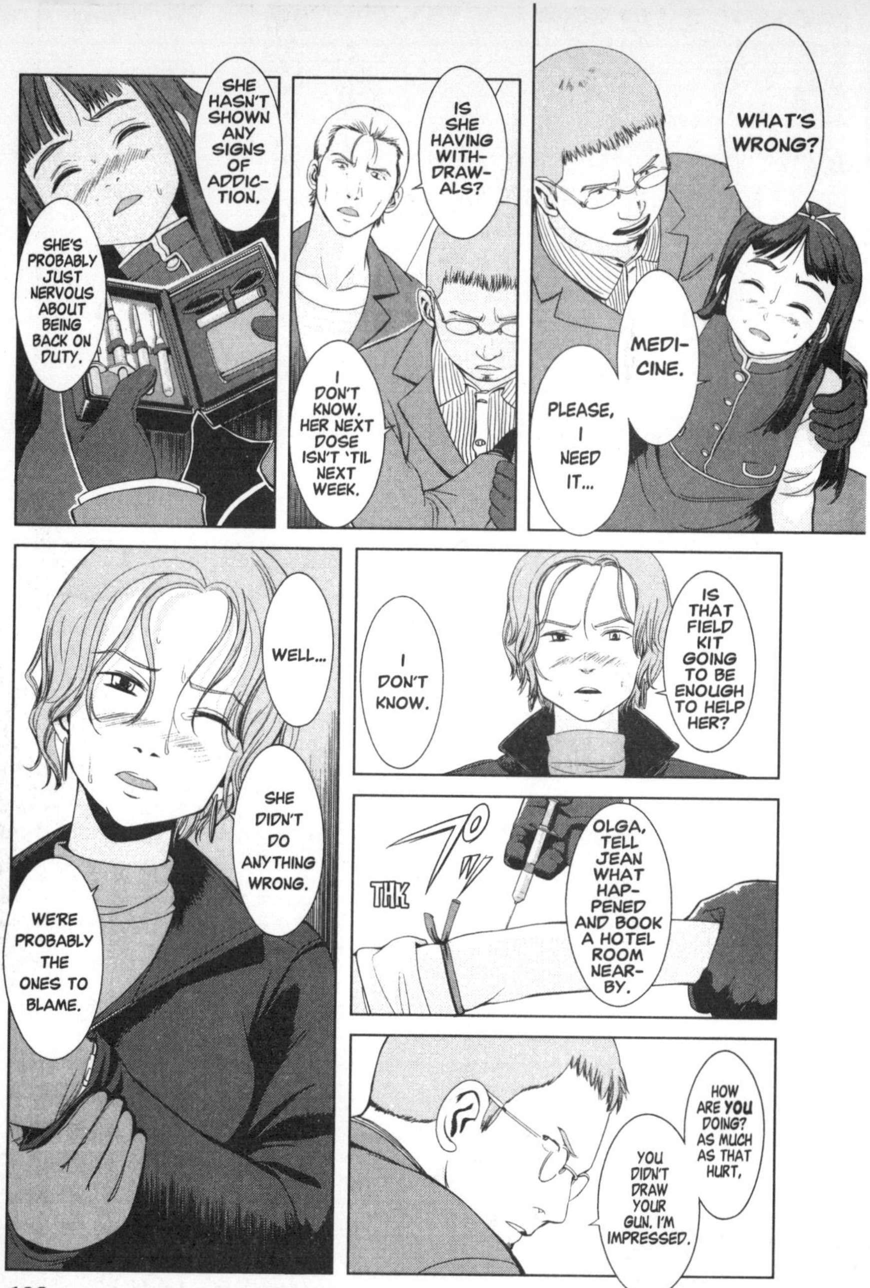
WHAT'S WRONG?
MEDICINE.
PLEASE, I NEED IT...
IS SHE HAVING WITHDRAWALS?
I DON'T KNOW. HER NEXT DOSE ISN'T 'TIL NEXT WEEK.
SHE HASN'T SHOWN ANY SIGNS OF ADDICTION.
SHE'S PROBABLY JUST NERVOUS ABOUT BEING BACK ON DUTY.
IS THAT FIELD KIT GOING TO BE ENOUGH TO HELP HER?
I DON'T KNOW.
WELL...
SHE DIDN'T DO ANYTHING WRONG.
WE'RE PROBABLY THE ONES TO BLAME.
THK
OLGA, TELL JEAN WHAT HAPPENED AND BOOK A HOTEL ROOM NEARBY.
HOW ARE **YOU** DOING? AS MUCH AS THAT HURT,
YOU DIDN'T DRAW YOUR GUN. I'M IMPRESSED.

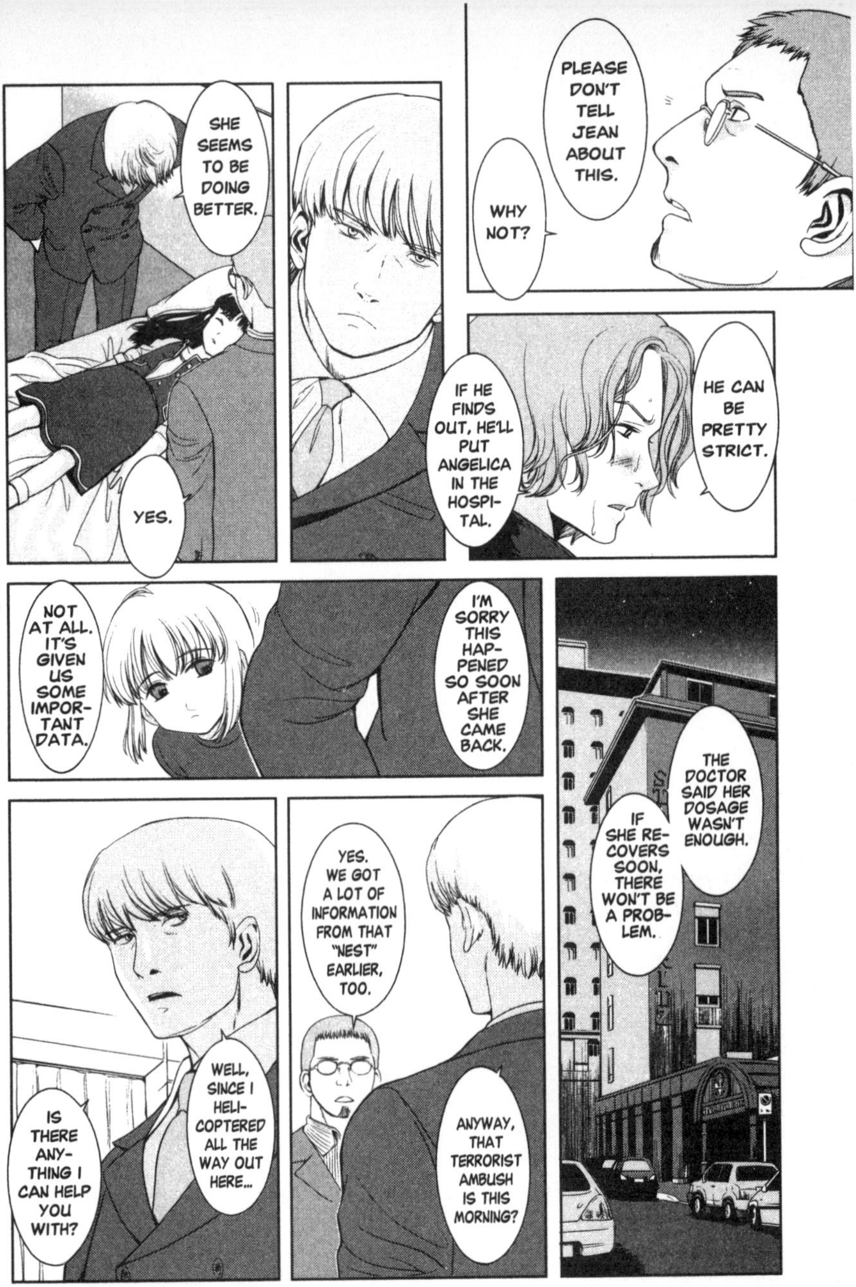

PLEASE DON'T TELL JEAN ABOUT THIS.
WHY NOT?
HE CAN BE PRETTY STRICT.
IF HE FINDS OUT, HE'LL PUT ANGELICA IN THE HOSPI-TAL.
SHE SEEMS TO BE DOING BETTER.
YES.
THE DOCTOR SAID HER DOSAGE WASN'T ENOUGH.
IF SHE RE-COVERS SOON, THERE WON'T BE A PROB-LEM.
I'M SORRY THIS HAP-PENED SO SOON AFTER SHE CAME BACK.
NOT AT ALL. IT'S GIVEN US SOME IMPOR-TANT DATA.
ANYWAY, THAT TERRORIST AMBUSH IS THIS MORNING?
YES. WE GOT A LOT OF INFORMATION FROM THAT "NEST" EARLIER, TOO.
WELL, SINCE I HELI-COPTERED ALL THE WAY OUT HERE...
IS THERE ANY-THING I CAN HELP YOU WITH?

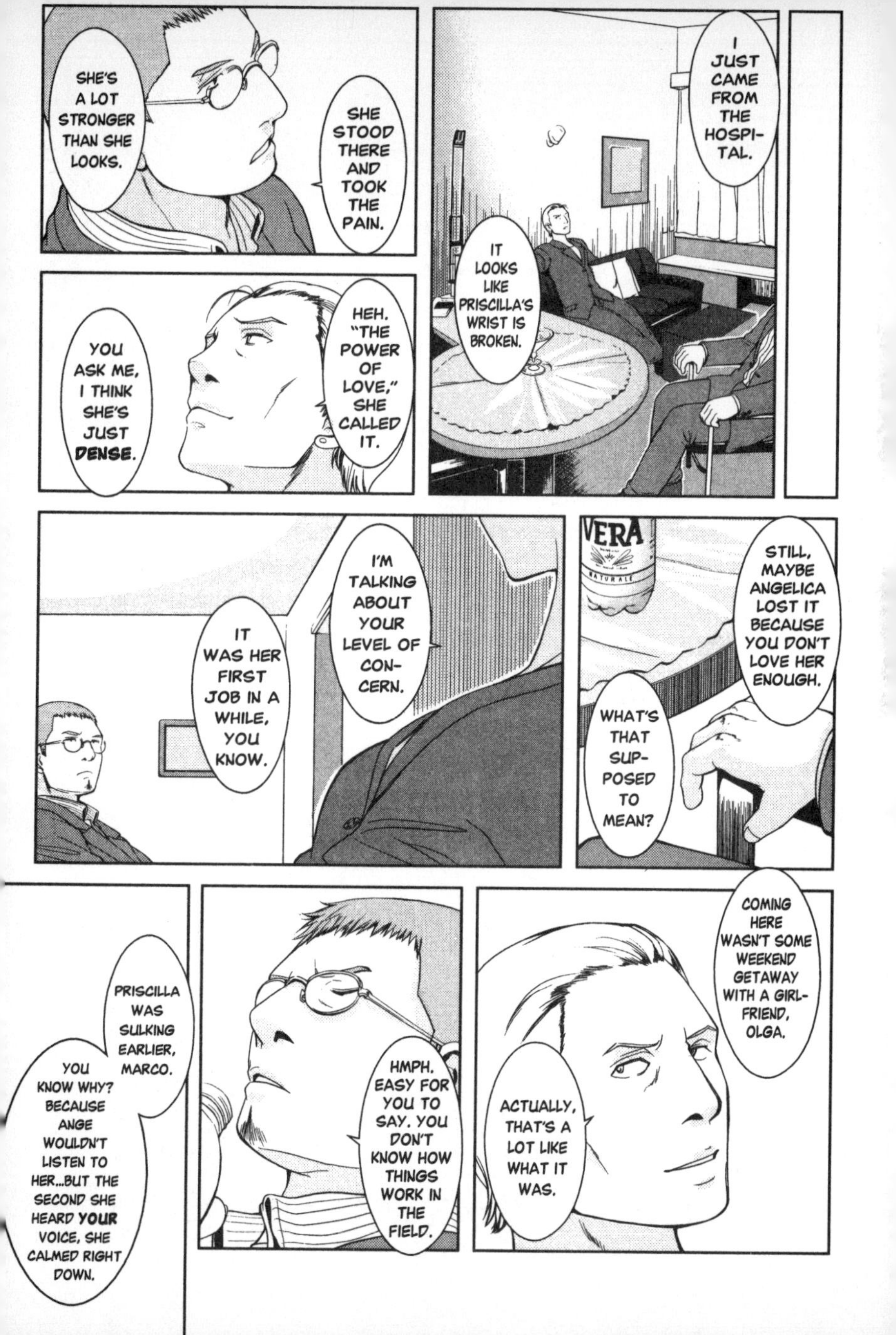
I JUST CAME FROM THE HOSPITAL.
IT LOOKS LIKE PRISCILLA'S WRIST IS BROKEN.
SHE STOOD THERE AND TOOK THE PAIN.
SHE'S A LOT STRONGER THAN SHE LOOKS.
HEH. "THE POWER OF LOVE," SHE CALLED IT.
YOU ASK ME, I THINK SHE'S JUST **DENSE**.
STILL, MAYBE ANGELICA LOST IT BECAUSE YOU DON'T LOVE HER ENOUGH.
WHAT'S THAT SUPPOSED TO MEAN?
I'M TALKING ABOUT YOUR LEVEL OF CONCERN.
IT WAS HER FIRST JOB IN A WHILE, YOU KNOW.
COMING HERE WASN'T SOME WEEKEND GETAWAY WITH A GIRLFRIEND, OLGA.
ACTUALLY, THAT'S A LOT LIKE WHAT IT WAS.
HMPH. EASY FOR YOU TO SAY. YOU DON'T KNOW HOW THINGS WORK IN THE FIELD.
PRISCILLA WAS SULKING EARLIER, MARCO.
YOU KNOW WHY? BECAUSE ANGE WOULDN'T LISTEN TO HER...BUT THE SECOND SHE HEARD **YOUR** VOICE, SHE CALMED RIGHT DOWN.

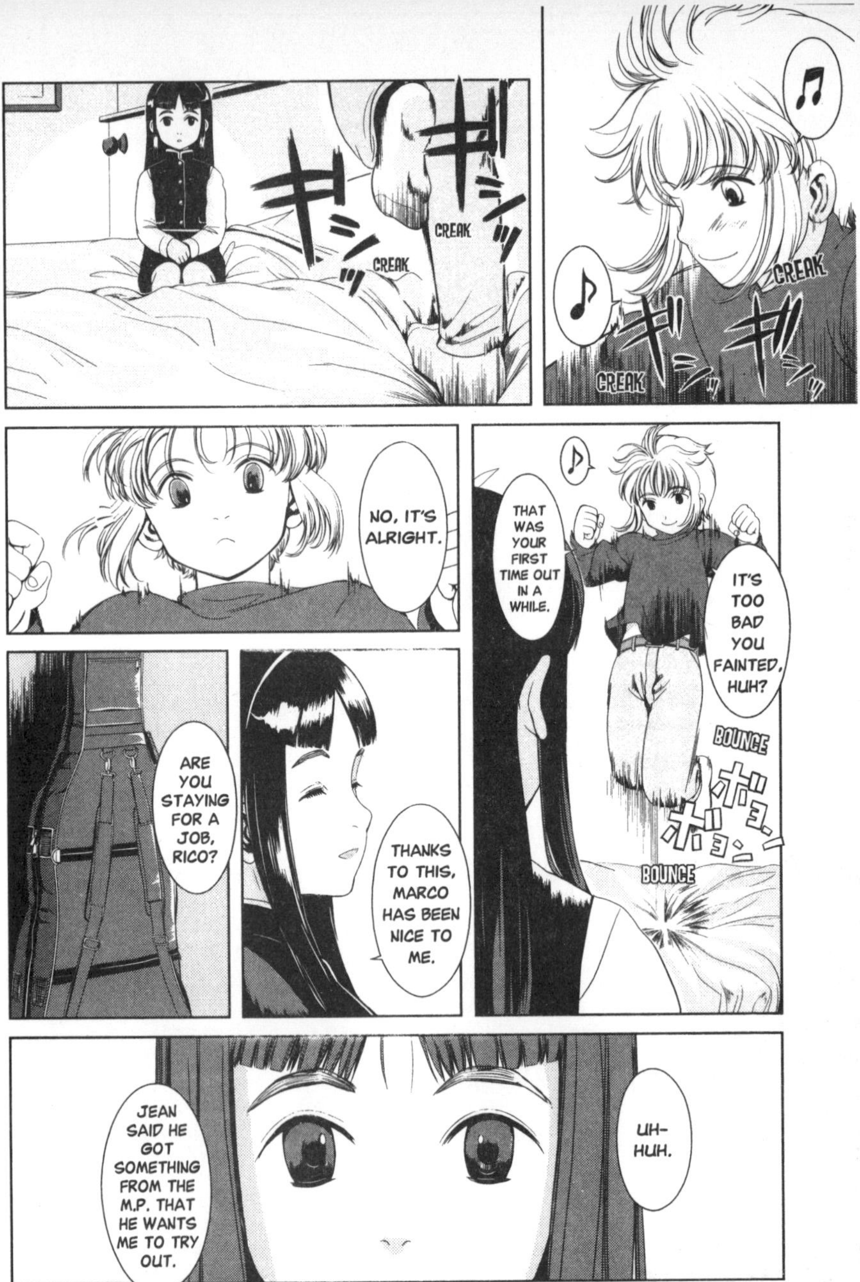

CREAK
CREAK
CREAK
CREAK
THAT WAS YOUR FIRST TIME OUT IN A WHILE.
IT'S TOO BAD YOU FAINTED, HUH?
BOUNCE
BOUNCE
NO, IT'S ALRIGHT.
THANKS TO THIS, MARCO HAS BEEN NICE TO ME.
ARE YOU STAYING FOR A JOB, RICO?
UH-HUH.
JEAN SAID HE GOT SOMETHING FROM THE M.P. THAT HE WANTS ME TO TRY OUT.

* M.P. = Military Police

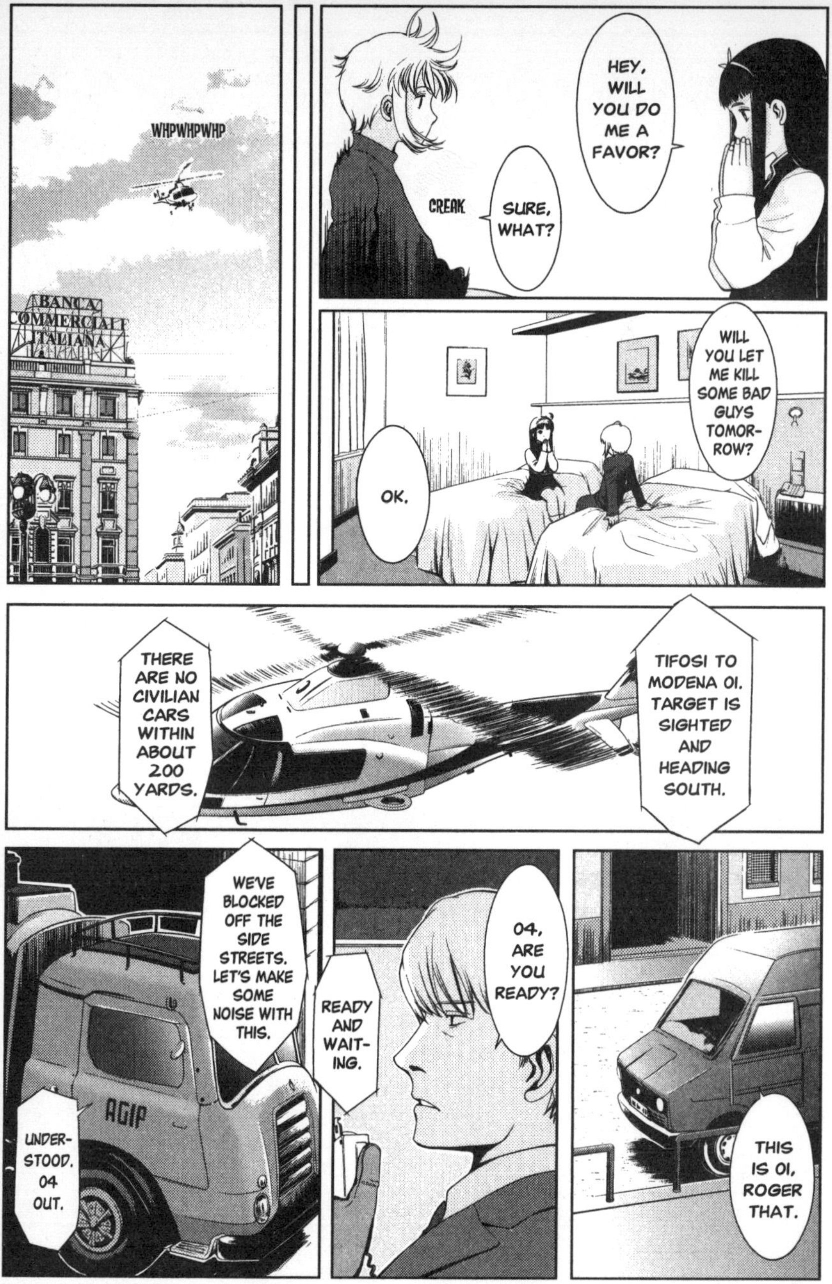
HEY, WILL YOU DO ME A FAVOR?
SURE, WHAT?
CREAK
WILL YOU LET ME KILL SOME BAD GUYS TOMOR-ROW?
OK.
WHPWHPWHP
BANCA COMMERCIALE ITALIANA
TIFOSI TO MODENA 01. TARGET IS SIGHTED AND HEADING SOUTH.
THERE ARE NO CIVILIAN CARS WITHIN ABOUT 200 YARDS.
THIS IS 01, ROGER THAT.
04, ARE YOU READY?
READY AND WAIT-ING.
WE'VE BLOCKED OFF THE SIDE STREETS. LET'S MAKE SOME NOISE WITH THIS.
AGIP
UNDER-STOOD. 04 OUT.

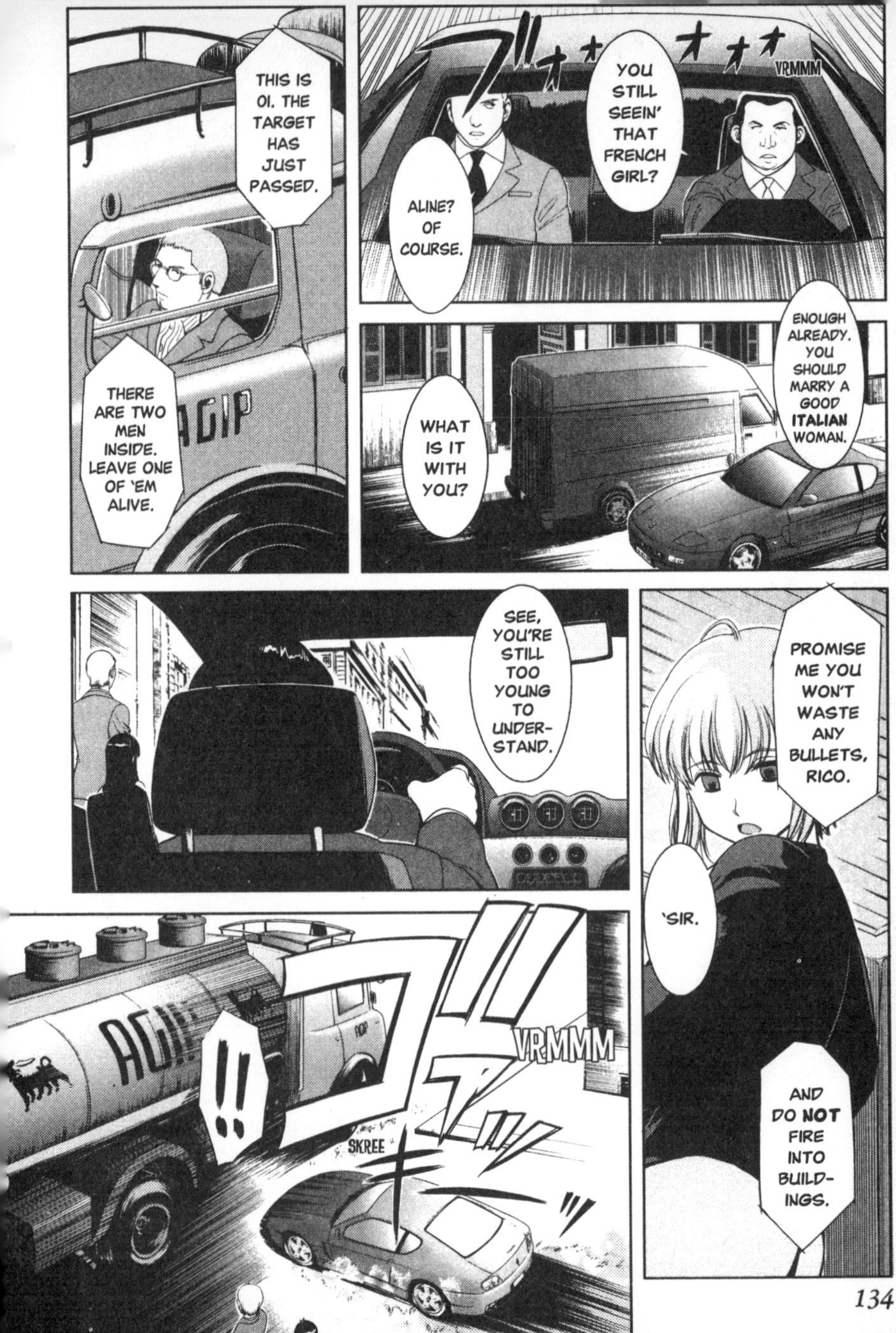
VRMMM
YOU STILL SEEIN' THAT FRENCH GIRL?
ALINE? OF COURSE.
THIS IS 01. THE TARGET HAS JUST PASSED.
THERE ARE TWO MEN INSIDE. LEAVE ONE OF 'EM ALIVE.
ENOUGH ALREADY. YOU SHOULD MARRY A GOOD ITALIAN WOMAN.
WHAT IS IT WITH YOU?
PROMISE ME YOU WON'T WASTE ANY BULLETS, RICO.
SEE, YOU'RE STILL TOO YOUNG TO UNDER-STAND.
'SIR.
AND DO NOT FIRE INTO BUILD-INGS.
VRMMM
!!
SKREE

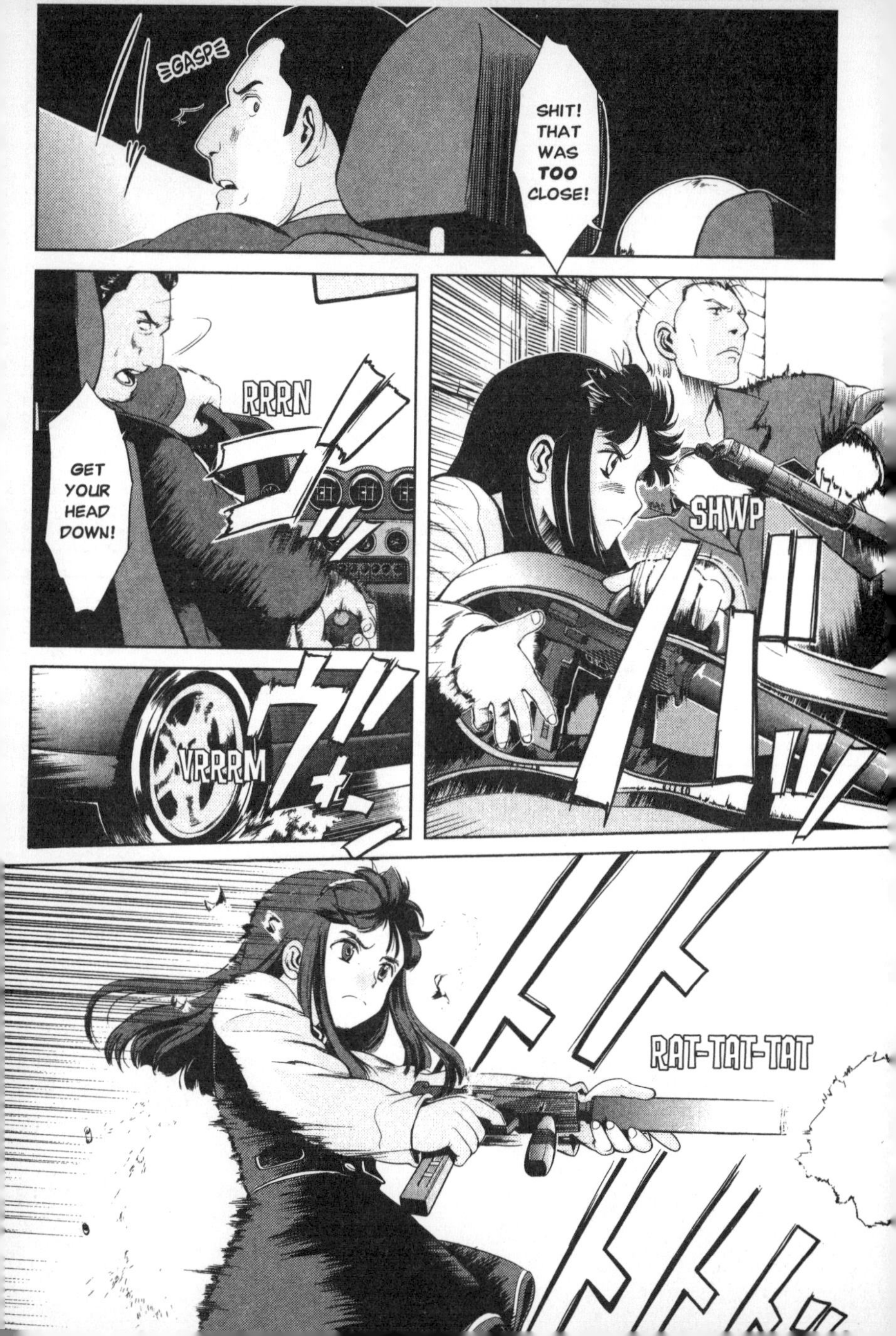
GASP
SHIT! THAT WAS TOO CLOSE!
RRRN
GET YOUR HEAD DOWN!
SHWP
VRRRM
RAT-TAT-TAT

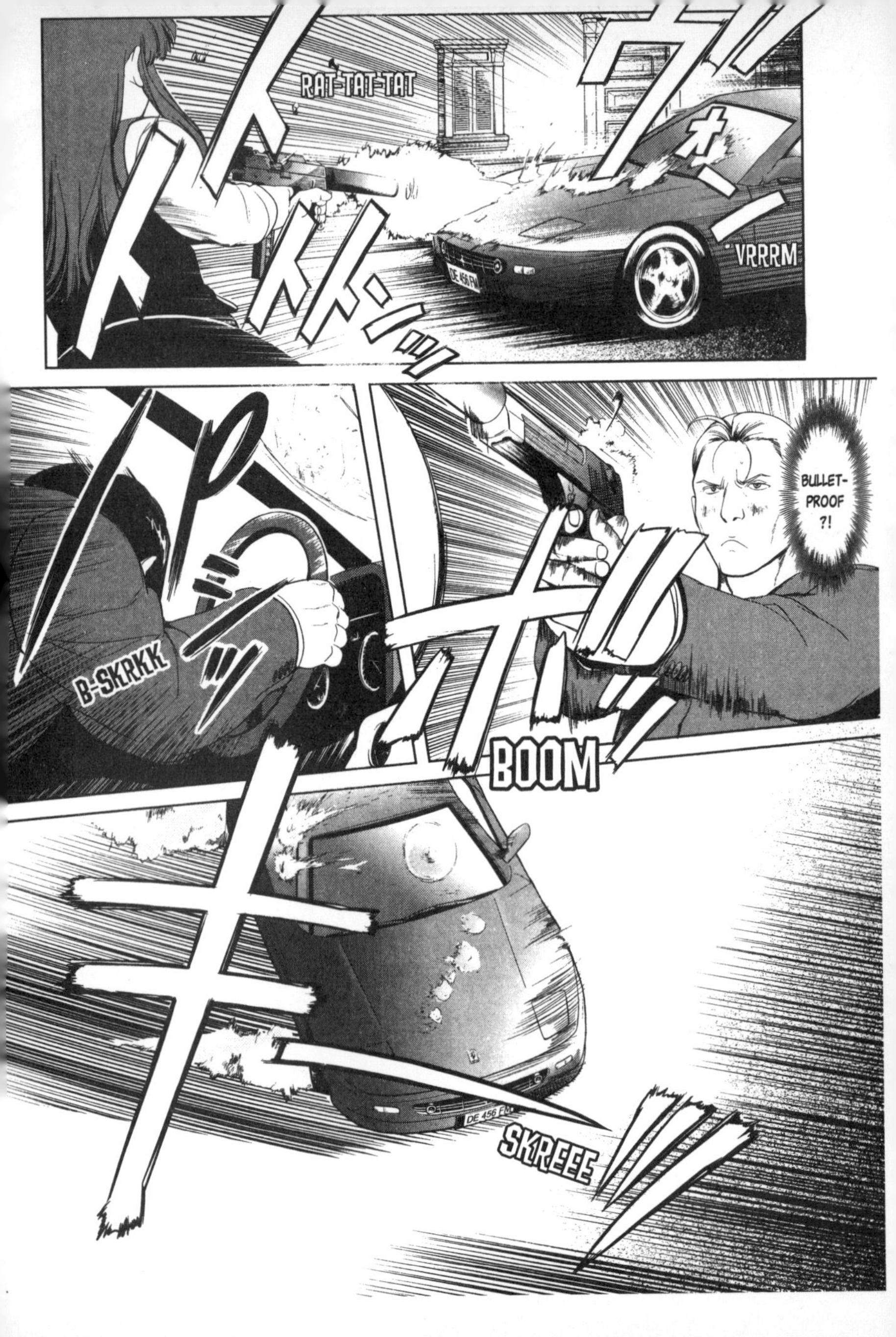
RAT-TAT-TAT
VRRRM
BULLET-PROOF ?!
B-SKRKK
BOOM
SKREEE

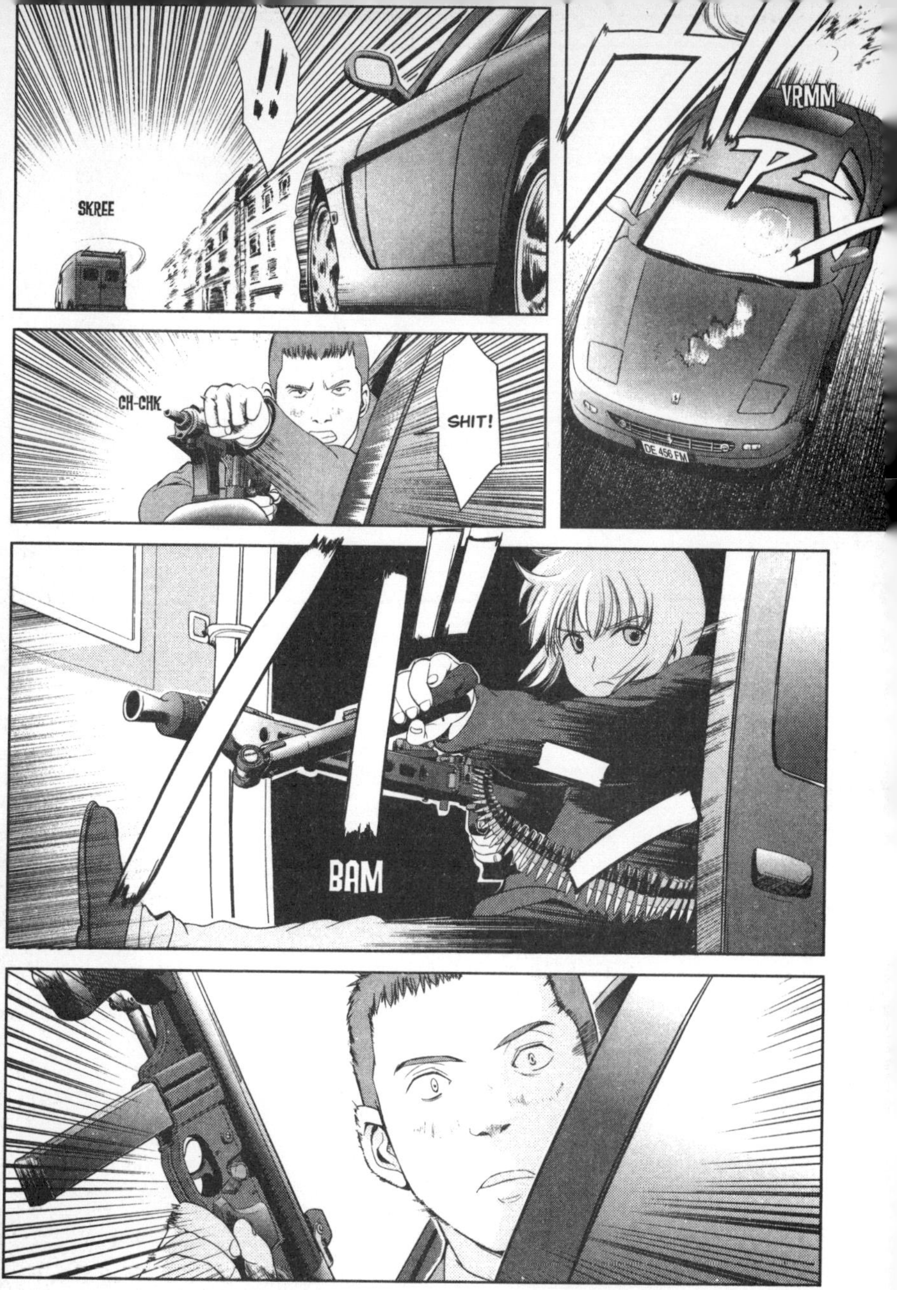
VRMM
DE 456 FM
!!
SKREE
SHIT!
CH-CHK
BAM

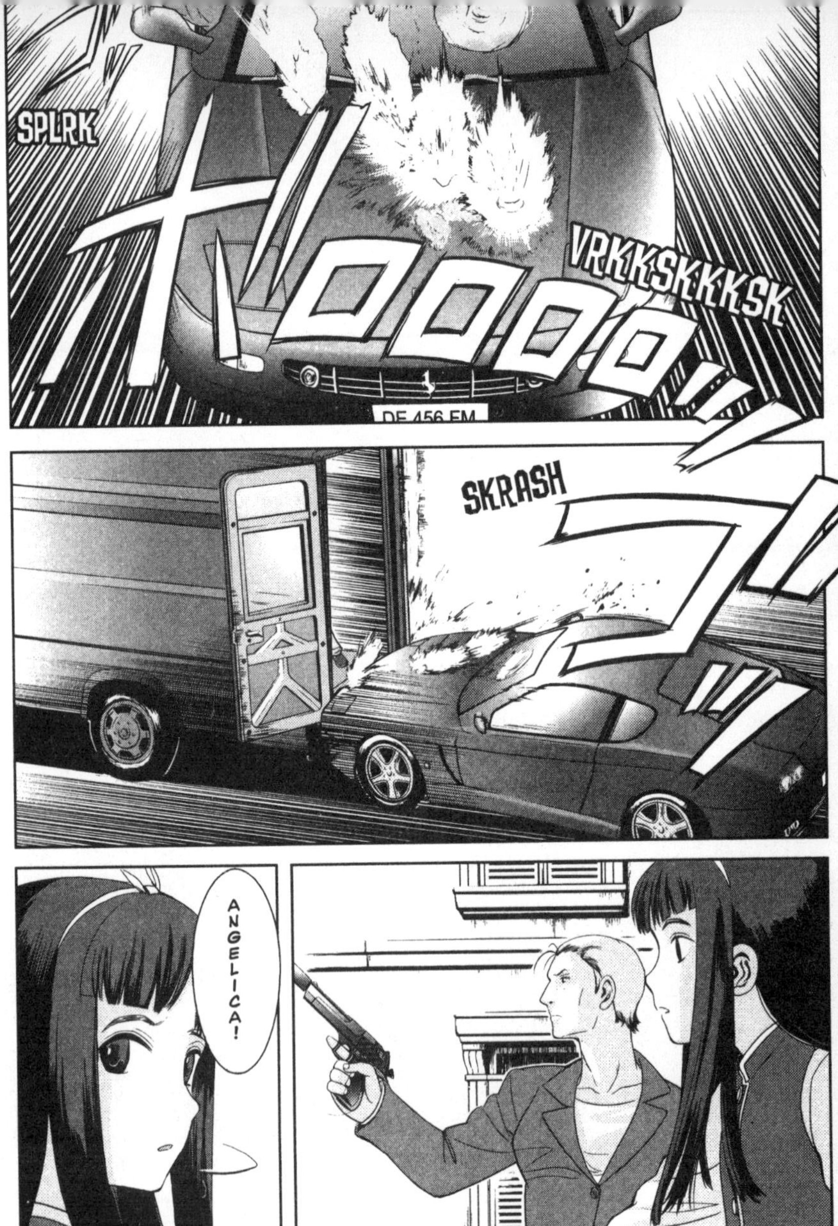
VRKKSKKKSK
SPLRK
DE 456 EM
SKRASH
ANGELICA!

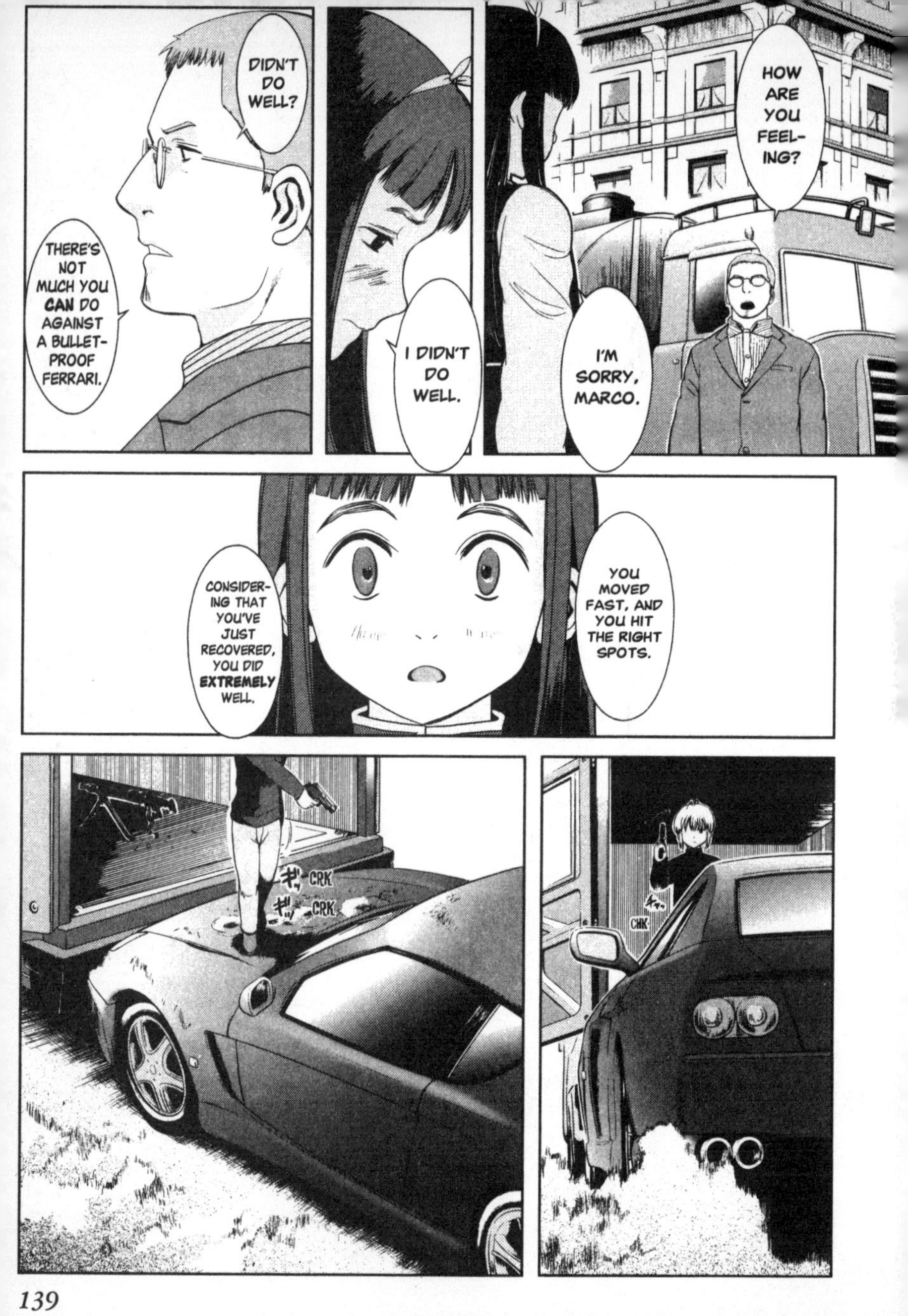
HOW ARE YOU FEELING?
I'M SORRY, MARCO.
I DIDN'T DO WELL.
DIDN'T DO WELL?
THERE'S NOT MUCH YOU **CAN** DO AGAINST A BULLET-PROOF FERRARI.
YOU MOVED FAST, AND YOU HIT THE RIGHT SPOTS.
CONSIDERING THAT YOU'VE JUST RECOVERED, YOU DID **EXTREMELY** WELL.
CHK
CRK
CRK

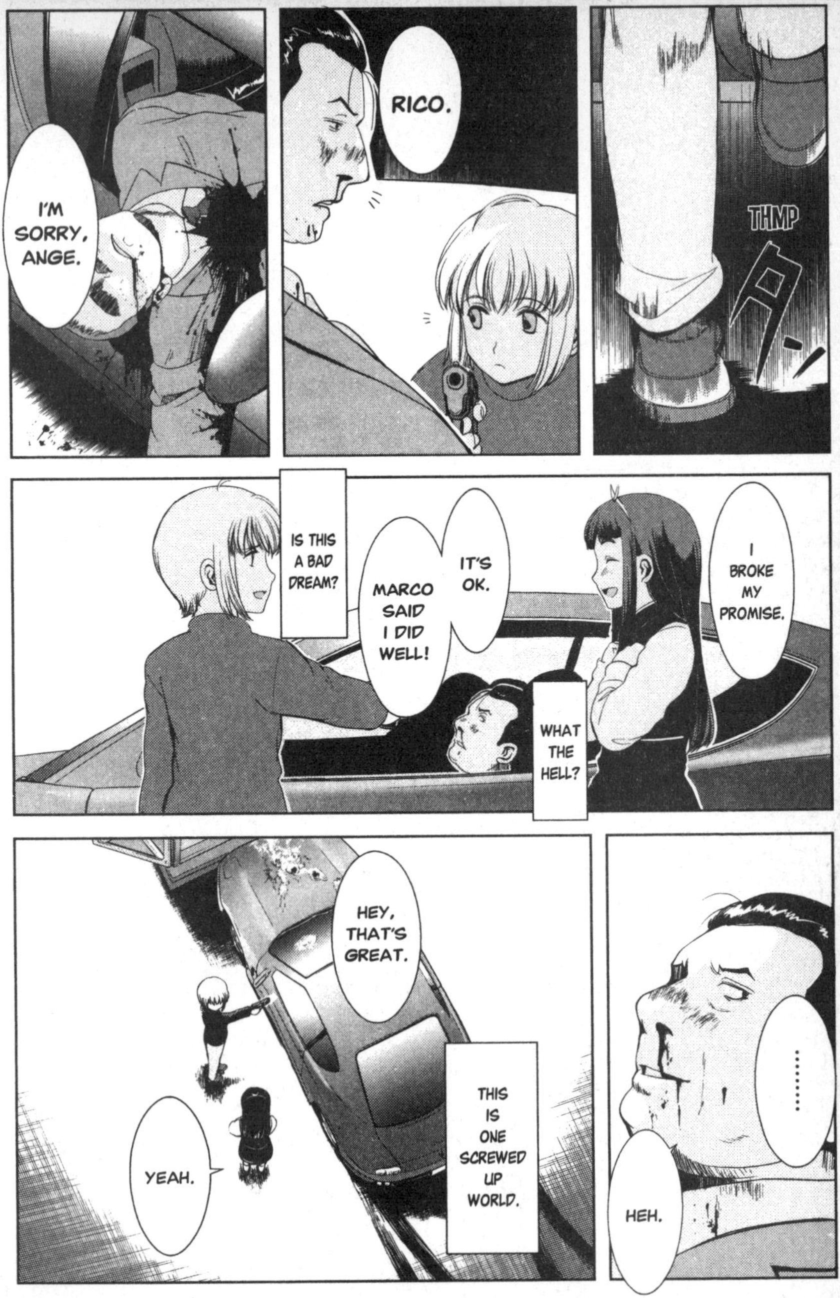

THMP
RICO.
I'M SORRY, ANGE.
I BROKE MY PROMISE.
WHAT THE HELL?
IT'S OK.
MARCO SAID I DID WELL!
IS THIS A BAD DREAM?
......
HEH.
HEY, THAT'S GREAT.
YEAH.
THIS IS ONE SCREWED UP WORLD.

GUNSLINGERGIRL.

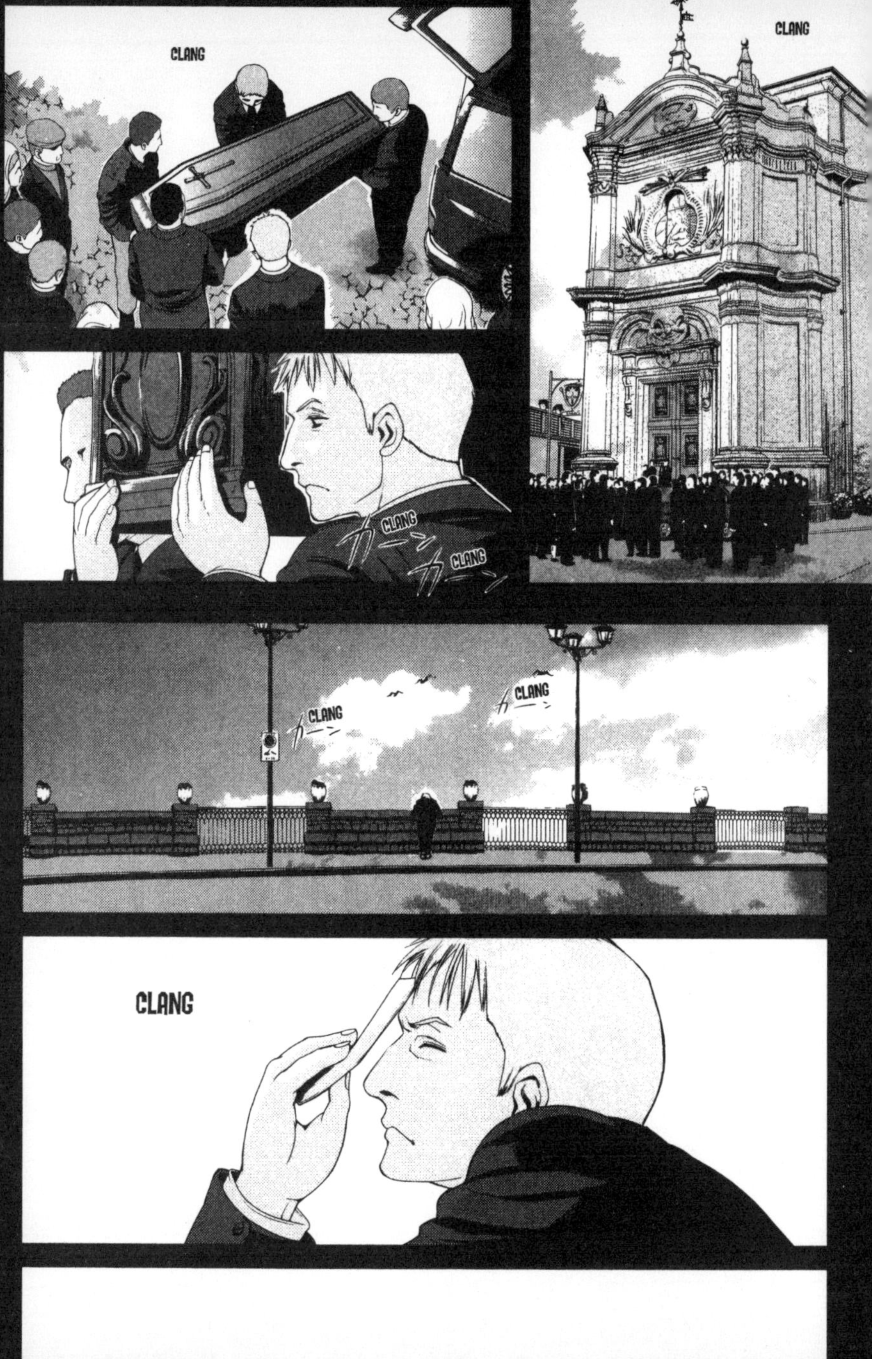
CLANG
CLANG
CLANG
CLANG
CLANG
CLANG
CLANG

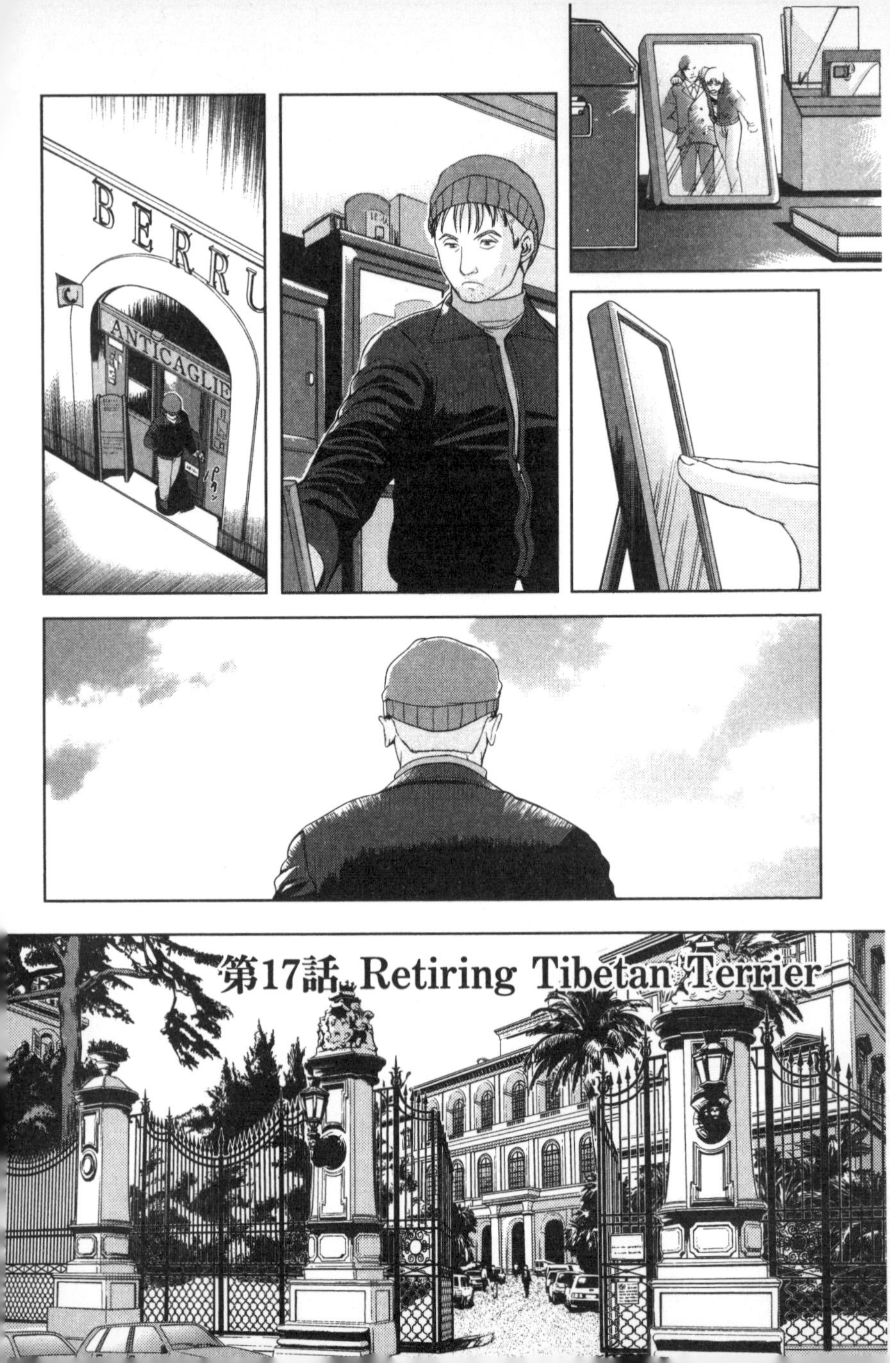
BERRU
ANTICAGLIE
パタン
第17話 Retiring Tibetan Terrier

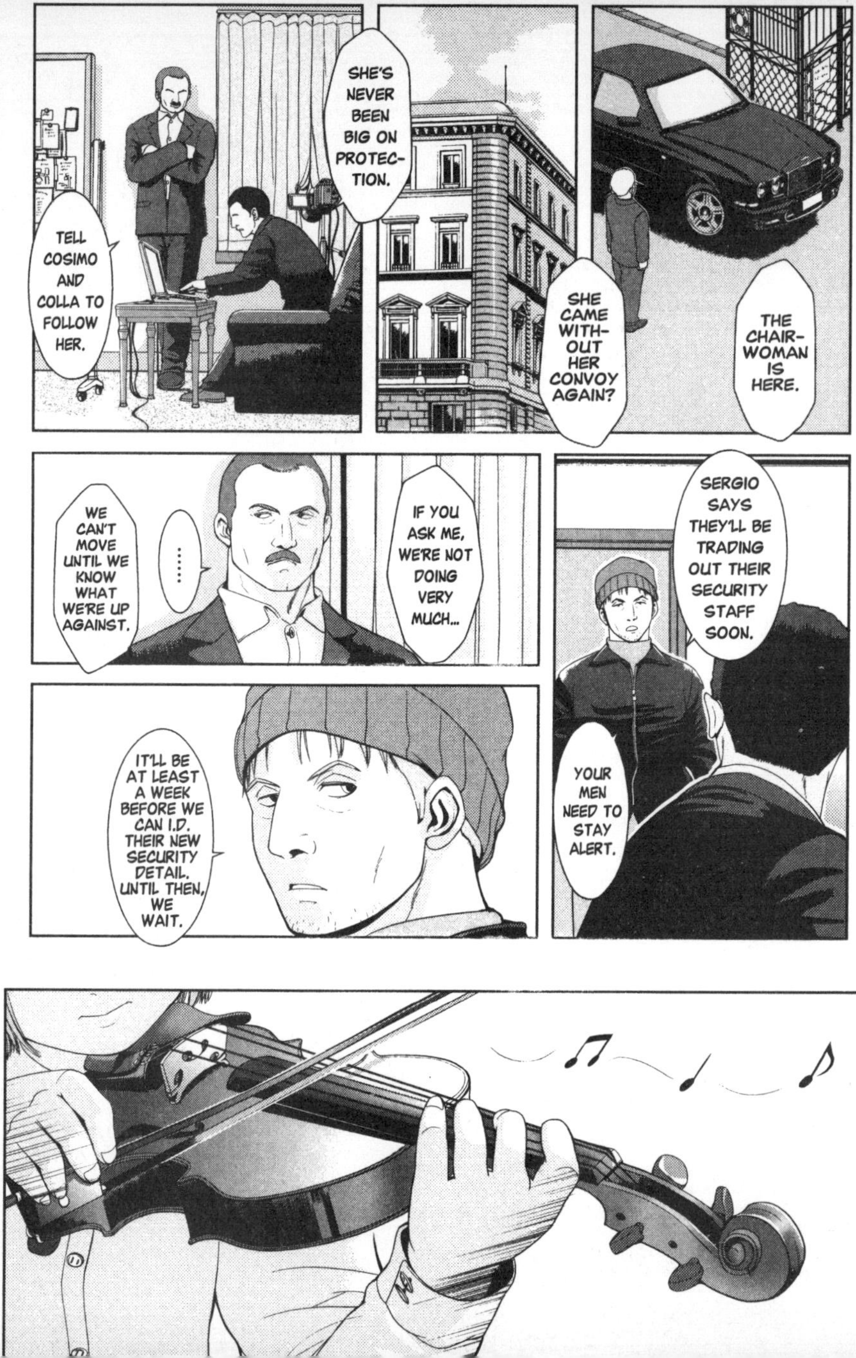
THE CHAIRWOMAN IS HERE.
SHE CAME WITHOUT HER CONVOY AGAIN?
SHE'S NEVER BEEN BIG ON PROTECTION.
TELL COSIMO AND COLLA TO FOLLOW HER.
SERGIO SAYS THEY'LL BE TRADING OUT THEIR SECURITY STAFF SOON.
YOUR MEN NEED TO STAY ALERT.
IF YOU ASK ME, WE'RE NOT DOING VERY MUCH...
......
WE CAN'T MOVE UNTIL WE KNOW WHAT WE'RE UP AGAINST.
IT'LL BE AT LEAST A WEEK BEFORE WE CAN I.D. THEIR NEW SECURITY DETAIL. UNTIL THEN, WE WAIT.

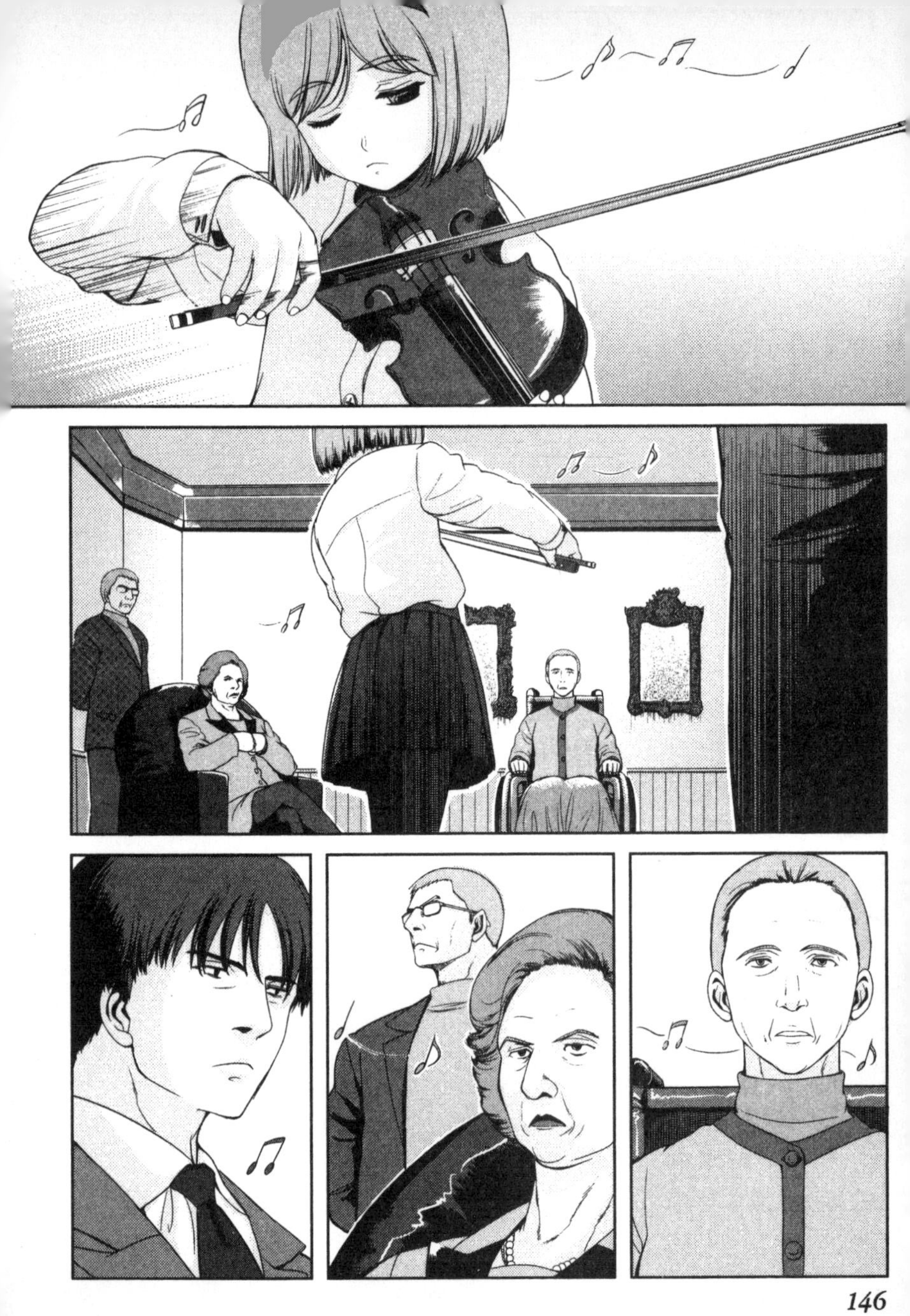

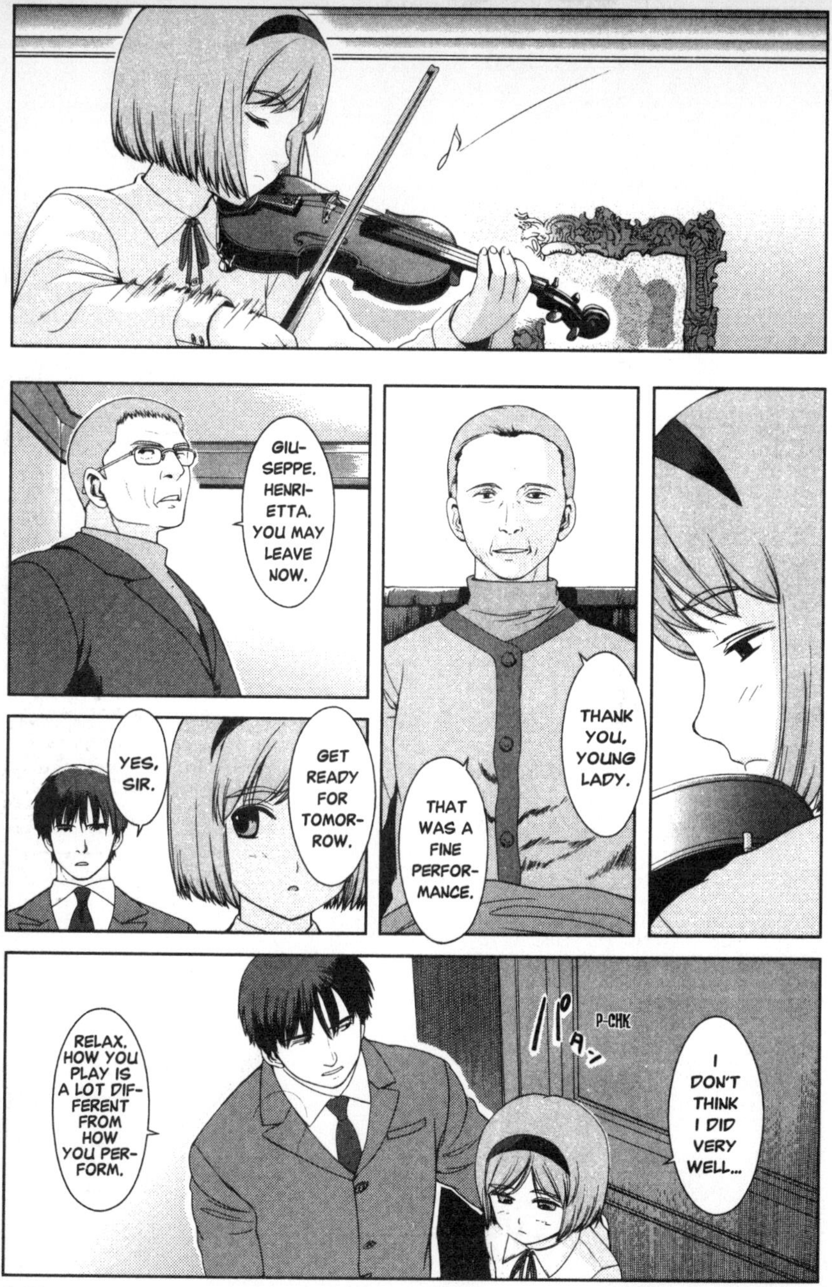
THANK YOU, YOUNG LADY.
THAT WAS A FINE PERFORMANCE.
GIUSEPPE. HENRIETTA. YOU MAY LEAVE NOW.
GET READY FOR TOMORROW.
YES, SIR.
I DON'T THINK I DID VERY WELL...
P-CHK
RELAX. HOW YOU PLAY IS A LOT DIFFERENT FROM HOW YOU PERFORM.

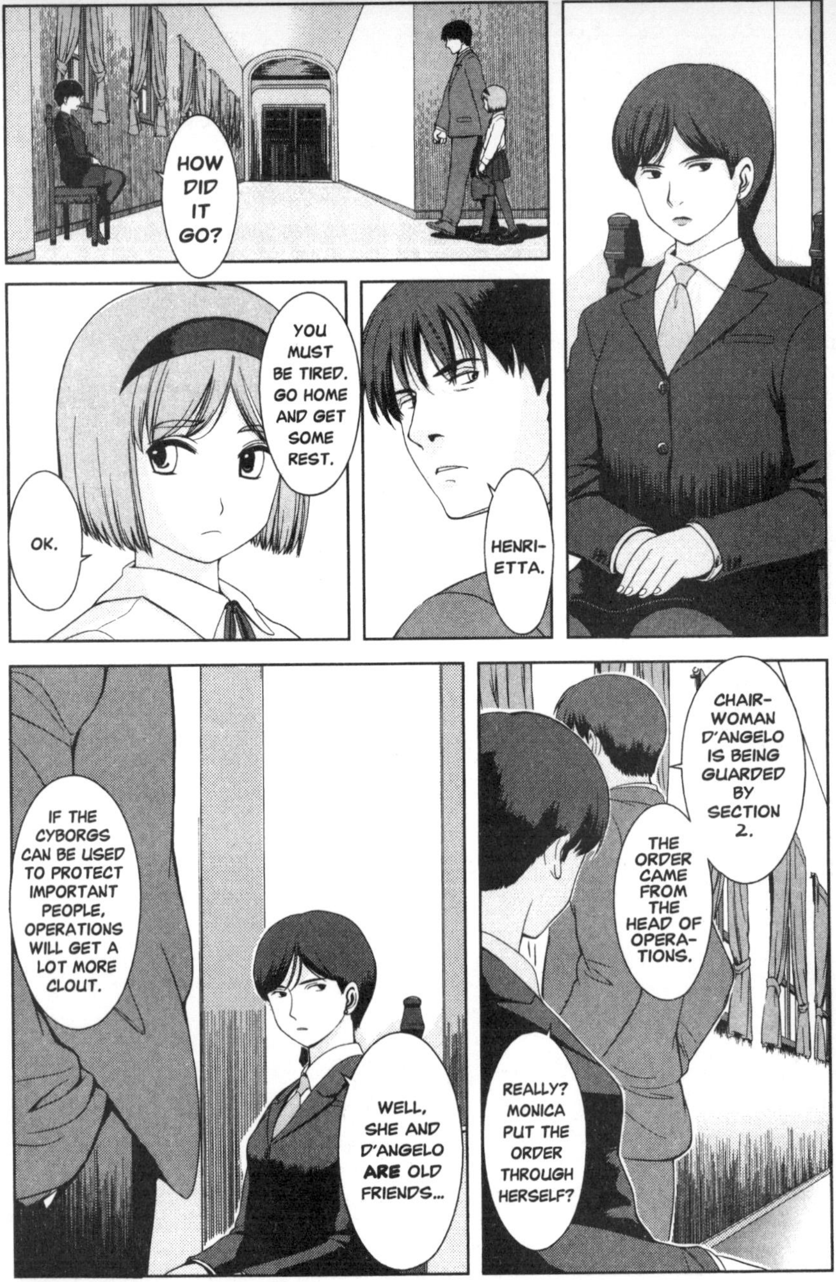
HOW DID IT GO?
HENRI-ETTA.
YOU MUST BE TIRED. GO HOME AND GET SOME REST.
OK.
CHAIR-WOMAN D'ANGELO IS BEING GUARDED BY SECTION 2.
THE ORDER CAME FROM THE HEAD OF OPERA-TIONS.
REALLY? MONICA PUT THE ORDER THROUGH HERSELF?
WELL, SHE AND D'ANGELO **ARE** OLD FRIENDS...
IF THE CYBORGS CAN BE USED TO PROTECT IMPORTANT PEOPLE, OPERATIONS WILL GET A LOT MORE CLOUT.

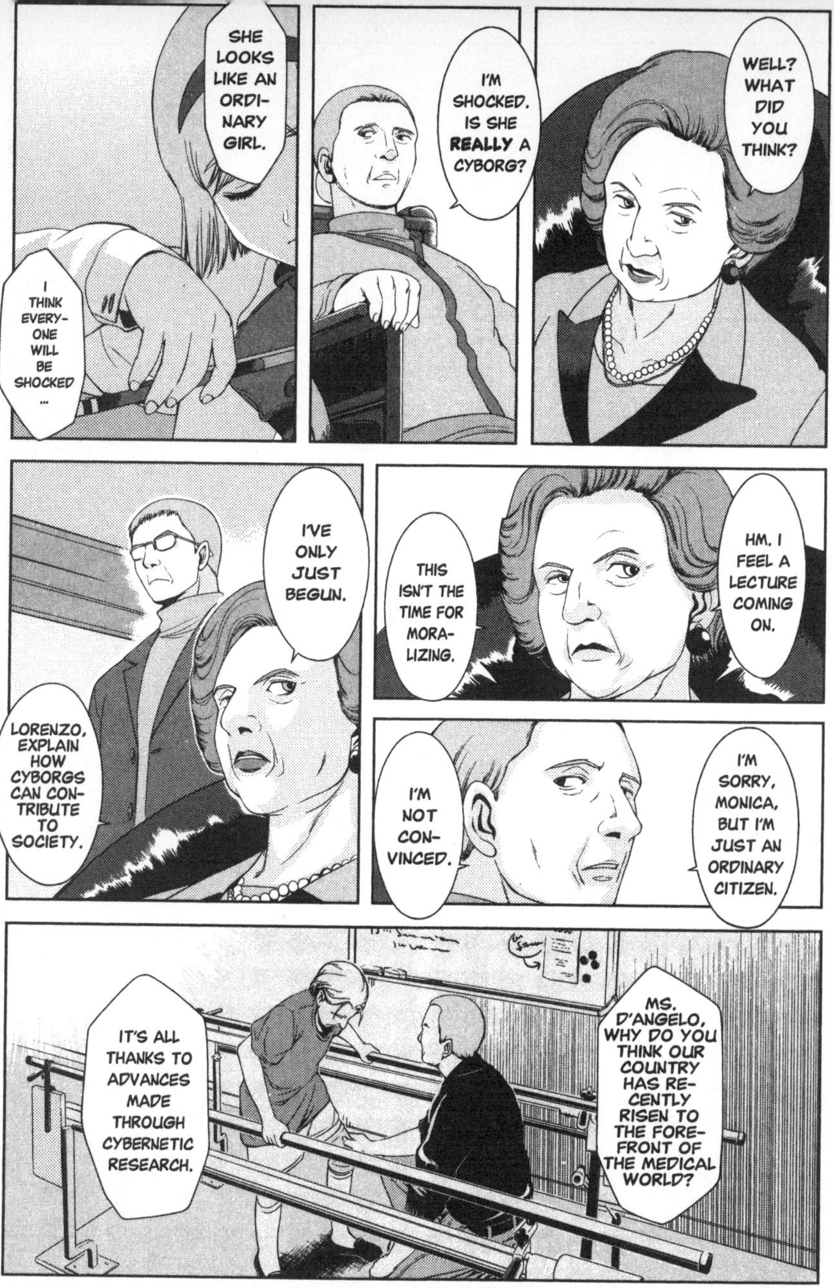
WELL? WHAT DID YOU THINK?
I'M SHOCKED. IS SHE **REALLY** A CYBORG?
SHE LOOKS LIKE AN ORDINARY GIRL.
I THINK EVERYONE WILL BE SHOCKED...
HM. I FEEL A LECTURE COMING ON.
THIS ISN'T THE TIME FOR MORALIZING.
I'M SORRY, MONICA, BUT I'M JUST AN ORDINARY CITIZEN.
I'M NOT CONVINCED.
I'VE ONLY JUST BEGUN.
LORENZO, EXPLAIN HOW CYBORGS CAN CONTRIBUTE TO SOCIETY.
MS. D'ANGELO, WHY DO YOU THINK OUR COUNTRY HAS RECENTLY RISEN TO THE FOREFRONT OF THE MEDICAL WORLD?
IT'S ALL THANKS TO ADVANCES MADE THROUGH CYBERNETIC RESEARCH.

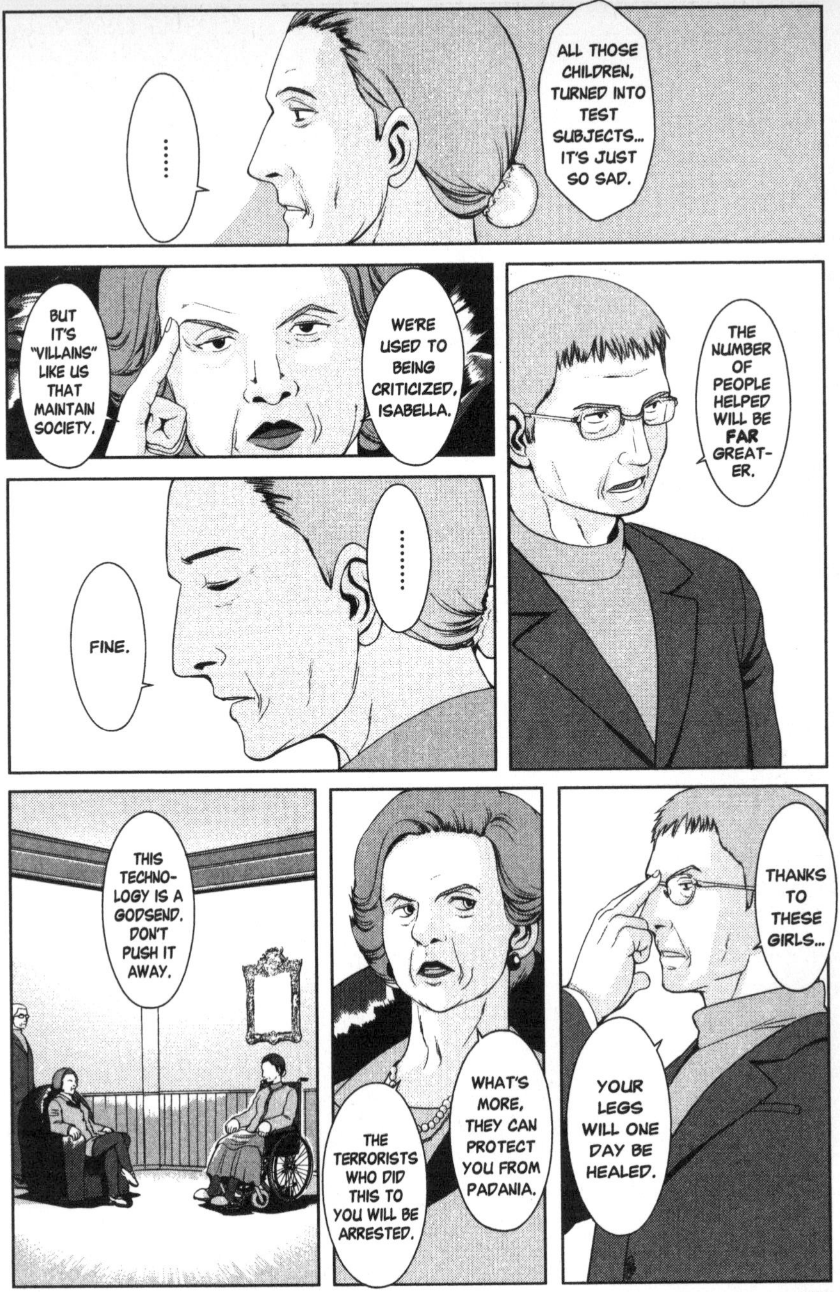
......
ALL THOSE CHILDREN, TURNED INTO TEST SUBJECTS... IT'S JUST SO SAD.
WE'RE USED TO BEING CRITICIZED, ISABELLA.
BUT IT'S "VILLAINS" LIKE US THAT MAINTAIN SOCIETY.
THE NUMBER OF PEOPLE HELPED WILL BE **FAR** GREAT-ER.
....
FINE.
THIS TECHNO-LOGY IS A GODSEND. DON'T PUSH IT AWAY.
THANKS TO THESE GIRLS...
YOUR LEGS WILL ONE DAY BE HEALED.
WHAT'S MORE, THEY CAN PROTECT YOU FROM PADANIA.
THE TERRORISTS WHO DID THIS TO YOU WILL BE ARRESTED.

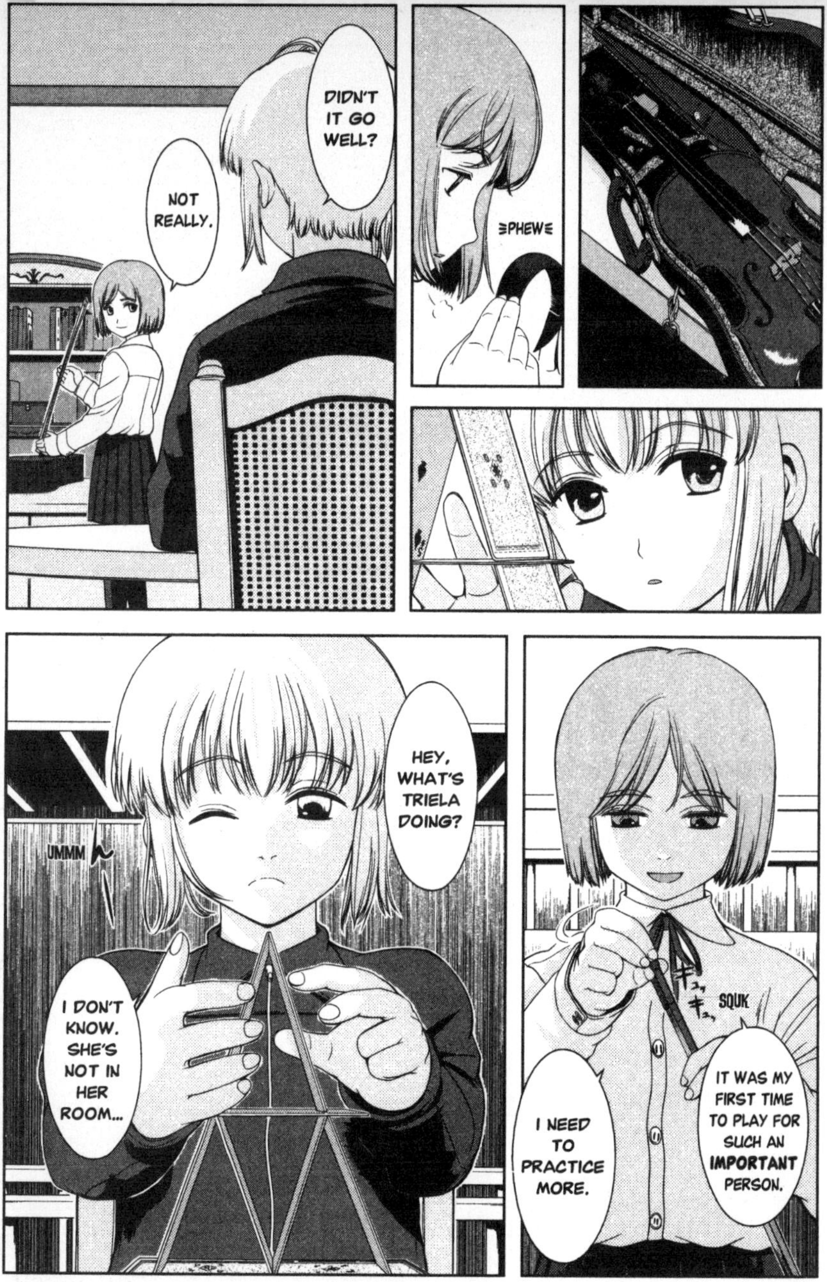

≡PHEW≡
DIDN'T IT GO WELL?
NOT REALLY.
SQUK
IT WAS MY FIRST TIME TO PLAY FOR SUCH AN **IMPORTANT** PERSON.
I NEED TO PRACTICE MORE.
UMMM
HEY, WHAT'S TRIELA DOING?
I DON'T KNOW. SHE'S NOT IN HER ROOM...

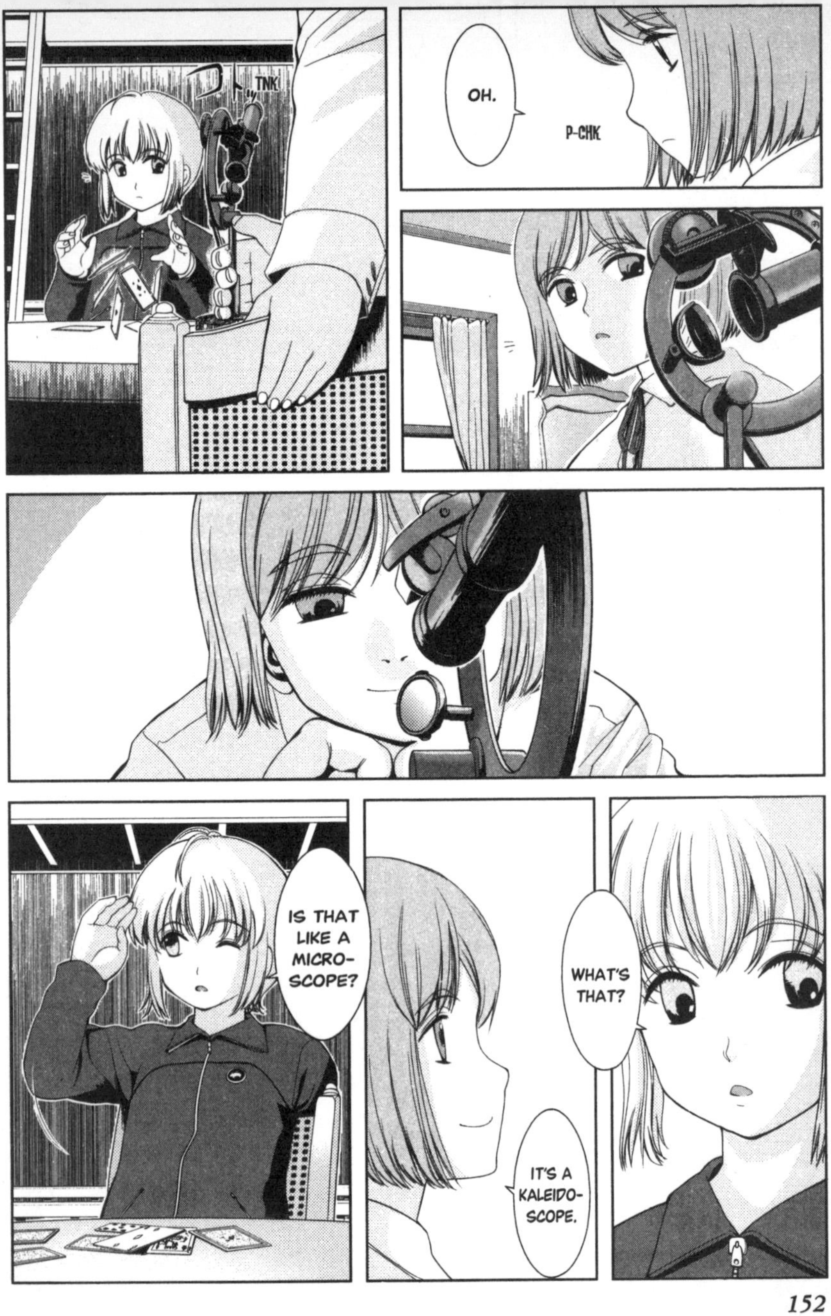
OH.
P-CHK
コト
TNK
WHAT'S THAT?
IT'S A KALEIDO-SCOPE.
IS THAT LIKE A MICRO-SCOPE?

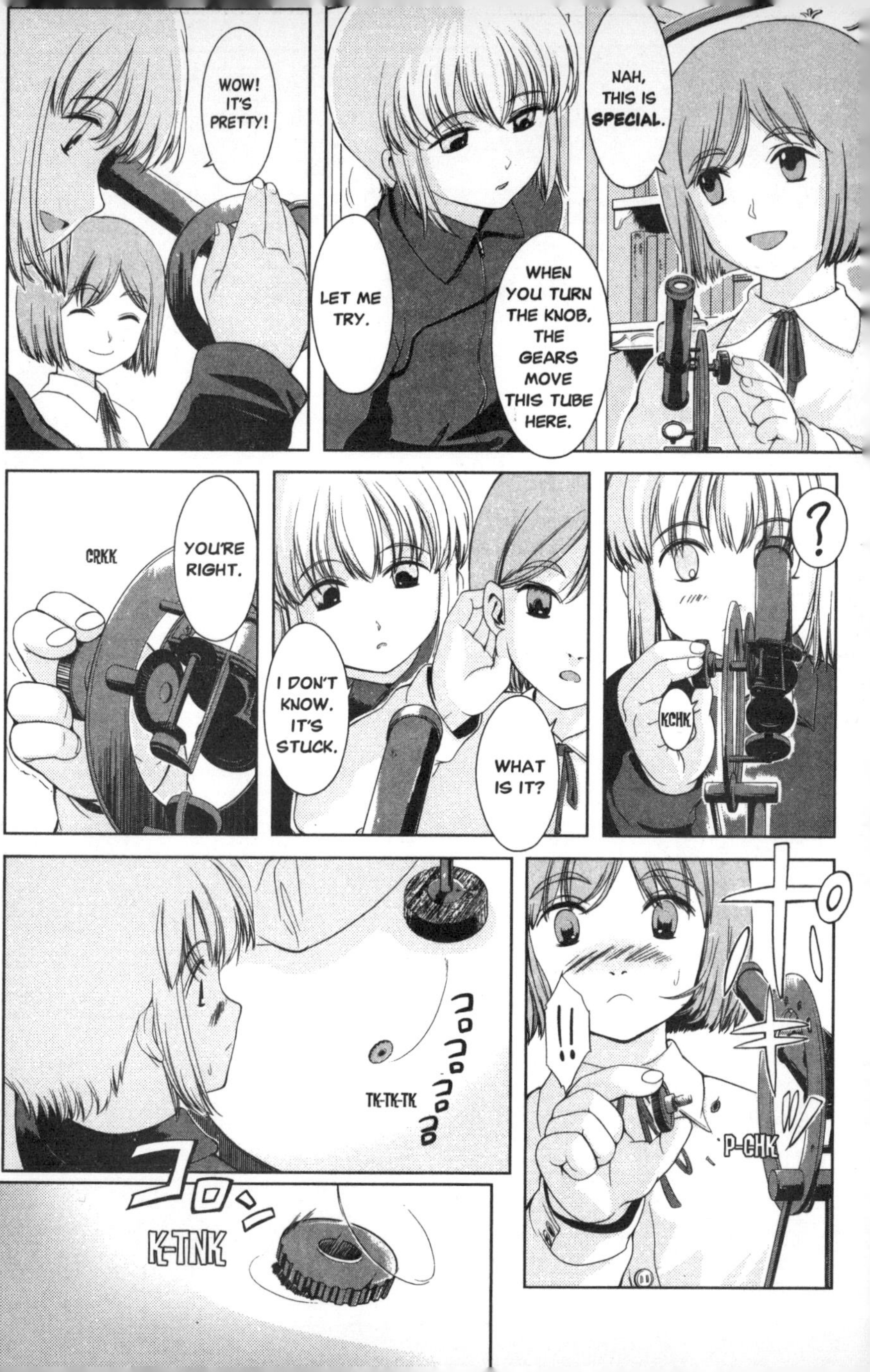
WOW! IT'S PRETTY!
NAH, THIS IS SPECIAL.
WHEN YOU TURN THE KNOB, THE GEARS MOVE THIS TUBE HERE.
LET ME TRY.
CRKK
YOU'RE RIGHT.
WHAT IS IT?
I DON'T KNOW. IT'S STUCK.
?
KCHK
TK-TK-TK
!!
P-CHK
K-TNK

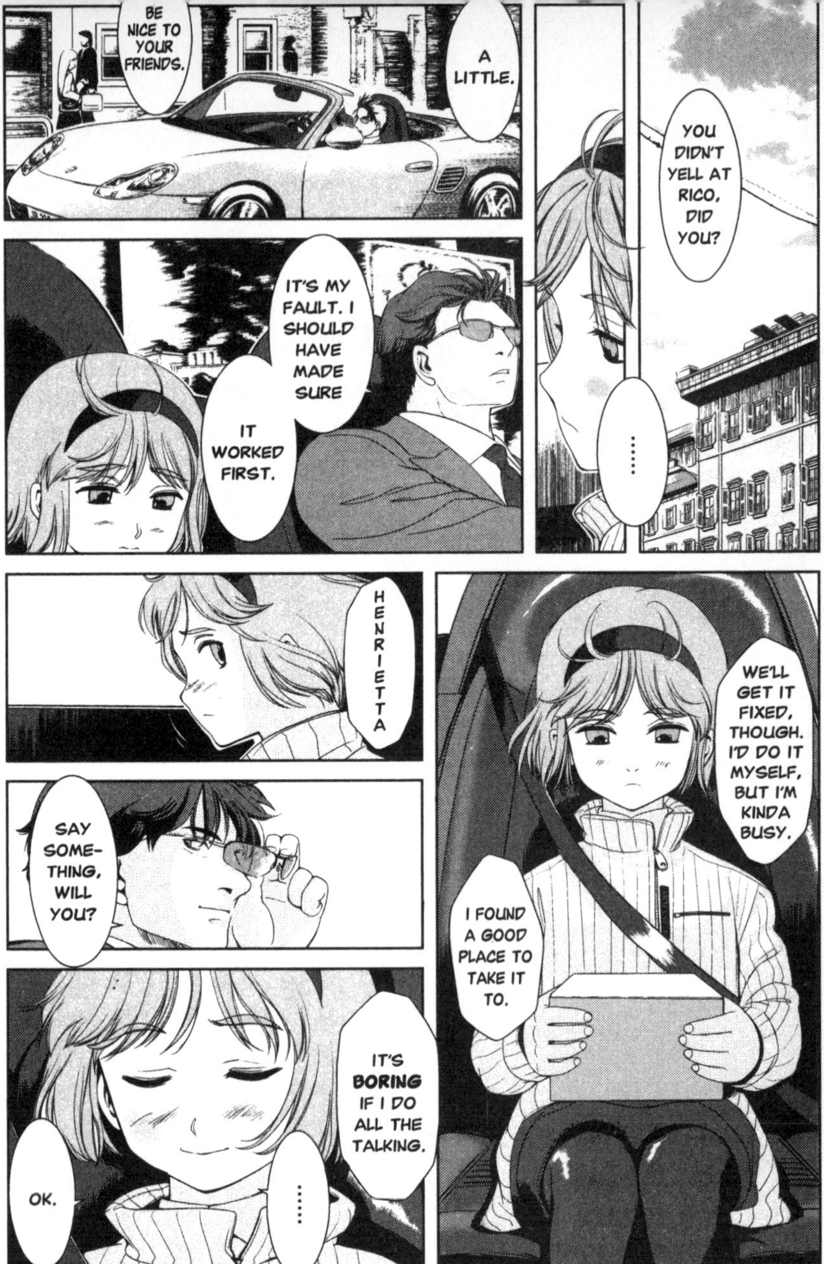
YOU DIDN'T YELL AT RICO, DID YOU?
......
A LITTLE.
BE NICE TO YOUR FRIENDS.
IT'S MY FAULT. I SHOULD HAVE MADE SURE
IT WORKED FIRST.
WE'LL GET IT FIXED, THOUGH. I'D DO IT MYSELF, BUT I'M KINDA BUSY.
I FOUND A GOOD PLACE TO TAKE IT TO.
HENRIETTA
SAY SOME-THING, WILL YOU?
IT'S **BORING** IF I DO ALL THE TALKING.
......
OK.

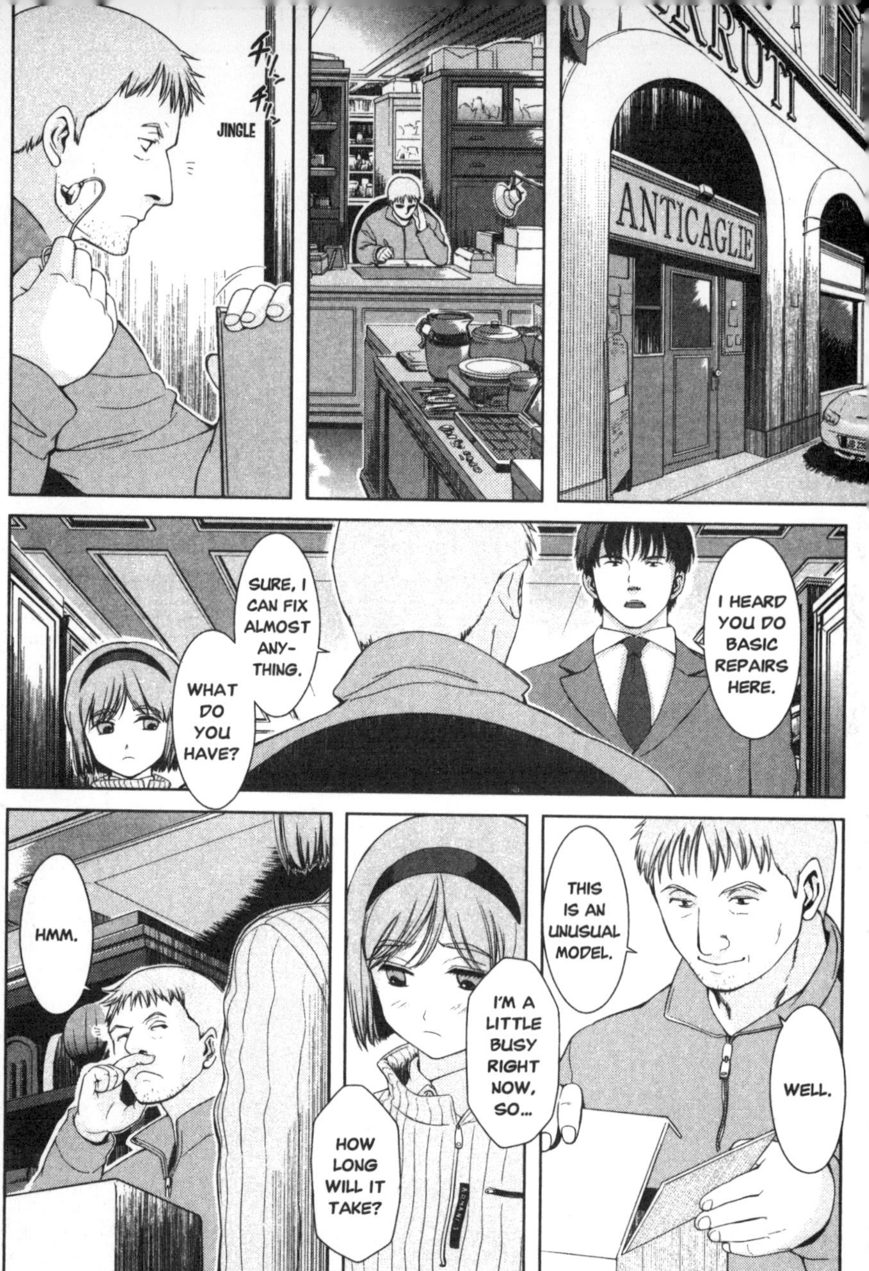
ANTICAGLIE
チリン チリン
JINGLE
I HEARD YOU DO BASIC REPAIRS HERE.
SURE, I CAN FIX ALMOST ANY-THING.
WHAT DO YOU HAVE?
WELL.
THIS IS AN UNUSUAL MODEL.
I'M A LITTLE BUSY RIGHT NOW, SO...
HOW LONG WILL IT TAKE?
HMM.

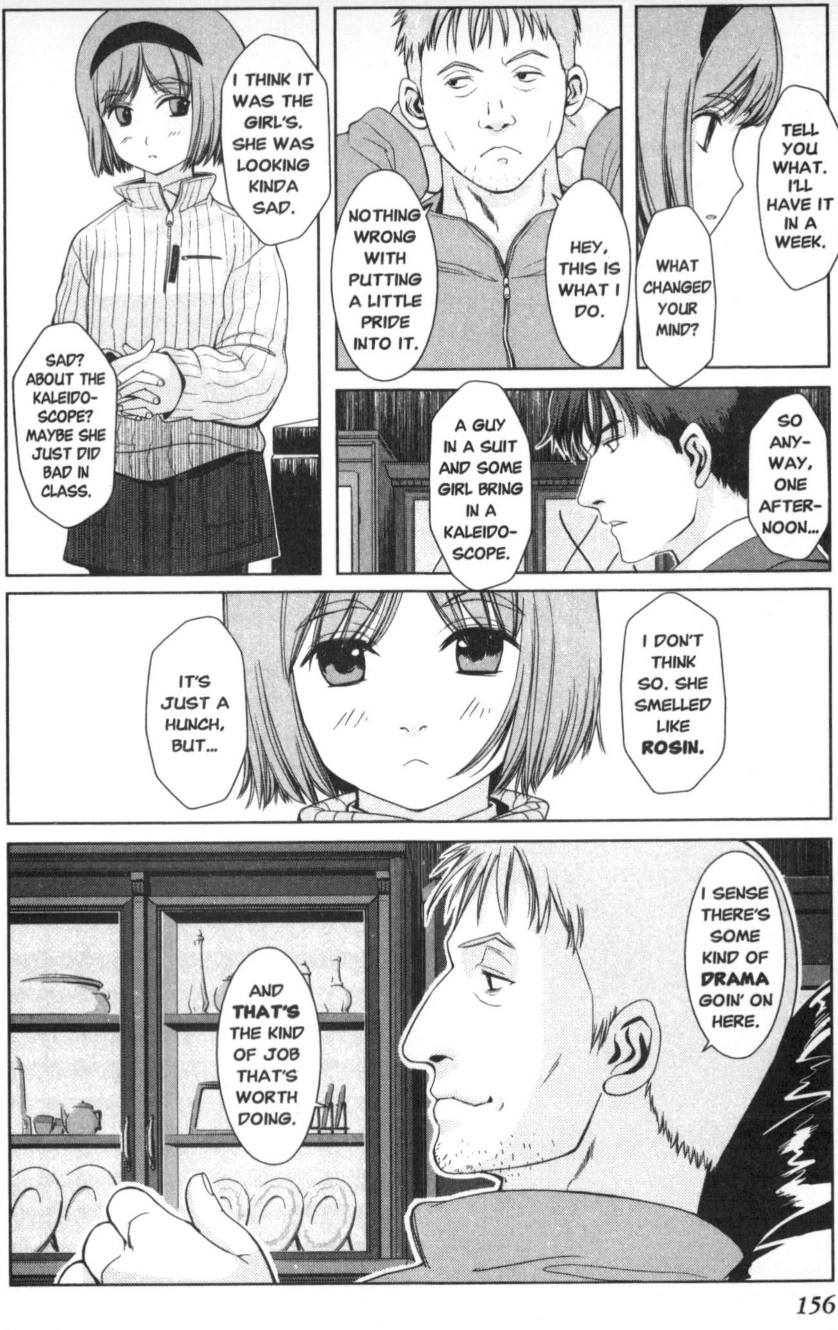
TELL YOU WHAT. I'LL HAVE IT IN A WEEK.
WHAT CHANGED YOUR MIND?
HEY, THIS IS WHAT I DO.
NOTHING WRONG WITH PUTTING A LITTLE PRIDE INTO IT.
SO ANYWAY, ONE AFTERNOON...
A GUY IN A SUIT AND SOME GIRL BRING IN A KALEIDOSCOPE.
I THINK IT WAS THE GIRL'S. SHE WAS LOOKING KINDA SAD.
SAD? ABOUT THE KALEIDOSCOPE? MAYBE SHE JUST DID BAD IN CLASS.
I DON'T THINK SO. SHE SMELLED LIKE **ROSIN.**
IT'S JUST A HUNCH, BUT...
I SENSE THERE'S SOME KIND OF **DRAMA** GOIN' ON HERE.
AND **THAT'S** THE KIND OF JOB THAT'S WORTH DOING.

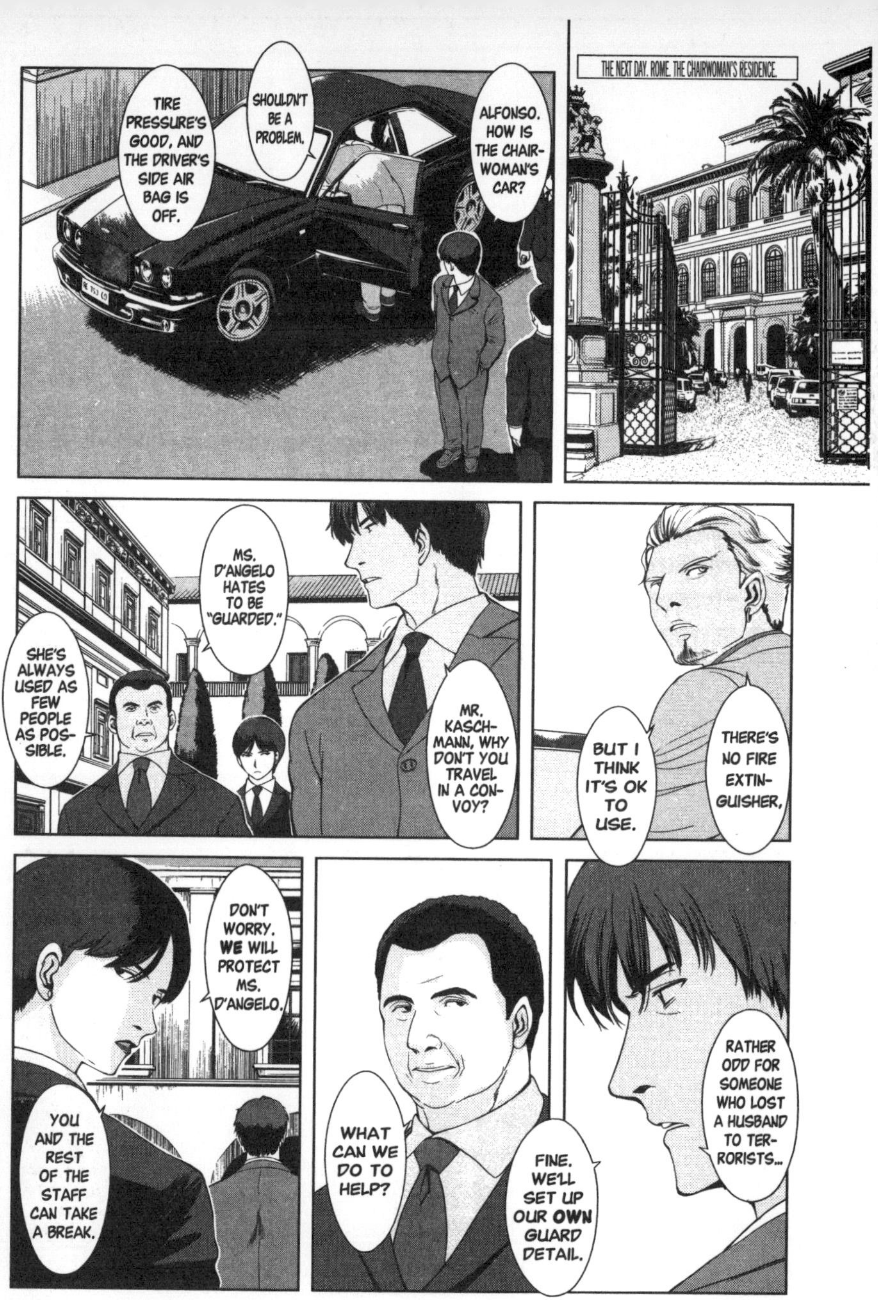
THE NEXT DAY. ROME. THE CHAIRWOMAN'S RESIDENCE.
ALFONSO. HOW IS THE CHAIRWOMAN'S CAR?
SHOULDN'T BE A PROBLEM.
TIRE PRESSURE'S GOOD, AND THE DRIVER'S SIDE AIR BAG IS OFF.
THERE'S NO FIRE EXTINGUISHER,
BUT I THINK IT'S OK TO USE.
MR. KASCHMANN, WHY DON'T YOU TRAVEL IN A CONVOY?
MS. D'ANGELO HATES TO BE "GUARDED."
SHE'S ALWAYS USED AS FEW PEOPLE AS POSSIBLE.
RATHER ODD FOR SOMEONE WHO LOST A HUSBAND TO TERRORISTS...
FINE. WE'LL SET UP OUR **OWN** GUARD DETAIL.
WHAT CAN WE DO TO HELP?
DON'T WORRY. **WE** WILL PROTECT MS. D'ANGELO.
YOU AND THE REST OF THE STAFF CAN TAKE A BREAK.

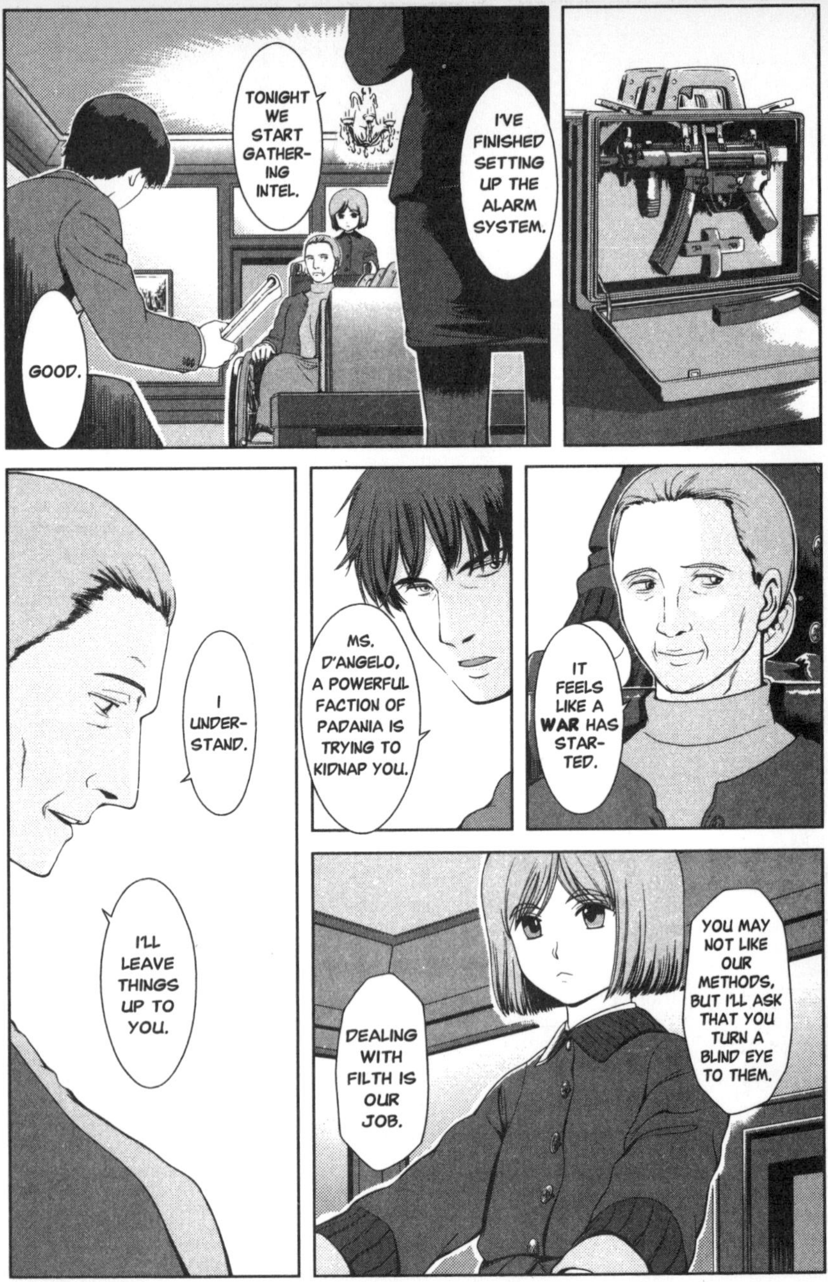
TONIGHT WE START GATHERING INTEL.
GOOD.
I'VE FINISHED SETTING UP THE ALARM SYSTEM.
MS. D'ANGELO, A POWERFUL FACTION OF PADANIA IS TRYING TO KIDNAP YOU.
IT FEELS LIKE A **WAR** HAS STARTED.
YOU MAY NOT LIKE OUR METHODS, BUT I'LL ASK THAT YOU TURN A BLIND EYE TO THEM.
DEALING WITH FILTH IS OUR JOB.
I UNDERSTAND.
I'LL LEAVE THINGS UP TO YOU.

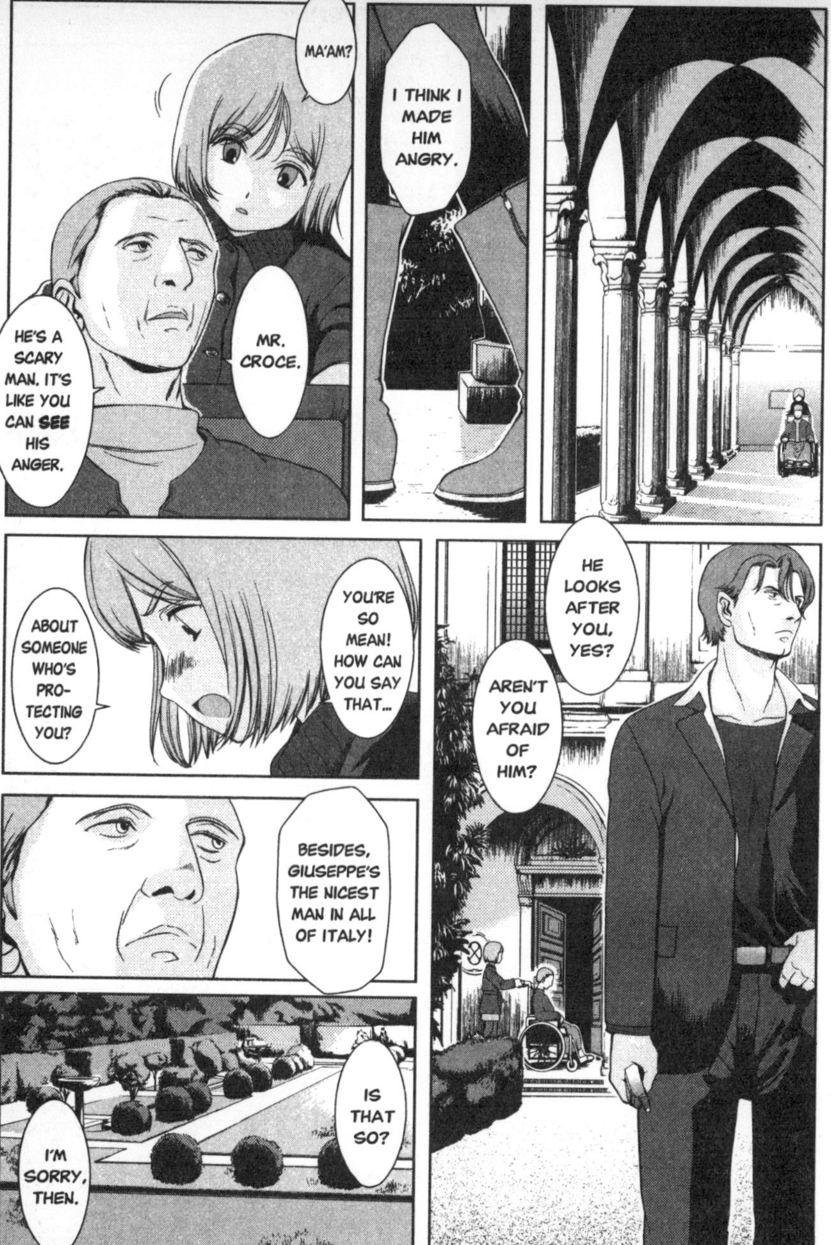
I THINK I MADE HIM ANGRY.
MA'AM?
MR. CROCE.
HE'S A SCARY MAN. IT'S LIKE YOU CAN **SEE** HIS ANGER.
HE LOOKS AFTER YOU, YES?
AREN'T YOU AFRAID OF HIM?
YOU'RE SO MEAN! HOW CAN YOU SAY THAT...
ABOUT SOMEONE WHO'S PRO-TECTING YOU?
BESIDES, GIUSEPPE'S THE NICEST MAN IN ALL OF ITALY!
IS THAT SO?
I'M SORRY, THEN.

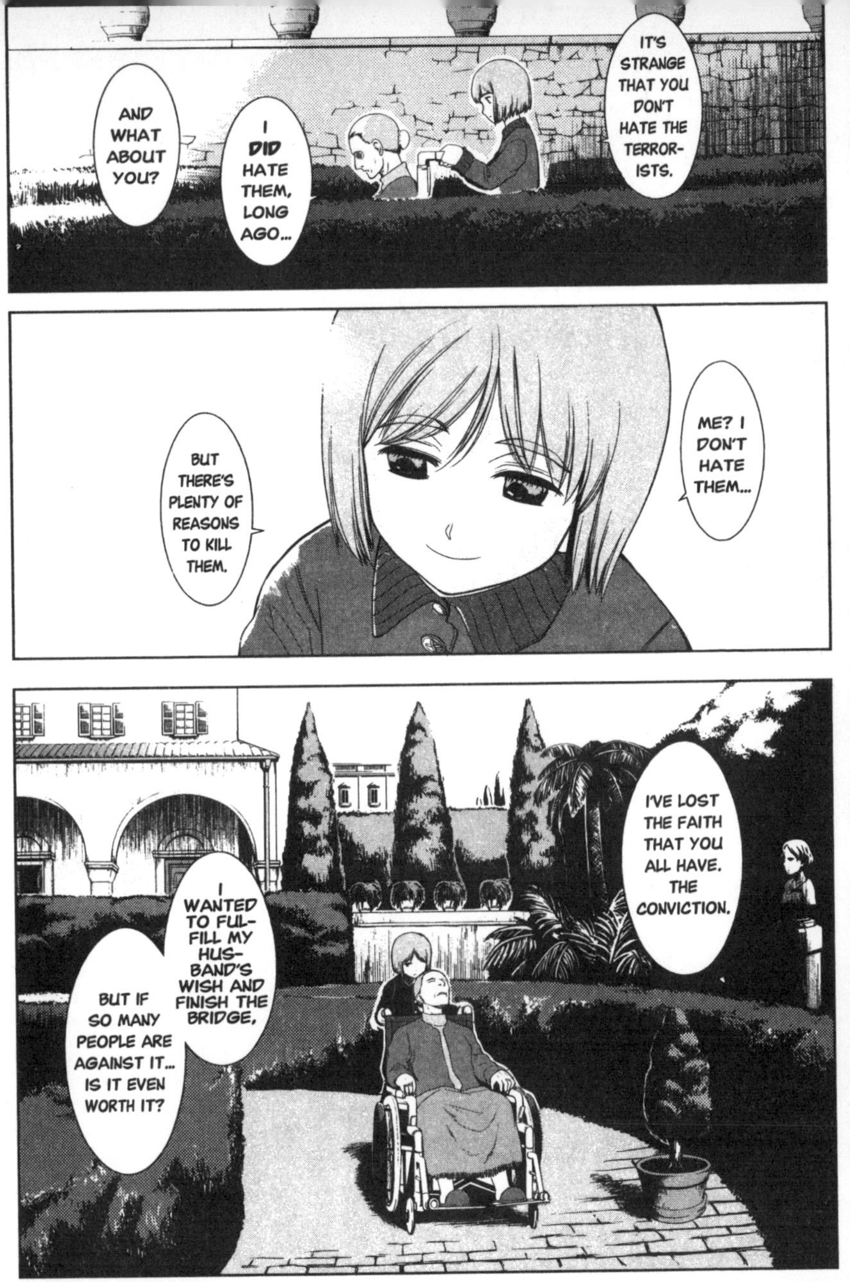
IT'S STRANGE THAT YOU DON'T HATE THE TERRORISTS.
I DID HATE THEM, LONG AGO...
AND WHAT ABOUT YOU?
ME? I DON'T HATE THEM...
BUT THERE'S PLENTY OF REASONS TO KILL THEM.
I'VE LOST THE FAITH THAT YOU ALL HAVE. THE CONVICTION.
I WANTED TO FULFILL MY HUSBAND'S WISH AND FINISH THE BRIDGE,
BUT IF SO MANY PEOPLE ARE AGAINST IT... IS IT EVEN WORTH IT?

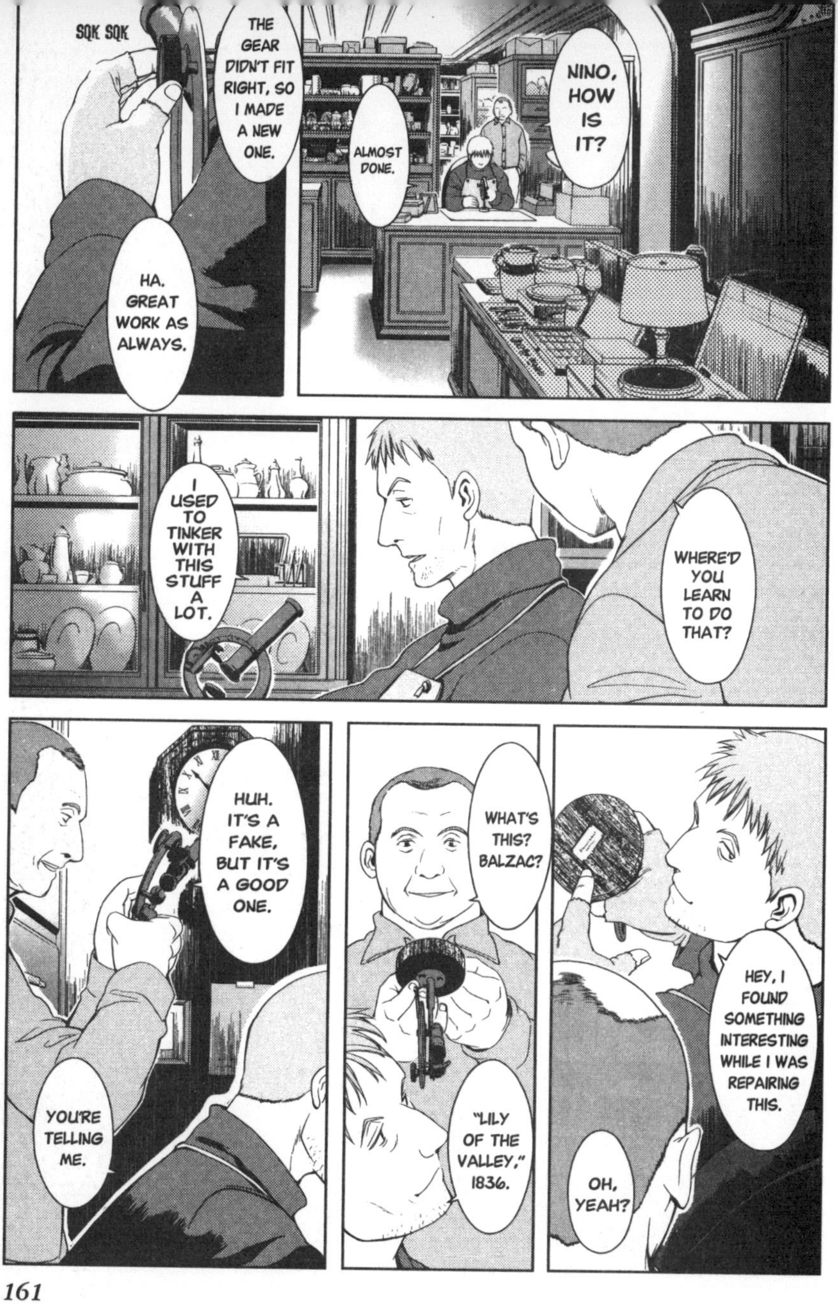
NINO, HOW IS IT?
ALMOST DONE.
THE GEAR DIDN'T FIT RIGHT, SO I MADE A NEW ONE.
SQK SQK
HA. GREAT WORK AS ALWAYS.
WHERE'D YOU LEARN TO DO THAT?
I USED TO TINKER WITH THIS STUFF A LOT.
HEY, I FOUND SOMETHING INTERESTING WHILE I WAS REPAIRING THIS.
OH, YEAH?
WHAT'S THIS? BALZAC?
"LILY OF THE VALLEY," 1836.
HUH. IT'S A FAKE, BUT IT'S A GOOD ONE.
YOU'RE TELLING ME.

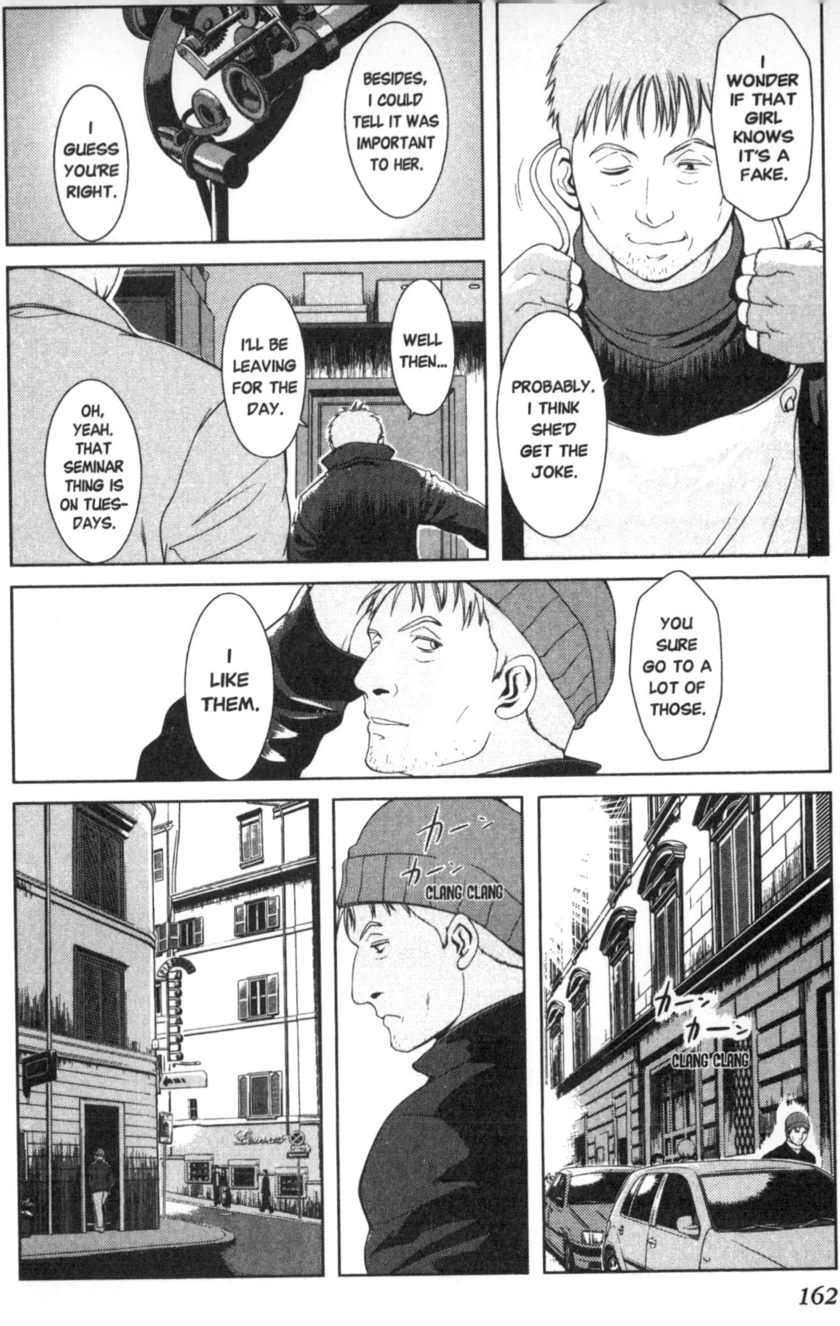
I WONDER IF THAT GIRL KNOWS IT'S A FAKE.
PROBABLY. I THINK SHE'D GET THE JOKE.
BESIDES, I COULD TELL IT WAS IMPORTANT TO HER.
I GUESS YOU'RE RIGHT.
WELL THEN...
I'LL BE LEAVING FOR THE DAY.
OH, YEAH. THAT SEMINAR THING IS ON TUES-DAYS.
YOU SURE GO TO A LOT OF THOSE.
I LIKE THEM.
カーン カーン
CLANG CLANG
カーン カーン
CLANG CLANG

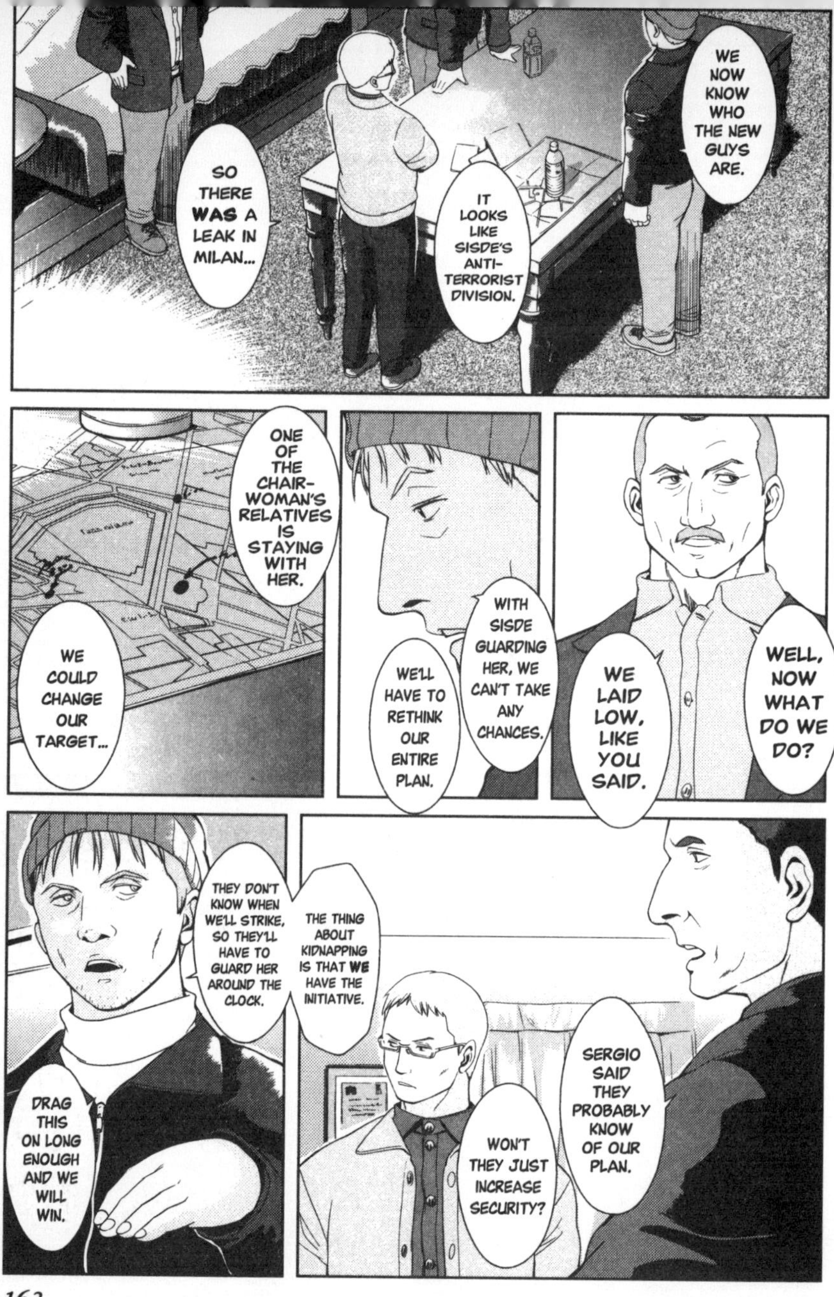
WE NOW KNOW WHO THE NEW GUYS ARE.
IT LOOKS LIKE SISDE'S ANTI-TERRORIST DIVISION.
SO THERE **WAS** A LEAK IN MILAN...
WELL, NOW WHAT DO WE DO?
WE LAID LOW, LIKE YOU SAID.
WITH SISDE GUARDING HER, WE CAN'T TAKE ANY CHANCES.
WE'LL HAVE TO RETHINK OUR ENTIRE PLAN.
ONE OF THE CHAIR-WOMAN'S RELATIVES IS STAYING WITH HER.
WE COULD CHANGE OUR TARGET...
SERGIO SAID THEY PROBABLY KNOW OF OUR PLAN.
WON'T THEY JUST INCREASE SECURITY?
THE THING ABOUT KIDNAPPING IS THAT **WE** HAVE THE INITIATIVE.
THEY DON'T KNOW WHEN WE'LL STRIKE, SO THEY'LL HAVE TO GUARD HER AROUND THE CLOCK.
DRAG THIS ON LONG ENOUGH AND WE WILL WIN.

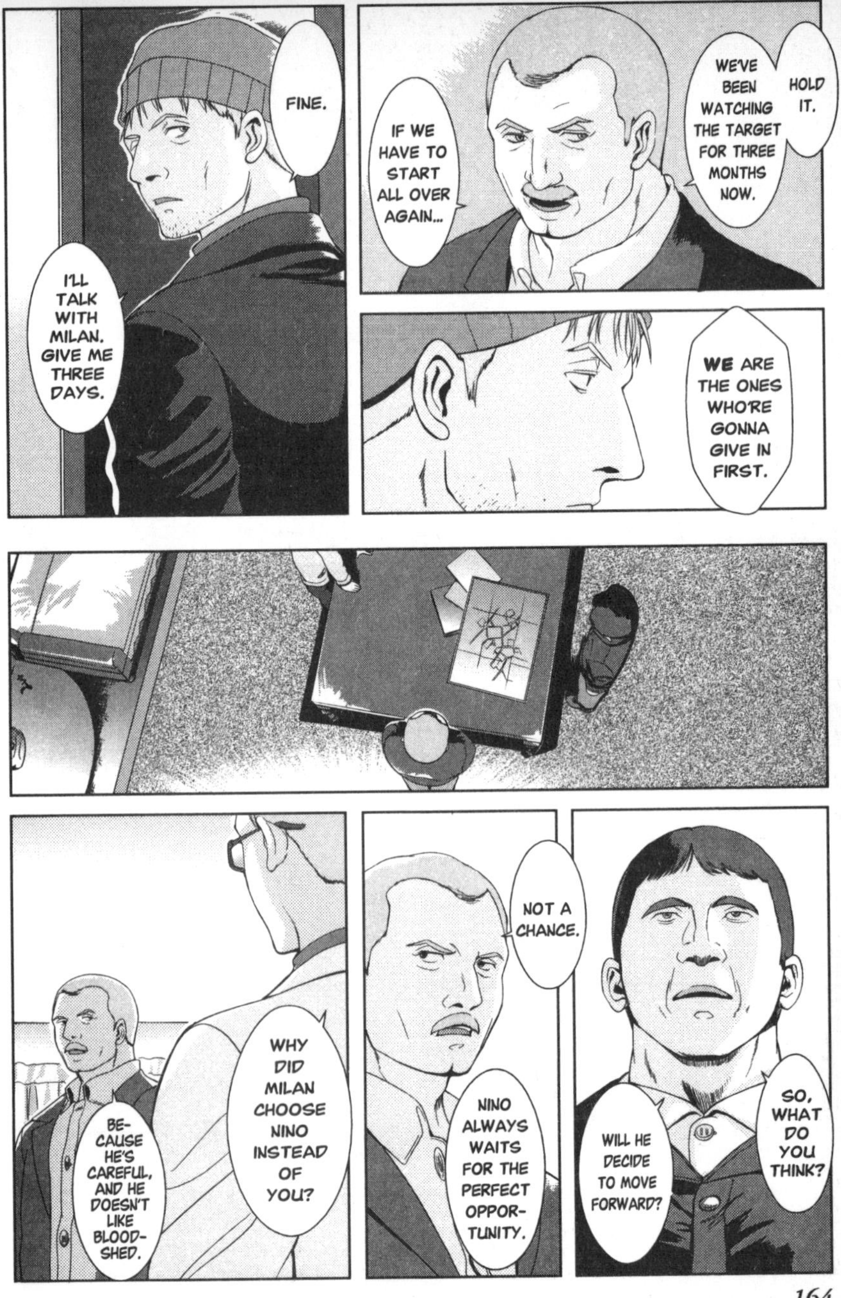
HOLD IT.
WE'VE BEEN WATCHING THE TARGET FOR THREE MONTHS NOW.
IF WE HAVE TO START ALL OVER AGAIN...
WE ARE THE ONES WHO'RE GONNA GIVE IN FIRST.
FINE.
I'LL TALK WITH MILAN. GIVE ME THREE DAYS.
SO, WHAT DO YOU THINK?
WILL HE DECIDE TO MOVE FORWARD?
NOT A CHANCE.
NINO ALWAYS WAITS FOR THE PERFECT OPPOR-TUNITY.
WHY DID MILAN CHOOSE NINO INSTEAD OF YOU?
BE-CAUSE HE'S CAREFUL, AND HE DOESN'T LIKE BLOOD-SHED.

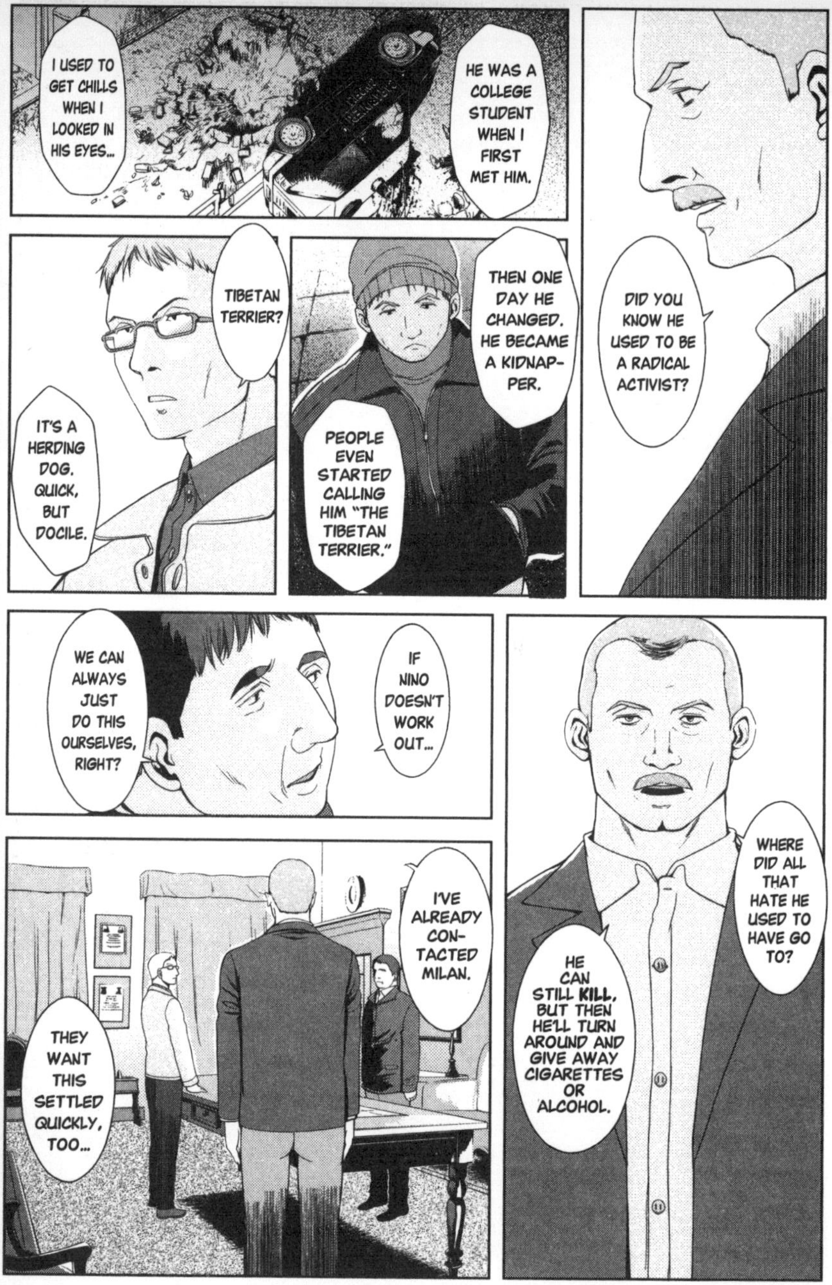
DID YOU KNOW HE USED TO BE A RADICAL ACTIVIST?
HE WAS A COLLEGE STUDENT WHEN I FIRST MET HIM.
I USED TO GET CHILLS WHEN I LOOKED IN HIS EYES...
THEN ONE DAY HE CHANGED. HE BECAME A KIDNAP-PER.
PEOPLE EVEN STARTED CALLING HIM "THE TIBETAN TERRIER."
TIBETAN TERRIER?
IT'S A HERDING DOG. QUICK, BUT DOCILE.
WHERE DID ALL THAT HATE HE USED TO HAVE GO TO?
HE CAN STILL **KILL**, BUT THEN HE'LL TURN AROUND AND GIVE AWAY CIGARETTES OR ALCOHOL.
IF NINO DOESN'T WORK OUT...
WE CAN ALWAYS JUST DO THIS OURSELVES, RIGHT?
I'VE ALREADY CON-TACTED MILAN.
THEY WANT THIS SETTLED QUICKLY, TOO...

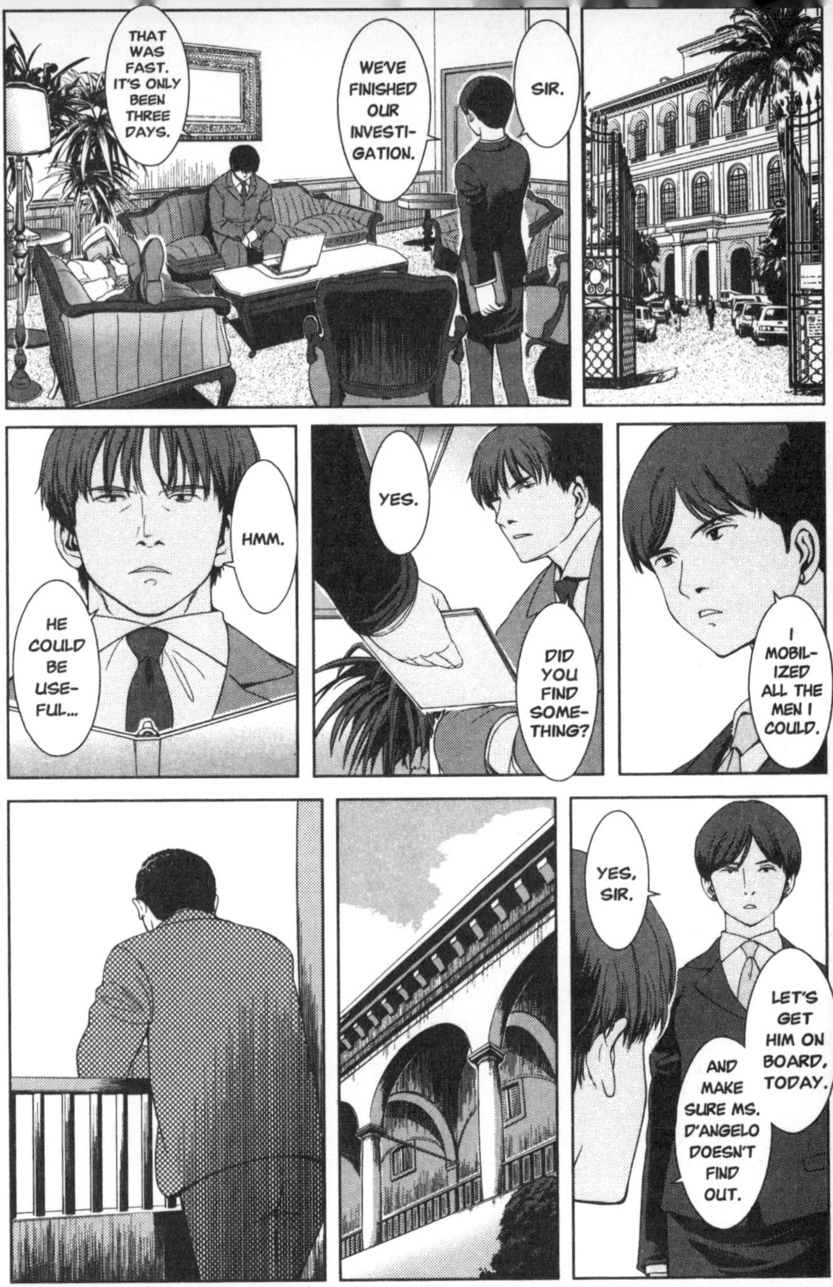
SIR.
WE'VE FINISHED OUR INVESTIGATION.
THAT WAS FAST. IT'S ONLY BEEN THREE DAYS.
I MOBILIZED ALL THE MEN I COULD.
DID YOU FIND SOMETHING?
YES.
HMM.
HE COULD BE USEFUL...
LET'S GET HIM ON BOARD, TODAY.
AND MAKE SURE MS. D'ANGELO DOESN'T FIND OUT.
YES, SIR.

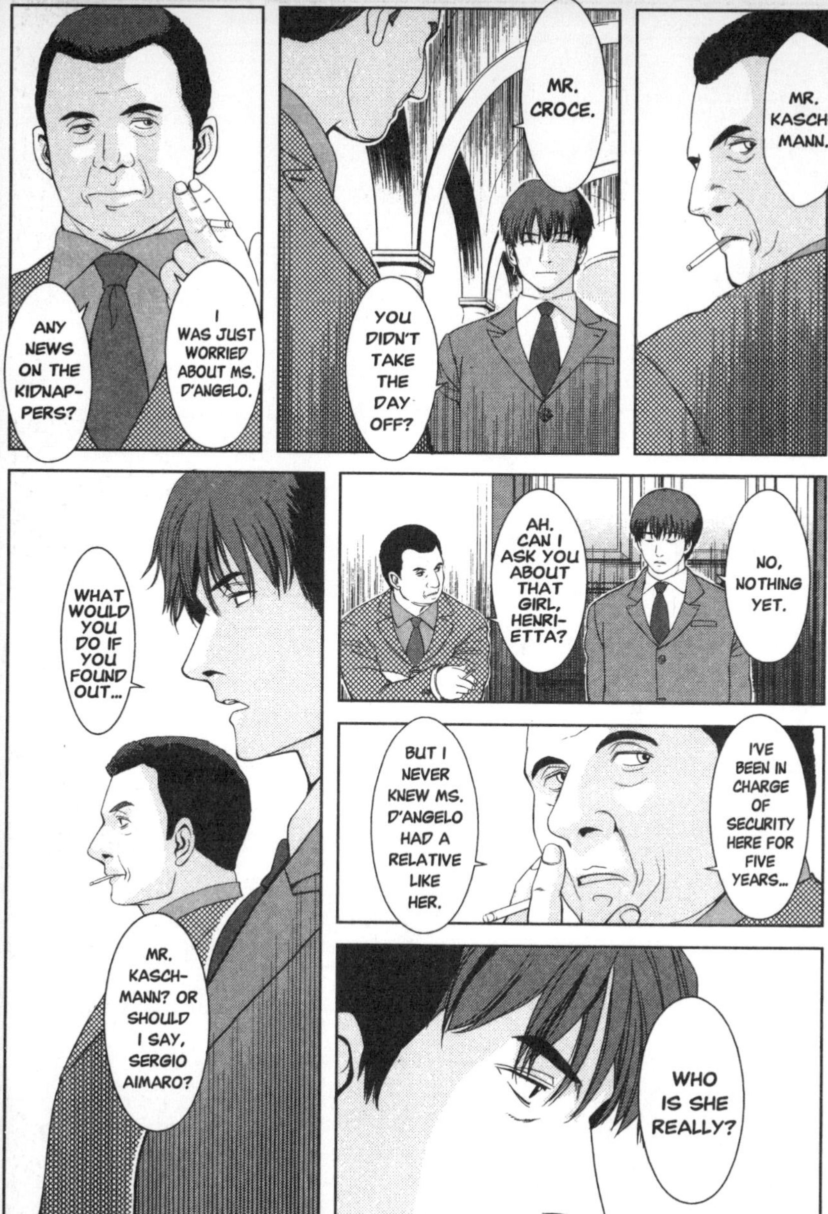
MR. KASCHMANN.
MR. CROCE.
YOU DIDN'T TAKE THE DAY OFF?
I WAS JUST WORRIED ABOUT MS. D'ANGELO.
ANY NEWS ON THE KIDNAPPERS?
NO, NOTHING YET.
AH. CAN I ASK YOU ABOUT THAT GIRL, HENRIETTA?
I'VE BEEN IN CHARGE OF SECURITY HERE FOR FIVE YEARS...
BUT I NEVER KNEW MS. D'ANGELO HAD A RELATIVE LIKE HER.
WHO IS SHE REALLY?
WHAT WOULD YOU DO IF YOU FOUND OUT...
MR. KASCHMANN? OR SHOULD I SAY, SERGIO AIMARO?

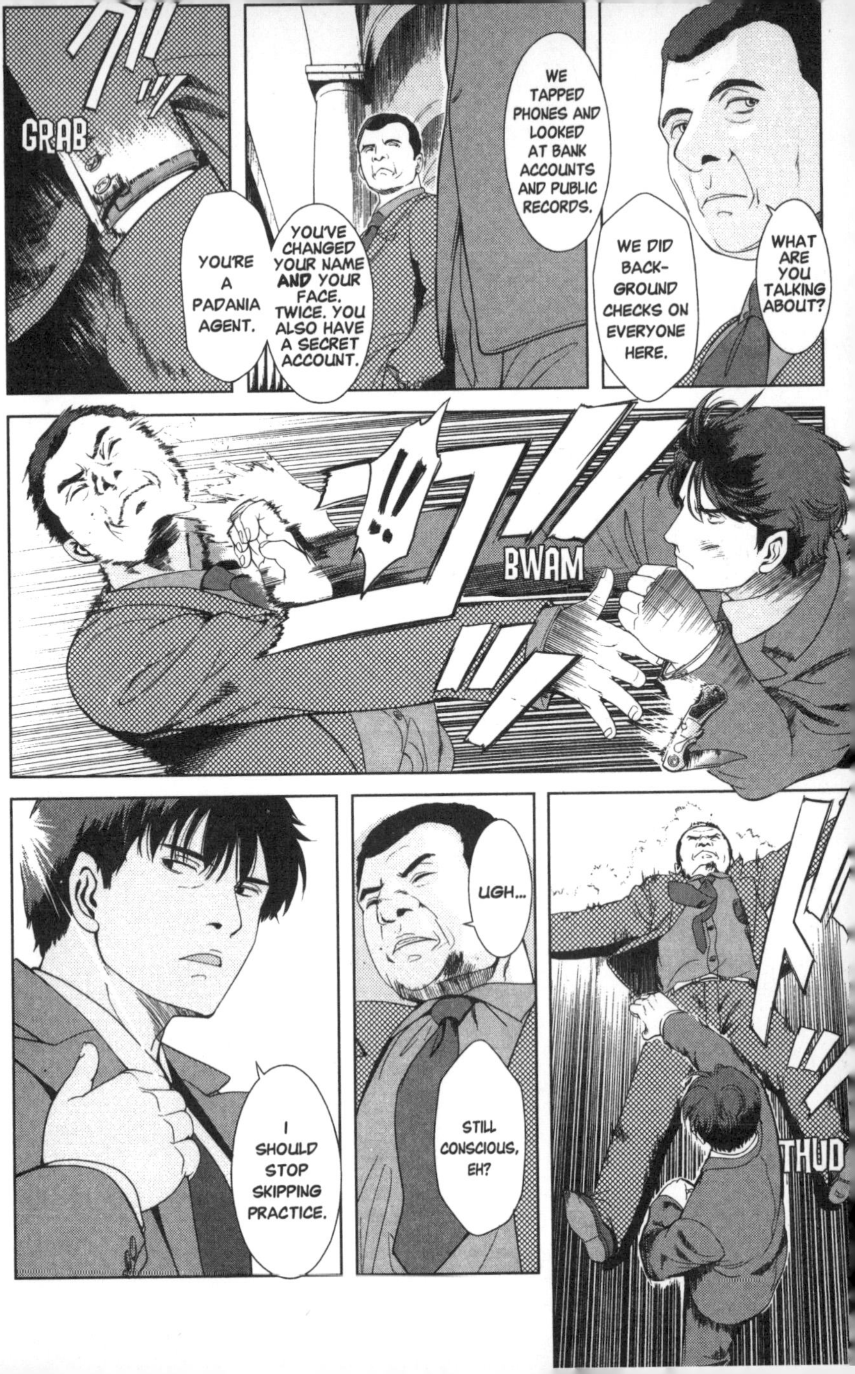
WHAT ARE YOU TALKING ABOUT?
WE DID BACK-GROUND CHECKS ON EVERYONE HERE.
WE TAPPED PHONES AND LOOKED AT BANK ACCOUNTS AND PUBLIC RECORDS.
YOU'VE CHANGED YOUR NAME AND YOUR FACE. TWICE. YOU ALSO HAVE A SECRET ACCOUNT.
YOU'RE A PADANIA AGENT.
GRAB
BWAM
THUD
UGH...
STILL CONSCIOUS, EH?
I SHOULD STOP SKIPPING PRACTICE.

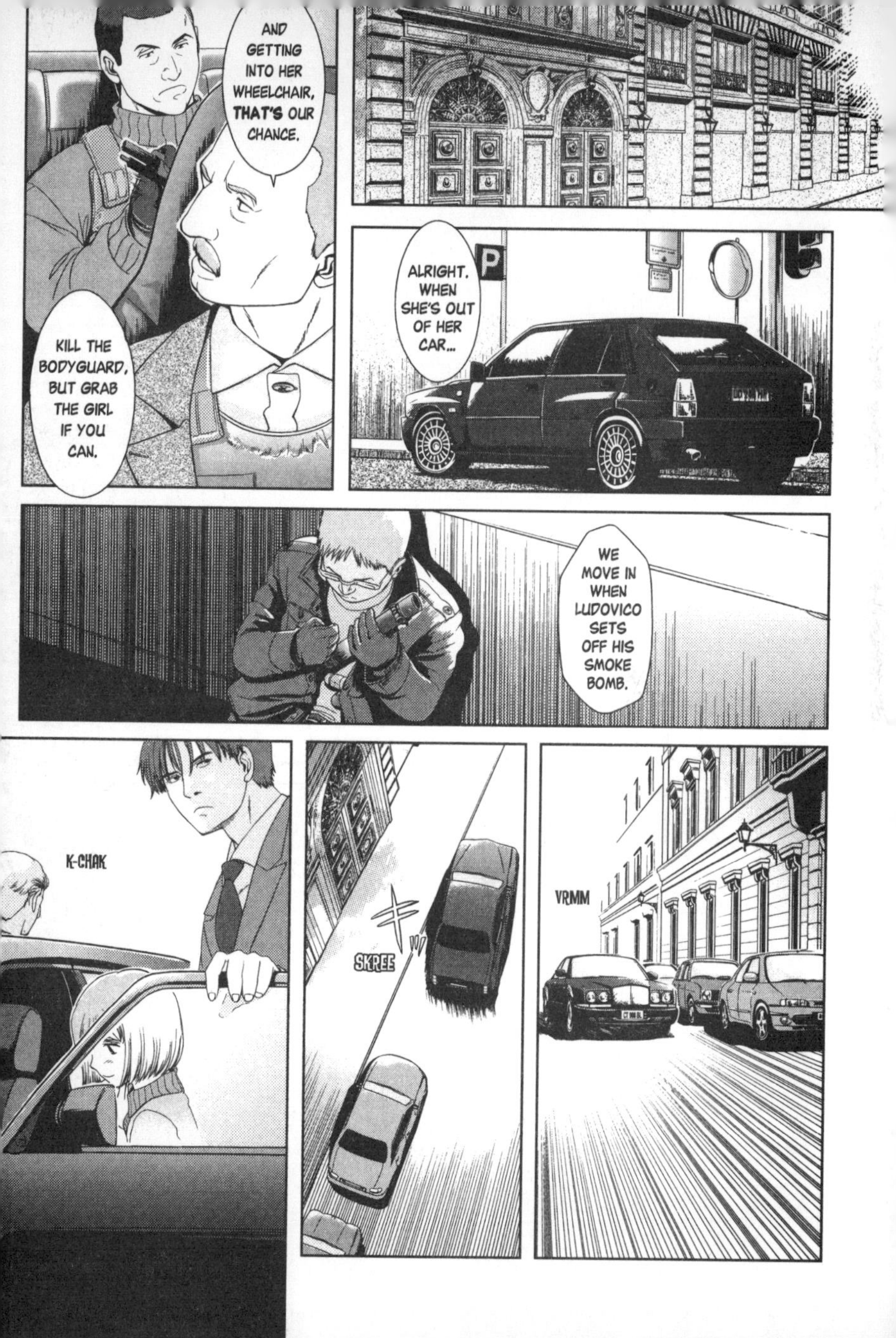
ALRIGHT. WHEN SHE'S OUT OF HER CAR...
AND GETTING INTO HER WHEELCHAIR, **THAT'S** OUR CHANCE.
KILL THE BODYGUARD, BUT GRAB THE GIRL IF YOU CAN.
WE MOVE IN WHEN LUDOVICO SETS OFF HIS SMOKE BOMB.
VRMM
SKREE
K-CHAK

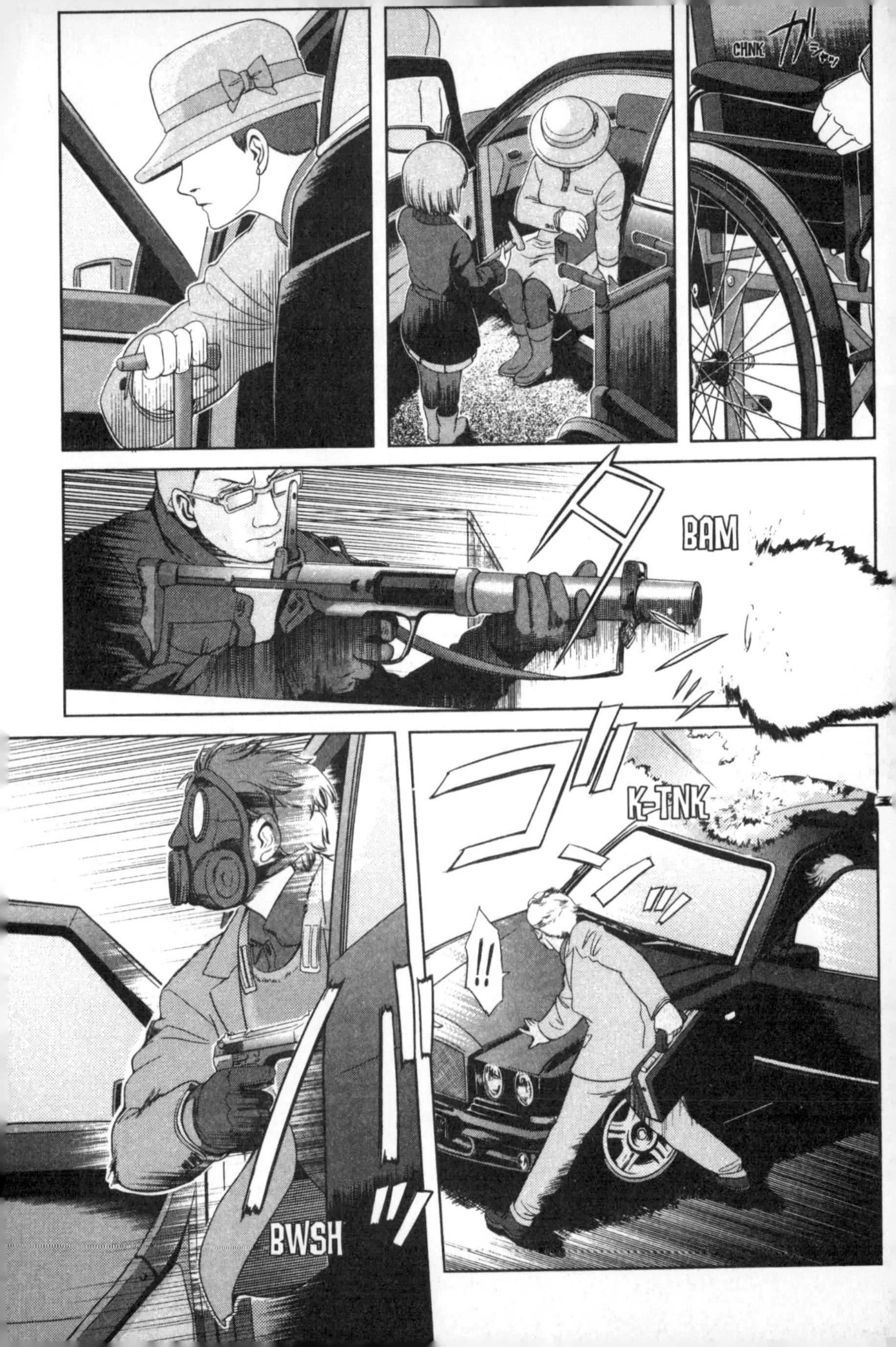
CHNK
ガシャッ
BAM
K-TNK
!!
BWSH

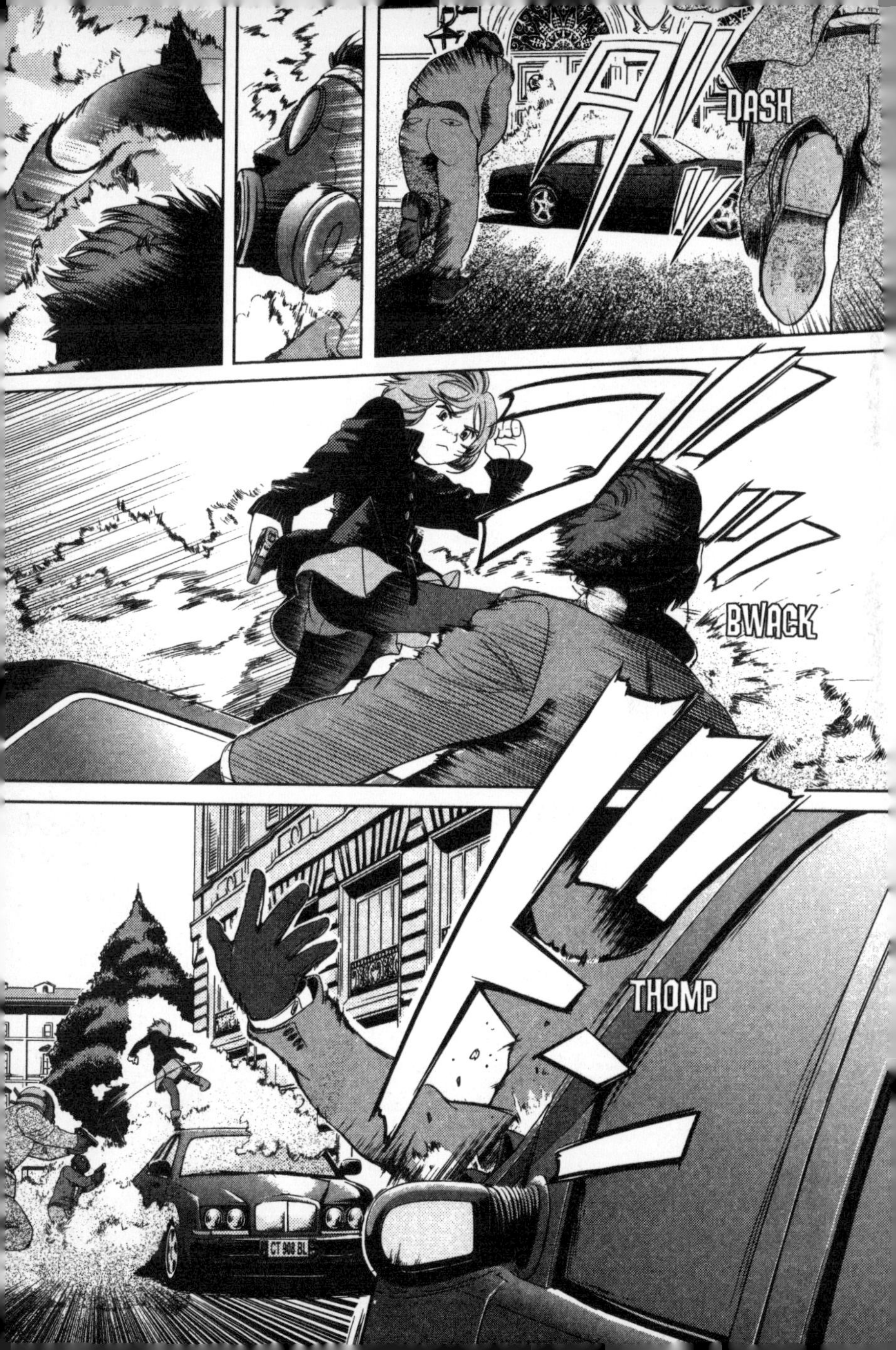
DASH
BWACK
THOMP
CT 908 BL

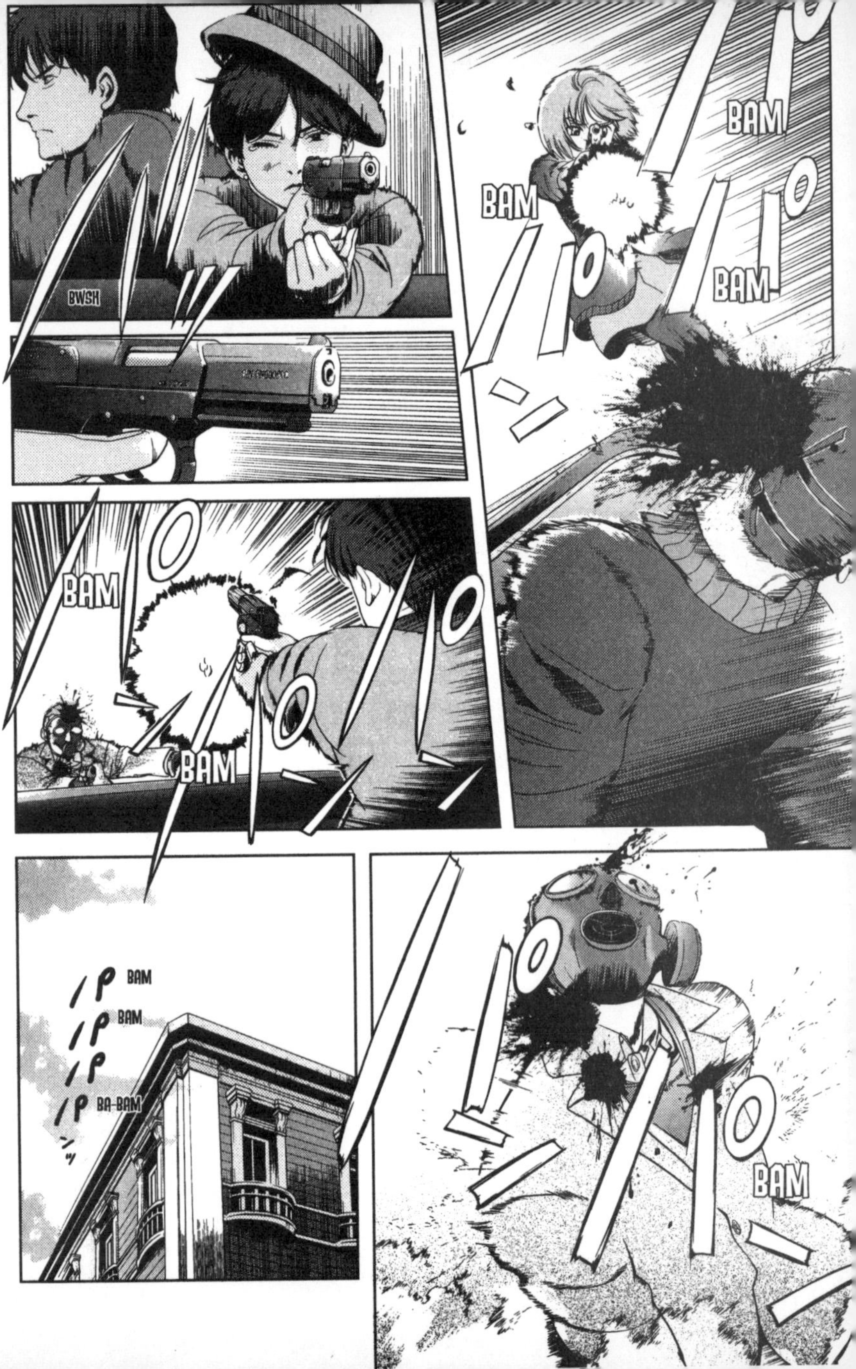
BAM
BAM
BAM
BWSH
BAM
BAM
BAM
BAM
BAM
BA-BAM

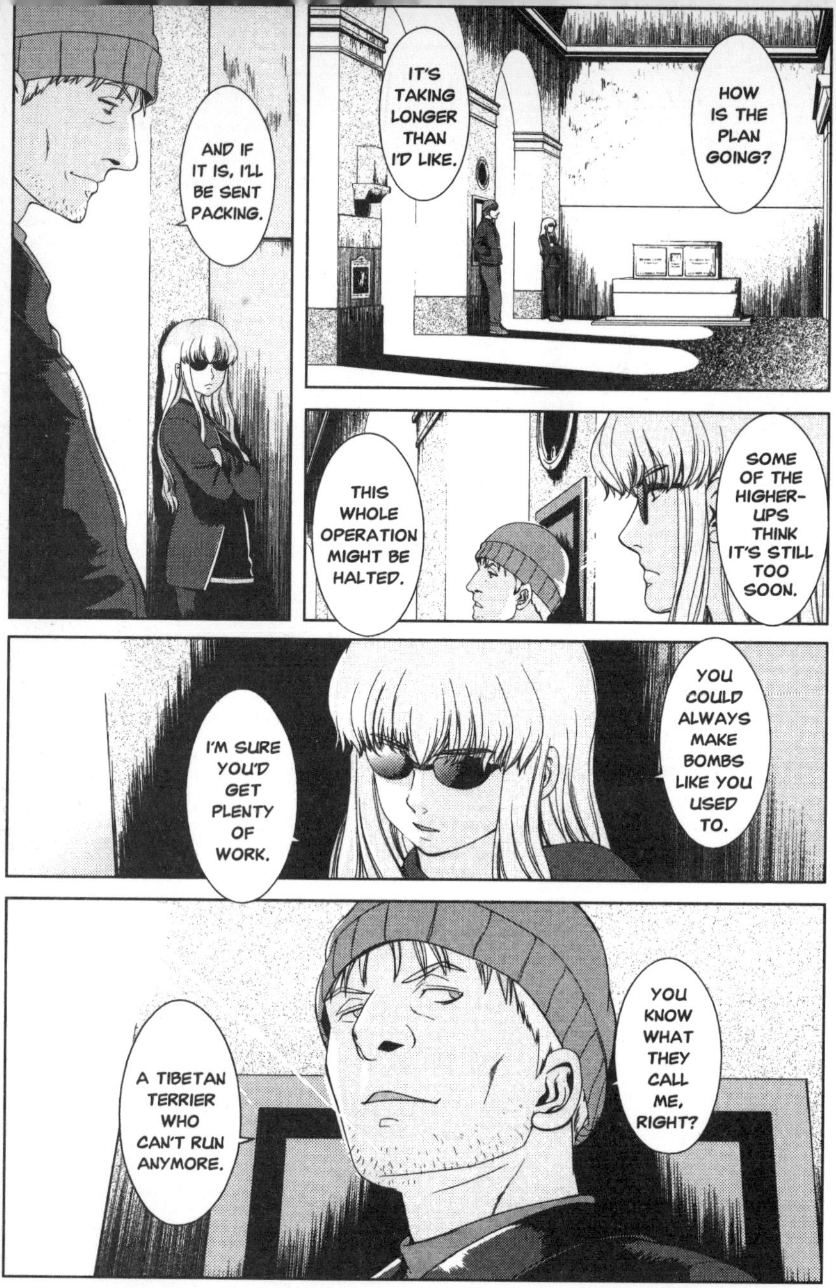
HOW IS THE PLAN GOING?
IT'S TAKING LONGER THAN I'D LIKE.
SOME OF THE HIGHER-UPS THINK IT'S STILL TOO SOON.
THIS WHOLE OPERATION MIGHT BE HALTED.
AND IF IT IS, I'LL BE SENT PACKING.
YOU COULD ALWAYS MAKE BOMBS LIKE YOU USED TO.
I'M SURE YOU'D GET PLENTY OF WORK.
YOU KNOW WHAT THEY CALL ME, RIGHT?
A TIBETAN TERRIER WHO CAN'T RUN ANYMORE.

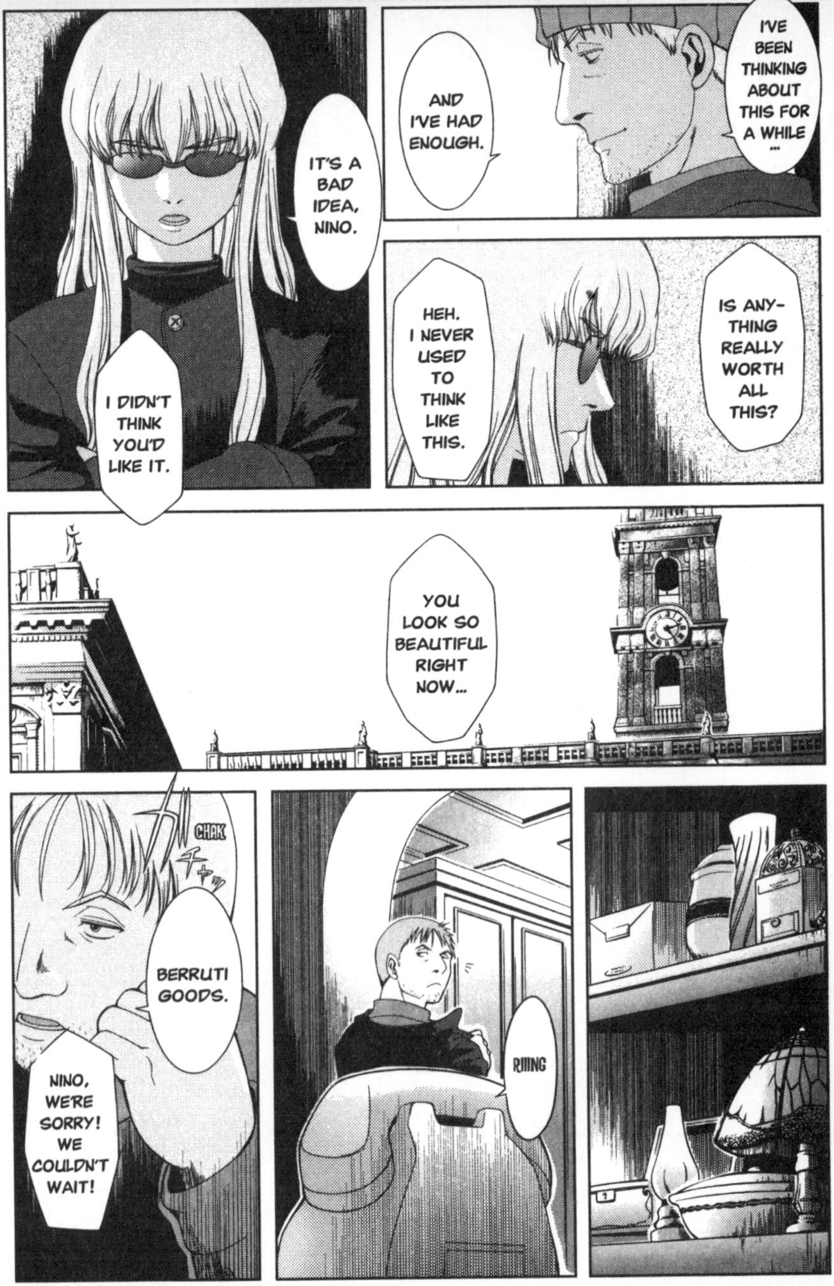
I'VE BEEN THINKING ABOUT THIS FOR A WHILE ...
AND I'VE HAD ENOUGH.
IT'S A BAD IDEA, NINO.
I DIDN'T THINK YOU'D LIKE IT.
IS ANY-THING REALLY WORTH ALL THIS?
HEH. I NEVER USED TO THINK LIKE THIS.
YOU LOOK SO BEAUTIFUL RIGHT NOW...
RIIING
CHAK
BERRUTI GOODS.
NINO, WE'RE SORRY! WE COULDN'T WAIT!

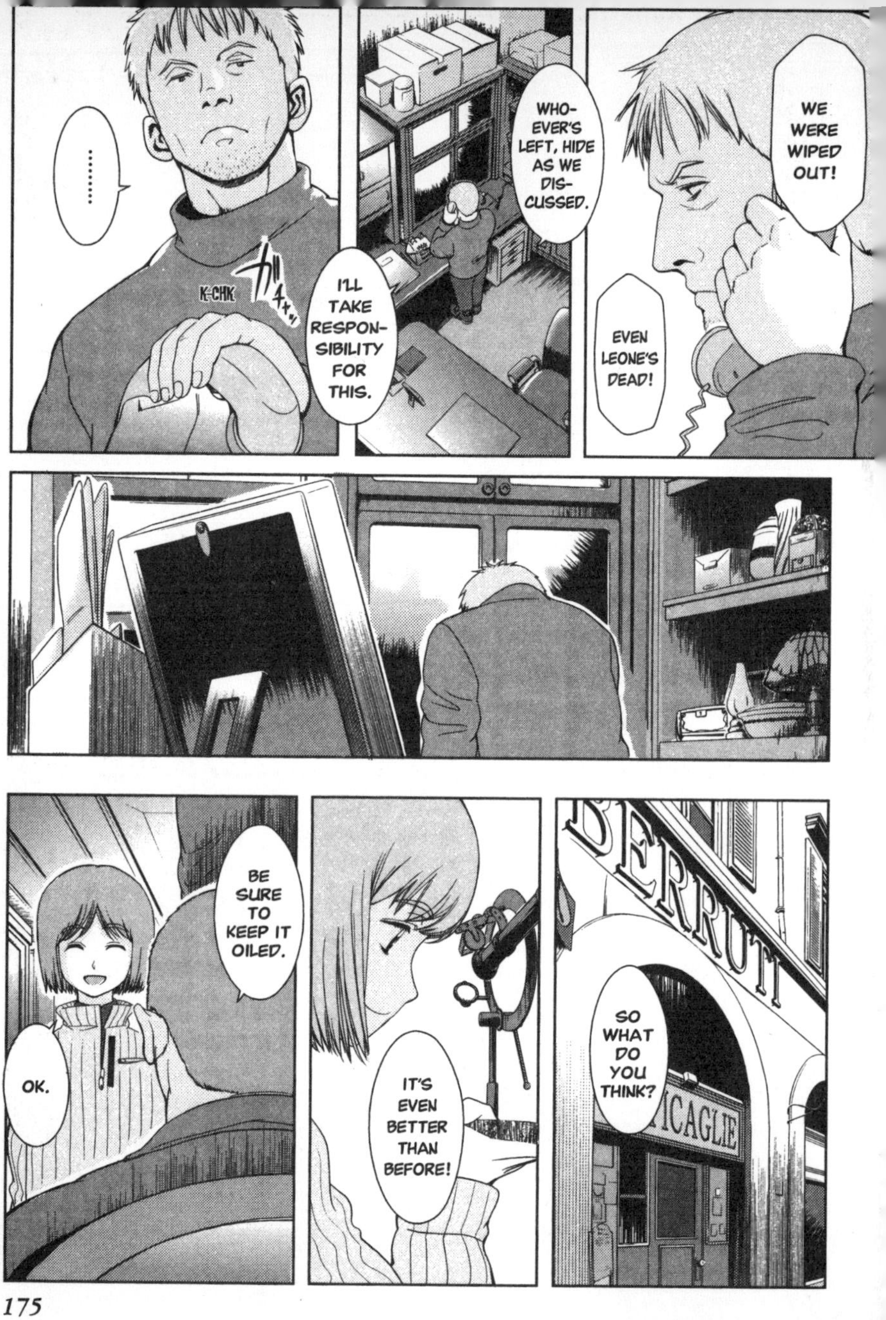
WE WERE WIPED OUT!
EVEN LEONE'S DEAD!
WHO-EVER'S LEFT, HIDE AS WE DIS-CUSSED.
I'LL TAKE RESPON-SIBILITY FOR THIS.
K-CHK
....
SO WHAT DO YOU THINK?
IT'S EVEN BETTER THAN BEFORE!
BE SURE TO KEEP IT OILED.
OK.

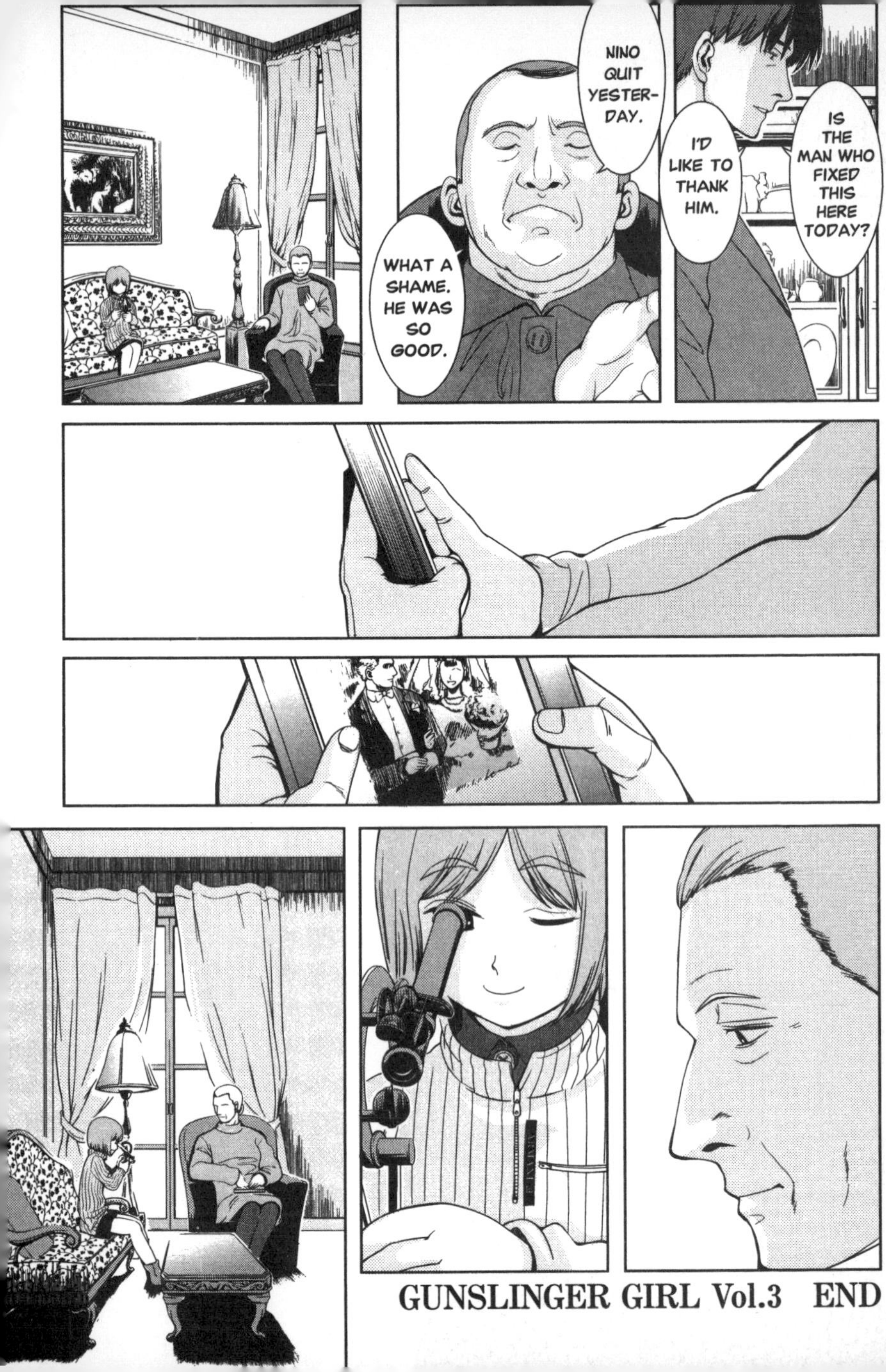
IS THE MAN WHO FIXED THIS HERE TODAY?
I'D LIKE TO THANK HIM.
NINO QUIT YESTER-DAY.
WHAT A SHAME. HE WAS SO GOOD.

GUNSLINGER GIRL Vol.3 END

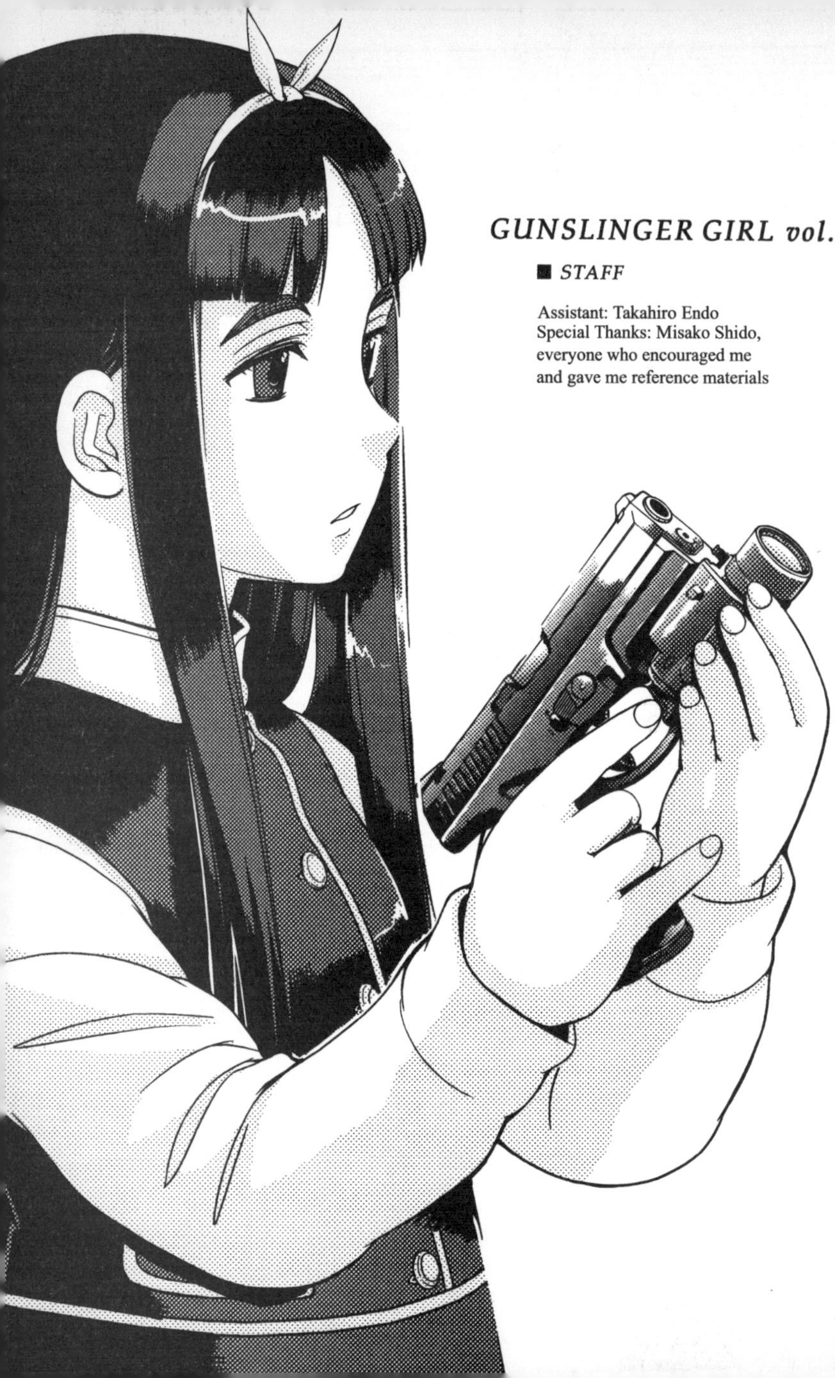

GUNSLINGER GIRL vol.3

■ *STAFF*

Assistant: Takahiro Endo
Special Thanks: Misako Shido,
everyone who encouraged me
and gave me reference materials

Gunslinger Girl Volume Three

© YU AIDA 2004
First published in 2004 by Media Works Inc., Tokyo, Japan.
English translation rights arranged with Media Works Inc.

Translator **AMY FORSYTH**
Translation Staff **KAY BERTRAND AND BRENDAN FRAYNE**
Editor **JAVIER LOPEZ**
Assistant Editor **SHERIDAN JACOBS**
Graphic Artists **HEATHER GARY AND NATALIA REYNOLDS**
Intern **MARK MEZA**

Editorial Director **GARY STEINMAN**
Creative Director **JASON BABLER**
Sales and Marketing **CHRIS OARR**
Print Production Manager **BRIDGETT JANOTA**
Pre-press Manager **KLYS REEDYK**

International Coordinators **TORU IWAKAMI, ATSUSHI KANBAYASHI, KYOKO DRUMHELLER AND AI TAKAI**

President, CEO & Publisher **JOHN LEDFORD**

Email: editor@adv-manga.com
www.adv-manga.com
www.advfilms.com

For sales and distribution inquiries please call 1.800.282.7202

ADU MANGA is a division of A.D. Vision, Inc.
10114 W. Sam Houston Parkway, Suite 200, Houston, Texas 77099

English text © 2005 published by A.D. Vision, Inc. under exclusive license.
ADV MANGA is a trademark of A.D. Vision, Inc.

ISBN: 1-4139-0274-X
First printing, June 2005
10 9 8 7 6 5 4 3 2 1
Printed in Canada

Gunslinger Girl Vol. 03

PG. 3
Steiff Bear
The very first of these classy (and expensive) stuffed bears was designed by Richard Steiff at his aunt Margaret's company in 1902. The following year, some 12,000 of them were sold at the World's Exhibition in St. Louis, and president Theodore Roosevelt was so taken with them that they would later be given the moniker "Teddy bear."

PG. 16
Louise Antoinette Laure
Also referred to as Louise-Antoinette-Laure De Berny. The "French author" mentioned here is Honoré de Balzac (see below), and Laure was his first mistress, whom he described as "more than a friend, more than a sister, almost a mother."

PG. 18
Balzac
Honoré de Balzac (1799-1850) was a modestly successful author credited with being one of the originators of realism in literature. The wildly prolific Balzac is best known for his *La Comédie Humaine* ("The Human Comedy"), a mammoth undertaking of nearly 100 novels and short stories and some 2,000 characters set amidst a backdrop of bourgeois France.

PG. 58
Padania
The name Padania (or Padana as it is spelled in Italian) refers to the valley in northern Italy formed by the river Po. Within the context of *Gunslinger Girl*, Padania is used synonymously with the Five Republics, a radical movement pushing for northern independence.

PG. 67
SCORPION
Constructed of aerospace-quality aluminum, this brand of silencer was designed for those times when "low profile, light weight, and world class sound suppression mean the difference between life and death."

PG. 102
(1) SIG
An abbreviation for *Schweizerische Industrie-Gesellschaft*. This Swiss company is one of the oldest and most widely-known manufacturers of small arms. "SIG" can be used to refer to any one of the many models the company makes.

Continued...

PG. 102

(2) Glock
Another small arms manufacturer, this one being founded in 1963 in Austria. It began producing its own firearms in the 1980s, when the Austrian army contracted the company to make a service pistol.

PG. 112

NOCS
NOCS (*Nucleo Operativo Centrale di Sicurezza*) is the national police unit roughly equivalent to the SWAT of the United States, being deployed in arrest, rescue and counterterrorist operations.

PG. 113

Carabinieri
Short for *il Carabinieri Nationale*, this is an old and highly-respected Italian military police force. Coincidentally, the first time the *Carabinieri* appeared in a piece of fiction was in *Pinocchio*.

PG. 116

(1) la Scala
This is the *Teatro alla Scala*, one of the world's oldest and most famous opera houses. Located in Milan, it was built from 1776-1778, and refurbished after the war in 1945-1946. By the time of this printing, it will have completed yet another refurbishment.

(2) Red Brigade
The *Brigate Rosse* is a terrorist movement founded on Communist principles. Largely inactive since 1989, the group at one time led a campaign of kidnappings and assassinations.

(3) CQB
Short for "Close Quarters Battle." This can include hand-to-hand fighting, as well as the use of knives, sticks, bayonets and so on.

PG. 181

Lily of the Valley
Written by Balzac in 1836, this is one of the stories comprising *The Human Comedy* (see above). As mentioned previously, the heroine's name is Henriette (or more properly, Madame Blanche-Henriette de Mortsauf).

PG. 183

SISDE
This stands for *Servizio per le Informazionie la Sicurezza Democratica.* It is an Italian security agency which reports directly to the Minister of the Interior.

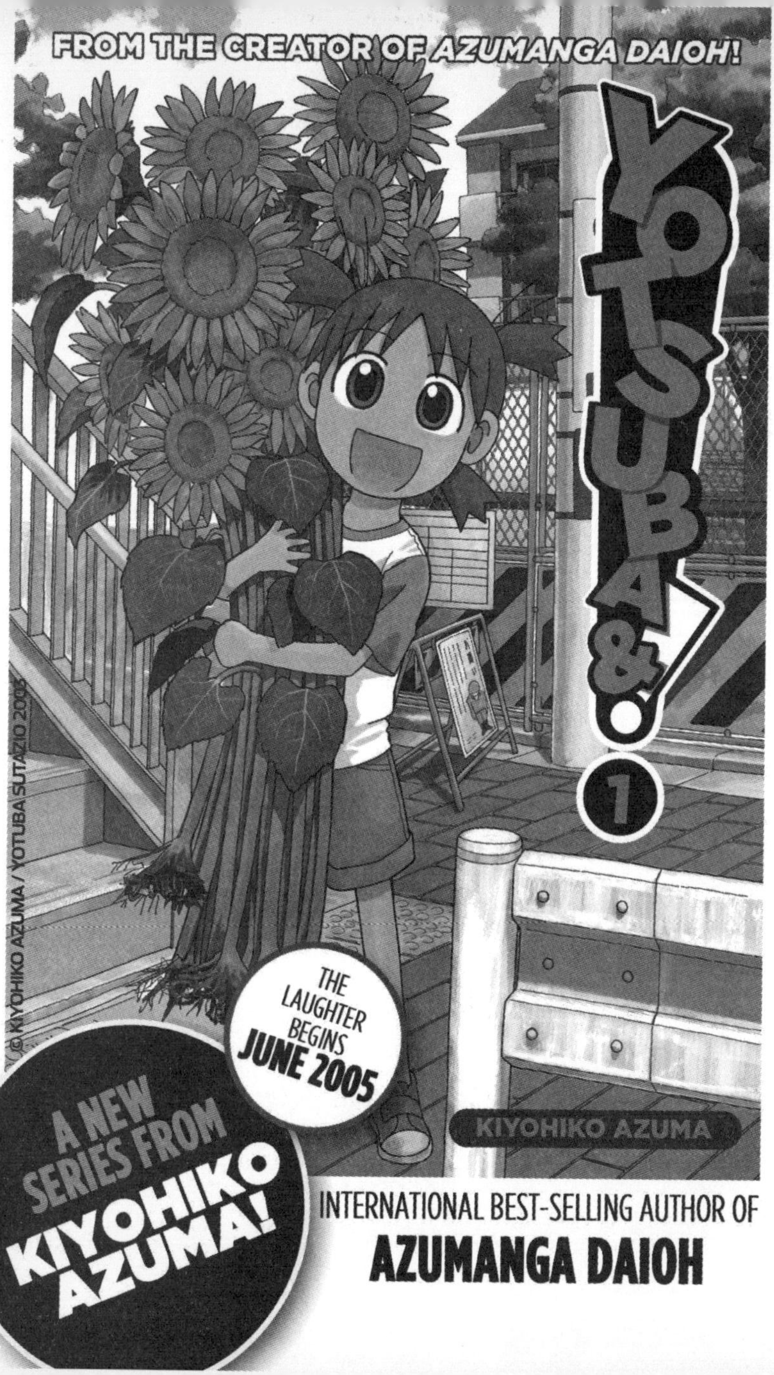
FROM THE CREATOR OF AZUMANGA DAIOH!
YOTSUBA&!
1
KIYOHIKO AZUMA
© KIYOHIKO AZUMA / YOTUBA SUTAZIO 2003
THE LAUGHTER BEGINS JUNE 2005
A NEW SERIES FROM KIYOHIKO AZUMA!
INTERNATIONAL BEST-SELLING AUTHOR OF
AZUMANGA DAIOH

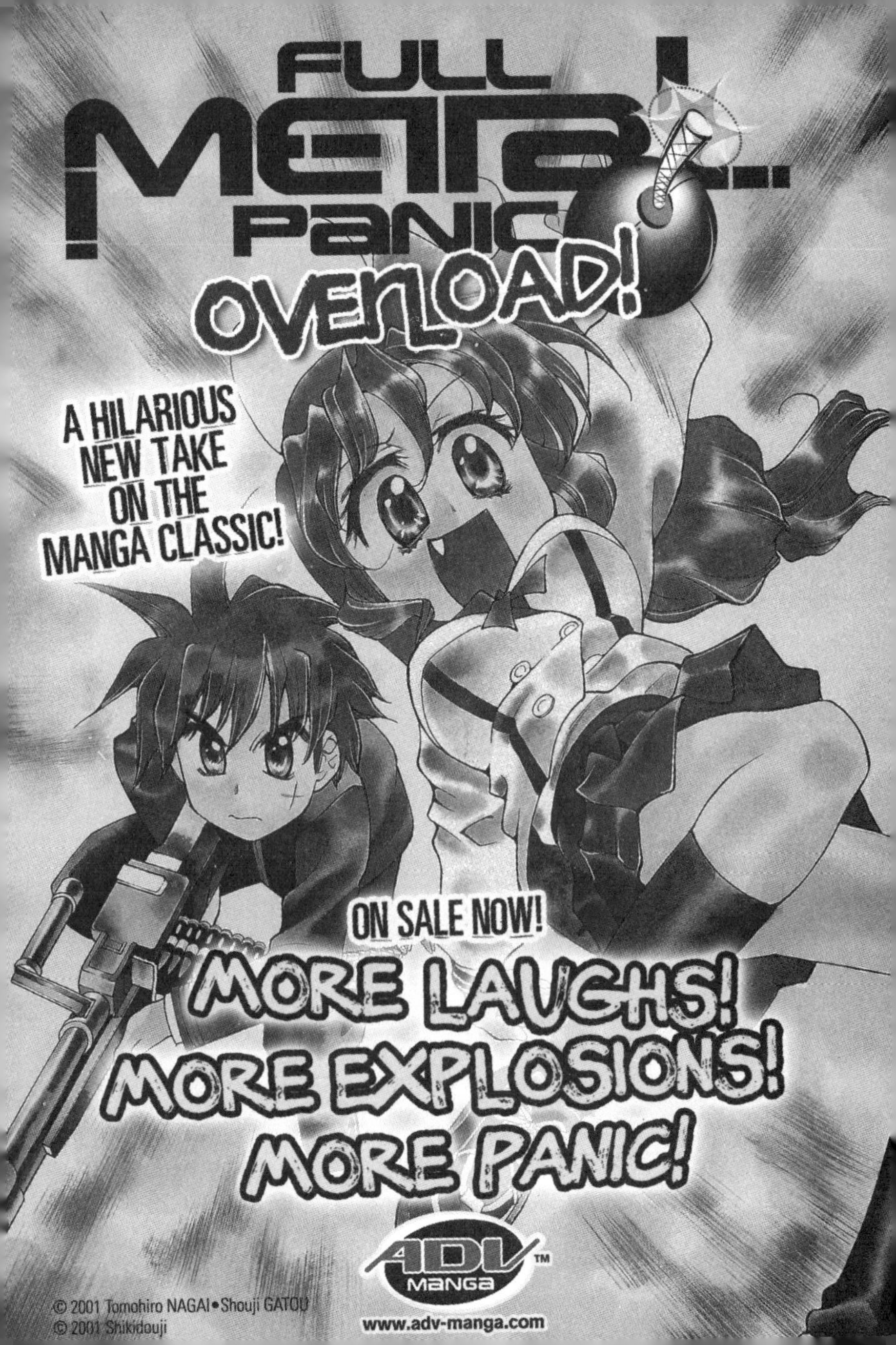
FULL METAL PANIC
OVERLOAD!
A HILARIOUS NEW TAKE ON THE MANGA CLASSIC!
ON SALE NOW!
MORE LAUGHS!
MORE EXPLOSIONS!
MORE PANIC!
ADV MANGA™
© 2001 Tomohiro NAGAI • Shouji GATOU
© 2001 Shikidouji
www.adv-manga.com

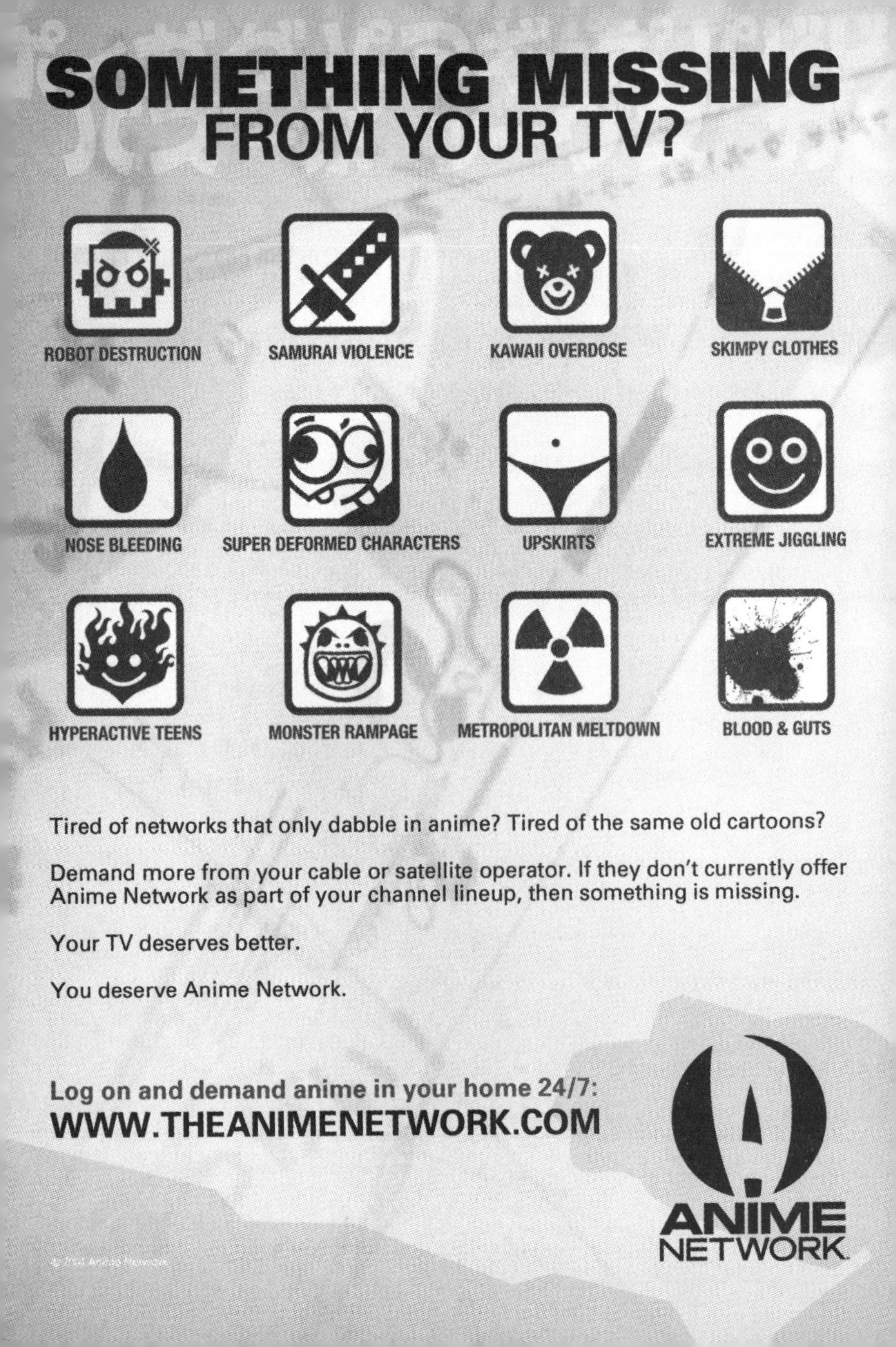
SOMETHING MISSING
FROM YOUR TV?
ROBOT DESTRUCTION
SAMURAI VIOLENCE
KAWAII OVERDOSE
SKIMPY CLOTHES
NOSE BLEEDING
SUPER DEFORMED CHARACTERS
UPSKIRTS
EXTREME JIGGLING
HYPERACTIVE TEENS
MONSTER RAMPAGE
METROPOLITAN MELTDOWN
BLOOD & GUTS
Tired of networks that only dabble in anime? Tired of the same old cartoons?
Demand more from your cable or satellite operator. If they don't currently offer Anime Network as part of your channel lineup, then something is missing.
Your TV deserves better.
You deserve Anime Network.
Log on and demand anime in your home 24/7:
WWW.THEANIMENETWORK.COM
ANIME NETWORK

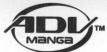

MANGA SURVEY

PLEASE MAIL THE COMPLETED FORM TO: EDITOR – ADV MANGA
c/o A.D. Vision, Inc. 10114 W. Sam Houston Pkwy., Suite 200 Houston, TX 77099

Name: ______________________________
Address: ______________________________
City, State, Zip: ______________________________
____
E-Mail: ______________________________
Male ☐ Female ☐ Age: ______________

☐ ***CHECK HERE IF YOU WOULD LIKE TO RECEIVE OTHER INFORMATION OR FUTURE OFFERS FROM ADV.***

All information provided will be used for internal purposes only. We promise not to sell or otherwise divulge your information.

1. Annual Household Income (*Check only one*)
- ☐ Under $25,000
- ☐ $25,000 to $50,000
- ☐ $50,000 to $75,000
- ☐ Over $75,000

2. How do you hear about new Manga releases? (*Check all that apply*)
- ☐ Browsing in Store
- ☐ Internet Reviews
- ☐ Anime News Websites
- ☐ Direct Email Campaigns
- ☐ Online forums (message boards and chat rooms)
- ☐ Carrier pigeon
- ☐ Other: ______________
- ☐ Magazine Ad
- ☐ Online Advertising
- ☐ Conventions
- ☐ TV Advertising

3. Which magazines do you read? (*Check all that apply*)
- ☐ Wizard
- ☐ SPIN
- ☐ Animerica
- ☐ Rolling Stone
- ☐ Maxim
- ☐ DC Comics
- ☐ URB
- ☐ Polygon
- ☐ Official PlayStation Magazine
- ☐ Entertainment Weekly
- ☐ YRB
- ☐ EGM
- ☐ Newtype USA
- ☐ SciFi
- ☐ Starlog
- ☐ Wired
- ☐ Vice
- ☐ BPM
- ☐ I hate reading
- ☐ Other: ______________

4. Have you visited the ADV Manga website?
- ☐ Yes
- ☐ No

5. Have you made any manga purchases online from the ADV website?
- ☐ Yes
- ☐ No

6. If you have visited the ADV Manga website, how would you rate your online experience?
- ☐ Excellent
- ☐ Good
- ☐ Average
- ☐ Poor

7. What genre of manga do you prefer?
(*Check all that apply*)
- ☐ adventure
- ☐ romance
- ☐ detective
- ☐ action
- ☐ horror
- ☐ sci-fi/fantasy
- ☐ sports
- ☐ comedy

8. How many manga titles have you purchased in the last 6 months?
- ☐ none
- ☐ 1-4
- ☐ 5-10
- ☐ 11+

9. Where do you make your manga purchases? (*Check all that apply*)
- ☐ comic store
- ☐ bookstore
- ☐ newsstand
- ☐ online
- ☐ other:_____
- ☐ department store
- ☐ grocery store
- ☐ video store
- ☐ video game store

10. Which bookstores do you usually make your manga purchases at?
(*Check all that apply*)
- ☐ Barnes & Noble
- ☐ Walden Books
- ☐ Suncoast
- ☐ Best Buy
- ☐ Amazon.com
- ☐ Borders
- ☐ Books-A-Million
- ☐ Toys Я " Us
- ☐ Other bookstore:
  _____

11. What's your favorite anime/manga website? (*Check all that apply*)
- ☐ adv-manga.com
- ☐ advfilms.com
- ☐ rightstuf.com
- ☐ animenewsservice.com
- ☐ animenewsnetwork.com
- ☐ Other:_____
- ☐ animeondvd.com
- ☐ anipike.com
- ☐ animeonline.net
- ☐ planetanime.com
- ☐ animenation.com

All information provided will be used for internal purposes only. We promise not to sell or otherwise divulge your information.